# A Photographic Guide to the
# BIRDS
## OF SOUTHEAST ASIA
### INCLUDING THE PHILIPPINES & BORNEO

Morten Strange

CHRISTOPHER HELM
LONDON

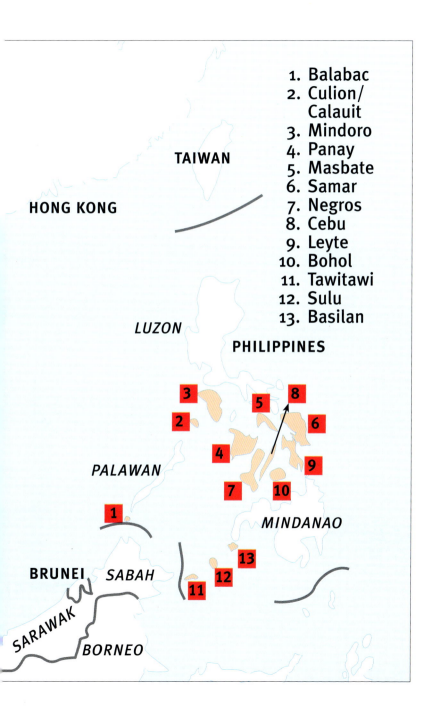

Published 2002 by Christopher Helm, an imprint of A&C Black Publishers Ltd.,
37 Soho Square, London W1D 3QZ

Copyright ©2000 by Periplus Editions (HK) Ltd.

ISBN 0-7136-6402-9

A CIP catalogue record for this book is available from the British Library.

All rights reserved. No part of this publication may be reproduced or used in
any form or by any means - photographic, electronic or mechanical, including
photocopying, recording, taping or information storage and retrieval systems
– without permission of the publishers.

A & C Black uses paper produced with elemental chlorine-free pulp, harvested
from managed sustainable forests.

Printed in Singapore

10 9 8 7 6 5 4 3 2 1

# CONTENTS

8 ACKNOWLEDGEMENTS

10 INTRODUCTION

24 HOW TO USE THIS BOOK

42 SYSTEMATIC SECTION

*NON-PASSERINES:*

42 Grebes – Podicipedidae
42 Pelicans – Pelecanidae
43 Boobies – Sulidae
44 Cormorants – Phalacrocoracidae
45 Darters – Anhingidae
46 Frigatebirds – Fregatidae
47 Herons, egrets, bitterns – Ardeidae
57 Storks – Ciconiidae
60 Ibises – Threskiornithidae
61 Geese, ducks – Anatidae
70 Osprey – Pandionidae
70 Hawks, eagles, vultures – Accipitrae
84 Falcons – Falconidae
85 Pheasants – Phasianidae
93 Buttonquail – Turnicidae
93 Cranes – Gruidae
94 Rails, crakes – Rallidae
99 Finfoots – Heliornithidae
100 Jacanas – Jacanidae
101 Paintedsnipe – Rostratulidae
101 Oystercatchers – Haematopodidae
102 Lapwings, plovers – Charadriidae
108 Curlews, sandpipers, snipe – Scolopacidae
124 Stilts, avocets – Recurvirostridae
125 Phalaropes – Phalaropidae
125 Thick-knees – Burhinidae
126 Pratincoles – Glareolidae
127 Gulls, terns – Laridae
134 Pigeons, doves – Columbidae
145 Parrots – Psittacidae
150 Cuckoos – Cuculidae
159 Barn Owls – Tytonidae
160 Owls – Strigidae
165 Frogmouths – Batrochostomidae
168 Nightjars – Caprimulgidae
170 Swifts – Apodidae
173 Treeswifts – Hemiprocnidae
174 Trogons – Trogonidae
177 Kingfishers – Alcedinidae
184 Bee-eaters – Meropidae
187 Rollers – Coraciidae
188 Hoopoe – Upupidae
189 Hornbills – Bucerotidae
196 Barbets – Megalaimidae
203 Honeyguides – Indicatoridae
204 Woodpeckers – Picidae

PASSERINES:

215 Broadbills – Eurylaimidae
218 Pittas – Pittidae
223 Larks – Alaudidae
224 Swallows – Hirundinidae
226 Cuckoo-shrikes, minivets
230 Ioras, leafbirds – Chloropseidae
234 Bulbuls – Pycnonotidae
249 Drongos – Dicruridae
253 Orioles – Oriolidae
255 Fairy Bluebirds – Irenidae
255 Crows, jays, magpies – Corvidae
260 Tits – Paridae
263 Nuthatches – Sittidae
264 Treecreepers – Certhiidae
264 Philippine Creepers – Rhabdornithidae
265 Babblers – Timaliidae
294 Thrushes – Turdidae
309 Warblers – Sylviidae
322 Flycatchers – Muscicapidae
333 Fantails – Rhipiduridae

# CONTENTS

- 335 Monarchs – Monarchidae
- 336 Whistlers, accentors – Pachycephalidae
- 338 Wagtails, pipits – Motacillidae
- 341 Wood–swallows – Artamidae
- 342 Shrikes – Laniidae
- 345 Starlings, mynas – Sturnidae
- 351 Sunbirds, spiderhunters – Nectariniidae
- 362 Flowerpeckers – Dicaeidae
- 366 White–eyes – Zosteropidae
- 368 Sparrows – Passeridae
- 369 Weavers – Ploceidae
- 371 Munias – Estrildidae
- 373 Finches – Fringillidae
- 375 Buntings – Emberizidae

- 376 GLOSSARY
- 379 BIBLIOGRAPHY
- 382 FURTHER INFORMATION

Opposite: *Female Great Hornbill feeding young inside nest.*

# Acknowledgements

In January 1997 something unusual happened to me. I had dropped by to visit the local bird park on the Indonesian island of Bali, and while I was waiting at the parking lot for a friend to pick me up, Eric Oey, the CEO of Periplus Editions, unexpectedly appeared. I have known Eric for almost ten years, having supplied his company with a few photographs and occasional texts on Southeast Asian wildlife.

Eric had decided to produce a new book on Southeast Asian birds, to be included in his Periplus Nature Guides series. Within 10 minutes, while standing there in the parking lot, the two of us had agreed on the concept for what later became *Tropical Birds of Southeast Asia*, Periplus Editions (1998).

As it turned out, Eric's ambitions went further than this small introductory volume. He planned to publish a complete (as possible) photographic coverage of the birds found in Southeast Asia and Indonesia. This would be produced in a guide book format that birdwatchers and nature enthusiasts in the region could use for identification purposes and to further their knowledge of the birds' locations and habits.

It is self-evident that in a photographic guide the photographs are of utmost importance. Since my reasonably comprehensive collection of photographs, acquired during fieldwork over the past fourteen years, were not enough for a monumental project like this, I appealed to my fellow photographers for help, and the response was overwhelming. Nearly forty percent of the photographs in this volume were produced by these wildlife photographers. Each frame has been selected to show the species in the best position possible, hence every shot used in this book is significant. All required considerable time and effort to produce, so I would like to thank these photographers for their most generous and valuable contributions.

I would like to single out a few people for special mention. One of the few women in the business, Ong Kiem Sian, has produced an impressive photographic collection of bird species, through extensive fieldwork in Singapore, Malaysia and Thailand. I much appreciated being allowed to tap into her outstanding collection. Apart from an impeccable technique, Sian has an unusual eye for composition and aesthetics in her photography. This is the first time a major selection of her pictures has been published, but it surely will not be the last.

It is particularly rewarding when local ornithologists take the trouble to photograph birds encountered during their travels to remote locations. In this way others may share their experiences and learn from their sightings. Alan OwYong, Allen Jeyarajasingam, Uthai Treesucon, Samson So, Atsuo Tsuji and others fall into this category, as does Dr. Pilai Poonswad of the Asian Hornbill Network. I would especially like to commend Dr. Poonswad for her dedication to the protection of Asian hornbills and to thank her for allowing me to work with her.

Some Western scientists and birdwatchers, whether on birdwatching visits to Southeast Asia or residing in the region, also produce rare and valuable photographs. They are well represented here and I would especially like to mention Pete Morris, a talented and hard-working young Briton with a remarkable insight into tropical birds and a photo collection to match. Tim Loseby from England, and Bernard van Elegem and some of his friends from Belgium, travel to this region especially to photograph birds and have produced some stunning images.

The gifted artist and scientist Kelvin Lim is surely destined for bigger things; his illustrations are a significant contribution to this volume.

Lim Kim Keang put his complete personal library of Southeast Asian ornithological references at my disposal during the information research phase of this book, and I thank him sincerely for that.

And many thanks to my long-time birding buddy Lim Kim Seng, himself an accomplished author on Southeast Asian birds, for checking through the manuscript for errors, and to my good friend Dr. Clive Briffett, who gave invaluable advice on format and content at the planning stage.

My special friend Ng Bee Choo, Managing Director of Nature's Niche in Singapore, provided contact with photo contributors, input on the content, and assistance through all the production stages. I particularly appreciate her vital support.

# INTRODUCTION

## The joy of birdwatching

Birds fascinate us more than any other group of fauna, perhaps because birds are found everywhere. They have colonised all corners of the earth, from the most inhospitable Arctic and Antarctic regions to bone-dry subtropical deserts and remote oceanic islands. Their dazzling power of flight never ceases to amaze us, and, perhaps most important of all, they are relatively easy to observe, since birds are usually active by day and thrive in our near surroundings. Also, their senses are much like our own—they rely mainly on eyesight and hearing—and therefore react much like we do and are easy for us to identify with.

You can watch birds from your window wherever you live. When you walk out into the nearby park or field there will be more birds to see. If you observe closely you will begin to recognise new species; some you see each time you go out, while others are rare and only turn up once in a while or at certain times of the year. Most birdwatchers develop a local patch where they go regularly. When you travel to another habitat, region, country, or even another altitude, you will find different birds to watch. It is this wonderful diversity that makes birdwatching so exciting.

Even though birds have been studied more thoroughly than any other class of animal, new information still surfaces every year. In 1991 a group of young Danish scientists found a new species of pheasant, the Udzungwa Forest-partridge, deep in the forests of Tanzania in Africa. This pheasant turned out to be related to the *Arborophila* hill-partridges of Southeast Asia, and was placed in its own monotypic genus when described in 1994. For details see del Hoyo et al. Vol 2 (1994). Other new species still turn up once in a while, adding to the 9,704 species already recognised by Collar et al (1994). And since taxonomic studies are on-going (see How to Use This Book) more discoveries and changes can be expected in future years.

The study and interpretation of bird behavior and habits also continues. For a marvellous worldwide collection of new and astonishing information see David Attenborough's television series, The Life of

Birds, produced by the BBC and the associated book, Attenborough (1998).

In our region, outstanding research has been conducted by the Asian Hornbill Network based at Mahidol University in Thailand, see Poonswad and Kemp (1993). After intensive initial research in Khao Yai National Park and later in Huai Kha Khaeng National Park in west Thailand, the project expanded into south Thailand, part of the Sunda subregion. During the 1998 breeding season, an astonishing 80 occupied hornbill nests, representing 6 different species, were observed in this area alone—a staggering number considering the huge and remote primary forest terrain that had to be covered. The observations and documentation of this network has completely transformed our insight into one of the most fascinating rainforest bird families of all. The network is currently expanding into other Southeast Asian countries such as Indonesia, Myanmar and Indochina.

## Birding techniques

Birdwatching can be enjoyed without much equipment, but a good pair of binoculars definitely helps. The technology is simple. Binoculars are described by two sets of numbers, the first being the magnification, and the second the front lens diameter in millimetres. In other words, looking at a bird through a 10x40 pair of binoculars makes a bird 10 metres away appear as if it were one metre in front of you, and the four-centimetre lenses should give a reasonably bright image. A 7x42 pair will produce a smaller, but significantly brighter, image.

Since binoculars have few mechanical parts, a pair will last you a long time—probably a lifetime, unless you lose them, since the top brands give a 30-year guarantee. Therefore it pays to select the best pair you can possibly afford, so that you won't waste money upgrading later. Selecting the appropriate pair can be difficult, because so many brands and types are available on the market. Consult an experienced birdwatcher or a dealer that you trust. Optical quality varies enormously; good resolution, clarity and colour reproduction is vital. As with most other things you get what you pay for, so pick a pair that is a little more expensive than what you had in mind and you will be happier in the long run.

A telescope, while slower to operate since a tripod is required to keep it steady, has the advantage of interchangeable eyepieces, allowing for different magnifications. Quality telescopes have fixed magnifications in the range of 20–30 times, and some zoom to 60x, but then the image is not as clear. A 'scope' is useful in open country and on remote mudflats, and can help pick out stationary forest birds. It is especially useful in group birdwatching as it allows more people to observe the bird once it is in the frame.

Birdwatching is a social exercise. Go with someone more experienced than yourself in the beginning, join a nature society and attend their outings. In this way you will be introduced to the best locations in your area. It is best to remain quiet and respect those in the group who take this hobby rather seriously. If you do go on your own, take a small note pad and make notes on any bird that you do not recognise. Look for diagnostic features such as bill and tail shape and distinct colour bands on head or wings, and write down details of what you see. You can always consult your field guide later, once the bird has flown off.

As you become more experienced you will find that bird identification is often done quickly, using the so-called 'jizz' of the bird. This slang expression used by birders is derived from 'gis', an achronym for General Impression and Shape, in US Air Force terminology. The jizz of that small garden bird hopping through the bushes lets you know right away that it is a tailorbird of some kind. Then, as you examine it more closely, the pale vent and elongated tail tells you that the bird is a male Common Tailorbird in breeding plumage.

You will find that birds are individuals and show some disparities, even within the same species. Some are more tame than others; during moulting the plumage might not be quite the usual colour, while some species include colour morphs—the Oriental Honey-buzzard varies from all-brown to almost snow-white. In fact you can learn to recognise individual birds which regularly visit your garden or balcony.

Some birdwatchers go on to study the subtle differences of subspecies. Others keep databases of all their observations, most importantly a world list of all species seen. Before you know it, adding to this list becomes something of a compulsive urge, and a so-called 'twitcher' is born—a birdwatcher who travels the globe in restless pursuit of new bird species.

Some birdwatchers carry tape recorders and collect bird calls, while others produce photographs and video recordings. Photographing birds is no easy task. Many birdwatchers have found out that twitching for new species or undertaking a serious survey is totally incompatible with the production of quality photographs, which requires that you walk slowly (the heavy equipment alone slows you down) or that you stay absolutely still in one place. At any rate, you seem to get the best results if you stop chasing the birds and let them come to you instead—by staying motionless or hiding by a fruiting or flowering tree, a forest clearing, in a tree canopy, by a pool of water, a nest or some suitable place that will attract one or more birds. You do not see that many different species this way, but you will get to know the ones you do see intimately, and most importantly you may produce rare documentary material that can be shared with others.

But strictly speaking, apart from binoculars, a birdwatcher really only needs one other tool to successfully pursue his hobby: a field guide identifying the birds in his area. This guide should be complete with all species that one could possibly come across illustrated in colour. Luckily, several such guides exist for parts of this region, notably Thailand, Malaysia, Singapore and Hong Kong.

Other important books are handbooks which are, in fact, large books with more detailed accounts of the bird habits than identification field guides provide, e.g. *Handbook of the Birds of the World.* Monographs featuring particular families also give more detailed information on a smaller selection of birds.

And then there are the photographic guides such as this volume. Complete photographic guides featuring every species are available for areas like Europe and Australia, but one for Southeast Asia, with over 1,400, species would not really be practical and, besides, photographs of all species are simply not available. What a photographic guide can do here is supplement the plates based on drawings in national field guides with photographs from the field. Even the best illustration will contain small discrepancies. Look at the bulbul plates in *Birds of Thailand* by Lekagul and Round (1991) and compare the Olive-winged Bulbul, Streak-eared Bulbul, Cream-vented Bulbul, Grey-eyed Bulbul and Buff-vented Bulbul there with what the birds really look like in this book and you will see my point. Photographs provide an invaluable source of reference, especially for hard-to-identify groups of bird with many similar species like bulbuls, babblers, warblers and shorebirds. In fact illustrators use (among other things) photographs when they produce field guide plates.

Photographic guides mainly feature those birds most likely to be met in the field—precisely because these are the species that will be available in photographs. The birds in the photos appear exactly as you will encounter them with no artistic adjustments.

## Habitats

One of the most fascinating aspects of birdwatching is the study of the way birds depend on their surroundings and the way birdlife changes with conditions. These changes are often gradual and many birds move between habitats—the Scaly-breasted Munia, for instance, can be found both in gardens, open country, wetlands and even beach-side grasses. Furthermore, definition of habitats are not always easy—the many types of lowland forest in this region, for example, makes it unsafe to generalise too categorically.

However, one also encounters many strictly stenotopic birds (birds confined to only one habitat), especially forest birds, mangrove species and birds occurring within narrow altitudinal ranges. Knowing which birds to expect within different habitat types makes the 'work' of identifying the many species much easier. We still find the habitats described in Strange and Jeyarajasingam (1993) the most relevant. There are five main categories.

**Gardens and Parks** are the most disturbed and artificial of all habitats of course, but they are highly productive, especially if managed sensitively. If you have your own garden, much can be done by planting a selection of fruiting trees to attract pigeons, bulbuls, starlings, the Black-naped Oriole and Coppersmith Barbet, and parrots if forest is nearby. Do not spray against insects if you can avoid it, to allow warblers and flycatchers to settle. Bushes with nectar-rich red flowers will attract sunbirds and if you are lucky a pair of Olive-backed Sunbirds might build their pouch nest in your garden or even in a potted plant on a balcony high above the roar of the traffic as they have been known to do.

Birds in parks and gardens often become used to plenty of human activity and become almost tame. Even shy raptors like the Shikra or the Japanese Sparrowhawk will visit parks, simply because of the abundance of small birds for them to catch. At night listen for the call of the Collared Scops-owl and the Large-tailed Nightjar, and during the winter season keep an eye out for rare visitors from the north, including certain forest birds that might turn up during migration.

**Open Country** is bee-eater, munia, coucal and shrike territory, although some birds such as the White-throated Kingfisher and others occur in both areas. Swifts and swallows fly overhead. A totally different avifauna inhabits the terrain around wet patches or open fresh water. Many species of heron, rail, duck and snipe are mainly or only found here. No wet field in Southeast Asia is complete without a party of foraging Cattle Egrets. If you are lucky you will locate a weaver colony—the Streaked Weaver prefers the tall grasses and low bushes, the Baya Weaver builds higher in trees and coconut palms, but either species provides captivating, non-stop action with birds calling, displaying, building and flying constantly to and fro.

At the **Coast** birds abound, especially on sheltered mudflats, and often where a large river joins the sea. Some species also occur around fresh water wetlands but most will be different species. Unless removed by developers, mangrove forests thrive along such sheltered shores and are home to a few specialised birds such as the Mangrove Pitta, Mangrove Blue Flycatcher, Ashy Tailorbird and Copper-throated Sunbird. Other mangrove birds such as the Pied Fantail, Mangrove Whistler, Collared Kingfisher and Laced Woodpecker are less specialised and turn up in nearby woodlands and gardens as well.

Storks are rare in this region, but this is the place to see them. At low tide, storks and many herons and egrets flock to feed on the exposed mudflats in front of the mangroves. Almost all shorebirds (plovers and sandpipers) in this region are migratory. The diversity can be somewhat confusing for the beginner (and for the experienced birder for that matter), especially since it is difficult to get close to shorebirds feeding far out on boggy mudflats. In fact, some birdwatchers get hooked on shorebirds and find the similarities and the differences a challenge. Exposed sandy seashores and rocky coastlines are less productive, but some plovers and sandpipers prefer this habitat, as does the resident Pacific Reef-egret. The Little Heron is likely to turn up wherever there is water.

Tropical Asia has few gulls, but further north in China they become more numerous although no species stay to breed in this area, except terns, which breed mainly on remote offshore islets. If you have a friend who owns a boat, catch a ride offshore in the South China Sea. Swim to some remote reef during April or May and there you can walk among the breeding sea birds, with terns screaming at you overhead, boobies with their young on the ground, and the majestic White-bellied Sea-eagle soaring in the distance—another of the great birding spectacles this region has to offer. Do not stay long though as the hot sun might damage exposed eggs and young.

**Lowland forests** are the prime habitat of all Southeast Asia. More birds can be found here than in any other environment and furthermore most are sedentary residents found here all year round, a great number of which are restricted to this region and parts of Indonesia.

Yes, birdwatching in the forest is as tough as it gets. In rainforest, the trees grow to a height of 30 metres or more, and the foliage is massive. Less than two percent of the outside light reaches the forest floor and the humidity stays near 100 percent, even in the afternoon. But then, forest birdwatching is also the most rewarding. You can walk the same forest trail twenty times, week after week, and then the twenty-first time you might see a species you have never seen before in your life, such is the diversity and the scarcity of forest residents.

Conditions are challenging, even in the somewhat lower deciduous forests further north. In addition to the poor viewing conditions the birds are shy and take off at the least disturbance. In general it is better to visit during the dry season, from December to February, and go where the forest is less dense and where many migratory warblers, thrushes and flycatchers augment the resident bird fauna.

Pheasants, hornbills, broadbills, woodpeckers, leafbirds, babblers and flowerpeckers are almost exclusively forest bird families; nightbirds, bulbuls, drongos, cuckoo-shrikes and flycatchers are also well represented.

As you proceed higher, the avifauna changes. At 900 metres you enter the **montane forest** where you will discover a totally different set of birds. This astonishing transformation is once again a highlight of birdwatching in this region. You can drive for a couple of hours from Kuala Lumpur to Fraser's Hill in Malaysia, or from Chiang Mai to Doi Inthanon in Thailand, and so profound is the change that you might well have crossed the ocean to another faunal region. You will then have to begin familiarising yourself with 50 or 60 new species that you simply will never find in the lowlands.

Insect life is abundant at montane elevations and insectivorous bird families such as babblers, warblers and flycatchers are especially well represented, but almost all the other forest bird families such as pigeons, bulbuls, broadbills, cuckoo-shrikes, thrushes, fantails, sunbirds and flowerpeckers have one or a few representatives in the mountains.

The higher reaches of the upper montane habitat, above 2,400 metres, and the alpine habitat near and above the tree limit are not of that much interest in this region, simply because there is little of it. It only exists in the Himalayan foothills of Myanmar and Yunnan (south China), which are not very accessible to tourists, and in Sabah within the Kinabalu National Park. At Kinabalu the subcamp at 3,400 metres is where the alpine habitat starts and this is really as far as birders need to go. Pushing all the way to the summit at 4,101 metres may bring you a nice view and a bout of altitude sickness, but no significant bird sightings apart from the occasional White-bellied Swiftlet, which is better observed at sea level.

# The bird year

The region covered by this book is above the Equator and is part of the northern hemisphere. Close to the Equator, from peninsular Thailand and the so-called Tenasserim part of Myanmar and south, tropical conditions prevail, with heavy rainfall all year round, and insignificant changes in the seasons. Even then, the breeding of resident birds is not evenly spread throughout the year. Surveys show that most birds breed at the beginning of the year, from February towards the end of the northeast monsoon season, which dumps more rain than usual over most of the area during the months from November to January. Breeding peaks between April and May, and lasts until June or July, with some birds such as seabirds breeding into August. It is rare to find any nests in the later part of the year.

Actually, it is not easy to find nests in the tropics. Many birds build high in remote forest areas and within dense foliage. But the breeding season is an important time for the birdwatcher, because males tend to mark their territory aggressively, so there are more calls and often the birds are somewhat bolder and easier to observe at this time. Towards the end of the breeding season juveniles appear and add to the activity. Passerines typically feed their young for some time after they fledge, and many breeding records are established by observing the feeding.

Above the 10th parallel, a change to a more seasonal climate occurs. The change is complete above the 20th parallel, where the climate is subtropical with a distinct hot and cold season. Significant local variations prevail, but in general these northern regions experience a cold season with little rainfall lasting from December to February. Over most parts of continental Thailand and Indochina, 80 percent of precipitation falls during the southwest monsoon from May to October, while the cold months are very dry. Breeding in this region is seasonal, with most forest birds breeding in the spring, which is typical for northern hemisphere birds. However, evidence suggests that waterbirds may locally prefer to nest during the end of the wet season, from July into January, but this needs further verification.

Southeast Asia lies towards the end of the East Asia migratory flyway.

Migrants from temperate, subarctic and arctic parts of Asia converge on the region during the northern winter. Some pass through during peak migration from September to November and on the return flight from March to April. Many others go no further and make the region their winter quarters.

The actual movement of flying birds is difficult to observe in this region, since most species tend to change location at night, or fly high, out of sight. However, they tend to follow the coastlines, and passage migrants and winter visitors can turn up anywhere depending on habitat requirements. Coastal mudflats (for the water-dependent species) and wooded areas just behind the beach (for arboreal birds) are particularly good places to birdwatch during the winter season.

In conclusion, the beginning of the year is a good time to visit Southeast Asia. At this time the northern subtropical areas experience cool, dry weather and many migrants augment the local avifauna. Towards the end of winter into early spring, the resident birds become more active and conspicuous. In tropical areas, the heavy rainfalls of December subside about this time and the many resident forest birds become more vocal and daring. Alternatively, try to visit from September to November after the subtropical rains, when the northern migrants arrive, but before the tropical monsoons begin. In the subtropics watch for breeding waterbirds.

## Places to go

Birds do not recognise political demarcations, so national boundaries are really not very useful when describing the avifauna of a region, however people do, and active birdwatchers keep lists, and tally species they have seen within certain countries. Within the region covered in this volume, some major political entities exist, thus in the following table we list the nations and territories most visited by birdwatchers. Endemics refer to restricted range species found only in that country, except for East Malaysia and Brunei where numbers refer to Borneo endemics.

Just how many birds can one see in total in this region? Obviously many of the species listed under countries will be repeats. For a measurement of the total diversity Robson (2000) lists 1,251 species, King et al (1975) list 62 additional ones for Taiwan, Hainan. MacKinnon & Phillipps list 37 species endemic to Borneo, and Dickinson et al. (1991) has 169 endemics for the Philippines. Calculated this way about 1,519 different birds are found in Southeast Asia. But if you see the 668 covered in this volume, you will have done well.

## Conservation

Many of the birds in this book are adaptable and prolific. The Yellow-bellied Prinia readily invades forest areas cleared for development; and the Common Myna visits gardens and even invades people's homes to grab food. These birds have no problem surviving, but others adapt poorly to changes in their environment, so if their forest is removed or their island built over, they have no place to go. They need our help if they are to survive.

'Conservation begins with enjoyment' says the English comedian and professional birdwatcher Bill Oddie. In the 1994 BirdLife International study, published in Collar et al. (1994), it was documented that no less than 1,111 bird species comprising 11 percent of the world's avifauna could be regarded as globally threatened with extinction. A further 875 (or nine percent) was near-threatened. In other words, one out of five of all birds in the world is doing poorly or about to disappear.

Even in this book, which mainly features the easy-to-see species, 29 birds are globally threatened, a further 31 birds fall into the near-threatened category, which totals nine percent of the species covered.

The BirdLife study also revealed that most of the threatened birds live in the tropics, in countries with relatively low national incomes. They are forest birds (65 percent) and the main causes for their decline are habitat loss, a small range or population, and hunting and trapping. Unfortunately, most birds are unable to defend themselves. This is where Bill Oddie's enjoyment factor comes in. Birdwatching is fun, exciting, intellectually stimulating and as more people take up the interest they will tend to appreciate the natural world more. This has happened in the West and is now happening in the East.

| Territory | Size (sq km) | Species | Endemics | Major sites |
|---|---|---|---|---|
| Myanmar | 676,552 | 970 | 4 | Chin Hills for montane forest birds; Inle Lake for waterbirds. |
| China | 9,596,961 | 1,244 | 59 | Ruili, Lijiang and Gaoligong in western Yunnan for Oriental forest birds. |
| Hong Kong | 1,074 | 458 | None | Tai Po Kau for forest birds; Mai Po for waterbirds. |
| Taiwan | 35,742 | 450 | 14 | Wushe and Hsitou for montane endemics; Tseng Wen Chi and Kenting for waterbirds. |
| Vietnam | 329,556 | 828 | 10 | Tam Dao and Cuc Phuong for northern and Da Lat Plateau and Nam Bai Cat Tien for southern forest birds. |
| Laos | 231,800 | 640 | None | Nakai-Nam Thuen and Phon Xang He in the center for forest birds; Xe Pian in the south for forest and wetland birds. |
| Cambodia | 181,035 | 899 | None | Dangkrek and Cardamom ranges for montane forest birds; Mekong River south of Stung Treng for lowland birds. |
| Thailand | 514,000 | 920 | 2 | Doi Inthanon for montane birds; Khao Yai for forest birds; Krabi and Khao Nor Chuchi for southern species. |
| Malaysia (Peninsular) | 330,000 132,000 | 725 638 | 39 2 | Taman Negara and Pasoh for lowland birds; Fraser's Hill for montane; Kuala Gula and Kuala Selangor for wetland birds. |
| (East) | 198,000 | 570 | 37 | Mulu, Bako and Niah in Sarawak; Kinabalu & Danum Valley in Sabah. |
| Singapore | 640 | 350 | None | Bukit Timah and Sime Road for forest birds; Sungei Buloh for wetland birds. |
| Brunei | 5,765 | 395 | 4 | Batu Apoi and Peradayan for forest birds. |
| Philippines | 300,000 | 565 | 169 | Quezon, Mt. Polis and Sierra Madre on Luzon;Balsahan and St. Paul on Palawan; Mt. Katanglad and Sitio on Mindanao. |

But first of all, reliable data is necessary before action can be taken. Together with BirdLife International, local nature societies and birdwatching clubs continuously document the status of selected species and sites as part of the Asian Red Data book project and surveys for Important Bird Area inventories.

In this era of globalisation, national efforts are not enough. The rich biodiversity is available for everybody to enjoy and likewise we all have a responsibility to monitor and protect it. Birdwatchers from elsewhere can visit Southeast Asia to enjoy what the region has to offer, and they should, in turn, make their expertise and observations available to national agencies. Once we know where to direct our priorities, we can initiate programs to reverse the decline of so many beautiful birds.

We must stop the indiscriminate developing of natural bird habitats, cease polluting the environment and start rebuilding what has already been damaged. We must heed the advice of those who have studied biodiversity and take into consideration the environmental effects of development just as seriously as we take the advice of economists and technicians before making decisions on how to progress.

In 1997, the Southeast Asian region experienced an economic setback partly due to an unbalanced and consumer-focused type of development. One hopes that the next bout of economic growth will be more sensitive to a total quality of life, including an appreciation for our natural heritage, the diversity of life, the health of the environment and the well-being of the other lifeforms around us—including the birds.

Opposite: *Baya Weaver at nest entrance.*

# HOW TO USE THIS BOOK

## Area covered

For the purpose of this book we have adopted the generally accepted system of dividing the world into 6 zoogeographical or faunal regions. Modified from Viney, Phillipps and Lam (1994) the regions are as follows:

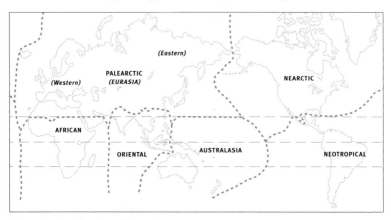

Figure 1: *Faunal regions of the world*

| Regions | Subregions |
|---|---|
| Australasian | Australia, New Zealand, New Guinea and Oceanic Islands |
| African | Africa and Madagascar |
| Neotropical | Central and South America |
| Nearctic | North American and Greenland |
| Oriental | South and Southeast Asia |
| Palearctic | Europe, North Africa and temperate Asia |

In the text, different sections of the Asian continent are referred to as in Figure 2 (opposite, top). The faunal region of special interest here is the Oriental region. This region is usually defined to include South and Southeast Asia from Pakistan east to Borneo and Bali. The northern limit is the Himalayan mountain range and south China. Inskipp, Lindsey and Duckworth (1996) use the Yangtze river as the northern boundary and

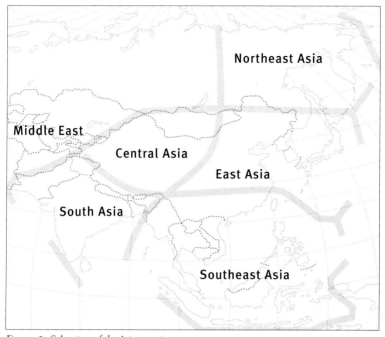

Figure 2: *Subregions of the Asian continent*
Figure 3: *The Oriental region*

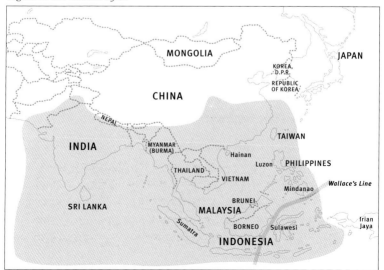

*Birding is a social activity.*

include the transitional subregion of Wallacea, i.e. Eastern Indonesia between Bali and Irian Jaya. Thus defined, the Oriental region has the extension as shown in Figure 3 (previous page, bottom).

Within the Oriental region, the book covers Southeast Asia, an area defined for this purpose to include the following countries and territories shown on the map on pages 2–3.

The term Southeast Asia usually includes the country of Indonesia. Indonesia however straddles two very different faunal regions and is treated separately in another volume.

## Nomenclature, taxonomy and sequence

For nomenclature, taxonomy and sequence our main reference was King, Dickinson and Woodcock (1975). Since this book does not include the latest taxonomic changes, small adjustments have been introduced, mainly following Lekagul and Round (1991) and MacKinnon and Phillipps (1993). Therefore we have placed fantails and monarch flycatchers in their own families, Rhipiduridae and Monarchidae respectively, a practice long ago accepted as standard.

Darters, barn owls, Asian barbets, fairy bluebirds, weavers, munias and buntings have also been allocated their own families.

We are aware of the considerably more radical taxonomic changes inspired by new DNA-based research into the relationships between birds. This information has led to a very different taxonomic system published in Sibley, G. and Monroe Jr. B. (1990), *Distribution and Taxonomy of Birds of the World*. This system was also adopted by Inskipp, Lindsey and Duckworth (1996), by Lim and Gardner (1997) and by Robson (2000). However, this taxonomy is by others deemed to be 'provisional and full of uncertainties' (Jürgen Haffer, *Handbook of the Birds of the World: Vol. 4* p. 22), so until the experts agree we believe it will be most reader-friendly to follow the established system.

Where names differ significantly between the different systems, the alternative name has been mentioned in brackets for easy reference. Efforts have been made to provide correct, brief and user-friendly information, but it is not necessarily complete. Therefore, this list of alternative names does not include names no longer in use or mainly used outside this area (e.g. in India). Please refer to the titles listed in Selected Bibliography for this information.

Regarding the order in which the bird species are listed, it is important to note that all our main reference sources for Southeast Asia uses the 'buntings-last' sequence, as is adopted here. Contrary to that, Andrew, P. (1992) *The Birds of Indonesia: A checklist (Peters' Sequence)* Indonesian Ornithological Society, Jakarta, which is re-printed in Jepson and Ounsted (1997), provides our main source of reference for our twin volume, *A Photographic Guide to the Birds of Indonesia*. This book therefore lists birds according to the somewhat different 'crows-last' sequence.

## Family and genus

The letter F: is short for family, and all Latin families end in '-idea'. The Latin family of the bird is rarely referred to during casual birdwatching. A birdwatcher would not say 'a member of the Apodidae family just flew over', he would use the term 'swift'. Nevertheless, the family of the bird is an important piece of information for the field observer and is therefore included. While almost all Pycnonotidae are labelled bulbuls in their common names, it might not be clear to readers that robins, shortwings, shamas, chats and forktails all belong to the Turdidae or thrush family. So only by looking at the Latin family name does their relationship become clearer.

Notice that mynas are part of the Sturnidae family, named after the starlings; these two groups are in fact closely related. Eagles, hawks, buzzards, kites, harriers and vultures are not different families, but all part of the large Accipitridae family.

Birds are divided into genera within each family. There is no English word for this subdivision, which can only be determined by studying the first of the Latin names. Only a few birds such as cochoas (F: Turdidae) and prinias (F: Sylviidae) use their genus name as their common name also, for example, the Green Cochoa, or *Cochoa viridis*.

It is useful to pay attention to at least the genus (the first part of the Latin name) as this establishes the relationship with other, often similar species. Note how *Merops* bee-eaters have so much in common in terms of build and habits, while *Nyctyornis* bee-eaters, within the same family Meropidae, differ from *Merops* bee-eaters, but are similar to each other.

Curlews, godwits, dowitchers, turnstones, sandpipers, stints and snipe all belong to the same large family Scolopacidae. But within this family notice how the Broad-billed Sandpiper, *Limicola falcinellus*, has a different genus name to the similar *Calidris* stints. Closer study reveals that it is in fact quite distinctive, just like the Ruff, *Philomachus pugnax*, is in many ways unlike the many similarly built *Tringa* sandpipers.

Some birds are unique, with no close relatives. They are monotypic, some form their own genus; this will usually be mentioned under the description of the bird. Very few birds are monotypic to the family level (in this book only the Osprey and the Hoopoe fall into this category), while others such as Oriental Darter, Masked Finfoot and Greater Painted-snipe are sole regional representatives of very small families.

The second part of the Latin name determines the species. Many birds occur in different distinct forms and are divided by taxonomists into separate subspecies or races designated by a third addition to the Latin name. In the Philippines, the resident subspecies Little Heron, *Butorides striatus carcinophilus*, is augmented by a migratory subspecies *B. s. amurensis* during winter. For this purpose only *B. striatus* is referred to. Only in a few instances, where differences are clearly noticeable in the field, are subspecies' characteristics mentioned here.

When birds are classified, families are split into subfamilies, and then grouped into suborders and orders, which together form the class Aves containing all birds. However fascinating the topic, we have deemed it outside the scope of this book, but the subject is thoroughly covered in some of the works listed in the Bibliography. We have, however, for the information of the readers, marked the beginning of the order Passeriformes—by far the largest order containing all the passerine (perching bird) families. These are regarded as the fastest evolving groups of birds. While some non-passerines have remained unchanged for millions of years, dating back almost to the dinosaurs, passerines are constantly developing; they are strong fliers, many males have bright colours or complex voices, and the young stay for longer in the nest, thus these birds are regarded as evolutionarily more advanced.

Each bird name is followed by the length of the species in centimetres. Within some species, notably many raptors in the Accipitridae family, the females are considerably larger than the males, but for brevity, an average size has been given for comparison. Only within the Phasianidae, where the male pheasant can sometimes be more than double the size of the female, have both sizes been included. Where extremely elongated tail feathers distort measurements, this has also been mentioned.

## Photographs

Each species is illustrated with a photograph, sometimes two. If the sex of the bird is not mentioned, the photograph shows an adult bird that cannot be identified with regard to sex. Where sexes differ, this is mentioned in the first paragraph of each entry (Description). The term 'sexes similar' is only used on occasions where most other species within the family are sexually dimorphic—for instance some flowerpeckers.

Unless otherwise mentioned, resident birds are shown in breeding plumage and migrants are shown in non-breeding or winter plumage. An additional photograph might show the other sex of the species or a bird in flight.

Most photographs are taken on location in Southeast Asia and show wild individuals. Where no authentic photograph was available, one showing a captive bird might be used, in which case it is mentioned in the description. We have done this consistently as we felt it was important for the reader to know that habitat, perch and surroundings might not appear as they would in the field. Only one species is shown held in the hand—the Coral-billed Ground-cuckoo.

## Description: bird topography

The description has been kept to a minimum. We have preferred to let the pictures do the talking and have only described what is not obvious, such as parts of the bird not visible in that particular pose or the appearance of the opposite sex. Efforts have been made, however, to point out so-called diagnostic features where appropriate. In the field there is often one single feature that distinguishes one species from all others. The Common Kingfisher has a tiny rufous dot behind the ear—once you spot that one all your worries are over! This technique enables trained birdwatchers to quickly put a name to most of the birds they see, leaving them more time to concentrate on the really tough groups with no (or very faint) diagnostic features.

Some species have no relatives that resemble them closely. These are easy to identify on all occasions, so have simply been labelled 'unmistakable'. Please bear in mind that this term and the diagnostic label only apply within the region covered. While the short bill of the Little Curlew is diagnostic in Southeast Asia, it is not enough as a single identification feature when compared with the Slender-billed Curlew of Eurasia or the Eskimo Curlew of the Americas, which both have fairly small bills. Parts of the bird are mentioned using the standard norm in bird books, but slightly modified for this specific purpose.

The upper surface of the entire body including the mantle, wings,

Figure 4: *The different parts of a bird*

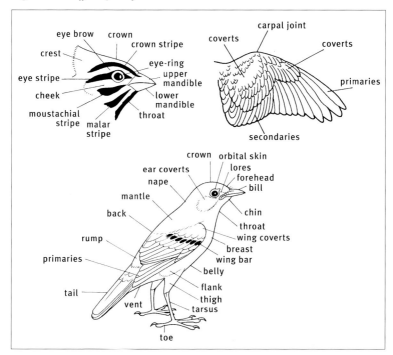

back and rump are often referred to collectively as upperparts, and likewise the entire under surface of the bird including the throat, breast, belly, flanks and vent is labelled collectively as underparts. Taxonomic variations and similar species not illustrated are also covered in this section.

## Voice

Calls follow our main references, especially Lekagul and Round (1991) and Lim and Gardner (1997), authors who have vast personal experiences studying bird vocalisation. Only in a few instances are descriptions modified slightly in accordance with our experiences.

Even using these authoritative sources for reference, verbalisation of bird calls is a tricky business. The frequently heard call by a common and noisy species like the Wood Sandpiper is variously described:

King, Woodcock and Dickinson (1975): fi-fi-fi or ziss, iss-iss

> Lekagul and Round (1991): chiff-chiff-chiff
> Lim and Gardner (1997): si-si-si
> MacKinnon and Phillipps: chee-chee-chee

From our own experience we chose wee-wee-wee as the best verbalisation.

> The less often heard Changeable Hawk-eagle is thus described:
> King, Woodcock and Dickinson (1975): yeep-yip-yip-yip
> Lekagul and Round (1991): kri-kri-kri-kri-kree-ah
> Lim and Gardner (1997): hwee-hwee-hwee
> MacKinnon and Phillipps: kwip-kwip-kwip-kwee-ah

Here we chose to follow Lim and Gardner (1997), partly from personal experience, partly from certainty that the author is very familiar with the call.

Despite these discrepancies in verbalisation, we felt it was important to include a voice description. Combining the call with observations can sometimes be crucial for identification. And while many families have similar calls within members—most bulbuls produce a similar soft chatter—other families are very diverse. The Bushy-crested Hornbill screams, the Rhinoceros Hornbill honks and the White-crowned Hornbill hoots. At least knowing that much is a help for the beginner.

However, in our experience, calls cannot be learned from a book. Audio tapes may help, but the best method is to go out there off the trails and find the bird making the call—often time and time again until the connection stays with you.

## Habits

This section includes an account of where the bird can be found and how it is likely to behave. Terms describing habitat are mainly self-explanatory except for forest birds. Since the exact distribution of different forest types in this region is a very complex subject, we have made a simple distinction between wet evergreen tropical rainforest and deciduous forests. Rainforest comprising mainly tall dipterocarp trees is the predominant vegetation type in the Philippines and in the Sunda subregion, including the Malay Peninsula and Borneo. It also grows with a slightly different tree composition in wet tropical parts of continental Thailand, Myanmar and Indochina where the term evergreen forest is often applied—please see Lekagul and Round (1991) for a more detailed explanation. In deciduous forest a majority of the trees shed their leaves during the dry winter months; this habitat type prevails in the northern drier and more seasonal subtropical areas. Although some species occur in both habitats there are also great differences in the respective avifaunas.

The terms primary and secondary forest have been used as defined in the Glossary. Secondary forest varies from low regrowth with few large trees remaining, to areas selectively logged decades back with many large trees remaining, or regrown forest, labelled mature secondary growth in this volume. Where canopies meet and form a continuous cover, even though some disturbance may have taken place, the term closed forest is sometimes applied. At the other end of the scale, where no large trees are left standing, the habitat is labelled scrub.

Forest changes composition with elevation, likewise does the associated avifauna. In the tropics this change is both profound and amazing. In the East Malaysian state of Sabah on Borneo it is possible to travel from the lowlands at Poring Hot Springs to the summit of Mount Kinabalu at 4,101 metres within a couple of days—a journey that has been compared to travelling overland from the Equator to the Arctic.

Very few birds occur across the whole altitudinal range. In fact most birds occur only in the lowland forest. A few are restricted to the extreme lowlands below 300 metres but many also move into the foothills or submontane elevations. At 900 metres elevation the composition of birds changes significantly as many different species can only be found in the lower and upper montane elevations. A few occur only in alpine habitats near the tree limit, which in the tropics is around 3,600 metres.

Therefore the altitudinal range of the bird is an important item of information. Where numbers are given, these are taken from our main sources of reference, sometimes rounded off to nearest the 100 metres. For a definition of the vocabulary used, please see Figure 5 (page 36).

Within the vast region covered by this book we have not found it appropriate to give specific directions to where a particular species can best be found. Only in a few special cases has this been done for species that in our experience are mainly reported from certain often-visited protected areas such as Khao Yai National Park in Thailand or Mount Kinabalu National Park in Sabah.

After a description of the habitat and preferred elevation, there follows a brief mention of where within the habitat the bird is likely to be spotted. Especially in the lowland tropical rainforest, birds are typically specialists and occupy narrow niches within the forest. A few families like flowerpeckers, sunbirds and leafbirds may have members that frequently move across all levels of the forest, but this is the exception. It is true to say that a barbet will never be found on the ground or a pheasant in the top of a tree.

We have followed Strange and Jeyarajasingam (1993) using terms describing the levels of the forest that are best illustrated as in Figure 6 (page 37).

Any relevant notes on feeding and breeding behavior follow at the end of this paragraph.

## Distribution and status

The distribution paragraph gives the extralimital range of the bird using the terms defined under 'Area Covered' in this chapter. Only a few species occur worldwide and most are restricted to the Oriental region. A few do not fit into the faunal regions as defined here, but this is explained. For instance, the Red-wattled Lapwing extends outside the Oriental region, without really spreading into the main Palearctic region, so the generally recognised area Middle East has been used.

Where nothing else is mentioned the bird is sedentary. For some groups with many migratory species, such as shorebirds, raptors and warblers, sedentary status is sometimes mentioned for clarification to emphasise that the species is an exception to the rule. But usually this is not the case, since large families like babblers and pheasants simply have no migratory members at all. The status of migratory species is, however, always explained. The term 'nomadic' refers to a species that moves outside its breeding range when not breeding, but not in the predictable north–south route followed by migratory birds.

For a few species their extralimital range falls within the area defined. This region does not have many restricted range or endemic species, but there are some and these are labelled 'Southeast Asia only' for clarification. They include small distribution species such as the Puff-throated, Stripe-throated and Grey-eyed Bulbul, Black-headed Sibia, Green-eared Barbet and Bar-bellied Pitta.

Most other small distribution range species also occur in Indonesia, as is the case for almost all the Sunda subregion endemic species. Even those endemic to Borneo usually extend into Indonesian Kalimantan. Since the rest of the Sunda subregion (Kalimantan, Sumatra, Java and Bali) is covered in *A Photographic Guide to the Birds of Indonesia*, the reader is advised to consult these two volumes together to get the larger picture of the distribution of most Southeast Asian birds.

Sometimes for clarification the term 'Eastern Indonesia' is used. This collectively refers to that part of Indonesia, which lies east of Borneo and Bali, i.e. east of Wallace's Line, an area that may or may not be regarded as part of the Oriental region. Please see *A Photographic Guide to the Birds of Indonesia* for further information.

Some species, such as the Green Peafowl and Pied Bushchat, have a discontinuous distribution and occur only in northern Southeast Asia and again on some Indonesia islands, in effect 'jumping over' the humid Sunda subregion. Here maps do not provide the full picture and again it has been necessary to explain further in the text.

After the full stop this paragraph covers the bird's local distribution and status. Where part of the bird's distribution falls outside the area covered—in other words the large majority of species—this has been clarified by the expression 'in region ... '. Region refers to the map on pages 2–3.

In general the wording is only meant as a supplement to the maps which are aimed at being self-explanatory. They have been drawn up using our references for source, but have been updated in a few instances

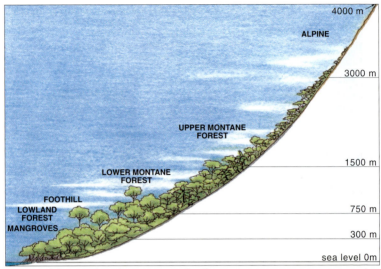

Figure 5: *The tropical rainforest at various altitudes*

according to the latest information published in Oriental Bird Club publications, please see Bibliography for details.

A simple colour-code has been applied to the maps:

- ■ blue indicating migratory/non-breeding visitor status only
- ■ red indicating breeding range.

Where breeding populations are augmented by migratory birds during the winter, this is explained in the text. Winter here refers to the northern hemisphere winter months December, January and February, the actual migratory season for most birds lasts from September to April. A few migrants can in fact be met with in winter quarters almost all months of the year.

Most migratory birds in Southeast Asia arrive on the so-called East Asian Flyway, following either the Malay Peninsula or the Philippine archipelago south, as illustrated in Figure 7 (page 40), which has been modified after Sonobe and Usui (1993).

We are aware that other authors, such as Lekagul and Round (1991) use a more elaborate system of four colour codes to distinguish between migratory and sedentary residents, and between passage

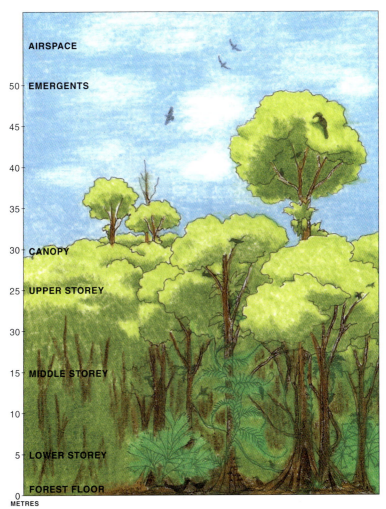

Figure 6: *Vertical levels of the rainforest*

migrants and winter visitors. This was deemed impractical in our case as it would only lead to a false sense of accuracy if applied here.

Since the maps are quite small it is not possible to accurately pick out Singapore, Hong Kong and Brunei. These areas are therefore mentioned specially in the text where appropriate, except for montane species which by definition will not occur in these lowlands.

Although not a country, Hong Kong has been singled out because of a long tradition of birdwatching in and around this territory. Otherwise the southern provinces of China are collectively referred to as south China except for Yunnan province, which is the only location in China for some Oriental region birds. The islands of Taiwan and Hainan can be identified on the map. Please see de Schauensee (1984) for a more detailed account of Chinese avifauna.

In Southeast Asia, there is a prolific trade in captive birds, and some individuals inevitably escape from their cages. Others are deliberately released during religious festivals. Lim and Gardner (1997) lists 58 species spotted in the wild in Singapore which are totally alien to that nation. In general these so-called escapees are not included in ornithological literature and are also not covered here. A few species, however, establish viable breeding populations in this way outside their natural range. These are referred to here as introduced species.

## Abundance code

We have tried to provide the reader with some idea of how common the bird is and how likely it is to be found in the field. It must be said that this is a highly subjective exercise and any label attached can only serve as a rough guideline.

The usual reference books are not very reliable for this purpose. Note that MacKinnon & Phillipps (1993) describe the Bushy-crested Hornbill as an 'Abundant hornbill ... in Borneo', Legagul & Round (1991) has it as a 'Fairly common resident' in Thailand. Contrary to that, Poonswad and Kemp (1993) list this species as rare in Indonesia and endangered with local extinction in Thailand.

For this purpose I have relied as much on published trip reports and personal comments by fellow birdwatchers as my own experiences. Since I have never seen a Bushy-crested Hornbill, despite travelling through prime habitat in both Thailand and East Malaysia for days and weeks, I simply labelled it as 'generally scarce', although it must be said that it appears to be locally fairly numerous in parts of Peninsular

Malaysia. Lekagul and Round (1991) describe the Plain-backed Sparrow as 'very common resident' in Thailand, yet birdwatchers have commented to me that they have travelled for weeks through that country working hard to find one or two individuals. Therefore it is listed here as 'uncommon'.

It could be that field guides are either written by very capable ornithologists who easily locate scarce birds, or that they tend to copy from other outdated references. Newer publications like Sun et al. (1998) tend to provide a more realistic picture on status. At any rate, it has been my experience that resident rainforest birds especially are few in number and are usually infrequently encountered, therefore many of those have been 'down-graded' to uncommon status here, which I hope will give the reader a more realistic expectation of birdwatching conditions in the region. In montane forest habitat, the diversity is lower, but the density tends to be higher, and more montane residents thus have been labelled fairly common or even common.

Where there appears to be a great discrepancy in status within range, this has been differentiated between the countries. Please note that references to status do not apply to Myanmar, where very little current information is available.

Some terms used:

**Widespread** means that the bird occurs over a wide geographical area and in a variety of habitat types.

**Local** is the antonym for widespread and is used where a species is restricted to a special habitat within a small geographical area.

The term **scarce** indicates that a bird occurs in low numbers (while an uncommon bird although uncommonly encountered could be locally and seasonally numerous or might be numerous elsewhere in extralimital range).

**Numerous** is the antonym of scarce, a species occurring in large numbers.

**Abundant** is very numerous, occurring in very large numbers, sometimes dense flocks.

Figure 7: *Southeast Asia migration routes*

Modified from Viney, Phillipps and Lam (1994) and Lim and Gardner (1997) we have used the following colour codes to indicate abundance of birds:

● Common. Encountered with at least 90 percent certainty in preferred habitat.

◉ Fairly common. Encountered with between 50 percent and 90 percent certainty in preferred habitat.

- ⊙ Uncommon. Encountered with less than 50 percent certainty in preferred habitat.

- ○ Rare. Encountered once a year or less in preferred habitat.

## Globally threatened status

We have included a code for globally threatened status. It follows the important BirdLife International study, which was published in Collar et al. (1994), please consult this book for more detailed information. Briefly, this survey operates with four main categories, which have been adopted unchanged here:

- ● Critically endangered; 50 percent chance of becoming extinct in five years.

- ◉ Endangered; 20 percent chance of becoming extinct in 20 years.

- ⊙ Vulnerable; 10 percent chance of becoming extinct in 100 years.

- ○ Near-threatened; close to qualifying for the categories above.

*The author in freshwater wetlands.*

## LITTLE GREBE (Red-throated Little Grebe)
### *Tachybaptus ruficollis* 25 cm  F: Podicipedidae

**Description**: Unmistakable. Note yellow spot near bill in breeding plumage; non-breeding plumage is duller, breast and hind neck pale brown.

**Voice**: A sharp *ke-ke-ke-ke*.

**Habits**: Like all grebes, a strictly aquatic bird rarely seen flying. Swims in ponds and lakes near or among reeds and dives when disturbed. Feeds on fish and aquatic invertebrates. Disperses outside breeding season, small flocks sometimes gather at prime locations.

**Distribution**: Africa, Eurasia into New Guinea; partly migratory. A widespread and generally common resident throughout mainland Southeast Asia; fairly common in Hong Kong; uncommon in the Philippines; rare in Singapore.

## SPOT-BILLED PELICAN
### *Pelecanus philippensis* 140 cm  F: Pelecanidae

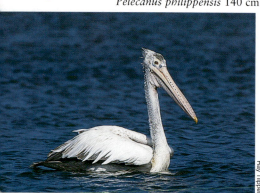

**Description**: Distinguished from other pelicans by spotted upper mandible on bill; also grey-tinged to white plumage.

**Voice**: Generally quiet.

**Habits**: Frequents a variety of shallow wetlands, from inland marshes and lakes, to brackish estuaries near the coast. Swims on surface and dives for fish, often in flocks with other water birds. Formerly widespread, numerous and locally abundant, with millions of birds in Myanmar alone. During the last few decades has declined drastically; now scarce throughout its range and vulnerable to global extinction.

**Distribution**: Oriental region. A confirmed resident in Cambodia only; a rare visitor to Myanmar, Thailand, Vietnam, southeast China, excluding Hong Kong; vagrant in Laos, the Philippines and Peninsular Malaysia.

## MASKED BOOBY
*Sula dactylatra* 86 cm  F: Sulidae

**Description**: Distinguished from other boobies by black facial mask contrasting with yellow bill; distinguished from Brown Booby also by large size and white (not brown) neck and wing coverts.

**Voice**: Quiet during migration; honks and whistles near nest.

**Habits**: A pelagic bird, sometimes found 1,000 km from nearest land. Only visits remote offshore islets to breed, however even these sites are not too remote for fishermen who collect eggs and young. Populations have been greatly reduced in Southeast Asia, but are still sizable in other regions such as the Pacific Ocean. Makes spectacular dives into the sea for large fish.

**Distribution**: Worldwide tropical oceans; roams widely outside breeding season. A rare visitor to the region and scarce resident in the Sulu Sea, the Philippines and off Sabah, Malaysia.

## RED-FOOTED BOOBY
*Sula sula* 71 cm  F: Sulidae

**Description**: Note diagnostic white tail. Also distinguished from previous species by smaller size, yellowish head and lack of mask.

**Voice**: Quiet during migration; honks and whistles near nest.

**Habits**: A pelagic bird that flies up to 150 km from breeding colony to forage on small flying fish and squid; never seen near the mainland. Mostly reduced in numbers in Southeast Asia, but over a million individuals are still found in the Pacific Ocean region, the Caribbean and off Australia.

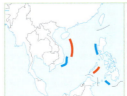

**Distribution**: Worldwide 1tropical oceans; roams widely outside breeding season. Within the region, a scarce resident around the Sulu Sea, the Philippines, the Paracel Islands and the South China Sea; vagrant in Malaysia.

# BROWN BOOBY
## *Sula leucogaster* 74 cm  F: Sulidae

**Description:** Note diagnostic chocolate-brown upper parts and neck contrasting with white belly.

**Voice:** Quiet during migration; quacking calls near nest.

**Habits:** The most widespread member of its family in Southeast Asia. Occasionally seen near the mainland coast flying low, with characteristic shallow wing beats. Although no longer a resident in Thailand and other areas, still locally numerous on islands in the Malacca Strait, South China Sea and off the Philippines. A large colony is located on the Layang-Layang Islands, where this photograph was taken. Can be reached by direct flight from Kota Kinabalu in Sabah.

**Distribution:** Worldwide tropical oceans; wanders widely, reaching Japan. Within the region, a very local resident in offshore Malaysia, the Philippines, and on the Spratly and Paracel Islands. A widespread but uncommon visitor elsewhere.

# GREAT CORMORANT (Cormorant)
## *Phalacrocorax carbo* 81 cm  F: Phalacrocoracidae

**Description:** Large size is diagnostic. Note whitish cheeks and throat.

**Voice:** Generally silent, although it grunts and groans at breeding sites.

**Habits:** Like other cormorants, it swims low in the water, diving for fish; between dives it often sits near water's edge drying off. A strong flyer, this species is trained to assist fishermen in China.

**Distribution:** Worldwide. Within the region, an uncommon resident in Indochina, Myanmar and south China; an uncommon, non-breeding visitor in Thailand, Malaysia, Brunei and the Philippines.

# LITTLE CORMORANT
*Phalacrocorax niger* 52 cm  F: Phalacrocoracidae.

**Description:** Distinguished with some difficulty from the generally less common Indian Shag, *P. fuscicollis* (64 cm), by its smaller size and shorter bill.

**Voice:** Usually silent, although it grunts and groans at breeding sites.

**Habits:** Lives around ponds, swamps and flooded fields, often near the coast, extending into tidal mangroves. Locally abundant in prime habitat, such as the wetlands south of Bangkok; often seen flying between its feeding grounds and its breeding colonies, located in low trees surrounded by water. Also perches in the open to dry out plumage after diving for fish.

**Distribution:** Worldwide. Within the region, a common resident locally in Myanmar, Thailand and Vietnam; an uncommon resident in Cambodia, Laos and south China; a rare, non-breeding visitor in Peninsular Malaysia.

# DARTER (Oriental Darter)
*Anhinga melanogaster* 91 cm  F: Anhingidae

**Description:** Unmistakable. Note the long, thin neck and pale streaks in plumage. A unique species; an American species is the only other member of this family.

**Voice:** Usually silent.

**Habits:** Found in inland swamps, overgrown reservoirs and rivers, often with wooded surroundings. Swims low in the water with only the head and neck above surface. Dives for fish as well as aquatic amphibians, reptiles and invertebrates. Suns itself like a cormorant, see photo.

**Distribution:** Africa, Oriental region, Australasia. Within the region, a widespread but rare resident in Myanmar, Thailand, Indochina, the Philippines, East Malaysia and Brunei; also possibly found in south China and Peninsular Malaysia.

## GREAT FRIGATEBIRD
*Fregata minor* 94 cm  F: Fregatidae

**Description**: Photo shows male; note complete lack of white in plumage. Female has white chest. Immature bird also has light brown head.

**Voice**: Silent; makes clappering noises when breeding.

**Habits**: A strictly pelagic bird, like all members of this small family. Only visits the shores of remote islets during breeding season, where it nests in colonies in low trees. Otherwise roams widely, surface dipping for fish and squid.

**Distribution**: Tropical oceans worldwide. Within the region, an uncommon resident off the shores of the Philippine islands and south China; a rare non-breeding visitor off Vietnam, Thailand and Peninsular Malaysia; a vagrant off Brunei.

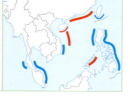

## LESSER FRIGATEBIRD
*Fregata ariel* 76 cm  F: Fregatidae

**Description**: Photo shows male. Distinguished from previous species by smaller size and white spots under wings. Female has white chest. Immature bird also light brown head.

**Voice**: Silent during migration.

**Habits**: This pelagic bird picks up fish and squid from surface waters far offshore and is rarely found near the coast. As well, some of this species, mostly females, chase terns and steal their fish. A very elegant flyer, this bird moves about singly or in small flocks, and is found at a few remote islets, sometimes in huge congregations.

**Distribution**: Tropical oceans worldwide. Within the region, an uncommon non-breeding visitor in offshore waters, including the waters near Singapore and Brunei. No breeding record.

## GREAT-BILLED HERON
*Ardea sumatrana* 115 cm  F: Ardeidae

**Description**: Huge size and grey plumage are diagnostic. Immature bird is more brownish and lacks the breeding adult's narrow, whitish plumes.

**Voice**: Sometimes a harsh croak.

**Habits**: A quiet and shy bird, usually seen standing alone and motionless along muddy seashores or offshore islets, on the lookout for fish and crustaceans. During high tide it rests among mangrove trees. Occasionally follows rivers inland. Flies off low across the water. Not numerous at any location.

**Distribution:** Southeast Asia, south to northern Australia; sedentary. A rare resident along remote coastlines within the region.

## GREY HERON
*Ardea cinerea* 95 cm  F: Ardeidae

**Description**: White neck and head with grey upper parts are diagnostic.

**Voice**: Deep, guttural honks while in flight or at breeding site.

**Habits**: Occurs along coastal mudflats but also in freshwater swamps and along inland rivers. Feeds mainly on fish and other aquatic prey, but also on reptiles and rodents. Flies slowly, high above habitat. Breeds in dense colonies located in low, inaccessible trees near water.

**Distribution:** Africa and Eurasia; northern populations migrate. Resident in south China, Vietnam, Myanmar, Malaysia and Singapore; fairly common migrant throughout the region.

## PURPLE HERON
*Ardea purpurea* 90 cm  F: Ardeidae

**Description**: Look for diagnostic purple head and neck. Note how head is pulled back during flight.

**Voice**: A harsh croak, mainly uttered within breeding colony and when taking off.

**Habits**: An aquatic bird, usually seen near overgrown freshwater rivers and reservoirs, less often at the coast. Feeds on fish, which it stalks patiently at the water's edge. Forms dense colonies during the breeding season, often mixing with other herons.

**Distribution:** Africa and Eurasia; northern populations migrate. Winter visitor and resident throughout much of the region, including Hong Kong, Singapore and probably Brunei.

## LITTLE HERON (Striated Heron)
*Butorides striatus* 45 cm  F: Ardeidae

**Description**: A small heron with crouching stance. Immature bird is brown with pale streaks. A unique, monotypic genus.

**Voice**: A loud *kweak...kee-kee-kee-kee* when taking off.

**Habits**: As a resident, most commonly found near the coast, where it nests in low mangrove trees, but occurs in all kinds of wetlands, including freshwater marshes and canals. Sometimes walks conspicuously out in the open along the water's edge.

**Distribution:** Tropics worldwide; partly migratory. A common resident in all countries of the region. Locally very numerous, especially during winter when local populations are augmented by northern migrants.

## CHINESE POND-HERON
*Ardeola bacchus* 45 cm  F: Adeidae

**Description:** Photo shows non-breeding plumage. During breeding, the head and breast are dark chestnut, the back is black and wings flash white in flight.

**Voice:** Normally silent. Low croaks during breeding.

**Habits:** An attractive small heron usually found at overgrown ponds, marshes and paddy fields, where it walks along slowly, looking for aquatic prey. Less common in mangroves. Breeds in colonies with other herons.

**Distribution:** China and Southeast Asia; partly migratory. Resident in south China, including Hong Kong and parts of Indochina. A common migrant within the rest of the region, although rare on Borneo and the Philippines.

## JAVAN POND-HERON
*Ardeola speciosa* 45 cm  F: Ardeidae

**Description:** Note the diagnostic pale chestnut breast and whitish head of breeding plumage; white wings flash brightly during flight. In non-breeding plumage is not easily distinguished from the Chinese Pond-heron.

**Voice:** Similar to previous species.

**Habits:** Moves about freshwater wetlands, flooded fields and sometimes among coastal mangroves, singly or in loose groups. A rather shy bird that walks slowly or stands waiting quietly for aquatic prey to appear.

**Distribution:** Southeast Asia; sedentary. Resident within the region; fairly common locally in central Thailand and southern Indochina. Vagrant in Malaysia, Brunei and the Philippines.

# CATTLE EGRET
*Bubulcus ibis* 50 cm  F: Ardeidae

**Description**: Small, stocky shape and yellow bill are diagnostic. A unique, monotypic genus. Orange plumes on head, chest and back during breeding season (see photo, bird in background).

**Voice**: Usually silent, although croaks at nest.

**Habits**: Numerous locally in open country and on cultivated fields; does not visit mudflats and beaches. Associates with grazing domestic animals, catching the insects, frogs and lizards that the cattle disturb. Large flocks form at communal roosts in the evenings and at breeding sites. A successful and expanding species.

**Distribution:** Worldwide; prefers warm climates; nomadic. A fairly common resident and non-breeding visitor throughout the region.

# PACIFIC REEF-EGRET (Reef Egret)
*Egretta sacra* 58 cm  F: Ardeidae

**Description**: Medium-sized egret with dull yellow bill; note dark tip on upper mandible (top). Northern birds often occur in a slate-black colour phase (bottom).

**Voice**: Sometimes a harsh arrk when disturbed.

**Habits**: A strictly coastal egret that ventures only occasionally up tidal estuaries and canals. Prefers exposed sandy and rocky seacoasts; sometimes found on mudflats feeding on small fish in shallow waters during low tide, usually alone or in small groups. Nests on the ground on remote coastal outcrops.

**Distribution:** East Asia into Australasia; sedentary. A fairly common resident throughout the region.

## CHINESE EGRET
*Egretta eulophotes* 68 cm  F: Ardeidae

**Description**: Photo shows breeding plumage; long crest and bright yellow bill and toes are diagnostic; orbital skin blue. In winter, only its longer legs and narrow bill distinguish it from the previous species.

**Voice**: Generally silent.

**Habits**: Occupies a narrow niche of tidal mudflats near estuaries; does not occur inland or on rocky shorelines. Confusion with the Pacific Reef-Egret is possible during winter months, although this species feeds more actively, sometimes running through shallow water with open wings to stir up prey.

**Distribution**: Breeds in northern China and Korea; winters in Southeast Asia. Formerly resident in Hong Kong; a rare winter visitor at certain locations within the region. World population is only about 2,000 individuals.

## GREAT EGRET
*Egretta alba* 90 cm *(Casmerodius albus)*  F: Ardeidae

**Description**: Huge size, long neck and strong bill are diagnostic. Bill is yellow (photo) during non-breeding season. During breeding season, bill is black and legs are reddish.

**Voice**: Sometimes a low, crow-like *kraa-a* when taking off.

**Habits**: Occurs in all types of wetlands, including coastal mangroves, estuaries and wet fields. Walks slowly or stands quietly, singly or in a small group, on the lookout for aquatic prey. Scattered groups may gather together at prime locations during winter months and can be very numerous locally.

**Distribution**: Worldwide; prefers warm climates; partly migratory. A fairly common, non-breeding visitor throughout the region and reported from all countries and territories. Also resident at certain locations.

## PLUMED EGRET *(Intermediate Egret)*
*Egretta intermedia* 70 cm, *Mesophoyz intermedia* F: Ardeidae

**Description**: A medium-sized bird. Its fairly short yellow bill is diagnostic.

**Voice**: Usually silent, except for a deep *kroa-kr* when taking off.

**Habits**: Found in the company of other egrets, mostly in freshwater marshes and fields, but also on tidal mudflats and along estuaries. Generally less numerous than the Great Egret and Little Egret. Walks slowly in the search of small fish, frogs and insects.

**Distribution**: Africa, the Oriental region, Australasia; partly migratory. A non-breeding visitor throughout all countries and territories within the region; resident in parts of Indochina, Myanmar and southwest China.

## LITTLE EGRET
*Egretta garzetta* 60 cm F: Ardeidae

**Description**: A small and slender egret. Note diagnostic thin, black bill and yellow feet. Feet black in Javan *(nigripes)* race which occurs in Singapore and Malaysia.

**Voice**: Usually silent, except for croaking calls at its nest.

**Habits**: The most common of the egrets, numerous at both freshwater and tidal wetlands. An attractive bird that feeds by walking quickly or running through shallow water, stirring up and chasing aquatic prey. Flocks disperse while feeding, but congregate at evening roosts and in breeding colonies.

**Distribution**: Africa, Eurasia and Australasia; northern populations migrate south. Within the region, a common resident and migrant on the mainland; less common in Borneo and the Philippines.

## BLACK-CROWNED NIGHT-HERON
### *Nycticorax nycticorax* 61 cm  F: Ardeidae

**Description**: Unmistakable; legs red during breeding. Immature bird is brown, dotted with white.

**Voice**: A penetrating, deep *wo-ok* when taking off.

**Habits**: Spends the day roosting in trees above water in mangroves or swamps. In early evening flocks disperse, flying slowly, high in the sky, on their way to feed in ponds and marshes during the night, returning during the morning. Huge breeding colonies in the region have been known to contain tens of thousands of birds.

**Distribution:** Worldwide, except in Australasia; partly migratory. Within the region, a fairly common resident on the mainland, including Singapore and Hong Kong; a migrant elsewhere.

## MALAYAN NIGHT-HERON
### *Gorsachius melanolophus* 48 cm  F: Ardeidae

**Description**: Photo shows immature plumage. The adult is a uniformly dark rufous colour with a blackish cap, missing on the similar Japanese Night-Heron, *G. goisagi*, which is sometimes seen in the region.

**Voice**: A series of deep *oo* notes.

**Habits**: Very secretive, staying inside flooded forests and overgrown lowland swamps. Also seen near cultivation during migration. Feeds mainly on insects, molluscs, small amphibians, reptiles and sometimes fish. Nocturnal and not often observed; breeding habits and movements little studied.

**Distribution:** Oriental region; partly migratory. A generally scarce resident in the Philippines and on parts of the mainland; uncommon winter visitor in Peninsular Malaysia; rare visitor to Singapore; vagrant in Taiwan and Borneo, including Brunei.

## YELLOW BITTERN
### *Ixobrychus sinensis* 38 cm  F: Ardeidae

**Description**: Small, slender, pale bittern. Note diagnostic black wingtips. Immature bird streaked with brown.

**Voice**: A short *kakak-kakak* when taking off.

**Habits**: Prefers freshwater swampland habitat. Lives among tall, dense marsh and riverside vegetation, where it climbs around at the bottom of the reeds, stalking aquatic invertebrates and tiny fish. Secretive and crepuscular in habit; sometimes seen clearly when it flies briefly out of the vegetation.

**Distribution**: Oriental region; East Asia, east to New Guinea; northern populations migrate. A common resident and migratory visitor throughout the region.

## SCHRENCK'S BITTERN
### *Ixobrychus eurhythmus* 38 cm  F: Ardeidae

**Description**: Photo shows female. Male has uniformly pale brown under-parts contrasting with dark brown upper-parts.

**Voice**: Low squawks in flight.

**Habits**: As a resident, it is most common near the coast, where it nests in low mangrove trees. During migration it occurs in all types of wetland, including freshwater marshes and canals. Sometimes walks conspicuously out in the open along the water's edge. Not numerous anywhere within its range.

**Distribution**: Breeds in northern East Asia, winters in Southeast Asia. An uncommon winter visitor in much of the region; not recorded in Brunei and Cambodia.

## CINNAMON BITTERN
*Ixobrychus cinnamomeus* 38 cm  F: Ardeidae

**Description**: Photo shows female. Male has uniformly pale rufous under-parts and darker upper-parts with no scales. In flight, uniformly rufous wings are characteristic.

**Voice**: Sometimes a low croak on take-off.

**Habits**: Found in freshwater swamps and along lakesides with some vegetation cover, never in tidal areas. An adaptable species that seems to prefer flooded grasslands and extensive paddy fields. Numerous, but never abundant. Not easy to observe as it searches for small aquatic prey near cover. Usually seen flying low over the grass before dropping back into cover.

**Distribution**: Oriental region; partly migratory. A widespread, generally common resident throughout the region; a winter visitor to all countries and territories.

## BLACK BITTERN
*Dupetor flavicollis* 54 cm  F: Ardeidae

**Description**: Note very dark plumage and some pale streaks on neck; in flight appears all black.

**Voice**: Sometimes a deep croak on take-off; also a booming call during breeding.

**Habits**: A wetland bird that prefers wooded swamps with tall reeds and trees nearby. Also visits flooded rainforest and tidal areas during migration. Rarely seen in open fields. Feeds secretively on fish, frogs and invertebrates, usually during low light periods. Often spotted making short flights and sometimes perching in trees.

**Distribution**: Oriental region, Australasia; northern populations migrate south. A fairly common resident in northern parts of the region; an uncommon winter visitor in Malaysia, Singapore, Brunei and Hong Kong.

# GREAT BITTERN
## *Botaurus stellaris* 76 cm  F: Ardeidae

**Description:** Unmistakable. Note massive size and sandy-brown, barred plumage.

**Voice:** Quiet during migration.

**Habits:** This secretive wetland bird requires extensive swamps with vast reed beds to thrive, but during migration it might turn up at smaller ponds or cultivated areas. Feeds quietly on small animals and in spite of its size is difficult to spot. Freezes or walks away when approached and prefers not to fly during the day.

**Distribution:** Breeds in temperate Eurasia; winters in subtropical Africa and Asia. Within the region, a widespread but scarce winter visitor on the mainland, including Hong Kong; rare in the Philippines, Peninsular Malaysia and Singapore.

# MILKY STORK
## *Mycteria cinerea* 92 cm  F: Ciconiidae

**Description:** Note diagnostic white under-parts and under-wing coverts; also yellow bill and red face.

**Voice:** Silent.

**Habits:** A shy mangrove bird that feeds on the mudflats for about two hours each day during low tide, catching mudskippers and other fish, as well as snakes and frogs. Nests in small colonies in trees in remote mangrove forests.

**Distribution:** Southeast Asia; sedentary. A rare resident in south Vietnam, Cambodia and the state of Perak, Malaysia. Vulnerable to global extinction.

## PAINTED STORK
*Mycteria leucephala* 102 cm  F: Ciconiidae

**Description**: Blackish breast-band and wings are diagnostic. Captive photo.

**Voice**: Silent.

**Habits**: Unlike the similar Milky Stork, this freshwater bird feeds in marshes, lakes and occasionally wet fields, mainly on fish, but also catches frogs, reptiles and insects. Breeds in colonies in trees near the water, often in the company of other storks and herons.

**Distribution**: Patchy occurrence within the Oriental region; most common in India; partly nomadic. Status in region largely unknown; numbers much reduced in Thailand.

## ASIAN OPENBILL
*Anastomus oscitans* 81 cm  F: Ciconiidae

**Description**: Smallest of the Asian storks. Size and a peculiar bill that does not close are diagnostic.

**Voice**: Generally silent.

**Habits**: Feeds almost exclusively on apple snails in freshwater marshes and wet fields, extracting snails with its specialized bill. Best place to see this species is the spectacular breeding colony in Wat Phai Lom, Thailand from November to April, when the semi-tame birds can be observed from special viewing towers. Populations disperse outside breeding season.

**Distribution**: Indian subcontinent and SE Asia. Within the region, a few colonies exist in Vietnam and Thailand; may breed in Cambodia and Myanmar.

# BLACK STORK
## *Ciconia nigra* 100 cm  F: Ciconiidae

**Distribution**: Breeds in temperate Eurasia; winters in subtropical Asia and Africa. Within the region, a rare winter visitor in northern parts of the mainland, including Hong Kong; vagrant in Taiwan.

**Description**: Black neck, wings and mantle are diagnostic; also note red bill. Captive photo.

**Voice**: Silent.

**Habits**: Found in marshes, along large rivers and around ponds behind the coast. Often occurs in somewhat vegetated areas, but during migration avoids closed forest. Feeds mainly on fish, but also takes a variety of other small aquatic and terrestrial prey. Recorded infrequently during the northern winter months from November to March. Seems to have declined in numbers in recent years.

# WOOLLY-NECKED STORK
## *Ciconia episcopus* 91 cm  F: Ciconiidae

**Distribution**: African and Oriental regions. Within the region, a rare resident in Myanmar, Cambodia, Vietnam, and possibly Thailand; an uncommon resident in the Philippines.

**Description**: Note diagnostic white extending across whole neck. The rare Sunda subregion resident subspecies is often treated as a full species. Storm's Stork, *C. stormi*, has black lower neck and yellow (not blue) facial skin.

**Voice**: Silent.

**Habits**: Occurs in marshes and wet fields in the lowlands that often have some trees, but is not found in forest. Also found behind estuaries and mangroves, but not on tidal mudflats, walking slowly, picking up fish, frogs, reptiles and large insects. Usually solitary and not numerous anywhere. Seems to have declined in numbers. Rarely observed.

# BLACK-NECKED STORK
## *Ephippiorhynchus asiaticus* 132 cm  F: Ciconiidae

**Description:** Note huge size, massive black bill and white back.

**Voice:** Silent.

**Habits:** Frequents marshes, monsoon-flooded savanna forest, and coastal swamps and lagoons; occasionally found in tidal mangroves. Feeds mainly on fish, but also takes frogs, reptiles and insects. Seems to require extensive, undisturbed wetlands to thrive, and has declined almost to extinction in Southeast Asia. In India and Australia, where it lives near villages and farmlands, it has adapted better to disturbed conditions.

**Distribution:** India, Southeast Asia, New Guinea and Australia. Within the region, a rare resident in Vietnam, possibly also Cambodia and Myanmar; a vagrant in Laos and Thailand.

# GREATER ADJUTANT
## *Leptoptilos dubius* 145 cm  F: Ciconiidae

**Description:** Distinguished from following species by larger size, and grey panel in wing and neck pouch. Captive photo.

**Voice:** Silent.

**Habits:** Occurs around freshwater marshes and large lakes, also in fields and drier grassland areas. Feeds on carrion; also catches fish, reptiles and injured animals. An abundant bird in the 19th century, with millions reported in India and Myanmar. Even in the early 20th century it was numerous, entering villages to feed on garbage and resting on rooftops. Now numbers have decreased alarmingly and the species is considered endangered with global extinction.

**Distribution:** Oriental region. A rare resident in Vietnam, possibly also Cambodia, Laos and Myanmar; an almost annual visitor in Thailand.

## LESSER ADJUTANT
*Leptoptilos javanicus* 114 cm  F: Ciconiidae

**Description**: A large stork with massive build. Note diagnostic orange neck and dark underwings.

**Voice**: Silent.

**Habits**: In SE Asia restricted to the mangrove habitat, feeding on exposed mudflats at low tide. Nests in trees in remote forest patches over the water, usually in small colonies near other water birds. Feeds on mudskippers, crustaceans and also carrion. A shy bird, but seen clearly when flying, sometimes flapping its huge wings slowly, at other times soaring high like an eagle.

**Distribution**: Oriental region; sedentary. A rare resident at certain mangrove sites; very rare in Myanmar; vagrant in Hong Kong; extinct in Singapore.

## BLACK-HEADED IBIS
*Threskiornis melanocephalus* 80 cm  F: Threskiornithidae

**Description**: Unmistakable, as is the only white ibis in this region.

**Voice**: Silent.

**Habits**: Found in freshwater marshes and wet fields behind the coast, less often on tidal mudflats. Feeds on frogs and aquatic invertebrates, also some fish. Always moves in flocks; nests in colonies in tall trees such as coconut palms near water and sometimes in villages.

**Distribution**: Oriental region; partly migratory. Resident in Vietnam and Cambodia; an uncommon winter visitor in much of region; vagrant in Taiwan and north Borneo. Population in Singapore are escapees.

## GLOSSY IBIS
### *Plegadis falcinellus* 64 cm F: Threskiornithidae

**Description**: Small size and all-black colouration are diagnostic.

**Voice**: Silent.

**Habits**: Occurs in marshy areas, mainly shallow freshwater lakes and flooded fields, but also in coastal wetlands and tidal lagoons. Nests in colonies in low trees near fresh water. A social species that breeds and feeds in flocks, often with other water birds. Walks along feeding on aquatic invertebrates, sometimes also small fish and frogs.

**Distribution**: Worldwide tropical and subtropical regions; nomadic. Within the region, resident in Myanmar, south Vietnam, Cambodia, Mindanao (Philippines) and possibly south China; vagrant in Thailand, Singapore and Hong Kong.

## GREY-LAG GOOSE
### *Anser anser* 84 cm  F: Anatidae

**Description**: Distinguished from the rarer Bean Goose, *A. fabalis,* by its paler neck and breast, pink (not orange) feet and pale (not dark) bill. Distinguished in flight by distinctive pale forewing.

**Voice**: Honks like a domesticated goose.

**Habits**: The only goose in the region likely to appear regularly in any great numbers. Often found swimming in marshes and in nearby fields where it feeds on grasses and grain. This genus is one of the few groups of birds able to digest the cellulose in ordinary grass. An elegant flier, its flocks form characteristic V-shaped formations during their long travels.

**Distribution**: Breeds in temperate Eurasia and winters in the subtropics. Within the region, an uncommon winter visitor to the northern parts of the mainland; vagrant in Hong Kong.

# LESSER TREEDUCK (Lesser Whistling-duck)
## *Dendrocygna javanica* 41 cm   F: Anatidae

**Description**: Light brown plumage and scaly wings are diagnostic. Rounded wings in flight. Distinguished from other tree-ducks by lack of white streaks on flanks.

**Voice**: Its alternative name indicates a vocal duck, constantly uttering a high-pitched, three-note whistle during flight.

**Habits**: An attractive small duck found in freshwater habitats such as marshes, reservoirs and lakes with plenty of vegetation; visits ponds, but never brackish or tidal areas. Forms dense flocks outside of breeding season, locally numbering thousands. A crepuscular feeder that visits paddy fields at night. Its nest is built in trees or among dense lakeside reeds.

**Distribution**: Oriental region; nomadic outside breeding season. A common resident on much of the mainland; an uncommon resident in Singapore

# WANDERING TREEDUCK (Wandering Whistling-duck)
## *Dendrocygna arcuata* 45 cm   F: Anatidae

**Description**: Note dark rufous wing coverts and black flight feathers in flight. Previous species appears much paler brown. On the water white flanks show prominently.

**Voice**: A high-pitched whistle, often during flight.

**Habits**: Prefers freshwater habitats such as marshes and lakes; also fish ponds just behind the coast, but never saline water. Often feeds at night by dabbling for plant food on the water surface or just below. Roosts in tall grass near water, seldom in trees.

**Distribution**: Southeast Asia into northern Australia. Within the region, a fairly common resident in the Philippines only.

## RUDDY SHELDUCK
### *Tadorna ferruginea* 64 cm  F: Anatidae

**Description**: Unmistakable. Picture shows captive female. Male has thin black collar.

**Voice**: Goose-like honks.

**Habits**: Found on lakes, marshes and flooded fields, where it feeds on vegetable matter and invertebrates. Dabbles in water as well as feeding on land, nibbling grass and picking out larvae.

**Distribution:** Breeds in central Asia; migrant in Oriental region. Within the region, a rare migrant in northern parts of mainland; vagrant in Taiwan and Laos; not recorded in Cambodia.

## COMMON PINTAIL (Northern Pintail)
### *Anas acuta* 56 cm  F: Anatidae

**Description**: Male unmistakable (left). The female's long, pointed tail is diagnostic. Captive photo.

**Voice**: Usually silent.

**Habits**: Mainly frequents freshwater ponds and lakes, and sometimes visits brackish coastal wetlands. Feeds by dabbling and up-ending to search the shallow bottom for food.

**Distribution:** Breeds worldwide in northern temperate to arctic climate zones, migrating into the subtropics. Within the region, a fairly common winter visitor in northern parts, but rarer further south; vagrant in north Borneo.

## COMMON TEAL
*Anas crecca* 38 cm  F: Anatidae

**Description:** Male unmistakable. Female (feeding in foreground of photo) distinguished with some difficulty from the Gargany duck by lack of pale eyebrow.

**Voice:** A short melodic *krick*.

**Habits:** Frequents freshwater ponds and lakes; also visits tidal lagoons during migration. Feeds on vegetable matter in shallow water. Like all dabbling ducks, it takes off vertically from the water's surface when disturbed and flies rapidly to another pond.

**Distribution:** Breeds worldwide in northern temperate to arctic climate zones, migrating into the subtropics. Within the region, a common winter visitor in northern parts, including Hong Kong, but rarer further south; vagrant in Malaysia and Singapore.

## SPOT-BILLED DUCK
*Anas poecilorhyncha* 61 cm  F: Anatidae

**Description:** Note diagnostic yellow tip of bill; also look for fine black eye-stripe and white patch in closed wing.

**Voice:** A Mallard-like *quack*.

**Habits:** Occurs in shallow freshwater ponds and lagoons where it feeds by dabbling for vegetable matter along vegetated edges. An adaptable species also found in flooded fields and rice paddies. Much hunted, but recovers quickly in protected areas.

**Distribution:** Breeds in temperate and subtropical East Asia; northern populations migrate south. Within the region, a fairly common resident in southeast China, including Hong Kong; an uncommon winter visitor further south.

## PHILIPPINE DUCK (Philippine Mallard)
*Anas luzonica* 53 cm  F: Anatidae

**Description**: Unmistakable; sexes similar.

**Voice**: A Mallard-like *quack-quack* both in flight and on the water.

**Habits**: The most numerous duck in the country, both in the lowlands and at montane elevations. Although still seen regularly in freshwater marshes, lakes, ponds and rivers where it feeds by dabbling on the water's surface, it has declined in numbers. Its habits have been little studied. Seems to breed year round, but its nest has never been found in the wild.

**Distribution**: A Philippine endemic; sedentary. A fairly common resident on most major Philippine islands.

## MALLARD
*Anas platyrhynchos* 58 cm  F: Anatidae

**Description**: Male unmistakable, with green head and chestnut breast. Female (photo) distinguished with difficulty from other ducks by facial pattern and short tail.

**Voice**: Quacks like a domestic duck.

**Habits**: The most widespread and numerous of all ducks in the world and the wild form of the domestic duck. Adaptable and tolerant to human disturbance. Frequents freshwater marshes, lakes and ponds; seen less often on tidal river estuaries. Avoids tropical conditions and is not successful in this region.

**Distribution**: Breeds worldwide in northern temperate to sub-arctic climate zones, migrating into the subtropics. An uncommon winter visitor to Myanmar and south China, including Hong Kong; rare in Vietnam and east Malaysia; vagrant in the Philippines.

# GADWALL
### *Anas strepera* 51 cm  F: Anatidae

**Description**: Top photo shows female on location in Singapore. Note diagnostic wing pattern. Male has bluish-grey flanks and pale head.

**Voice**: Usually silent.

**Habits**: Found in freshwater ponds and lakes, where it feeds by dabbling through the water surface, picking out vegetable matter such as seeds, leaves and roots of aquatic plants. Flight is fast, strong and direct.

**Distribution**: Breeds worldwide in northern temperate climates; winters in the subtropics. An uncommon winter visitor in northern parts of the region; vagrant in Singapore and the Philippines.

# GARGANEY
### *Anas querquedula* 41 cm  F: Anatidae

**Description**: Small size and rapid flight are characteristic. Breeding male has prominent white eyebrows. Female has pale brown plumage, with diagnostic light brown stripes across its head.

**Voice**: Usually silent; sometimes a slight *kwak*.

**Habits**: By far the most widespread and numerous migratory duck in the region. Found in prime habitats during the northern winter, sometimes by the thousands. Frequents lakes and reservoirs, also tidal ponds and coastal lagoons, feeding on both vegetable and animal aquatic food found at the water's surface

**Distribution**: Breeds in temperate Eurasia; winters in Africa and the Oriental region. A common winter visitor throughout the region; reported in all countries and territories.

## NORTHERN SHOVELER
*Anas clypeata* 52 cm  F: Anatidae

**Description**: Photo shows male in captivity. Female is a uniform scaly-brown, but its peculiar bill is always diagnostic.

**Voice**: A Mallard-like *quack*.

**Habits**: Frequents freshwater lakes and reservoirs, but seen less often in coastal wetlands. Feeds by dabbling through the water's surface, extracting both vegetable and tiny animal food with its specialised bill.

**Distribution**: Breeds worldwide in northern cold climate zones; winters in the subtropics. A common winter visitor to northern parts of region; uncommon in Thailand; vagrant in Malaysia, Singapore and Borneo.

## COMMON POCHARD
*Aythya ferina* 44 cm  F: Anatidae

**Description**: Male (photo) unmistakable. Note pale grey body and reddish-brown head. Female is a nondescript brown; lacks the white wing bar in flight.

**Voice**: Usually quiet; sometimes a low hissing call.

**Habits**: Found in vegetated freshwater ponds and lakes. Often moves out to coastal lagoons and tidal estuaries in winter. Unlike previous species (dabbling ducks in genus *Anas*) this species belongs to a small group of diving ducks. It feeds on plants and small invertebrates on the water's surface, but readily dives and can swim several metres under water.

**Distribution**: Breeds in temperate Eurasia; winters to the south, reaching the subtropics. Within the region, an uncommon winter visitor to Myanmar and south China, including Hong Kong; rare in Vietnam, Luzon (Philippines) and Thailand.

## TUFTED DUCK
### *Aythya fuligula* 43 cm  F: Anatidae

**Distribution:** Breeds in temperate and subarctic Eurasia, winters in the south, reaching the subtropics. Within the region, an uncommon winter visitor to northern parts of the mainland and Philippines; rare in Thailand and Malaysia.

**Description:** Female (photo) distinguished by small tuft and whitish patch at base of bill. Male has black body contrasting sharply with white planks.

**Voice:** Usually quiet; during courtship a soft whistling and cooing.

**Habits:** Frequents freshwater lakes with plenty of vegetation cover and often moves to lagoons and tidal river estuaries, nearer to the coast, during winter. Swims and dives for aquatic plants and insects. A strong flier, like other diving ducks, with a rapid, direct flight. Runs across water surface before lift-off. Dabbling ducks take off vertically.

## MANDARIN DUCK
### *Aix galericulata* 48 cm  F: Anatidae

**Distribution:** Breeds in NE Asia; threatened with near extinction in the wild, but does well in captivity. Within the region, resident in Taiwan; winter visitor to southern China, including Hong Kong; vagrant in Myanmar and Thailand.

**Description:** Male unmistakable. Female (behind) has diagnostic white 'spectacle'. Captive photo.

**Voice:** Soft whistle.

**Habits:** Frequents lakes and pools that are often surrounded by deciduous forest. Also found along flowing rivers, and has a preference for little islands in streams. Feeds by dabbling through the surface water for vegetable food and aquatic invertebrates. The pair forms a strong bond. The nest is built inside a cavity in a tree.

## COTTON PYGMY GOOSE
*Nettapus coromandelianus* 33 cm  F: Anatidae

**Description**: Note diagnostic white head of male (left). Female is pale brown.

**Voice**: Soft, melodic quacking.

**Habits**: Not related to and does not resemble a goose, in spite of its name. This small duck frequents lakes and vegetated ponds, where it grazes on floating vegetation. A retiring and shy bird, it is not easy to view clearly. Sometimes seen perching on branches. Nests inside tree-hollows.

**Distribution:** Oriental region, Australasia; mainly sedentary. Within the region, a fairly common resident locally in much of mainland; rare in Singapore; a non-breeding visitor to Luzon (Philippines) and East Malaysia; vagrant in Hong Kong and Taiwan.

## WHITE-WINGED DUCK
*Cairina scutulata* 75 cm  F: Anatidae

**Description**: A large duck with unmistakable plumage and pale head. In flight displays prominent white wing coverts. Captive photo.

**Voice**: Short honks.

**Habits**: A shy and retiring duck rarely seen in the wild. Total world population may number less than 1,000 birds. Found around forested ponds and streams in the lowlands and at submontane elevations. Feeds mainly at night and spends the day among dense vegetation along banks.

**Distribution:** Oriental region; patchy occurrence from eastern India to Sumatra; sedentary. Within the region, a rare resident at selected forest locations and much reduced in numbers; vagrant in Peninsular Malaysia.

## OSPREY
*Pandion haliaetus* 55 cm  F: Pandionidae

**Description:** Long, narrow wings, pale underparts and dark mask across eyes are diagnostic.

**Voice:** Usually silent, but near its nest, a loud, plaintive whistle.

**Habits:** Only member of family. A successful species specialising wholly in catching live fish, often diving spectacularly into the water from a great height. Fishes in the sea, but also in fresh-water sources. Avoids montaneous regions.

**Distribution:** Worldwide; partly migratory. Fairly common to uncommon winter visitor throughout the region. Some birds seem to stay all year but breeding has not been confirmed.

## JERDON'S BAZA
*Aviceda jerdoni* 46 cm  F: Accipitridae

**Description:** Note broad wing shape and barring under wing and body. At rest, long wings and crest combined with rufous barring are diagnostic.

**Voice:** A soft, airy *pee-weeow*.

**Habits:** Occurs in primary forest and along forest edges. Seems to prefer low hills, although it has been recorded to 1,400 metres during migration. A low-density species, not often observed, although sometimes seen soaring low over the forest. Perches in large trees and pounces on small prey, mainly large insects, on the ground; some frogs and reptiles are also taken.

**Distribution:** Oriental region; northern populations are partly migratory. Rare within the region and the Philippines; possibly resident in Laos, Malaysia and Brunei; not recorded in Cambodia.

## BLACK BAZA
*Aviceda leuphotes* 33 cm  F: Accipitridae

**Description**: Note diagnostic rounded wings and black band across breast. Long, thin crest visible when perched.

**Voice**: A soft, airy 1- to 3-noted scream.

**Habits**: Frequents open woodlands, often perching in large trees near clearings and villages. Gregarious during migration and forms scattered flocks in winter quarters. Flies low with flapping wings when hunting insects and small vertebrate prey; soars high when shifting location.

**Distribution**: Oriental region; northern populations migrate south. An uncommon resident within the region, but numerous locally during migration.

## ORIENTAL HONEY-BUZZARD (Crested Honey-buzzard)
*Pernis ptilorhynchus* 50 cm  F: Accipitridae

**Description**: Plumage varies from dark brown to almost white; look instead for flight silhouette with diagnostic long neck and tail, small head and fairly long wings.

**Voice**: Silent during migration; a high-pitched call during breeding.

**Habits**: Occurs in all types of forested habitat, from submontane rainforest (residents) to open woodlands (migratory birds). Moves about singly, but will form flocks during peak migration. Has a unique preference for raiding beehives and feeding on the larvae inside.

**Distribution**: Oriental region and NE Asia; northern populations migrate. Resident race (with a crest) is uncommon within the region, but the migratory race is a very numerous winter visitor.

# BLACK-SHOULDERED KITE (Black-winged Kite)
## *Elanus caeruleus* 30 cm  F: Accipitridae

**Description**: A small, elegant raptor. Plumage and behaviour are unmistakable.

**Voice**: Short, soft whistle.

**Habits**: Frequents open woodlands, savanna and forest edges, where it sits on an exposed perch. Patrols the terrain, flying low with lifted wings or hovering low over the ground before dropping into the grass to catch insects and small vertebrate prey. The nest is built of sticks in a tree, at a height of 2 to 20 metres.

**Distribution**: Africa and Oriental region; sedentary. Within the region, a common resident on the mainland, including Singapore; an uncommon resident in the Philippines; vagrant in Borneo, Brunei and Hong Kong.

# BLACK KITE
## *Milvus migrans* 65 cm  F: Accipitridae

**Description**: Shape, large size and overall dark plumage are diagnostic. Tail is slightly forked when closed.

**Voice**: A rather faint, prolonged scream.

**Habits**: Frequents open country, often populated areas, villages and the outskirts of towns. Moves near the coast during migration. Feeds on all kinds of meat, both live prey and carrion, often scavenging at garbage dumps and fishing areas.

**Distribution**: Africa, Eurasia, Australasia; partly migratory. Within the region, the most common raptor in South China and a fairly common winter visitor further south; vagrant in the Philippines and Borneo.

## BRAHMINY KITE
*Haliastur indus* 45 cm  F: Accipitridae

**Description**: A relatively small hawk; bright chestnut brown upperparts and black wing-tips are diagnostic. Immature bird is mottled brown.

**Voice**: A nasal, mewing call.

**Habits**: Usually a coastal bird found in mangroves, estuaries and harbour areas, but also occurs in wooded lowlands far from water. An opportunistic feeder, it takes all meats, often picking up debris from the water's surface or catching live fish. Also hunts small terrestrial prey. Its nest is built high in a large tree, often near water.

**Distribution:** Oriental region, Australasia; sedentary. A common resident in much of the region, including Singapore and Brunei; less common to the north; vagrant in Hong Kong.

## WHITE-BELLIED SEA-EAGLE (White-bellied Fish-Eagle)
*Haliaeetus leucogaster* 70 cm  F: Accipitridae

**Description**: Massive size, grey upperparts and V-shaped lifted wings when soaring are diagnostic; immature bird is brownish.

**Voice**: Loud, honking call used frequently around nesting site.

**Habits**: A coastal bird often found on offshore islands far from the mainland; also ventures up large rivers and to reservoirs some distance from the sea. Picks large fish out of the water in spectacular swoops without getting wet; also takes a variety of other prey and scavenges along the shoreline. The nest is a massive structure in a large tree or on an offshore rock.

**Distribution:** Oriental region and Australasia; sedentary. A widespread but not very numerous resident within the region. Found throughout coastal districts including Singapore, Hong Kong and Brunei.

## GREY-HEADED FISH-EAGLE
### *Ichthyophaga ichthyaetus* 68 cm  F: Accipitridae

**Description**: Distinguished from the similar and sympatric Lesser Fish-eagle, *I. humilis* (58 cm), only by larger size and distinct white base to tail.

**Voice**: A wailing scream with short, chuckling notes heard at dawn and dusk.

**Habits**: This shy forest bird frequents large rivers in the lowland and lower montane forest areas; also found around stagnant ponds and reservoirs. Usually seen as it takes off from its forest edge perch and flies low out of sight along the river. Seems to feed almost exclusively on freshwater fish; feeding and breeding habits little studied.

**Distribution**: Oriental region; sedentary. A widespread but generally rare resident in Myanmar, Thailand, parts of Indochina, Malaysia, Singapore, Brunei and the Philippines.

## HIMALAYAN GRIFFON
### *Gyps himalayensis* 130 cm  F: Accipitridae

**Description**: Unmistakable; largest of all raptors with a massive 10-kg body and 3-metre wingspan. Photo shows two immature birds.

**Voice**: Usually silent.

**Habits**: Resident from 1,500 to 4000 metres. Immature birds seem to disperse in small groups and may be found near forested hills. Soars on motionless, outstretched wings, covering ground and shifting elevation with incredible swiftness and speed.

**Distribution**: Breeds in the Himalayas, from northern India and Nepal into China; immature birds are somewhat nomadic. Within the region they have been recently reported as vagrant in Thailand, Peninsular Malaysia and Singapore.

## WHITE-RUMPED VULTURE (White-backed Vulture)
### *Gyps bengalensis* 89 cm  F: Accipitridae

**Description**: Distinguished from the similar and sympatric Long-billed Vulture *G. indicus* by blackish (not sandy brown) wings and prominent white rump.

**Voice**: Usually silent.

**Habits**: Feeds on carrion, mainly cattle carcasses. Remarkably tolerant of the human presence, often seen feeding on busy rubbish dumps and nesting in large trees in villages. Previously numerous in much of the region, but numbers are now much reduced, even in its stronghold of northern India, for reasons not fully understood.

**Distribution:** Oriental region; mainly sedentary. A rare resident in Myanmar, Thailand, parts of Indochina, south China and northern Peninsular Malaysia; a single recording from Brunei.

## RED-HEADED VULTURE
### *Sarcogyps calvus* 81 cm  F: Accipitridae

**Description**: Note diagnostic red head and feet.

**Voice**: Usually silent.

**Habits**: Much reduced in numbers and no longer occurs near human habitation anywhere within this region. Mainly found as territorial pairs in remoter areas, especially along forested river valleys, from the lowlands to 2,000 metres. Shyer and less gregarious than other vultures. Feeds on carcasses of large mammals, often together with other scavengers.

**Distribution:** Oriental region; sedentary. A rare resident in Myanmar, Thailand, parts of Indochina, south China and northern Peninsular Malaysia.

# CRESTED SERPENT-EAGLE
## *Spilornis cheela* 81 cm  F: Accipitridae

**Description**: Somewhat scaly plumage and small crest are diagnostic (left); note white wing band on flying bird (right).

**Voice**: A penetrating *wheew-wheew* when soaring carries far. Vocal.

**Habits**: Essentially a forest bird that seems to prefer mature secondary growth along forest edges and clearings. Sits motionless on a mid-storey branch watching for prey, mostly tree snakes, but also some small mammals and birds. Often soars high over the forest on late morning thermals.

**Distribution**: Oriental region; sedentary. A fairly common resident throughout region including Hong Kong, Brunei and Palawan (Philippines); rare in Singapore.

# PHILIPPINE SERPENT-EAGLE
## *Spilornis holospilus* 56 cm  F: Accipitridae

**Description**: Unmistakable within its range. Recently accepted as a full species. Distinguished from previous species by more well-defined spots on underparts and wings.

**Voice**: Similar to previous species.

**Habits**: Occurs in forest and along forest edges, often seen in clearings and river valleys. Tolerant of environmental disturbance and often seen soaring over nearby open areas. Feeds on amphibians, reptiles and other live prey. Otherwise little studied and its nest has not yet been described.

**Distribution**: A Philippine endemic. A widespread and common resident on all large islands within the country, other than Palawan.

## EASTERN MARSH-HARRIER
*Circus spilonotus* 50 cm  F: Accipitridae

**Description**: Photo shows immature bird; the underparts of immature and female birds are less streaked than other harriers. The male is pale grey with black wing coverts.

**Voice**: Usually silent.

**Habits**: Found in open country, especially in extensive marshes, reed beds, tall grass areas and wet fields. The most numerous harrier (genus: *Circus*) in the region. Flies low, hugging the contours of the terrain, flapping briefly and gliding intermittently. Dives into the grass to catch slow-moving birds and rodents.

**Distribution**: Breeds in NE Asia and winters SE Asia. Within the region, a fairly common winter visitor on the mainland; uncommon in the Philippines and north Borneo.

## JAPANESE SPARROWHAWK
*Accipiter gularis* 27 cm  F: Accipitridae

**Description**: Photo shows female bird. The male is smaller and has more rufous underparts with thin barring. The immature bird has a streaked (not barred) chest.

**Voice**: Usually silent.

**Habits**: Typical *Accipiter* raptor. Flies low with amazing agility when hunting for prey, almost exclusively small passerine birds surprised and caught in flight. Found during winter in all types of wooded habitat, from forest edges to semi-open country and around villages. Sometimes soars high, late in the morning or during migration.

**Distribution**: Breeds in NE Asia; migrates south, reaching Indonesia. A common passage migrant and winter visitor on the mainland and Borneo; uncommon in the Philippines.

# BESRA
### *Accipiter virgatus* 33 cm  F: Accipitridae

**Description**: Plumage variable with sex, age and subspecies. Photo shows female. Distinguished with great difficulty from previous species by heavier streaks on its throat.

**Voice**: Usually silent.

**Habits**: A forest bird found in a variety of wooded habitats, often in elevated areas up to 2,400 metres. Status somewhat uncertain as this species is very difficult to distinguish in the field from previous migratory species. Feeds on small birds caught on the wing; less often on reptiles and small mammals hunted on the ground. Its small nest is built high in a large forest tree.

**Distribution**: Oriental region; mainly sedentary. An uncommon resident on parts of the mainland including Hong Kong, the Philippines and Sabah (East Malaysia); vagrant in Singapore and Brunei.

# CRESTED GOSHAWK
### *Accipiter trivirgatus* 40 cm  F: Accipitridae

**Description**: Note the short, rounded wings and streaked/barred underparts; crest hardly noticeable.

**Voice**: A shrill, prolonged scream *he-he-he-he-he*.

**Habits**: A forest hawk found in lowland and submontane rainforest and along forest edges. Flies low to hunt for squirrels, lizards, birds and large insects. Sometimes soars on thermals over its territory, screaming loudly.

**Distribution**: Oriental region; sedentary. Resident in much of region including Hong Kong, Singapore and Brunei; common on parts of the mainland and less common on Borneo; uncommon in the Philippines.

# SHIKRA
*Accipiter badius* 32 cm  F: Accipitridae

**Description**: Male (photo) has diagnostic bluish wings and back. Female is larger with brownish upperparts.

**Voice**: A high-pitched *kyeew* near its nest, otherwise silent.

**Habits**: Frequents woodlands and nearby open country, often seen near plantations, roads and villages. Hunts from a perch by dashing out to catch lizards, small mammals and large insects on nearby branches or in the grass below; does not chase flying birds.

**Distribution**: Africa and the Oriental region; sedentary. Within the region, a common resident on much of the mainland; vagrant in Peninsular Malaysia.

# COMMON BUZZARD
*Buteo buteo* 55 cm  F: Accipitridae

**Description**: Note broad tail, short neck and diagnostic black spot on carpal joint (shoulder) of wing.

**Voice**: Usually silent during migration.

**Habits**: Found along forest edges and in wooded areas and open country from lowlands to montane altitudes, usually alone. Often seen soaring high. Perches on an open branch or hovers in the air to swoop down and catch prey in grass below.

**Distribution**: Breeds in Eurasia; migrates to Africa and the Oriental region. Within the region, a fairly common winter visitor in northern parts of the mainland; vagrant in Peninsular Malaysia, Singapore and the Philippines.

# BLACK EAGLE
*Ictinaetus malayensis* 69 cm  F: Accipitridae

**Description**: Plumage a uniform blackish colour. Unique; the only member of its genus. Distinguished from the following species by characteristic flight silhouette with wings narrowing in at the body.

**Voice**: Silent during migration.

**Habits**: A low-density species preferring the montane forest habitat, from the foothills to 2,500-metre elevations. Sometimes ventures into lowlands and forest edges. Soars low over the treetops on the lookout for prey such as birds, reptiles, frogs and small mammals. Especially adept at raiding other birds' nests and picking up roosting bats. Like other eagles, the pair engages in acrobatic display flights near their large nest built in a tall tree on a forested slope.

**Distribution**: Oriental region; mainly sedentary. A widespread but scarce resident in much of region, including Brunei, but excluding Singapore and Hong Kong; vagrant in Taiwan.

# GREATER SPOTTED EAGLE
*Aquila clanga* 68 cm  F: Accipitridae

**Description**: Immature bird (top) has white spots in plumage. Adult is a uniform black. Note wings are held straight out, plank-like, in flight.

**Voice**: Silent during migration.

**Habits**: The most common of the majestic *Aquila* eagles in the region and very conspicuous in the air. Usually found in open country near wetlands, especially in large marshy areas and grasslands behind the coast. Perches in large trees and flies out to feed on all kinds of vertebrate prey; also scavenges. Much reduced in numbers worldwide and now vulnerable to global extinction.

**Distribution**: Breeds in central and northern Asia; winters in the subtropics. Within the region, an uncommon winter visitor in much of the mainland, including Singapore and Hong Kong; vagrant in Taiwan.

## STEPPE EAGLE
*Aquila nipalensis* 81 cm  F: Accipitridae

**Description**: A magnificent large eagle with uniformly dark brown plumage. Immature (photo) bird is light brown with a diagnostic broad white band in wings when held out straight from body (typical for *Aquila* eagles).

**Voice**: Silent during migration.

**Habits**: Immature birds roam widely and are seen in this region occasionally. Frequents open country, feeding mostly on small mammals. During migration immature birds often feed on carrion.

**Distribution:** Breeds in central Asia; winters in Africa and south Asia. Within the region, a rare winter visitor to Myanmar and south China; vagrant in Vietnam, Thailand, Peninsular Malaysia and Singapore.

## PHILIPPINE EAGLE
*Pithecophaga jefferyi* 92 cm  F: Accipitridae

**Description**: Unmistakable. Huge eagle with pale appearance. A monotypic genus.

**Voice**: No information.

**Habits**: A forest specialist occurring in primary montane rainforest, from the foothills to 2,000 metres. Sometimes found in the lowlands or seen soaring along forest edges. Mostly moves inside or below the canopies hunting for tree-dwelling prey such as monkeys, civet cats, squirrels, bats, flying lemurs and large birds and reptiles. The species has been extensively studied, but is now very rare due to habitat clearance and hunting. Less than 200 individuals believed to survive in the wild.

**Distribution:** Philippine endemic. A rare resident on Luzon, Leyte, Mindanao and the Samar islands. Critically endangered with global extinction.

## RUFOUS-BELLIED EAGLE
### *Hieraaetus kienerii* 51 cm  F: Accipitridae

**Description**: Note diagnostic rufous underparts contrasting with white chest and throat.

**Voice**: A high-pitched scream, preceded by preliminary notes.

**Habits**: Found in primary and mature secondary lowland and submontane rainforest. Soars in low circles over the trees. An elegant flyer, swooping like a falcon through the air to catch birds and small mammals. Little studied and generally an uncommon species.

**Distribution**: Oriental region; somewhat nomadic. An uncommon resident in much of the region. A non-breeding visitor to Peninsular Malaysia and Singapore; no records from Cambodia.

## CHANGEABLE HAWK-EAGLE
### *Spizaetus cirrhatus* 68 cm  F: Accipitridae

**Description**: Plumage variable; photo shows pale morph. Subspecies from India has longer crest than Southeast Asian birds. Dark morph has uniformly dark brown plumage.

**Voice**: A series of ascending shrill screams *hwee-hwee-hweeee*.

**Habits**: A low-density forest species occurring in the lowlands, but also found at submontane elevations; in Thailand up to 2,000 metres. Prefers primary forest and closed secondary growth, but also strays into nearby disturbed areas. Sometimes soars over trees like the more common Crested Serpent-eagle. Can be recognised by its longer call, size and lack of wing-bars.

**Distribution**: Oriental region; sedentary. A widespread but generally scarce resident in southern parts of the mainland, Malaysia, Brunei and Philippines; a rare resident in Singapore.

## MOUNTAIN HAWK-EAGLE
### *Spizaetus nipalensis* 66 cm  F: Accipitridae

**Description**: A large hawk-eagle. Note banded underparts and very broad wings.

**Voice**: Three shrill notes, *tlueet-weet-weet*.

**Habits**: Restricted to forests at montane and lower montane elevations, from 600 to 4,000 metres; also found in foothills at lower elevations, outside of breeding season. Best seen late in the morning, soaring high over the forest. Will hunt mammals and large birds from a perch at forest's edge.

**Distribution**: Oriental region; somewhat nomadic outside breeding season. An uncommon resident in montane parts of the region; vagrant in Hong Kong.

## BLYTH'S HAWK-EAGLE
### *Spizaetus alboniger* 52 cm  F: Accipitridae

**Description**: Note slaty-black plumage with barred underparts and tail; long crest visible at rest.

**Voice**: Various shrill whistles and high-pitched notes.

**Habits**: A lower montane rainforest specialist found from the foothills to 1,700 metres, usually between 600 and 1,200 metres. Seen circling low over the forest or sitting on a concealed perch just below canopy level, on the lookout for prey such as squirrels, birds and reptiles.

**Distribution**: Sunda subregion, mainly sedentary; immature birds are somewhat nomadic. Within the region, an uncommon resident in south Thailand and Malaysia; vagrant in Singapore and Brunei.

## COLLARED FALCONET
### *Microhierax caerulescens* 19 cm  F: Falconidae

**Description**: Note full white neck; only falconet within its range.

**Voice**: No information.

**Habits**: Occurs in forest and along forest edges, often near rivers and clearings, from the lowlands to 1,800 metres. A lively and agile small raptor, often seen sitting on an open perch or flying out to catch insects in the air, mostly butterflies and moths taken at dusk. Also gleans insects and other small prey from foliage. The nest is built inside an abandoned woodpecker or barbet hole.

**Distribution**: Oriental region. A generally scarce resident in Myanmar, Thailand and parts of Indochina.

## BLACK-THIGHED FALCONET
### *Microhierax fringillarius* 15 cm  F: Falconidae

**Description**: Distinguished from the White-fronted Falconet, *M. latifrons,* (endemic to Sabah, Malaysia) by its black (not white) forehead. The Philippines has an endemic member of this genus, the Philippine Falconet *M. erythrogenys.*

**Voice**: Piercing cries, *yak yak yak.*

**Habits**: Occurs in forest habitats, but is tolerant of disturbance and prefers clearings and forest edges with large trees, from the lowlands into lower montane elevations at 1,500 metres. This sparrow-size raptor is the smallest bird of prey in the world. Often sits in the open on a dead branch and flies out to catch various insects, making it fairly easy to see.

**Distribution**: Sunda subregion. Within the region, a generally scarce resident in south Thailand, Myanmar, Peninsular Malaysia, and Sarawak (East Malaysia); common in Brunei; rare in Singapore.

# EURASIAN KESTREL
## *Falco tinnunculus* 34 cm   F: Falconidae

**Description**: Note pointed wings and black wingtips; male (photo) has grey head; female has more black spots on upperparts and a brown head.

**Voice**: Piercing cries, *yak yak yak*.

**Habits**: Mainly an open country species found in grassland, scrub fields and at the edge of villages. A strong flier that hovers for long periods in the air, while searching the ground; drops down to grab rodents and other small prey.

**Distribution**: Africa and Eurasia; partly migratory. Within the region, a fairly common resident and migrant in the northern parts of the mainland including Hong Kong; an uncommon winter visitor in Malaysia, Singapore, Brunei and the Philippines.

# BLACK WOOD-PARTRIDGE (Black Partridge)
## *Melanoperdix nigra* 24 cm   F: Phasianidae

**Description**: Male (captive photo) unmistakable. Female is dark brown with black bars on rufous wings. A unique bird; the only species in its genus.

**Voice**: A double whistle.

**Habits**: Found in primary lowland rainforest; in Peninsular Malaysia to 600 metres, in Sarawak mainly at lower montane elevations. It walks along the forest floor, feeding on insects, grubs and fallen seeds. Previously reported as not uncommon in certain areas, especially where Bertam Palms are present. Rarely seen, so numbers are difficult to gauge. BirdLife International regards it as near-threatened with global extinction.

**Distribution**: Sunda subregion, Malaysia and Indonesia only. Within the region, a rare resident in Peninsular Malaysia and Sarawak (East Malaysia); extinct in Singapore.

# BLUE-BREASTED QUAIL
## *Coturnix chinensis* 15 cm  F: Phasianidae

**Distribution:** Oriental region and Australasia. A widespread and fairly common resident locally, in all countries and territories within the region, except Hong Kong.

**Description:** Male (captive photo) unmistakable. Female is buff-brown with thin, black barring; difficult to distinguish in the field from the 3 species of Buttonquail (Turnicidae) that also occur in region.

**Voice:** A trisyllabic whistle, *twi-ti-yu*.

**Habits:** Usually found in rural cleared areas with long grass, such as overgrown fields with some bushes. Seen often on wet ground, sometimes in cultivated fields, from the coast inland to 1,300 metres. Quite a successful and numerous species, but difficult to see clearly, as it feeds on the ground and runs into cover at the least disturbance. Flies only short distances.

# BAR-BACKED PARTRIDGE
## *Arborophila brunneopectus* 28 cm  F: Phasianidae

**Distribution:** Southeast Asia only. An uncommon resident in montane parts of the mainland.

**Description:** Note the diagnostic head pattern. Captive photo shows the Sunda subspecies (Sumatran Hill-partridge, *A. orientalis*) that is sometimes regarded as a full species. Northern birds have more barring on flanks.

**Voice:** A throaty *ti-hu* and a low *wut-wit*.

**Habits:** A submontane bird found in primary forest, from 500 to 1,400 metres. All members of this family walk on the ground and the species is notoriously difficult to see. In prime habitat it is quite a common bird locally. Once its call is learned it can be located and, with some patience, viewed.

## SCALY-BREASTED PARTRIDGE (Chestnut-breasted/Chestnut-necklaced)
### *Arborophila charltonii* 29 cm  F: Phasianidae

**Description**: Note the characteristic scaly head pattern and chestnut upper breast of this captive individual. The taxonomy of this species is disputed. Its name here follows King et al (1975). Today the group is split into 2 or more full species, depending on the author.

**Voice**: A low, soft double whistle.

**Habits**: A forest bird found in primary forest and sometimes in nearby cultivated areas, from the lowland to 1,300 metres. It moves along the ground, feeding on seeds and termites. Little information is available and only one nest has been recorded.

Frank Lambert

**Distribution**: Southeast Asia. Within the region, an uncommon resident in parts of the mainland and Sabah (East Malaysia).

## FERRUGINOUS WOOD-PARTRIDGE (Ferruginous Partridge)
### *Caloperdix oculea* 26 cm  F: Phasianidae

**Description**: Diagnostic small white and black scales in an otherwise dark chestnut plumage. A monotypic genus. Captive photo.

**Voice**: An ascending and accelerating trill, eventually ending in 2 to 4 harsher notes.

**Habits**: A forest bird occurring in lowland and submontane primary rainforest; also sometimes seen in adjacent scrub where it moves on the ground picking up seeds, fallen fruit and insects. Little studied. Rarely seen or heard during surveys.

Morten Strange

**Distribution**: Sunda subregion. Within the region, a rare resident in south Thailand and Malaysia.

## CRESTED WOOD-PARTRIDGE (Crested Partridge)
*Rollulus rouloul* 26 cm  F: Phasianidae

**Description:** Unmistakable; a unique bird. Photo shows captive male. Female is pale green with chestnut wings. A monotypic genus.

**Voice:** A shrill, plaintive whistle *si-il;* quite vocal at early dawn.

**Habits:** One of a very few pheasant species that might be seen during a walk in the lowland rainforest. Moves in small parties along the ground, often found below fruiting trees. Runs off quickly when disturbed.

**Distribution:** Sunda subregion. Within the region, a fairly common resident locally in Malaysia and Brunei; rare in south Thailand.

## KALIJ PHEASANT
*Lophura leucomelana* ♂ 74 cm, ♀ 51 cm  F: Phasianidae

**Description:** Captive male. Distinguished from the similar Silver Pheasant, *L. nycthemera,* of southeast China and Indochina by its smooth (not scaly) mantle and white streaks on flanks. The female is brown with prominent white scales on black underparts.

**Voice:** A thin whistling and grunting call; in alarm, a distinctive *whoop-keet-keet.*

**Habits:** Found in closed rainforest and drier deciduous forest, from the lowlands to 1,200 metres. Moves on the forest floor in small parties, but disappears into cover as soon as approached, often before it can be spotted.

**Distribution:** Oriental region. Within the region, an uncommon resident in Myanmar and western Thailand.

## CRESTLESS FIREBACK
*Lophura erythropthalma* ♂ 48 cm, ♀ 43 cm  F: Phasianidae

**Description**: Photo shows female at nest. Male has greyish mantle. Distinguished from the following species by its red (not blue) facial skin and lack of crest.

**Voice**: Male has low croaking call and whirls wings in display.

**Habits**: A lowland rainforest specialist found below 300 metres, inside closed primary and mature secondary forest. Shy and retiring, but is occasionally spotted walking quietly across the trail in the early morning. Feeds on fallen fruits and invertebrates in about equal proportions. Broods for 24 days on a clutch of 3 to 6 eggs, in a nest among buttress roots.

**Distribution**: Sunda sub-region. Within the region, a rare resident in Peninsular Malaysia and Sarawak (East Malaysia); a single sight record from Brunei; extinct in Singapore. Vulnerable to global extinction.

## CRESTED FIREBACK
*Lophura ignita* ♂ 67 cm, ♀ 56 cm  F: Phasianidae

**Description**: Female (captive photo) has diagnostic brown crest and scaly white flanks. Male has blue facial skin with crest; dark blue belly/white tail (Malay Peninsula race); and chestnut belly/yellow tail (Borneo race).

**Voice**: Male has a croaking call, followed by a shrill chirp.

**Habits**: A lowland rainforest specialist found in primary and mature secondary forest, often near rivers and streams. Much reduced in numbers due to hunting and forest clearance. A shy bird rarely seen and little studied.

**Distribution**: Sunda subregion. Within the region, a rare resident in south Thailand, Malaysia and Brunei. Vulnerable to global extinction.

## SIAMESE FIREBACK
*Lophura diardi* ♂ 80 cm, ♀ 60 cm  F: Phasianidae

**Description**: Note the diagnostic pale grey breast and long greenish-black tail of this male. The female has diagnostic black bars across its wings and tail.

**Voice**: No information; male whirls wings in display.

**Habits**: Occurs in primary forest from the lowlands to 800 metres; also comes out along forest edges to feed on insects and fallen fruits. Much reduced in numbers due to the clearing of forests, but can be seen in several protected reserves within its range, such as the Khao Yai National Park in Thailand, where this rare photo was taken.

**Distribution**: Southeast Asia. A rare resident endemic to parts of east Myanmar, Thailand and Indochina. Vulnerable to global extinction.

## RED JUNGLEFOWL
*Gallus gallus* ♂ 79 cm, ♀ 42 cm  F: Phasianidae

**Description**: Female (photo). Male similar to the purebred domestic chicken, with distinct white ear patch.

**Voice**: Call of the male similar to that of the domestic chicken, but with more abrupt ending.

**Habits**: The most successful member of its family in Southeast Asia and ancestor to the domestic chicken. Found in all types of forest and along forest edges. Also ventures into nearby plantations and scrub; runs or takes a short flight into cover when disturbed. Omnivorous, often seen foraging in small parties.

**Distribution**: Southeast Asia. A rare resident endemic to parts of east Myanmar, Thailand and Indochina. Vulnerable to global extinction.

## MALAYSIAN PEACOCK-PHEASANT
*Polyplectron malacense* ♂ 50 cm, ♀ 40 cm  F: Phasianidae

**Description**: Picture shows captive male. The female is smaller with less green in plumage and no crest.

**Voice**: A melancholy, disyllabic, rising whistle.

**Habits**: Strictly a primary lowland rainforest resident; does not venture above 300 metres and is usually found below 150 metres. Rarely seen and little is known of its feeding habits and movements. Only 4 nesting records; clutch is a single egg. Adapts poorly to disturbance and logging activities.

**Distribution:** Malay Peninsula only. A rare resident in Peninsular Malaysia; very rare, possibly extinct in Thailand.

## PALAWAN PEACOCK-PHEASANT
*Polyplectron emphanum* ♂ 50 cm, ♀ 40 cm  F: Phasianidae

**Description**: Unmistakable; photo shows captive male. Female is smaller and plain brown with pale face.

**Voice**: No information.

**Habits**: A shy terrestrial denizen of closed rainforest. Originally a lowland species, today found mainly at less disturbed lower montane elevations to 600 metres. Said to feed on fallen fruits and invertebrates, but no confirmed information about feeding or breeding habits in the wild. Much reduced in numbers due to habitat destruction, hunting, and trapping for the captive bird trade.

**Distribution:** Philippine endemic. An uncommon resident on the island of Palawan. Endangered with global extinction.

## GREAT ARGUS
*Argusianus argus* ♂ 120 cm, ♀ 60 cm  F: Phasianidae

**Description:** Unmistakable huge pheasant; male has elongated tail feathers. The female is a uniform chestnut brown. Monotypic genus.

**Voice:** A powerful and explosive *kow-wow* that carries far in the forest.

**Habits:** Travelers in the Malaysian forest often hear the call of this magnificent bird, but few manage to see it. The male displays on the ground in front of the female at a hidden dancing ground, deep inside primary or mature lowland rainforest.

**Distribution:** Sunda subregion. Within the region, a fairly common resident in Malaysia and Brunei; uncommon in south Thailand.

## GREEN PEAFOWL
*Pavo muticus* ♂ 210 cm, ♀ 120 cm  F: Phasianidae

**Description:** Unmistakable within its range. Distinguished from the better known Indian Peafowl, *P. cristatus,* by its green (not blue) neck. Photo shows female; male has longer tail.

**Voice:** Male has a loud call, *aow-aaw,* and often calls early morning and evening.

**Habits:** This spectacular bird is much reduced throughout its range due to hunting and forest clearance. Still relatively numerous in Myanmar, but in Cambodia only recorded at one site; a few recorded in Laos, Vietnam and Yunnan (China). In Thailand a population of 300 persists within the huge Huai Kha Khaeng reserve, which has a suitable habitat of dry forests and wide riverbanks.

**Distribution:** Oriental region. Within the region, a rare resident in selected locations on the mainland. Previously resident in Malaysia, now possibly extinct on the Malay peninsula.

## BARRED BUTTONQUAIL
*Turnix suscitator* 17 cm  F: Turnicidae

**Description**: Distinguished from other buttonquails and the female Blue-breasted Quail by prominent barring on underparts. Also note white eyebrow of this male. Female has large, black throat patch.

**Voice**: A 3-note whining call; also a soft whooping call accelerating and stopping abruptly.

**Habits**: A terrestrial bird that runs along the ground in areas with long grass, in open country and in areas under cultivation. Seldom flies and runs into cover as soon as disturbed. The male incubates the eggs and raises the chicks alone. The most widespread and numerous member of this small family in the region.

**Distribution:** Oriental region. A locally common resident throughout the mainland, including Singapore and parts of the Philippines; a rare winter visitor to Hong Kong.

## COMMON CRANE
*Grus grus* 115 cm  F: Gruidae

**Description**: Captive photo. Diagnostic facial pattern and overall dark grey plumage. Flies with neck stretched out like a stork.

**Voice**: A penetrating, high-pitched call.

**Habits**: Found in open country, often around marshes and freshwater wetlands. Feeds on fields and grasslands nearby. Feeds mainly on grain and other vegetable matter during the winter. Often seen in small groups, flying high between roosting and feeding grounds.

**Distribution:** Breeds in temperate Eurasia; winters in subtropical Eurasia and northern Africa. Within the region, an uncommon winter visitor to south China, Myanmar and Vietnam; vagrant in Hong Kong.

# SARUS CRANE
## *Grus antigone* 152 cm  F: Gruidae

**Description:** Distinguished from previous species by its massive size and red skin on head. Captive photo.

**Voice:** A high-pitched call, louder than any other crane.

**Habits:** Found in marshes and wet fields. Walks slowly in wet or drier fields picking up plant matter and small prey. In India birds have adapted to cultivated habitats, but in Southeast Asia the population has decreased markedly since 1960. The out-dated range described in King et al. (1975) shows how fast the decline has happened. Still present at a few wetland locations in the Mekong Delta, where efforts are being made to protect it.

**Distribution:** Oriental region, also northern Australia. Somewhat nomadic. Within the region, a rare resident in Cambodia and Vietnam only; probably extinct Myanmar, Thailand, south China, Laos, Philippines and Peninsular Malaysia.

# SLATY-BREASTED RAIL
## *Gallirallus striatus* 25 cm  F: Rallidae

**Description:** Diagnostic white barring on all upperparts; also chestnut neck contrasting with slaty-black breast.

**Voice:** A harsh *gelek* repeated 10 to 15 times.

**Habits:** Found in freshwater marshes and denser, drier vegetation near reeds, where it feeds on insects and seeds. A secretive and shy bird that sneaks into cover when disturbed. Rarely seen, although widespread and probably quite numerous. Crepuscular and most visible early in the morning.

**Distribution:** Oriental region. A fairly common resident throughout the region including Singapore, Brunei and Hong Kong; uncommon in the Philippines.

# RED-LEGGED CRAKE
## *Rallina fasciata* 25 cm  F: Rallidae

**Description**: Diagnostic red legs combined with reddish head and reddish-brown mantle.

**Voice**: A loud series of nasal *pek* calls.

**Habits**: A shy and secretive rail that prefers wooded areas with wet ground, streams in lowland rainforest, disturbed forest edges and sometimes nearby cultivation. Emerges in poor light, at dawn and dusk, and calls at night. Moves along the ground, sometimes briefly perching low in trees. Diet unknown. Nest has never been described. May disperse outside breeding season, but this has not been studied.

**Distribution**: Oriental region, extending into eastern Indonesia. Within the region, an uncommon resident in Myanmar, Thailand and Malaysia; a rare resident of the Philippines and Singapore, possibly also Brunei and southern Vietnam.

# BAILLON'S CRAKE
## *Porzana pusilla* 18 cm  F: Rallidae

**Description**: Smallest crake in the region. Note diagnostic white streaks on back and wings.

**Voice**: A short *krek-krek*.

**Habits**: Found in freshwater marshes and along densely vegetated edges of lakes and reservoirs. Often walks out on floating vegetation, but rarely out of cover. Feeds mostly on aquatic insects and their larvae. Rarely flies by day, preferring to run away when approached.

**Distribution**: Africa, Eurasia and Australasia; northern populations migrate south. A generally uncommon migrant and winter visitor in much of the region; vagrant in Hong Kong and Taiwan.

## RUDDY-BREASTED CRAKE (Ruddy Crake)
### *Porzana fusca* 21 cm  F: Rallidae

**Description**: Note diagnostic uniformly dark red underparts; faint barring under tail only.

**Voice**: Usually quiet; sometimes makes a long rattle.

**Habits**: Found in a variety of freshwater wetland habitats, from lakeside reed beds to wet fields, grasslands and nearby dry scrub. Usually stays inside cover, rarely flies and is not often seen. Mainly crepuscular and secretive.

**Distribution**: East Asia and Oriental region; northern populations migrate. A fairly common resident locally, and a winter visitor in much of region; migrant in Hong Kong; vagrant in Borneo.

## WHITE-BROWED CRAKE
### *Porzana cinerea* 20 cm  F: Rallidae

**Description**: Prominent white eyebrow is best diagnostic feature.

**Voice**: Vocal during breeding season with soft, high-pitched piping.

**Habits**: Found in freshwater marshes in the lowlands or near the coast, often walking on floating vegetation; occurs less often in mangroves and fields. Resident pairs usually seen together, feeding mainly on aquatic invertebrates. Quite shy; walks quietly into cover when disturbed.

**Distribution**: Southeast Asia into Australasia; sedentary. A fairly common resident in Malaysia, Singapore, Brunei and the Philippines; uncommon in Thailand and Cambodia.

## WHITE-BREASTED WATERHEN
*Amaurornis phoenicurus* 33 cm  F: Rallidae

**Description**: Unmistakable; the only rail with white breast.

**Voice**: A series of peculiar croaking and grunting chuckles lasting several minutes; also a high-pitched, single-note alarm call. Vocal, especially during dawn and dusk.

**Habits**: A very successful bird, more common and more conspicuous than other rails. Occurs in freshwater wetlands, coastal mangroves as well as drainage canals, scrub, fields, villages and gardens. Comes out into open spaces and flies readily, but dives into cover when disturbed.

**Distribution**: Oriental region; mostly sedentary. A common resident throughout the region; present in all countries and locally abundant; fairly common in the Philippines.

## WATERCOCK
*Gallicrex cinerea* 40 cm  F: Rallidae

**Description**: A large rail. Male in breeding plumage (photo) is unmistakable; non-breeding male and female are light brown with dark, scaly black upperparts.

**Voice**: Usually silent; a booming call during breeding.

**Habits**: Found in extensive freshwater marshes with dense vegetation, ponds, rivers and flooded fields. Found in tidal estuaries and brackish swamps during migration. Shy and secretive, but seen clearly sometimes when flying over the reeds.

**Distribution**: East Asia and Oriental region; northern populations migrate. A generally fairly common resident and winter visitor within the region; uncommon in Hong Kong and Borneo.

## COMMON MOORHEN
### *Gallinula chloropus* 33 cm  F: Rallidae

**Description**: Unmistakable; immature bird is brown with pale underparts.

**Voice**: An abrupt, metallic *pruuk*.

**Habits**: Frequents freshwater wetlands, both large marshes and small ponds. Walks conspicuously along the water's edge or swims out onto the water, feeding mainly on plant matter and some insects and larvae. Forms a strong pair bond; the nest is a mound of aquatic plants piled near to or out in the water.

**Distribution**: Worldwide, except Australasia; northern populations migrate. A fairly common resident and winter visitor throughout most of the region; a non-breeding visitor to north Borneo.

## PURPLE SWAMPHEN
### *Porphyrio porphyrio* 43 cm  F: Rallidae

**Description**: Unmistakable. A massive rail with purple plumage, red bill and frontal shield.

**Voice**: A variety of grunts and hoots and an explosive *wak*.

**Habits**: Found in freshwater marshes but requires large open spaces to thrive. Walks out onto floating vegetation covering large lakes and reservoirs, looking mainly for vegetable food. Usually seen in pairs or a small group. Sometimes flies short distances across the wetlands.

**Distribution**: Africa, Eurasia and Australasia; somewhat nomadic. A fairly common resident locally in much of the region, including Singapore; uncommon in the Philippines; vagrant in Hong Kong.

## COMMON COOT
### *Fulica atra* 40 cm  F: Rallidae

**Description:** Unmistakable. Note prominent white bill and facial shield.

**Voice:** Quite vocal, with a variety of penetrating calls, often a sharp *kik kik*.

**Habits:** A mainly aquatic rail that swims like a duck out on the surface of freshwater lakes and ponds. Found along tidal estuaries during migration. Also dives under water in search of food, mainly plants. Often flies, running across the water to become airborne.

**Distribution:** Africa, Eurasia and Australasia; northern populations migrate. A fairly common winter visitor to northern parts of the region; rare in Peninsular Malaysia and the Philippines; vagrant in Singapore and Borneo.

## MASKED FINFOOT
### *Heliopais personata* 53 cm  F: Heliornithidae

**Description:** Unmistakable. Its large size, behaviour and coloration are all distinctive.

**Voice:** A bubbling or gargling call.

**Habits:** Found in a variety of vegetated wetlands, from narrow, forested rivers to mangrove creeks and freshwater swamps. Prefers muddy banks with overhanging vegetation, where it walks. Swims low in the water. Movements, feeding and breeding habits little understood. A low-density species regarded as vulnerable to global extinction due to its small, fragmented population, and habitat disturbance and loss.

**Distribution:** Oriental region; possibly partly migratory. Scarce and presumed resident in Myanmar, Thailand, Cambodia, Vietnam and possibly Peninsular Malaysia, where it is recorded infrequently year round.

## PHEASANT-TAILED JACANA
*Hydrophasianus chirurgus* 33 cm  F: Jacanidae

**Distribution**: Oriental region; partly migratory. A fairly common resident locally; a winter visitor in much of the region; uncommon in Peninsular Malaysia and Singapore; vagrant in Hong Kong.

**Description**: Photo shows non-breeding plumage; during breeding season, the body is black, wings white, tail feathers elongated.

**Voice**: A loud, mewing alarm call.

**Habits**: Frequents freshwater marshes, reservoirs, ponds and flooded fields. Mostly seen walking on lotus leaves, water hyacinths, lily pads and other floating weeds. Builds its nest on this surface, far from the bank. Roams widely during migration. Flies low like a rail with legs trailing behind.

## BRONZE-WINGED JACANA
*Metopidius indicus* 28 cm  F: Jacanidae

**Distribution**: Oriental region; sedentary. A locally common resident in Myanmar and Thailand; rarer in parts of Indochina and Yunnan (China); vagrant in Peninsular Malaysia.

**Description**: Unmistakable. The only species in its genus. Note glossy blackish body with bronze wings and distinctive white supercilium.

**Voice**: Piping and low, guttural notes.

**Habits**: Found in overgrown freshwater marshes, ponds and canals. An adaptable species that also moves into wet cultivated grasslands and paddy fields. In a suitable habitat it can become numerous. Easily observed running along on floating vegetation, picking up vegetable and animal food. The nest is built on floating vegetation or among nearby grasses, and is better hidden than the nest of the previous species.

## GREATER PAINTEDSNIPE (Greater Painted Snipe)
*Rostratula benghalensis* 25 cm  F: Rostratulidae

**Description**: Photo shows female. Male has rufous-tinged areas replaced with dull brown.

**Voice**: Usually silent; during breeding the female utters a penetrating *kook-kook-kook* at dawn and dusk.

**Habits**: Found in marshy areas, wet fields and tidal estuaries with plenty of vegetation cover. Secretive and largely nocturnal. Not numerous anywhere. The female leaves the nest right after laying, leaving the male to incubate the eggs and raise the young. This bird and a South American relative are the only members of their family placed somewhere between the Rallidae and Scolopacidae.

**Distribution:** Africa, Oriental region, East Asia and Australasia; sedentary. A widespread but uncommon resident throughout the region, including Singapore and Hong Kong; not recorded in Brunei.

## COMMON OYSTERCATCHER
*Haematopus ostralegus* 45 cm  F: Haematopodidae

**Description**: Unmistakable, note prominent red bill and wing band.

**Voice**: A penetrating *ky-bik*.

**Habits**: A strictly coastal shorebird found on sheltered mudflats, and exposed rocky coasts with sandy beaches. Moves in small flocks during migration. Feeds by probing the sand with its strong bill, for mussels, crabs and worms.

**Distribution:** Breeds in temperate Eurasia; winters in Africa and south Asia. Within the region, a rare winter visitor to parts of Myanmar and south China; vagrant in Hong Kong and Peninsular Malaysia.

## NORTHERN LAPWING
*Vanellus vanellus* 30 cm  F: Charadriidae

**Description**: Note diagnostic underwing pattern and breast band; has a long crest; upperparts a uniform dark green with whitish spots in winter plumage.

**Voice**: A penetrating *wi-ip*.

**Habits**: During migration found in open country with short grasses, often near marshes, but also in drier areas and open fields. Feeds in typical plover-style by running forward abruptly, picking up invertebrate prey suddenly, then standing motionless for a while.

**Distribution**: Breeds in temperate Eurasia; winters in the subtropics. Within the region, an uncommon winter visitor in northern parts of the mainland, including Hong Kong; rare in Thailand.

## GREY-HEADED LAPWING
*Vanellus cinereus* 35 cm  F: Charadriidae

**Description**: Distinguished from following species by a uniformly grey head.

**Voice**: A sharp *peep* in flight.

**Habits**: On breeding grounds in northern China, Russia and Japan it prefers remote and secluded inland swamps and river banks. Seeks a similar habitat during migration; also found in cultivated fields and coastal lagoons. Not as numerous as many other shorebirds and seems to have declined in numbers. Currently regarded as near-threatened with global extinction.

**Distribution**: Breeds in northern East Asia; winters in Oriental region. Within the region, a generally uncommon winter visitor throughout the mainland, including Hong Kong; vagrant in Malaysia, Singapore, Brunei and the Philippines.

# RED-WATTLED LAPWING
### *Vanellus indicus* 33 cm  F: Charadriidae

**Description**: Distinguished from other lapwings by its black head and breast, contrasting with a white patch behind the eye; note also red wattle.

**Voice**: A loud *did-he-do-it*.

**Habits**: Found in dry fields and bush country, often near marshes and rivers. Seen sometimes far from water. Runs forward in sudden jerks, plover-style, and pecks for insects in the short grass. Often a resident pair vigorously defends their territory, flying past the intruder and calling out persistently. The 3 to 4 eggs are laid in a shallow scrape on the ground, lined with small stones and debris.

**Distribution:** Middle East and Oriental region; mainly sedentary. Within the region, a widespread and common resident throughout the mainland; uncommon in Peninsular Malaysia; a rare visitor to Singapore.


# RIVER LAPWING
### *Vanellus duvaucelii* 30 cm  F: Charadriidae

**Description**: Note pale sides of head, contrasting with black cap and throat; legs are black.

**Voice**: A penetrating *keck*.

**Habits**: A river specialist found in river valleys and around wide, flowing streams with sand bars and shingle beds. Occasionally visits nearby fields. Never found near stagnant water. This low-density species is unable to adapt to new opportunities and is not common anywhere. Feeds on invertebrates such as insects, worms and crustaceans. Nests on the stony riverbanks.

**Distribution:** Oriental region; sedentary. A generally scarce resident in parts of mainland SE Asia, from south Thailand to south China.

## GREY PLOVER
### *Pluvialis squatarola* 28 cm  F: Charadriidae

**Description**: A large plover with dark grey upperparts mottled with white.

**Voice**: A slurred whistle *kwee-u-ee;* often calls in flight.

**Habits**: During migration this shorebird prefers exposed seashores, probably similar to its barren high arctic breeding grounds. Found on remote sandy beaches and less often on mudflats. Not as numerous as some shorebirds. Usually seen with just a few companions, picking worms from the sand.

**Distribution**: Worldwide; breeds high in the arctic; winters in the tropics. A fairly common passage migrant and winter visitor throughout the region.

## PACIFIC GOLDEN PLOVER (Lesser Golden Plover)
### *Pluvialis fulva* 25 cm  F: Charadriidae

**Description**: Distinguished from the Grey Plover by its golden brown upperparts faintly dotted with orange. Shown here with a common Redshank on the right.

**Voice**: A clear and penetrating whistle, *tu-ee*.

**Habits**: Found in a variety of wetland and open country habitats, from tidal mudflats to grasslands and fields far from the shore. One of the most numerous shorebirds in the region. During periods of peak migration, dense flocks may appear. Some birds are present most months of the year.

**Distribution**: Breeds in Siberia and Alaska; winters in the tropics and subtropics in Asia and Australasia. A common migrant and winter visitor in all countries of the region.

## COMMON RINGED PLOVER
*Charadrius hiaticula* 19 cm  F: Charadriidae

**Description**: Photo shows almost full breeding plumage; during non-breeding season, its black collar is duller with more brown; note lack of eye ring.

**Voice**: Soft whistle, *tu-weet*, when flying.

**Habits**: Habits: Frequents coastal mudflats during migration, often singly or together with other shorebirds. Migration route seems to bypass the region, but possibly this is a somewhat overlooked species.

**Distribution:** Breeds in temperate and arctic Eurasia; winters mainly in Africa. Within the region, an uncommon passage migrant in Peninsular Malaysia and Singapore; rare in Myanmar and Hong Kong; vagrant in the Philippines, Thailand and north Borneo.

## LITTLE RINGED PLOVER
*Charadrius dubius* 18 cm  F: Charadriidae

**Description**: Yellow orbital ring is diagnostic; photo shows non-breeding plumage; during breeding has brown breastband and black facial mask.

**Voice**: Descending whistle *pe-ou*.

**Habits**: Breeds up country along sandy riverbanks. Found in all types of wetlands during migration, often in flocks along tidal mudflats, along the edges of mangrove forests and prawn ponds, but also in marshes and fields far from the coast. An active feeder; runs forward quickly, then stops abruptly to pick in the mud.

**Distribution:** Breeds in temperate and subtropical Eurasia; winters in Africa and tropical Asia. An uncommon resident in the region, but a common migrant and winter visitor; locally abundant.

## KENTISH PLOVER
### *Charadrius alexandrinus* 15 cm F: Charadriidae

**Description**: Picture shows non-breeding plumage; note diagnostic black legs and big brown spot on side of breast.

**Voice**: A soft *twit*.

**Habits**: During migration this tiny shorebird is mainly found on the coast, along sandy beaches and mudflats. It occurs less often inland, along rivers and wet fields. Locally it can congregate in flocks of 20 to 30 birds, but often just a few are seen together, picking invertebrates from the mud.

**Distribution**: Worldwide, except Australasia; northern populations migrate. Within the region, a fairly common winter visitor to the mainland, including Hong Kong; uncommon in Singapore, the Philippines and Borneo.

## MALAYSIAN PLOVER
### *Charadrius peronii* 15 cm F: Charadriidae

**Description**: Male (top) has diagnostic thin, black band across its neck; the female's band (bottom) is rufous brown; note its pale legs.

**Voice**: Like a Kentish Plover.

**Habits**: Found exclusively on sandy beaches and those with washed up coral debris, usually in remote and tranquil areas with little human activity. Feeds close to the water's edge, usually in pairs. The nest is a depression in the sand further up the beach. Little else is known about this species; it is not numerous anywhere.

**Distribution**: Southeast Asia; sedentary. A scarce resident in tropical parts of the region. Near-threatened with global extinction.

## MONGOLIAN PLOVER (Lesser Sand-plover)
*Charadrius mongolus* 20 cm  F: Charadriidae

**Description**: Photo shows non-breeding plumage; in breeding plumage has rufous breast band and black facial mask.

**Voice**: A short trilling *dri-it*.

**Habits**: Found along all types of coastline, often on mudflats near mangroves and around commercial prawn ponds; also on exposed sandy beaches. Always in flocks; birds spread out when feeding, but congregate in dense flocks when roosting during high tide.

**Distribution**: Breeds in the arctic and temperate northeast and central Asia; migrates south, reaching Australia. A passage migrant and winter visitor throughout the region; rare in Hong Kong, but locally abundant further south.

## GREATER SAND-PLOVER
*Charadrius leschenaultii* 23 cm  F: Charadriidae

**Description**: Similar to the Mongolian Plover, but can be recognised by its longer legs and stronger bill.

**Voice**: Sometimes a soft *trrrt*.

**Habits**: Habits: Similar to the Mongolian Plover, in fact the two species often mix; this species seems to prefer the more open, sandy coastlines while the Mongolian is often more numerous on sheltered mudflats.

**Distribution**: Breeds in central Asia; migrates to the tropics and south to Australia. A generally common passage migrant and winter visitor within the region, including Hong Kong; less numerous on the Malay peninsula.

# EURASIAN CURLEW
## *Numenius arquata* 57 cm  F: Scolopacidae

**Description:** Distinguished from the following species by a much larger bill and lack of black crown-stripe; in flight, its pale rump best distinguishes it from the rarer Eastern Curlew.

**Voice:** Voice: In flight a fluty and plaintive *cour-li*.

**Habits:** During migration it is found at remote mudflats seaward of mangrove forests; also along more exposed beaches and offshore islets, usually mixing with other shorebirds, as this photo of roosting flocks shows. The flocks are concentrated along the shoreline during high tide, then spread out, as the tide retreats. It feeds using its specialised bill for probing deep into the soft mud for worms and crustaceans.

**Distribution:** Breeds in temperate Eurasia; winters to the south, reaching Indonesia. A widespread but generally scarce winter visitor throughout most of region, including Hong Kong, Singapore and Brunei.

# WHIMBREL
## *Numenius phaeopus* 43 cm  F: Scolopacidae

**Description:** Distinguished from previous species by shorter bill and black crown-stripe.

**Voice:** A fluty and penetrating *tu-tu-tu-tu* when taking off.

**Habits:** Frequents a variety of wetlands, mostly mudflats, mangroves and estuaries, but also sandy shores and even freshwater marshes and fields some distance behind the coast. Walks with long strides and probes its curved bill deep into the mud for worms and crustaceans.

**Distribution:** Worldwide; breeds in temperate northern hemisphere; winters in the south. Widespread within the region, and a common migrant and winter visitor throughout; can be found almost any month of the year.

## LITTLE CURLEW
### *Numenius minutus* 30 cm  F: Scolopacidae

**Description:** A small version of Whimbrel; note diagnostic short bill.

**Voice:** Fluty *di-di-di* in flight.

**Habits:** Found near the coast in dry, open country with short grass, often airport areas and sometimes golf courses. Seen more rarely on tidal mudflats. Walks among the short vegetation, picking up insects and other invertebrates.

**Distribution:** Breeds in eastern Siberia; migrates mainly east of Borneo to winter in Australasia, especially northern Australia. Within the region: a rare passage migrant in Hong Kong, Taiwan and Philippines; vagrant in Borneo, Thailand and Singapore.

## EASTERN CURLEW
### *Numenius madagascariensis* 59 cm  F: Scolopacidae

**Description:** Very similar to the Eurasian Curlew; a diagnostic feature is its dark (not pale) rump, visible on take-off. Latin name derives from an error by scientist Linnaeus, who named it in 1766.

**Voice:** Like Eurasian Curlew.

**Habits:** Breeds in subarctic freshwater marshes, but during migration is found mostly near the coast. It feeds in small flocks on the mudflats along estuaries and coastal lagoons. In this area it is extremely timid, and takes off at 200 metres distance or more, which makes good observations difficult. The photo was taken in Australia, the only place this species congregates in any great numbers. Near-threatened with global extinction.

**Distribution:** Breeds in eastern Siberia; winters mainly in Australasian region, reaching New Zealand. Within the region: a scarce passage migrant in south China, including Hong Kong, the Philippines, Vietnam, Malaysia, Singapore and Brunei.

## BLACK-TAILED GODWIT
*Limosa limosa* 40 cm  F: Scolopacidae

**Description**: A large shorebird; in winter plumage look for very long straight bill and smooth grey upperparts; in flight, black tail tip contrasts with white wing band.

**Voice**: Usually quiet; occasionally a loud *kell-kell-kell* when taking off.

**Habits**: Found on coastal mudflats, usually in small flocks; occasionally seen upcountry along large rivers and lakes. Spreads out and feeds with the other shorebirds at low tide, but congregates into dense groups at high tide roosting sites.

**Distribution**: Breeds in temperate and subarctic Eurasia; winters in the subtropics and tropics. A fairly common passage migrant and winter visitor in much of the region, including Hong Kong; uncommon in Singapore and the Philippines.

## BAR-TAILED GODWIT
*Limosa lapponica* 37 cm  F: Scolopacidae

**Description**: Distinguished from the Black-tailed Godwit by its slightly upturned bill, scaly upperparts, barred tail (in flight) and lack of wingbar.

**Voice**: Usually quiet; in flight, a soft *kit-kit-kit*.

**Habits**: During migration frequents extensive mudflats on remote shorelines; does not come into sandy areas or marshes. This active feeder walks continuously forward, probing deep into the mud for invertebrate prey.

**Distribution**: Breeds in arctic Eurasia and Alaska; winters in the tropics and subtropics. A locally fairly common passage migrant and winter visitor within the region, but generally less widespread and numerous than many other shorebirds.

## SPOTTED REDSHANK
*Tringa erythropus* 30 cm  F: Scolopacidae

**Description:** Distinguished with difficulty from the following species by its longer, thinner bill and paler underparts in winter plumage; best diagnostic feature is lack of white in wing on take-off.

**Voice:** A penetrating *te-wit*.

**Habits:** Breeds far to the north on the tree-less tundra. During migration it is seen in scattered flocks on sheltered shores and tidal mudflats, also sometimes on marshes and ponds far from the coast. Feeds in shallow water and occasionally swims. Before the return journey in April, some birds can be seen in handsome breeding plumage, with all-black underparts and fine white spots on wings.

**Distribution:** Breeds in arctic Eurasia; winters in subtropical and tropical Africa and Asia. A common passage migrant and winter visitor in south China, including Hong Kong; rarer further south; vagrants reaching Malaysia, Singapore and Brunei.

## COMMON REDSHANK
*Tringa totanus* 28 cm  F: Scolopacidae

**Description:** Shown in photo with Terek Sandpiper (on the left) for comparison (top); note red legs and brownish upperparts; in flight (bottom) note prominent white secondaries.

**Voice:** A series of loud, ringing notes *teu-hoo* when taking off.

**Habits:** During migration frequents prawn farms and mudflats along sheltered beaches and mangrove edges; only rarely seen inland at rivers and wet fields. Locally abundant; forms dense flocks along high tide roosting sites; individuals spread out when feeding at low tide.

**Distribution:** Breeds in temperate Eurasia; winters in subtropical and tropical Africa and Asia. A common passage migrant and winter visitor in most of the region; uncommon in the Philippines.

# MARSH SANDPIPER
*Tringa stagnatilis* 23 cm  F: Scolopacidae

**Description**: In non-breeding plumage (photo); pale grey upperparts and needle-thin, black bill are diagnostic; more slender, paler and smaller than Common Greenshank.

**Voice**: A high-pitched *tyeuk*.

**Habits**: Found during migration with other shorebirds at tidal mudflats, estuaries and prawn ponds; seen less often around freshwater wetlands behind the coast. Often just a few are found together, however, at prime sites they congregate in flocks of several hundred birds. It probes the mud surface frantically at low tide for minute invertebrate prey.

**Distribution**: Breeds in central and northern Asia; migrates south, reaching South Africa and Australia. Within the region: A locally common migrant and winter visitor to the mainland, including Hong Kong; uncommon in the Philippines and Borneo.

# COMMON GREENSHANK
*Tringa nebularia* 35 cm  F: Scolopacidae

**Description**: Non-breeding plumage (photo), with Ruddy Turnstone; like Marsh Sandpiper, but somewhat darker upperparts, larger size and stronger bill are diagnostic.

**Voice**: A penetrating *teu-teu* when taking off.

**Habits**: Usually found on tidal mudflats, along mangrove edges, around prawn cultivation areas and along exposed, sandy beaches. This shorebird also regularly moves up country to rivers, freshwater marshes and reservoirs far from the coast. Often seen singly or a few together, rarely in larger groups and never in vast flocks.

**Distribution**: Breeds in subarctic Eurasia; migrates south to South Africa and Australia. Widespread and common, although not abundant; a passage migrant and winter visitor in all of the region.

## NORDMANN'S GREENSHANK (Spotted Greenshank)
*Tringa guttifer* 33 cm  F: Scolopacidae

**Description**: Distinguished with some difficulty from previous species by shorter legs and thicker, two-tone bill; also paler plumage, in breeding with heavy black spots on chest.

**Voice**: Less vocal than preceding species; sometimes a very different scream, *keyew*.

**Habits**: During migration settles on sheltered coastlines with mudflats and sandflats near estuaries and lagoons. Feeds during the retreating tide; takes many crabs plus a variety of other aquatic invertebrates and small fish. This rare bird is endangered with global extinction and seems be declining further in numbers; its world population is estimated at 1,000 individuals. Hong Kong still a good place to observe it.

**Distribution:** Breeds east Russia pacific coast area, migrates south to Oriental region. Rare winter visitor to south China incl. Hong Kong, also some years Malay Peninsula, vagrant in Singapore, where not recorded since 1981.

## GREEN SANDPIPER
*Tringa ochropus* 24 cm  F: Scolopacidae

**Description**: Distinguished from following species by darker, finely spotted upperparts, contrasting with bright white rump in flight; also distinguished by call.

**Voice**: A ringing *tlu-eet-weet*.

**Habits**: During breeding this shorebird prefers forested moors; nests in trees (not on the ground as other waders). During migration it does not form dense flocks at mudflats. Instead it scatters inland and settles singly or a few together at small vegetated ponds and canals. Shy, it flies off abruptly and quickly when disturbed.

**Distribution:** Breeds temperate and subarctic Eurasia, migrates south. In the region, a widespread and common winter visitor in northern parts incl. Hong Kong, stragglers reach Malaysia, Singapore and Brunei.

## WOOD SANDPIPER
*Tringa glareola* 23 cm  F: Scolopacidae

**Description**: Photo shows non-breeding plumage; note scaly upperparts and white supercilium.

**Voice**: A high-pitched, shrill *wee-wee-wee*.

**Habits**: During migration this shorebird favours all kinds of wetlands from sheltered mudflats, to marshes and flooded fields far inland. It rarely congregates in dense flocks, preferring instead to move singly or in loose groups, feeding in shallow water.

**Distribution**: Breeds in temperate and subarctic Eurasia; migrates to the tropics, south to Africa and Australia. A widespread and common passage migrant and winter visitor throughout the region.

## TEREK SANDPIPER
*Tringa cinereus* 24 cm (*Xenus cinereus*)  F: Scolopacidae

**Description**: Similar to a small Common Redshank, but note its orange legs, smooth grey upperparts and long, thin, slightly up-turned bill.

**Voice**: A loud trill, *twee-hwee-hwee*.

**Habits**: A strictly coastal shorebird frequenting tidal mudflats and estuaries; also more exposed beaches and sandy shores. Moves singly or in small flocks, picking invertebrates out of the mud surface at a frantic pace. Bunches together at high tide roosting sites.

**Distribution**: Breeds in temperate and subarctic Eurasia; migrates south, reaching South Africa and Australia. A fairly common passage migrant and winter visitor in much of the region; uncommon in Hong Kong and the Philippines.

## COMMON SANDPIPER
*Tringa hypoleucos* 20 cm (*Actitis hypoleucos*)  F: Scolopacidae

**Description**: Unmistakable; note chocolate brown upperparts and solid build; bobs tail incessantly; flies off low across the water on whirling wing beats.

**Voice**: A penetrating *twee-wee-wee* when taking off.

**Habits**: Most widespread and adaptable of all shorebirds. Found where water is nearby, from the usual mudflats and sandy shores near harbour areas and city drainage canals, to inland reservoirs and forested rivers. A restless feeder, it runs along the water's edge constantly, picking up minute prey.

**Distribution**: Breeds across Eurasia, from the subarctic to subtropical zones; winters south to Africa and Australia. A widespread and common migrant and winter visitor throughout the region; can be seen almost any month of the year.

## GREY-TAILED TATTLER
*Tringa brevipes* 25 cm (*Heteroscelus brevipes*)  F: Scolopacidae

**Description**: Built and moves like a Common Redshank, but smooth prey upperparts, greenish legs, and lack of white in wing when flying are diagnostic.

**Voice**: Sharp whistle, *too-weet*.

**Habits**: Strictly coastal during migration and prefers somewhat exposed beaches, sandy shores and coves with washed up coral debris. Does not mix much with other waders; moves singly or in small flocks, feeding at low tide, roosting on higher ground between feeds.

**Distribution**: Breeds in northeastern Siberia; migrates along an easterly flyway to winter mainly in Australia. A locally common passage migrant in the Philippines; uncommon or rare in the rest of the region.

# RUDDY TURNSTONE
## *Arenaria interpres* 23 cm  F: Scolopacidae

**Description**: Unmistakable in all plumages. White bands (on wings, tail and back) flash prominently in flight (bottom).

**Voice**: A metallic *ti-ti-ti-ti-ti* when taking off.

**Habits**: A strictly coastal bird found mostly on sandy shores, rocky offshore islands and concrete embankments. Also sometimes seen on the dry edges of mudflats, usually singly or in small groups, rarely with other shorebirds. The Ruddy Turnstone actually does turn over small stones to flush out marine invertebrates.

**Distribution**: Worldwide; breeds in high arctic region; winters in the south. A fairly common passage migrant and winter visitor throughout the region.

# ASIAN DOWITCHER
## *Limnodromus semipalmatus* 35 cm  F: Scolopacidae

**Description**: Distinguished with some difficulty from the Bar-tailed Godwit by its stocky build, upright stance and powerful, all-black bill.

**Voice**: Usually silent; sometimes a quiet *miau*.

**Habits**: Frequents mudflats and estuaries, where it feeds with peculiarly wooden movements, penetrating the mud with a stiff neck somewhat like a sewing machine. Usually just a few are seen together; a generally scarce species, not really numerous anywhere except Indonesia.

**Distribution**: Breeds in sub-arctic Siberia; winters in Southeast Asia into northern Australia. A rare winter visitor on the mainland, including Hong Kong and Singapore; vagrant in Borneo and the Philippines. Considered near-threatened with global extinction.

## SWINHOE'S SNIPE
### *Gallinago megala* 28 cm  F: Scolopacidae

**Description**: Similar to Pintail Snipe, *G. stenura,* but note its diagnostic long tail extending beyond folded wings.

**Voice**: A short, rasping cry when taking off.

**Habits**: During migration frequents freshwater wetlands, marshes and wet fields, often near the coast, but rarely seen at tidal mudflats. Usually stays inside cover but will come out to feed in the open when undisturbed.

**Distribution**: Breeds in Mongolia and Siberia; winters in tropical Asia and Australasia. A fairly common passage migrant and winter visitor in parts of the region; vagrant in Thailand; absent from Indochina, but possibly overlooked.

## COMMON SNIPE
### *Gallinago gallinago* 27 cm  F: Scolopacidae

**Description**: Distinguished from other *Gallinago* snipes by a black eye-stripe, broader at base of bill; in flight, a fine white trailing edge on secondaries is sometimes visible.

**Voice**: An explosive rasping cry when flushed.

**Habits**: Found in freshwater wetlands with tall grass and swampy areas; also visits paddy fields and sometimes tidal estuaries. Stays inside cover until flushed – shoots away abruptly in fast, erratic flight.

**Distribution**: Worldwide, northern hemisphere; breeds in the north, winters south to the Equator. Within the region, a common winter visitor on the mainland; uncommon in the Philippines and Borneo.

# RED KNOT
## *Calidris canutus* 24 cm  F: Scolopacidae

**Description:** Note stocky build; photo shows non-breeding plumage; during breeding the grey is replaced with a warm rufous colour.

**Voice:** A muted *chut-chut* and a whistling *twit-wit* when taking off.

**Habits:** Occurs at mudflats and estuaries; is known to form dense flocks, but in this region just a few are usually seen together, sometimes seen with Great Knot. Feeds typical *Calidris* style walking forward and pecking rapidly in the mud from side to side for minute invertebrates.

**Distribution:** Worldwide; breeds in the high arctic, migrates to the extreme south of southern continents. A widespread but rare passage migrant and winter visitor in the region including Kong Kong, Brunei and Singapore.

# GREAT KNOT
## *Calidris tenuirostris* 30 cm  F: Scolopacidae

**Description:** Largest of all *Calidris* shorebirds; distinguished from previous species by larger size and stockier build; shown here with Little Tern and Common Redshank behind.

**Voice:** Usually silent; sometimes a low *chucker-chucker*.

**Habits:** This Asian shorebird has a limited distribution; most individuals overfly the Oriental region to the east, to winter further south. Therefore only small groups turn up at coastal mudflat locations, usually 2 to 10 together, and always with other shorebirds. Larger flocks reported only from Hong Kong during return migration in April.

**Distribution:** Breeds in northeastern Siberia; winters mainly in Australia. A generally scarce passage migrant within the region, including Kong Kong, Brunei and Singapore.

## RUFOUS-NECKED STINT
*Calidris ruficollis* 15 cm  F: Scolopacidae

**Description**: In non-breeding plumage; note greyish upperparts and diagnostic short, black legs; has a rufous head and breast only in breeding season.

**Voice**: A soft *chit-chit-chit*.

**Habits**: During migration, this tiny shorebird is found only on the coast, on mudflats near mangroves, prawn ponds and along sandy beaches near estuaries. Feeds actively. Runs continuously across the mud, pecking frantically. When disturbed, the birds bunch together and manoeuvre rapidly across the coastline in a dense flock.

**Distribution**: Breeds in northeast Siberia; migrates south, reaching New Zealand. A widespread and common passage migrant and winter visitor throughout the region; locally abundant.

## LITTLE STINT
*Calidris minuta* 15 cm  F: Scolopacidae

**Description**: In winter, very similar to previous species, but note scaly wings and distinct white V-shaped marking on mantle.

**Voice**: A sharp *stit-it*.

**Habits**: During migration found at tidal mudflats; usually a few are seen together with other *Calidris* shorebirds. This region constitutes the southeastern limit of the range of this species, which is abundant at other locations further west. Possibly overlooked, but not easily identified along the extensive shorelines where it is found.

**Distribution**: Breeds in northern Siberia; winters mainly in Africa and South Asia. Within the region: a rare winter visitor to Hong Kong and Vietnam; vagrant in the Philippines, Thailand and Peninsular Malaysia.

# TEMMINCK'S STINT
### *Calidris temminckii* 15 cm  F: Scolopacidae

**Description**: Distinguished from other stints in winter plumage by smooth, brownish (not grey or scaly) upperparts and pale yellowish legs.

**Voice**: A distinctive, high-pitched trill *tirrrr* on take-off.

**Habits**: During migration this is the stint most likely to be found far from the coast at freshwater marshes and irrigated fields. It also occurs at coastal lagoons and tidal ponds, but is never seen on exposed beaches. An unobtrusive, quiet wader; easily overlooked. Often moves singly or just a few together. Reported in Hong Kong, in larger flocks numbering up to 30 birds.

**Distribution**: Breeds in arctic Eurasia; winters mainly in Africa and the Oriental region, not crossing the Equator. Within the region: a fairly common winter visitor to northern areas including Hong Kong; rarer further south, including Singapore and Brunei.

# LONG-TOED STINT
### *Calidris subminuta* 16 cm  F: Scolopacidae

**Description**: Note brownish, rather scaly upperparts and fairly long, greenish legs; shown here with a Terek Sandpiper on the right for size comparison.

**Voice**: A soft *chi-rup* on take-off.

**Habits**: During migration found on coastal mudflats and estuaries, but generally near the shore in drier areas, and sometimes also around freshwater ponds behind the coast. Tends to feed closer to vegetation than other *Calidris* shorebirds and does not form dense flocks. Usually a few move together in loose groups.

**Distribution**: Breeds in Siberia; winters mainly in Southeast Asia. A few reach Australia. A fairly common passage migrant and winter visitor throughout the region.

## SHARP-TAILED SANDPIPER
*Calidris acuminata* 22 cm  F: Scolopacidae

**Description**: Somewhat similar to the previous species, but note its larger size and black streaks on its bright rufous upperparts.

**Voice**: A soft *pleep*.

**Habits**: After breeding in the arctic tundra, this shorebird flies south, practically non-stop, to the wintering grounds in Australia. During the slower return journey in Feb-May, small flocks stop over in this area, where they sometimes can be seen at coastal mudflats with other shorebirds.

**Distribution**: Breeds in northern Siberia; winters mainly in the Australasian region reaching New Zealand. An uncommon passage migrant in south China, including Hong Kong and the Philippines. Rare in Thailand, Malaysia, Singapore and Brunei.

## DUNLIN
*Calidris alpina* 19 cm  F: Scolopacidae

**Description**: Photo shows breeding plumage; in non-breeding plumage, similar to Curlew Sandpiper; shorter bill and darker upperparts are diagnostic.

**Voice**: A soft, trilling *trree* when taking off.

**Habits**: During migration frequents coastal mudflats; also sometimes found inland along riverbanks and lakeshores. Moves in small flocks, often near groups of other shorebirds, spreading out when feeding and bunching up when flying and roosting.

**Distribution**: Worldwide, northern hemisphere. Breeds in temperate and subarctic zones. Winters in the south, mainly in the subtropics. A fairly common winter visitor in northern parts of the region; rare in Thailand. Vagrant in Laos, Malaysia and Singapore.

## CURLEW SANDPIPER
### *Calidris ferruginea* 21 cm  F: Scolopacida

**Description**: Note silver-grey non-breeding plumage and long, decurved bill.

**Voice**: A liquid *chirrip*.

**Habits**: During migration frequents seacoasts; feeds along tidal mudflats, estuaries and in commercial prawn pond areas. Flies across the coast in closed flocks, landing on the exposed mud, to feed frantically as the tide retreats. Roosts on high gravel banks when the tide returns.

**Distribution**: Breeds in high arctic Siberia; migrates south, reaching South Africa and New Zealand. A fairly common passage migrant and winter visitor in much of region, especially Malay Peninsula where it is locally abundant during peak migration.

## SANDERLING
### *Calidris alba* 20 cm  F: Scolopacidae

**Description**: Unmistakable; note very white appearance in non-breeding plumage, contrasting with black upperparts.

**Voice**: A distinctive *cheep cheep* when taking off.

**Habits**: Strictly coastal at all times. During migration prefers remote sandy beaches resembling its barren breeding grounds; rare along estuaries and never found at sheltered mudflats. Feeds by running in small groups, following the exact edge of the surf at a frantic pace.

**Distribution:** Worldwide; breeds on the highest arctic land masses close to the North Pole; winters in the south. A widespread and locally fairly common passage migrant and winter visitor in most of the region. Rare in the Philippines.

## BROAD-BILLED SANDPIPER
### *Limicola falcinellus* 18 cm  F: Scolopacidae

**Description**: In non-breeding plumage (photo), distinguished with some difficulty from Dunlin by its striped head pattern. A unique and monotypic genus.

**Voice**: A metallic *chee-reep* on take-off.

**Habits**: An inconspicuous shorebird; feeds on sheltered mudflats or in tidal marshes just behind the beach. Often solitary or a few are found together, mixing with other similar waders; never seen in flocks. This is a widespread but globally fairly scarce species that is not really numerous anywhere.

**Distribution:** Breeds in subarctic and arctic Eurasia; winters in the south, reaching South Africa and Australia. An uncommon and scarce passage migrant and winter visitor within the region.

## RUFF
### *Philomachus pugnax* 28 cm  F: Scolopacidae

**Description**: In non-breeding plumage (photo) the stance, shape of bill combined with brown, scaly upperparts are diagnostic. A unique, monotypic genus.

**Voice**: Usually silent; sometimes a low *chuck-chuck*.

**Habits**: During migration it frequents tidal mudflats, estuaries and drier areas with short grass just behind the coast. A quiet and inconspicuous wader, sometimes spotted singly or mixing with other shorebirds. Males display and fight each other on leks near northern breeding grounds.

**Distribution:** Breeds in temperate to arctic Eurasia; winters mainly in Africa and south Asia. A widespread but uncommon to rare passage migrant and winter visitor throughout the region.

## BLACK-WINGED STILT
*Himantopus himantopus* 38 cm  F: Recurvirostridae

**Description**: Unmistakable in all plumages; distinguished by long pinkish red legs and needle-thin bill; photo shows immature birds; male has all-white head and black wings; the female's wings are dull brown.

**Voice**: A penetrating *kik-kik-kik* in flight.

**Habits**: Found in coastal wetlands, especially freshwater lagoons and marshes just behind tidal estuaries. Truly looks as if it walks on stilts, as it feeds on minute aquatic prey in shallow water.

**Distribution**: Worldwide tropics and subtropics; northern populations migrate south. An uncommon mainly winter visitor within the region; a few pairs breed in Thailand and Indochina.

## PIED AVOCET
*Recurvirostra avosetta* 43 cm  F: Recurvirostridae

**Description**: Unmistakable, with pied plumage and upturned bill.

**Voice**: A clear *kly-yt*.

**Habits**: Occurs in extensive saline marshes where it feeds in the shallow waters of both tidal estuaries and freshwater lagoons behind the coast. This elegant bird walks forward, swinging its bill from side to side in the water's surface, picking out tiny invertebrate prey. Occasionally swims.

**Distribution**: Breeds in temperate and subtropical Eurasia; winters mainly in Africa. An uncommon winter visitor to Myanmar, Taiwan and southern China, including Hong Kong; vagrant in Vietnam, Thailand and the Philippines.

## RED-NECKED PHALAROPE
*Phalaropus lobatus* 18 cm  F: Phalaropidae

**Description**: Unmistakable, with small size and needle-like bill; shown in non-breeding plumage; note pied colouration.

**Voice**: A short *chek*.

**Habits**: Breeds in freshwater marshes, but spends the non-breeding season at sea, often in loose flocks far from the shore. Can also turn up at coastal mudflats and coral reefs where it is often quite approachable. Feeds while swimming around restlessly, high in the water, constantly pecking the surface for minute prey.

**Distribution**: Breeds worldwide in the arctic and subarctic climate zones; winters in tropical seas. Within the region, a widespread winter visitor; locally fairly common in Hong Kong, the Philippines and Borneo, but rarely observed elsewhere.

## BEACH THICK-KNEE
*Esacus magnirostris* 51 cm  F: Burhinidae

**Description**: Unmistakable; the only thick-knee within its range. Previously considered conspecific with the similar Great Thick-knee, *E. recurvirostris*, of mainland Southeast Asia and South Asia.

**Voice**: A loud, high-pitched *pee-pee-pee*.

**Habits**: Found on offshore islands and sometimes on remote mainland beaches. Frequents a wide range of coastal habitats, from rocky coral reefs to sandy beaches and mudflats near estuaries. A low density species, with resident pairs spread out over remote coastal expanses. Feeds almost exclusively on crustaceans, especially crabs, which it stalks like a heron on the mud.

**Distribution**: Oriental region, Australasia; sedentary. A generally scarce resident in coastal regions of south Thailand, Malaysia, Singapore, Philippines and Brunei.

## ORIENTAL PRATINCOLE
### *Glareola maldivarum* 25 cm  F: Glareolidae

**Description**: Note black border around throat.

**Voice**: A sharp *chek-chek*.

**Habits**: Found in open country; builds its nest on the ground in dry fields. During migration it congregates in flocks, settling around airports and coasts, near or mixing with proper shorebirds. Behaves sometimes like a wader, feeding while running on mudflats and short grass; at other times it feeds like a swallow, catching flying insects on warm thermals.

**Distribution**: Breeds in northern parts of the Oriental region and East Asia; migrates south, reaching northern Australia. A fairly common resident and passage migrant throughout the region; may breed in the Philippines and Borneo.

## SMALL PRATINCOLE
### *Glareola lactea* 18 cm  F: Glareolidae

**Description**: Note its uniformly pale grey plumage and the diagnostic white bar in wing during flight (bottom).

**Voice**: A low, harsh note.

**Habits**: Found in open country, especially near large rivers with sandy shores and shingle banks; also seen at freshwater marshes, lake-side mud banks and sea coasts during migration. Nests in small colonies, the 2 to 3 eggs are laid in a small scrape in the sand. Like other pratincoles, it feeds on insects caught on the ground or in the air.

**Distribution**: Oriental region: outside the breeding season, somewhat nomadic. Within the region: an uncommon resident and winter visitor in parts of the mainland. Vagrant in Singapore

## COMMON BLACK-HEADED GULL
*Larus ridibundus* 38 cm  F: Laridae

**Description**: Brown (not black) head of breeding plumage (photo) replaced by black spot behind ear in winter plumage; wing tips almost pure white.

**Voice**: A harsh *kwar*.

**Habits**: During migration mainly coastal, often sitting on kelong poles some distance from the shore; can also turn up at inland rivers. Feeds by swimming or flying over the water's surface, lifting out invertebrates and fish; also walks along the beach and mudflats picking up food.

**Distribution**: Breeds in temperate Eurasia; winters in the south, reaching the Equator. A widespread and locally fairly common winter visitor, especially in northern part of the region; rarer in the south; the only gull recorded in the Philippines.

## BROWN-HEADED GULL
*Larus brunnicephalus* 46 cm  F: Laridae

**Description**: Noticeably larger, heavier and slower bird than previous species; in flight black wingtips are diagnostic.

**Voice**: A harsh *gek, gek*.

**Habits**: Breeds on islands in large lakes in the interior of Asia. During winter months (October-April) migrates to the coast and is locally numerous within the region. It is the only gull occurring in this range in any significant numbers. Prefers coastal marshes and tidal mudflats near mangroves. Seen less often inland, at rivers and lakes. Feeds on fish and aquatic invertebrates while swimming in shallow water.

**Distribution**: Breeds in central Asia; winters in the Oriental region. A locally common winter visitor in Myanmar, Thailand and northwest Peninsular Malaysia; rarer in Indochina.

## HERRING GULL
### *Larus argentatus* 60 cm  F: Laridae

**Description**: Upper wing is silvery grey; note diagnostic pinkish-red feet; shown here with Common Gull, *L. canus* (40 cm), another winter visitor to south China; immature bird is mottled brown.

**Voice**: A loud *gi-au* and *ga-ga-ga*.

**Habits**: Found mainly along seashores, estuaries and harbour areas, also seen on occasion along inland lakes. A conspicuous bird and omnivorous feeder, taking practically all edible matter, even garbage, but mainly a variety of fish and other marine food.

**Distribution**: Worldwide, northern hemisphere; breeds in temperate to arctic climate zones; winters south to subtropics. Within the region: A fairly common winter visitor to south China, including Hong Kong. Rare in Thailand and Vietnam.

## WHISKERED TERN
### *Chlidonias hybridus* 26 cm  F: Laridae

**Description**: Note diagnostic short bill, head pattern and pale wings in non-breeding plumage; tail only slightly forked.

**Voice**: A short, harsh *kitt*.

**Habits**: Breeds in freshwater marshes. During migration found in a variety of wetlands from reservoirs and flooded fields far inland to tidal estuaries, mudflats, prawn ponds and seashores. Elegant flier that picks aquatic prey, including small fish, from the surface water; also catches insects in mid-air.

**Distribution**: Africa, Eurasia, the Oriental region and Australasia; northern populations migrate south. Common passage migrant and winter visitor in most of the region; locally abundant; rare in Singapore.

## WHITE-WINGED TERN
### *Chlidonias leucopterus* 23 cm  F: Laridae

**Description**: In non-breeding plumage (top). Its dark wings and black dot behind ear are diagnostic. During breeding season is unmistakable with black body and pale wings (bottom).

**Voice**: A sharp *kwek-kwek*.

**Habits**: During migration frequents sheltered seacoasts, estuaries, tidal mudflats; also seen at inland ponds and reservoirs. During peak migration, flocks numbering hundreds of birds sometimes congregate at prime locations. Feeds on the wing by hawking for insects or by flying slowly against the wind, picking up invertebrates from the water's surface; rarely plunges in.

**Distribution**: Breeds in temperate Eurasia; migrates south, reaching South Africa and Australia. A widespread, common passage migrant and winter visitor throughout the region; locally abundant.

## GULL-BILLED TERN
### *Gelochelidon nilotica* 38 cm  F: Laridae

**Description**: Photo shows individual in winter plumage with other terns; note large size and diagnostic heavy, black bill; during breeding its cap is black. A unique bird and the only member of its genus.

**Voice**: A soft *kuw-ik*.

**Habits**: Found at coastal mudflats and along estuaries and mangrove edges. Sometimes seen at saline marshes behind the coast, but never on exposed beaches. Often a few group together, but never in dense flocks. Feeds by flying slowly over the mud or dry land, diving down for insects, worms, small reptiles and amphibians.

**Distribution**: Worldwide tropics and subtropics, northern populations migrate south. In the region, mostly a widespread but uncommon visitor occuring in fairly small numbers.

## CASPIAN TERN
### *Sterna caspia* 53 cm  F: Laridae

**Description**: Unmistakable; note huge size, red bill in all plumages and black wing tips; cap deep black when in breeding plumage.

**Voice**: A crow-like *kraaaah*.

**Habits**: During migration frequents coastal regions, mudflats and estuaries; during breeding season also found around inland seas and large lakes with sandbanks, where it nests in colonies. Catches fairly large fish by diving spectacularly into the water from a great height.

**Distribution**: Worldwide; northern populations migrate. Within the region, a locally fairly common resident and winter visitor to South China, including Hong Kong; rare elsewhere; vagrant in the Philippines and Brunei.

## COMMON TERN
### *Sterna hirundo* 35 cm  F: Laridae

**Description**: Medium-sized tern with deeply forked tail and strong, elastic wing-beats; in non-breeding plumage its upper wings are dark grey (photo); in breeding plumage, cap (including forehead) is black.

**Voice**: A harsh *keer-ar*.

**Habits**: During migration frequents coastal waters, mudflats, estuaries and, on occasions, inland rivers. Congregates in loose flocks in prime habitat. Perches on kelong poles or floating logs near the shore and dives into the water for small fish.

**Distribution**: Worldwide; breeds in northern temperate climate zones; winters to the south. A widespread passage migrant and winter visitor within the region; during peak passage locally abundant; uncommon in the Philippines.

## BLACK-NAPED TERN
### *Sterna sumatrana* 31 cm  F: Laridae

**Description:** Note white cap, black nape and very pale prey upperparts.

**Voice:** A sharp *kick*.

**Habits:** A strictly offshore bird, although it is often seen near the shore. Breeds in dense, but small, colonies on remote, uninhabited islets. Lays two eggs on bare rock or in coral debris. Local populations may be declining, however more studies needed on this. Catches small fish by plunge-diving.

**Distribution:** Tropical seas from the Indian Ocean to the Pacific; nomadic outside breeding season. A widespread and locally common offshore resident throughout the region, including Singapore and Brunei.

## BRIDLED TERN
### *Sterna anaethetus* 37 cm  F: Laridae

**Description:** Distinguished (with difficulty) from the rarer Sooty Tern, *S. fuscata,* by its narrow, white forehead extending back behind the eye, and dark brown (not black) upperparts.

**Voice:** A harsh alarm call, *kee-errr-krr*.

**Habits:** Strictly offshore, but usually found within 15 km of land and sometimes much closer. Breeds in colonies on remote islets; pairs are often spread out, with eggs well hidden among rocks and grass; often seen with the previous species in mixed colonies. An elegant flier, it feeds on small fish and squid by surface-dipping, sometimes resting on floating objects.

**Distribution:** Worldwide tropical oceans; disperses to sea outside the breeding season. A widespread but generally scarce resident throughout region, including Brunei. An uncommon visitor to Singapore, Cambodia and Hong Kong.

## LITTLE TERN
*Sterna albifrons* 23 cm  F: Laridae

**Description:** Its very small size and rapid wing-beats are diagnostic; in breeding plumage (top) the bill is yellow; in non-breeding plumage (bottom), the bill is black.

**Voice:** A high-pitched *kik-kik*.

**Habits:** Frequents coastal regions, often fishing in the sea near mudflats, estuaries and exposed sandy beaches but also inland at rivers and reservoirs. Breeds in loose colonies on remote sandy beaches or riverine shingle banks. Hovers in the air close to the water's surface and plunges in for small fish.

**Distribution:** Africa, Eurasia and Australasia; northern populations migrate south. A fairly common winter visitor and local resident throughout the region; has bred in the Philippines and Brunei.

## GREAT CRESTED TERN
*Sterna bergii* 45 cm  F: Laridae

**Description:** A large, slow-flying tern; note yellowish bill and dark grey upperparts.

**Voice:** A sharp *kirrik*.

**Habits:** A strictly coastal tern; is often seen outside the breeding season in small flocks or with other terns near the shore, resting on kelong poles and on the beach, but never lives permanently on land. During the breeding season it retreats offshore to nest on remote uninhabited reefs and islets. Plunges from a great height into the water for fish.

**Distribution:** Tropical and subtropical seas, from Africa to the Pacific; outside the breeding season, somewhat nomadic. Within the region, a widespread resident on offshore reefs; a common winter visitor to Malaysia and Singapore; vagrant in Hong Kong.

# LESSER CRESTED TERN
## *Sterna bengalensis* 40 cm  F: Laridae

**Description:** Distinguished with some difficulty from *T. bergii* by orange bill, smaller size and paler upperparts.

**Voice:** A loud *kirrik*.

**Habits:** A strictly coastal and offshore species. Moves in small flocks, often together with the Great Crested Tern, but in smaller numbers. Rests on offshore fishing equipment or on tidal sandbanks. Plunge-dives for fish from a medium height, often submerging completely in the water.

**Distribution:** Tropical seas from Africa to Australia; nomadic outside breeding season. An uncommon winter visitor to southern coast lines within the region. Vagrant off south China and Cambodia.

# BROWN NODDY
## *Anous stolidus* 42 cm  F: Laridae

**Description:** Unmistakable, apart from the much rarer Black Noddy, *A. minutus,* which is vagrant in region; distinguished from that species by its larger size, pale cap which gradually (not sharply) contrasts with brownish (not blackish) back.

**Voice:** Quiet, harsh croaks near nest.

**Habits:** This pelagic tern is known to breed in colonies on Pulau Penang off Peninsular Malaysia, as well as on remote islets in the South China Sea, the Sulu Sea, and the Philippines. Appears to be extirpated from islands off Thailand. Stays offshore, far from the mainland, feeding on small fish, flying fish and squid that it picks from the water's surface. It does not dive.

**Distribution:** Worldwide tropical seas; somewhat nomadic. Resident in Malaysia, Philippines and south China. An offshore visitor elsewhere.

## YELLOW-VENTED PIGEON
*Treron seimundi* 30 cm  F: Columbidae

**Distribution:** Southeast Asia. An uncommon resident in Laos, Vietnam and Peninsular Malaysia only. Vagrant in Thailand. Near-threatened with global extinction.

**Description:** Very similar in appearance and habits to the Pin-tailed Pigeon, *T. apicauda*, of the northern mainland; distinguished from this species by its shorter tail and yellow vent; photo shows female; male has small maroon patch on shoulder.

**Voice:** No information.

**Habits:** A lower montane specialist found in forest, from the foothills into lower montane elevations. May wander into lowlands to feed on occasion. Observed feeding in the canopy of tall fruiting trees. Otherwise not often recorded and little studied; its nest has never been described.

## WEDGE-TAILED PIGEON
*Treron sphenura* 33 cm  F: Columbidae

**Distribution:** Oriental region. Within the region, a generally scarce resident in montane parts of the mainland. Not recorded in Cambodia.

**Description:** Note distinctive maroon patch on the wing of this male (missing in the female); photo shows Peninsular Malaysia subspecies. The northern Wedge-tailed Pigeon has more maroon on wings, extending across its mantle.

**Voice:** Deep, hooting notes.

**Habits:** A strictly montane pigeon found in forest from 800 to 1,700 metres in Malaysia; further north, found from 600 to 2,800 metres elevation; at higher elevations, it is the most numerous *Treron* pigeon in the forest, but never abundant. Seen in fruiting trees or flying past quickly, at canopy level. The nest is a flimsy structure of twigs; the first Malaysian nest, described in 1992, was built by the bird in this photo.

## THICK-BILLED PIGEON (Thick-billed Green Pigeon)
*Treron curvirostra* 27 cm  F: Columbidae

**Description**: Photo shows male; female is green with a yellow stripe in wing and a distinct, bluish eye-ring.

**Voice**: A soft, throaty *cloo-cloo*.

**Habits**: A forest bird found in a variety of wooded habitats, from coastal mangroves to submontane rainforest. Locally numerous in mature secondary growth, where it congregates in fruiting fig trees. Often seen flying quickly and directly to and from fruiting trees.

**Distribution**: Oriental region. A widespread and fairly common resident in much of the region including Singapore and Brunei. Vagrant in Hong Kong.

## POMPADOUR PIGEON
*Treron pompadora* 26 cm  F: Columbidae

**Description**: Distinguished best from both sexes of previous species by lack of blue orbital ring; photo shows female.

**Voice**: Soft cooing and nasal whistling calls.

**Habits**: A forest bird found in a variety of wooded habitats, often along disturbed edges and second growth. Mainly a lowland species, seen regularly at 800 metres elevation, sometimes to 1,200 metres. Previously described as common, now appears to have declined in numbers in Southeast Asia. Feeds in large trees on fruits and berries, often mixing in small flocks with other pigeons.

**Distribution**: Oriental region. Within the region, a generally scarce resident in parts of the mainland and the Philippines.

## LITTLE GREEN PIGEON
*Treron olax* 20 cm  F: Columbidae

**Description**: Its small size is diagnostic; photo shows male; female is a dull green with faintly greyish cap and a yellow stripe in its wing.

**Voice**: Soft cooing; higher-pitched than other pigeons.

**Habits**: A forest bird found mainly in lowland primary rainforest and mature secondary growth with plenty of fruiting trees. Also recorded in nearby cultivated areas, and at lower montane elevations to 1,400 metres. Usually seen flying quickly and low over the canopy in the early morning; later in the day seen feeding in fruiting trees in small groups, as the photo shows.

**Distribution**: Sunda subregion. Within the region, a locally fairly common resident in Malaysia and Brunei; rare in south Thailand and Singapore.

## PINK-NECKED PIGEON (Pink-necked Green Pigeon)
*Treron vernans* 25 cm  F: Columbidae

**Description**: Male (top) has greyish head and pink breast (not neck); female (bottom) is uniformly green with a yellow stripe in wing.

**Voice**: Some chuckling and gurgling notes.

**Habits**: An arboreal pigeon from the coastal forest that has successfully invaded disturbed habitats such as secondary growth, plantations, parks, gardens and even ornamental trees in cities. A few birds feed together on fruits and berries in tall trees and in low bushes; when disturbed, it flies off with noisy wing beats.

**Distribution**: Southeast Asia. A locally common resident in parts of the region, including Singapore and Brunei.

## WHITE-EARED BROWN-DOVE
### *Phapitreron leucotis* 24 cm  F: Columbidae

**Description**: The sexes are similar. Distinguished with difficulty from the much rarer and montane Amethyst Brown-dove, *P. amethystina,* by its greenish neck and white vent. This genus with 3 species is unique to the Philippines.

**Voice**: A descending and accelerating *hoot-ho*.

**Habits**: An arboreal pigeon occurring in a variety of wooded habitats, from primary forest to disturbed forest edges and nearby cultivation, mainly in the lowlands and occasionally to 1,000 metres. Often seen with other frugiverous birds in fruiting trees and sometimes feeding low in small bushes. The nest is a flimsy platform of twigs high in a tree.

**Distribution:** A Philippine endemic. A generally common resident on all main islands except Palawan.

## YELLOW-BREASTED FRUIT-DOVE
### *Ptilinopus occipitalis* 31 cm  F: Columbidae

**Description**: A deep, resonant *hoowoo* in morning and late afternoon.

**Voice**: a sharp *ke-ke-ke-ke*.

**Habits**: A forest bird found mainly in primary forest, from the lowlands to 1,000 metres elevation, and occasionally to 1,800 metres. Somewhat tolerant of disturbance, has also been found mixing with other birds in nearby logged forest. Movements and feeding habits have not been studied. The nest has not been described.

**Distribution:** A Philippine endemic. Locally a fairly common resident on most main islands.

## JAMBU FRUIT-DOVE
*Ptilinopus jambu* 28 cm  F: Columbidae

**Description**: Note diagnostic pink-red face and breast on male (top), lacking in female plumage (bottom).

**Voice**: A quiet *hoo*.

**Habits**: Found in small numbers in coastal and lowland secondary rainforest; also in mangrove forests and plantations but not gardens. Also flies to offshore islands. Is generally an inconspicuous species usually seen feeding quietly on fruits in the canopies of large trees.

**Distribution**: Sunda subregion; somewhat nomadic with a small range. Within the region, an uncommon resident in south Thailand and Malaysia; a non-breeding visitor to Singapore; vagrant in Brunei.

## BLACK-NAPED FRUIT-DOVE
*Ptilinopus melanospila* 28 cm  F: Columbidae

**Description**: Female (photo) is dark green with a bluish face; male is unmistakable, with green body and pale grey face contrasting with black nape and yellow lower belly.

**Voice**: A ringing *awook-wook*.

**Habits**: A secretive fruit-dove usually seen sitting passively in mid-storey canopies. Best located by call. Mainly spotted when it flies quickly into the next tree or emerges on open branches to feed on fruits (see photo). Mostly a small island specialist, it has not been recorded from mainland Borneo.

**Distribution**: Southeast Asia, mainly Indonesia. Within the region, an uncommon resident on islands in the southern Philippines and off Sabah (East Malaysia).

## GREEN IMPERIAL PIGEON
*Ducula aenea* 45 cm  F: Columbidae

**Description**: A very large pigeon with green wings and grey underparts.

**Voice**: A loud *curr-hoo*.

**Habits**: A forest bird occurring in lowlands and lower montane rainforest and forest edges; locally also in mangroves. Has a conspicuous habit of flying high across the forest each morning towards fruiting trees, returning in the evening. Perches high in the largest trees of the forest; not easy to view clearly.

**Distribution**: Oriental region. A widespread and fairly common resident in most of the region, including Brunei; extinct in Singapore.

## PIED IMPERIAL PIGEON
*Ducula bicolor* 42 cm  F: Columbidae

**Description**: A fairly large pigeon with unmistakable black and white plumage.

**Voice**: A deep, chuckling *hu-hu-hu-hu*.

**Habits**: Specialises in living on islands; often seen flying to and from, and circling around islands near the mainland. It prefers larger islands with coastal hills. Usually moves in pairs or small groups, settling in mangrove and coastal woodlands. Feeds in fruiting trees.

**Distribution**: Southeast Asia east to New Guinea; may be somewhat nomadic. A widespread but not very numerous resident within the region; a non-breeding visitor to Singapore; vagrant in Brunei.

# MOUNTAIN IMPERIAL PIGEON
## *Ducula badia* 45 cm  F: Columbidae

**Description**: Distinguished from *D. aenea* by brown (not green) wings and back.

**Voice**: A deep, booming *oomp-oomp*.

**Habits**: Mostly found in montane and lower montane forests, from the foothills up to 2,200 metres elevation. Although resident in the mountains, this strong flier roams widely in search of food and can even turn up in coastal mangroves. It can be seen visiting fruiting trees, flying rapidly across the canopies or sitting at mid-storey level emitting its booming call.

**Distribution**: Oriental region. A locally fairly common resident in much of region, including Brunei.

# LITTLE CUCKOO-DOVE
## *Macropygia ruficeps* 30 cm  F: Columbidae

**Description**: A small sized bird; its rufous upperparts and pale underparts are diagnostic; Borneo race (photo) has dark-brown spots on breast.

**Voice**: A rapidly repeated *kroo-wuk*.

**Habits**: A denizen of the lower montane forest and montane elevations up to 2,000 metres. Occasionally feeds down to 300 metres. Sits low in the forest and seems to prefer open forest edges; also enters nearby cultivated areas. Feeds on fruit and berries low in trees or on the ground.

**Distribution**: Southeast Asia. Within the region, an uncommon to locally quite numerous resident in montane areas; not confirmed in Brunei.

## ORIENTAL TURTLE-DOVE
### *Streptopelia orientalis* 32 cm  F: Columbidae

**Description**: Distinguished from other doves by scaly wings, grey lower back and prominent stripes (not spots) on neck, all features showing well in the photo.

**Voice**: A 4-note cooing *croo croo-croo crooo*.

**Habits**: This adaptable dove is associated with forests throughout much of its range, but it also occurs in open country and farmlands. It finds most of its food (such as seeds, plant shoots and some fruit) on the ground. During migration it becomes sociable and flocks of several hundred birds have been reported at roosting sites, e.g. at the Mai Po Marshes, Hong Kong.

**Distribution:** Oriental region and north into the eastern Palearctic region; northern populations migrate south. A common resident and winter visitor, mainly in northern parts of the region, including Hong Kong; rarer further south.

## COLLARED DOVE
### *Streptopelia decaocto* 33 cm  F: Columbidae

**Description**: Note the pale, sandy-brown plumage and diagnostic narrow, black collar.

**Voice**: A deep, 3-tone *coo-cooo-coo*; also a nasal *churrr* on take-off.

**Habits**: In recent years this successful species has expanded its range from its strongholds in south Asia. It now occurs also in north Africa, Japan and north America (introduced). Originally an arboreal bird of open deciduous woodlands, it adapts readily to cultivated areas and even occurs in cities. Like other *Streptopelia* doves, it perches and nests in trees, but is also seen on the ground, feeding mainly on seeds. Its diet also includes some invertebrates.

**Distribution:** Eurasia and the Oriental region; sedentary. Within the region, resident in northern parts only, from Myanmar, east into the Fukien Province of China.

## RED TURTLE-DOVE (Red-collared Dove)
*Streptopelia tranquebarica* 23 cm  F: Columbidae

**Description**: Male (photos) unmistakable, with reddish plumage, black neck band and grey head; female has dull reddish brown colours in place of the male's bright colours.

**Voice**: A throaty, repeated *croodle-oo-croo*.

**Habits**: An open country pigeon that moves about in scrub, dry woodlands and open fields with some trees, usually in small flocks. Common in cultivated areas, but does not enter villages. A strong flier that shoots along in a speedy and direct manner. Mostly feeds on the ground, picking up seeds and grain at the edge of vegetation.

**Distribution**: Oriental region; partly migratory. Within the region, a common resident on the mainland, expanding into the Malay Peninsula; fairly common in the northern Philippines; migrant in Hong Kong; introduced in Singapore.

## SPOTTED DOVE
*Streptopelia chinensis* 30 cm  F: Columbidae

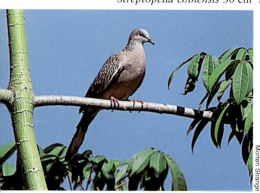

**Description**: Note diagnostic broad, black collar with white dots.

**Voice**: A soft *te-croo-crooo*.

**Habits**: An open country species that has benefited from widespread forest clearance in the region. Found in all types of open woodlands and cultivated areas; also enters villages, parks and gardens. Walks on the ground pecking up grain, but flies up to a high perch when disturbed. The nest is a flimsy structure built low in a tree. Is often kept as a pet.

**Distribution**: Oriental region. A widespread and common resident in all countries of the region.

## PEACEFUL DOVE (Zebra Dove)
*Geopelia striata* 21 cm  F: Columbidae

**Description**: Note small size and barred flanks; distinguished with difficulty from two similar Indonesian and Australian species by its unbarred, pink breast.

**Voice**: A soft, rolling *croo-croo-croo*.

**Habits**: Feeds on the ground in open country, coastal woodlands and around cultivated areas. Seen frequently on dry fields in rural areas and along roadsides, but does not come into towns. Flies up and perches in a tree when disturbed. Popular cage bird valued for its 'singing'.

**Distribution**: Southeast Asia. Within the region, native to the Malay Peninsula, including Singapore; introduced and common in central Thailand, the Philippines and Borneo, including Brunei.

## EMERALD DOVE (Green-winged Pigeon)
*Chalcophaps indica* 25 cm  F: Columbidae

**Description**: Note bright green wings and warm vinous underparts; photo shows female; male is brighter and has a grey cap.

**Voice**: A soft, deep *tu-hoop*.

**Habits**: A forest bird found in rainforest, in secondary growth and along forest edges up to lower montane altitudes. Usually seen singly or in pairs, flying low across the trail while navigating between the trees with amazing speed, like a green projectile. A shy bird that prefers to stay under cover, it feeds on the ground or perches low on fallen logs.

**Distribution**: Oriental region, Australasia. A widespread and locally fairly common resident in all territories in the region, including Hong Kong, Singapore and Brunei.

## LUZON BLEEDING-HEART
### *Gallicolumba luzonica* 30 cm  F: Columbidae

**Description**: Unmistakable; the only member of its genus within its range; grey and black stripes in wings visible from side view; one of 5 bleeding-heart pigeons, each endemic to various parts of the Philippine archipelago.

**Voice**: A low-pitched, clear and mournful *coo-oo*.

**Habits**: Occurs in primary and mature secondary rainforest, from sea level to 1,400 metres elevation. Moves along the forest floor feeding on seeds, fallen fruit and invertebrates, often near forest clearings, trails and along streams. Shy; flies off a short distance and runs into cover when disturbed. Roosts on a perch in a tree.

**Distribution:** Philippine endemic. An uncommon resident on the islands of Luzon and nearby Polillo and Catanduanes. Near-threatened with global extinction.

## MINDORO BLEEDING-HEART
### *Gallicolumba platenae* 30 cm  F: Columbidae

**Description**: Unmistakable; only member of its genus within its range; note tiny maroon patch on lower breast, visible from the front. Captive photo.

**Voice**: No information.

**Habits**: A lowland rainforest specialist only found inside closed forest below 400 metres elevation, a habitat fast disappearing on Mindoro. Habits presumably like previous species. Not observed in the wild by bird-watchers since 1991. Some reports since then by local people but further studies are required, as this species may possibly already be extinct.

**Distribution:** A Philippine endemic. A rare resident on the island of Mindoro. Critically endangered with global extinction.

## NICOBAR PIGEON
*Caloenas nicobarica* 40 cm  F: Columbidae

**Description**: Unmistakable; photo shows captive male; female's hackles are shorter. Unique; the only member of its genus.

**Voice**: Usually quiet.

**Habits**: A peculiar species restricted to small, forested offshore islands. It occasionally wanders onto larger islands or the mainland. Crepuscular or nocturnal in habit; feeds on the ground in dense vegetation. Rarely seen flying between islands. When disturbed, it takes off with noisy wing beats to perch low in a tree.

**Distribution**: Southeast Asia, east to New Guinea; makes nomadic movements between islands. Within the region, a rare resident offshore mainland Southeast Asia, north Borneo and the Philippines. Near-threatened with global extinction.

## BLUE-CROWNED RACQUET-TAIL
*Prioniturus discurus* 27 cm  F: Psittacidae

**Description**: Distinguished from 3 other *Prioniturus* parrots, partly sympatric to this species, by blue cap; note characteristic elongated tail unique to this genus.

**Voice**: A penetrating screech in alarm.

**Habits**: A forest bird found in closed rainforest, from coastal mangroves to lower montane forest at 1,750 metres elevation. Adapts to disturbed habitats and frequently flies into nearby orchards and banana plantations to feed on fruit. Moves about in small groups of 4 to 6, flying quickly and maneuvering rapidly between the trees. Up to 25 have been reported at evening roosts. The nest is built inside a forest tree, as the photo shows.

**Distribution**: A Philippine endemic. A locally fairly common resident on most major islands except Palawan (which has a similar endemic species).

# BLUE-NAPED PARROT
## *Tanygnathus lucionensis* 30 cm  F: Psittacidae

**Description**: Distinguished from similar and sympatric Blue-backed Parrot, *T. sumatranus*, by blue crown and orange-buff scales in wings.

**Voice**: Noisy, loud, frequent and far-reaching shrieks, both when flying and perched.

**Habits**: A rainforest bird found in closed forest, from the coast to 1,000 metres elevation. It visits fruiting and flowering trees in pairs or small groups of 4 to 9 birds. An adaptable species, often seen in cultivated areas and on small islands with little forest. However numbers have decreased markedly in recent years due to habitat loss and trapping for the captive bird trade.

**Distribution**: Southeast Asia, east to New Guinea; makes nomadic movements between islands. Within the region, a rare resident offshore mainland Southeast Asia, north Borneo and the Philippines. Endangered with global extinction.

# ALEXANDRINE PARAKEET
## *Psittacula eupatria* 51 cm  F: Psittacidae

**Description**: Distinguished from the following species (which has a similar head pattern) by its much larger size and maroon shoulder patch; photo shows male; female has all-green head and neck.

**Voice**: A loud, ringing scream.

**Habits**: Prefers open woodlands and mixed deciduous forest with plenty of flowering and fruiting trees. Found mainly in the lowlands and behind mangroves and coastal forest, also in the foothills to 800 metres elevation. Feeds in flocks on fruit and nectar, often visiting commercial orchards near the forest. Much reduced in numbers; presently scarce in this area mainly due to raiding of nest holes and capture for the bird trade.

**Distribution**: Oriental region. Within the region, a generally uncommon resident in Myanmar, Thailand and parts of Indochina.

## ROSE-RINGED PARAKEET
*Psittacula krameri* 36 cm  F: Psittacidae

**Description**: Distinguished from other parakeets by plain green plumage and black/pink collar (male only, refer photo); female sometimes shows faint emerald collar.

**Voice**: A frequent and high-pitched *heel* in flight.

**Habits**: Occurs in deciduous woodlands and secondary forest. Flies along in fast, noisy flocks. Settles in fruiting and flowering trees and clambers about, chewing into fruits, flower buds and young shoots. In some of its strongholds, e.g. India, it is abundant and raids commercial orchards. It does well in captivity and escapees have established small feral populations in many cities in Asia, Africa and even the USA.

**Distribution:** The Oriental region and Africa. Within the region, a fairly common resident in Myanmar; rare in south-east China and south Vietnam; a fairly common resident in Hong Kong and Singapore, where it has been introduced.

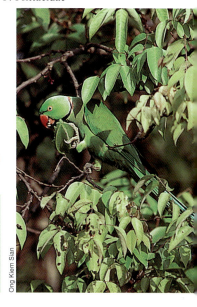

Ong Kiem Sian

## RED-BREASTED PARAKEET
*Psittacula alexandri* 36 cm  F: Psittacida

**Description**: Note diagnostic pinkish breast; the female (in front) is somewhat duller than the male.

**Voice**: A harsh, disyllabic chatter.

**Habits**: Occurs in dry, deciduous woodlands and along forest edges. Found mainly in the lowlands, locally to 1,600 metres elevation. Also visits nearby cultivated areas to feed, but does not appear as opportunistic as the previous species. Feeds mainly in tall, flowering trees; also eats other vegetable matter such as fruit, seeds and leaf buds. Although previously numerous, recently it appears to have declined in numbers throughout its range, mainly due to its capture as pets.

Tim Loseby

**Distribution:** The Oriental region, mainly Southeast Asia into parts of Indonesia. Within the region, a generally scarce resident in parts of the mainland; status in Hong Kong uncertain; introduced in Singapore.

## LONG-TAILED PARAKEET
*Psittacula longicauda* 40 cm  F: Psittacidae

**Distribution:** Southeast Asia. Within the region, a widespread and locally fairly common resident in Peninsular Malaysia, Singapore and Borneo, including Brunei; recorded in south Vietnam.

**Description:** All *Psittacula* parakeets have long tails, but note diagnostic head and breast patterns of this male; female has dull red bill and face.

**Voice:** A penetrating screech during flight.

**Habits:** Found along rainforest edges, in secondary growth and open coastal woodlands, mangroves and plantations, also parks and mature gardens. Always moves around in noisy flocks, when feeding in flowering or fruiting trees during the morning or gathering at communal roosts in the evening. Nests in colonies in cavities high in the trees.

## BLOSSOM-HEADED PARAKEET
*Psittacula roseata* 33 cm  F: Psittacidae

**Distribution:** Oriental region. Within the region, a generally scarce resident in Myanmar, Thailand and Indochina; possibly also south China.

**Description:** Note diagnostic features of this male: Fairly small size and tail, with slaty-grey head demarcated with yellow border; female has grey head.

**Voice:** Softer and less piercing than other parakeets.

**Habits:** A forest bird found in deciduous forest and along forest edges; also in nearby cultivated areas, from the lowlands to 900 metres elevation. Not as well studied as other members of this genus; little is known of its feeding and breeding habits. Like many of its relatives, it appears to have declined in numbers due to habitat loss, persecution as an agricultural pest and capture for the bird trade.

# BLUE-RUMPED PARROT
*Psittinus cyanurus* 18 cm  F: Psittacidae

**Description**: A small, compact parrot; male (photo) has blue rump, bluish head and red bill; female has brown head and bill.

**Voice**: A loud, metallic *chi-chi-chi*.

**Habits**: A lowland rainforest bird; flies far and is also found in mangroves and nearby plantations. Occurs in low densities and is not really numerous anywhere. Usually seen flying quickly and directly across the canopies; perches on high branches, so good views are difficult. Little is known about its feeding habits. The nest is built inside a natural cavity very high in a forest tree.

**Distribution:** Sunda subregion. Within the region, a rare resident in south Thailand and Singapore; locally fairly common in Malaysia and Brunei, but generally scarce. Near-threatened with global extinction.

# VERNAL HANGING-PARROT
*Loriculus vernalis* 13 cm  F: Psittacidae

**Description**: Unmistakable; the only Hanging Parrot within its range; distinguished from the following species by its red (not black) bill; photo shows female; male has blue throat.

**Voice**: A sharp, trisyllabic *chee-chee* in flight; a low chattering while feeding.

**Habits**: Occurs in primary and mature secondary forest, from the lowlands up to lower montane altitudes at 1,500 metres. Feeds high in the canopies of fruiting and flowering trees, as the photo shows. It also visits cultivated areas to feed, but nests inside the forest in a natural tree hollow in a dead branch.

**Distribution:** Oriental region. Within the region, a locally fairly common resident in parts of the mainland; rare in the southwest; possibly also in south-east China.

# BLUE-CROWNED HANGING-PARROT
## *Loriculus galgulus* 12 cm  F: Psittacidae

**Description**: The only Hanging Parrot within its range; note black bill and blue crown; male (photo) has red patch on chest.

**Voice**: A high-pitched *dzi* in flight.

**Habits**: Breeds in primary and mature secondary rainforest, from the lowlands up to lower montane altitudes. Flies far to feed along forest edges, in plantations and even gardens. Often seen flying quickly, low over the canopies, settling to feed in flowering and fruiting trees. Climbs around the branches using bill for support; often hangs upside down and even sleeps this way.

**Distribution**: Sunda subregion. Within the region, a locally common resident in south Thailand, Malaysia and Brunei; rare resident in Singapore.

# HODGSON'S HAWK-CUCKOO
## *Cuculus fugax* 29 cm  F: Cuculidae

**Description**: Distinguished from other hawk-cuckoos by plain grey head and streaked (not barred) underparts; in the Philippines, this subspecies is sometimes treated as the full species the Philippine Hawk-cuckoo, *C. pectoralis*.

**Voice**: A shrill *gee-weet* and a bubbling call.

**Habits**: This is a forest bird that occurs in a variety of wooded habitats, from dry, deciduous forest to dense rainforest. During migration it is also found in mangroves and cultivated areas. It usually stays low inside cover, feeding on caterpillars, beetles and some fruits. A skulking, low density species, it is rarely observed. Nest-parasitic on Small Niltava, Black-throated Babbler and other small passerines.

**Distribution**: Oriental region, East Asia; northern populations migrate south. Widespread but scarce resident and winter visitor throughout the region, including Singapore and Brunei; rare in the Philippines; vagrant in Hong Kong.

## INDIAN CUCKOO
*Cuculus micropterus* 33 cm  F: Cuculidae

**Description**: Distinguished from the following species and the Common Cuckoo, *C. canorus*, mainly by its call.

**Voice**: A diagnostic, penetrating, 4-note whistle with 4th note lower.

**Habits**: Adaptable species found in all wooded areas, from primary lowland rainforest to open coastal woodlands. Flies like a small hawk among the vegetation. Often perches high in the trees and is not easy to see well. Best located during breeding season by its repetitive and far-reaching call. Nest-parasitic; especially selecting various species of drongos, Dicruridae.

**Distribution**: Oriental region, East Asia; northern populations migrate south. A widespread and fairly common resident, passage migrant and winter visitor in most of the region; a common visitor to Singapore; rare in the Philippines.

## ORIENTAL CUCKOO
*Cuculus saturatus* 33 cm  F: Cuculidae

**Description**: Distinguished mainly by its call from the Common Cuckoo and the previous species.

**Voice**: Four mellow notes, *pup-poop-poop-poop*.

**Habits**: Breeds in forest. Within Malaysia, it is exclusive to the montane forest above 1,200 metres elevation. During migration, it turns up in a variety of wooded habitats, including open country with scattered trees. Perches inside the canopies, occasionally in the open as this photograph from Fraser's Hill in Malaysia shows. Not often observed, but possibly somewhat overlooked.

**Distribution**: Resident in East Asia and montane parts of the Sunda subregion. Northern populations migrate south reaching Australia. Resident in south China, Myanmar and Malaysia; an uncommon migrant elsewhere, including Hong Kong, Singapore and Brunei.

# PLAINTIVE CUCKOO

## *Cacomantis merulinus* 21 cm F: Cuculidae

**Distribution:** Oriental region; mainly sedentary. A widespread and locally common resident in all countries throughout the region, although not abundant.

**Description:** Distinguished from following species by full grey head and throat, and lack of eye-ring.

**Voice:** A mournful series of whistling notes, rising in pitch.

**Habits:** Found in all types of woodlands, except closed forest. Adapts well to cultivated areas, gardens and rural villages, often fairly tame. In spite of this, is not an easy bird to see well, as it feeds on larvae and insects inside bushes and trees. Nest-parasitic on warblers (Sylviidae), especially on prinias and tailorbirds.

# BRUSH CUCKOO

## *Cacomantis variolosus* 24 cm F: Cuculidae

**Distribution:** Southeast Asia into Australasia region. Within the region, an uncommon resident in south Thailand, Malaysia and Singapore; fairly common in the Philippines.

**Description:** Distinguished from previous species by larger size, prominent yellow orbital ring, and more rufous on upper breast; SE Asia race pictured here sometimes treated as separate species, the Rusty-breasted Cuckoo, *C. sepulcralis*.

**Voice:** A series of 10 to 15 rising, whistling notes.

**Habits:** Generally prefers more of a wooded area than the previous species; occurs in dense rainforest, mangroves and secondary growth; seen less often in scrub and plantations. Often found in the foothills to 1,200 metres elevation. A secretive bird best located by call. No less than 60 different host species have been identified, all small passerines.

## ASIAN EMERALD CUCKOO
### *Chrysococcyx maculatus* 18 cm  F: Cuculidae

**Description:** Photo shows male; female is similar to the following species, but has dull green upperparts and chestnut cap.

**Voice:** A whistled twitter; in flight, a sharp *chweek*.

**Habits:** Breeds in the forest, often in elevated areas from the foothills to 1,800 metres elevation. Seems to disperse widely outside the breeding season and turns up in lowland forest edges, cultivated areas and even gardens. This low density species moves quite high near canopy level feeding on insects and flying quickly from tree to tree so good views as in this extraordinary photograph are rare.

**Distribution:** Oriental region; partly migratory. Within the region, a generally uncommon resident and perhaps a winter visitor throughout most of the mainland, excluding Singapore; vagrant in Hong Kong.

Ong Kiem Sian

## VIOLET CUCKOO
### *Chrysococcyx xanthorhynchus* 17 cm  F: Cuculidae

**Description:** Photo shows female; male similar to previous species, but green is replaced with equally radiant violet.

**Voice:** A descending trill; also a loud *che-wick* in flight.

**Habits:** This is a forest bird occurring in closed forest and in open woodlands, mangroves and cultivated areas. Found mainly in the lowlands, rarely to 1,500 metres. A low density species sometimes seen flying high over the forest, calling or flying from tree to tree chasing insects. Nest parasitic, possibly on sunbirds, but its egg has never been found.

**Distribution:** Oriental region; possibly somewhat nomadic. A generally uncommon resident throughout much of the region, including Singapore and Brunei.

Ong Kiem Sian

## LITTLE BRONZE CUCKOO (Malayan Bronze Cuckoo)
*Chrysococcyx minutillus* 15 cm  F: Cuculidae

**Description:** Photo shows juvenile with host (Flyeater); adult has black bars across underparts.

**Voice:** A slow and descending whistle of 3 to 5 notes.

**Habits:** Mainly a mangrove and coastal forest bird; also ventures into nearby scrub, plantations and even mature gardens. An inconspicuous bird seen feeding on insects and larvae at medium level in the coastal woodlands, flying swiftly into the next tree. Nest-parasitic on the Flyeater and other members of the *Gerygone* genus.

**Distribution:** Oriental region and Australasia; Australian birds migrate north to Indonesia. A generally uncommon to locally common resident in southern parts of the region, including Singapore; vagrant in Brunei.

## DRONGO CUCKOO
*Surniculus lugubris* 25 cm  F: Cuculidae

**Description:** Similar to the Bronzed Drongo, but note thin bill and white barring under tail. This bird and the endemic Philippine Drongo Cuckoo, *S. velutinus,* are the only members of its genus.

**Voice:** 4 to 8 ascending whistling notes.

**Habits:** A denizen of lowland rainforest and forest edges. During the non-breeding season, also found in mangroves and disturbed habitats. Generally inconspicuous, but quite vocal during the breeding season. Catches insects and larvae at mid-storey level. Nest-parasitic; in this region, mainly on small members of the babbler family Timaliidae.

**Distribution:** Oriental region; partly migratory. A widespread but generally scarce resident and winter visitor within the region, including Singapore; vagrant in Brunei; not recorded in Hong Kong.

# COMMON ASIAN KOEL
*Eudynamys scolopacea* 42 cm  F: Cuculidae

**Description**: Large cuckoo; male (photo) all black; female brown with white spots.

**Voice**: A far-reaching *ko-wel* with stress on last syllable.

**Habits**: An adaptable bird found in mangroves, coastal woodlands and forest edges but also in parks and gardens attracted by fruiting trees. Unlike most other members of this family, the Koel is almost entirely frugivorous. Shy and secretive; stays inside cover of trees. Often calls loudly early in the morning before dawn. Nest-parasitic, especially on crows and orioles.

**Distribution:** Oriental region, Australasia; partly migratory. A widespread and locally common resident and winter visitor throughout the region, including Hong Kong and Singapore; uncommon in Borneo, including Brunei; vagrant in Taiwan.

# CHESTNUT-BELLIED MALKOHA
*Phaenicophaeus sumatranus* 40 cm  F: Cuculidae

**Description**: Distinguished from similar Black-bellied Malkoha, *P. diardi*, by chestnut belly and under tail coverts.

**Voice**: Usually quiet; a low *kok*.

**Habits**: Found in primary and secondary forest, from the lowlands to lower montane altitudes; also in mangroves and forest edges. Hops about inside canopies looking for large insects to prey on, usually in pairs. Makes short flights into next tree. Breeding habits little studied; the nest is a pile of sticks high in a forest tree.

**Distribution:** Sunda subregion. Within the region, an uncommon resident in south Thailand, Myanmar, Singapore and Brunei; locally fairly common in Malaysia.

## GREEN-BILLED MALKOHA
*Phaenicophaeus tristis* 55 cm  F: Cuculidae

**Description**: Most malkohas have green bills, but note very long tail and plain grey underparts.

**Voice**: Grunting or croaking notes.

**Habits**: A fairly adaptable forest bird found in most wooded areas from lowland primary rainforest to lower montane forest, up to 1,600 metres. Also seen in more open woodlands, disturbed forest edges and plantations. Feeds on insects, caterpillars and lizards often fairly low in the vegetation, frequently flying across the trail to another tree. The territorial pair builds its own nest.

**Distribution:** Oriental region. Within the region, a widespread and locally common resident on the mainland, excluding Hong Kong and Singapore.

## RAFFLES'S MALKOHA
*Phaenicophaeus chlorophaeus* 33 cm  F: Cuculidae

**Description**: Unmistakable malkoha; small size and chestnut plumage of male (top) are diagnostic; female (bottom) has a grey head and breast.

**Voice**: A soft, cat-like *kiaow-kiaow-kiaow*.

**Habits**: Occurs in primary and secondary lowland rainforest and in forest edges. Usually found in pairs. Climbs low inside canopies looking somewhat like a squirrel, constantly searching through the foliage for invertebrate prey. Only flies for short distances. Although a fairly easy bird to find, its nest has never been described.

**Distribution:** Sunda subregion. Within the region, a locally fairly common resident in south Thailand, Myanmar, Malaysia and Brunei; extinct in Singapore.

# RED-BILLED MALKOHA
## *Phaenicophaeus javanicus* 45 cm  F: Cuculidae

**Description**: Look for diagnostic red bill.

**Voice**: A quiet *kuk*.

**Habits**: Found in primary and mature secondary rainforest from the lowlands up to lower montane altitudes. Usually moves high in the middle storey or upper storey level, just below the canopy. Often seen in pairs. Hops and flies from branch to branch searching for large insects; rarely crosses open spaces.

**Distribution**: Sunda subregion. Within the region, a locally fairly common, but generally scarce resident in south Thailand, Myanmar, Malaysia and Brunei; extinct in Singapore.

# CHESTNUT-BREASTED MALKOHA
## *Phaenicophaeus curvirostris* 49 cm  F: Cuculidae

**Description**: Large malkoha; note the yellowish upper mandible on bill; underparts and the tip of tail are chestnut.

**Voice**: A deep *tok-tok-tok*.

**Habits**: Frequents lowland rainforest, secondary growth, forest edges and nearby scrub, and occasionally lower montane forest. Moves across the middle storey of the forest, jumping and crawling through the dense foliage, picking off large insects and small vertebrate prey. Flies briefly into the next tree. Two birds develop a tight bond, pair and build their own nest of twigs.

**Distribution**: Sunda subregion. Within the region, a fairly common to locally common resident in south Thailand, Myanmar, Malaysia, Brunei and parts of the Philippines.

# CORAL-BILLED GROUND-CUCKOO
*Carpococcyx renauldi* 69 cm  F: Cuculidae

**Description:** Unmistakable; this cuckoo, together with two endangered species endemic to Sumatra and Borneo respectively, form a peculiar genus unique to Southeast Asia.

**Voice:** A characteristic deep, rolling whistle.

**Habits:** Even though this photograph is far from perfect, it has been included here since this is a species many visitors to Thailand and Indochina want to see, and few succeed. Khao Yai is the usual place to watch for it. Found in primary forest and closed secondary growth, it walks like a pheasant on the ground and roosts low in trees where it builds its platform nest. Once its call is learned, it seems to be more numerous.

**Distribution:** Southeast Asia. An uncommon resident in parts of Thailand and Indochina only.

# GREATER COUCAL
*Centropus sinensis* 53 cm  F: Cuculidae

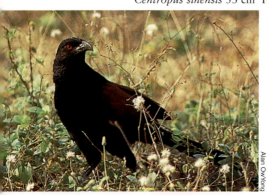

**Description:** Its large size and smooth plumage, without spots, are diagnostic.

**Voice:** A series of deep, booming *poop-poop-poop*.

**Habits:** Found along forest edges, in secondary growth, mangroves, riverbanks, savannah, grasslands and cultivated areas. Prefers a bit more vegetation cover than the Lesser Coucal. A shy and retiring bird, usually staying near the ground or inside cover where it creeps around, searching for vertebrate and invertebrate prey. Sometimes seen well when it emerges near rural roadsides.

**Distribution:** Oriental region. A widespread and fairly common to locally very common resident throughout the region; in the Philippines, an uncommon resident in the south only.

## LESSER COUCAL
### *Centropus bengalensis* 38 cm  F: Cuculidae

**Description**: Distinguished from the Greater Coucal by its smaller size and tiny white strands in duller plumage.

**Voice**: Hoots like the Greater Coucal, but more rapidly and with a higher pitch.

**Habits**: Mostly an open country species found in scrub, tall grassland and cultivation; especially numerous in marshy areas. Feeds by walking on the ground in search of insects, spiders, frogs and lizards. Suns itself in the open during early morning, otherwise best observed as it makes short flights low across the grass. The nest is a big ball of vegetation on or near the ground.

**Distribution:** Oriental region. A widespread and common resident in all countries of the region.

## BARN OWL
### *Tyto alba* 34 cm  F: Tytonidae

**Description**: Unmistakable; note its heart-shaped face; appears almost white in flight at night, like a 'ghost'.

**Voice**: Rasping and hissing sounds.

**Habits**: Roosts during the day in buildings, under bridges or in other man-made structures where it also nests; rarely in trees. Flies out silently at night to hunt for rats and mice in open country, plantations or villages. Often overlooked due to its nocturnal and quiet habits, but its range has expanded in recent years owing to the regional deforestation.

**Distribution:** Almost worldwide. Within the region, a widespread and locally fairly common resident on parts of the mainland, including Singapore.

# ORIENTAL SCOPS-OWL
## *Otus sunia* 19 cm  F: Strigidae

**Distribution:** East Asia, Oriental region; northern populations migrate south. An uncommon resident and winter visitor within the region; rare visitor to Singapore.

**Description:** Distinguished from following species by its smaller size, black streaks on underparts and yellow (not brown) eyes; most birds are grey (as shown in the photo) but a brown morph also occurs; sometimes included as a subspecies of the Common Scops-owl, *O. scops,* of Eurasia and Africa.

**Voice:** A tuneless *toik, toik-ta-toik*.

**Habits:** Breeds in deciduous forest and open woodlands, but during migration it turns up in a variety of wooded habitats, including parks and gardens. Perches fairly low on a large branch.

# COLLARED SCOPS-OWL
## *Otus lempiji* 23 cm *(Otus bakkamoena)*  F: Strigidae

**Distribution:** Oriental region. A widespread and common resident throughout the region except the Philippines.

**Description:** Small, brownish owl; ear tufts sometimes visible.

**Voice:** A soft *hoo-o* repeated at regular intervals.

**Habits:** A very adaptable and successful bird found in all kinds of wooded habitats, such as forests, parks and mature gardens, from lowland coastal areas to lower montane elevations. Very vocal during the breeding season; the most likely owl in the region to be heard or seen. Feeds on insects and small reptiles; nests in tree cavities.

## PHILIPPINE SCOPS-OWL
*Otus megalotis* 22 cm  F: Strigidae

**Description**: Note somewhat darker plumage than previous species and distinct ear tufts. Taxonomy disputed; some authors place with previous species. Dickinson, Kennedy & Parkes (1991) list this species and 6 other *Otus* species for the country.

**Voice**: 4 to 5 very distinctive, descending, barking notes.

**Habits**: A forest bird found in primary and secondary forest, from the lowlands to 1,600 metres elevation. Feeds on insects. Roosts during the day in a secure place near the trunk of a large forest tree. Breeding has been recorded from February to May.

**Distribution:** Philippine endemic. A widespread and fairly common resident on the major islands.

## BARRED EAGLE-OWL
*Bubo sumatranus* 48 cm  F: Strigidae

**Description**: Unmistakable within its range; note diagnostic barred underparts; a larger species, the Spot-billed Eagle-owl, *B. nipalensis,* replaces it in northern Southeast Asia.

**Voice**: Two deep hoots, *hu hu.*

**Habits**: Found in primary rainforest; sometimes ventures into forest edges and clearings in the evening. Appears at dusk and flies onto a perch, first gliding low across the ground. From there it drops down onto the ground to search for prey. Regularly seen near the bungalows in Taman Negara National Park, Malaysia.

**Distribution:** Sunda subregion. Within the region, a scarce resident in south Thailand, Myanmar, Malaysia and Brunei; extinct in Singapore.

## BROWN FISH-OWL
*Ketupa zeylonensis* 53 cm  F: Strigidae

**Description:** A large owl; distinguished from the following species by its paler sandy-brown plumage and fewer scales on wings; also note brown (not white) patch between eyes.

**Voice:** A soft, rapid *hup-hup*.

**Habits:** Found in open woodlands and fields with scattered trees, also along edges of coastal mangroves, from the lowlands to 800 metres elevation. Always lives near a stream, pond or small lake. Partly diurnal; it emerges mostly at dusk. Catches fish by night, as well as reptiles, small mammals and invertebrates.

**Distribution:** Oriental region. Within the region, a generally scarce resident in much of the mainland; rare in Peninsular Malaysia and Hong Kong.

## BUFFY FISH-OWL
*Ketupa ketupu* 50 cm  F: Strigidae

**Description:** Note diagnostic white patch above bill; also distinguished from previous species by generally darker plumage with thicker black streaks.

**Voice:** A soft *to-wee*.

**Habits:** Frequents forest edges near streams; also found in mangroves and near plantations and wet paddy fields. Usually rests in a tree during the day and flies out at dusk to feed on fish, frogs and crustaceans near streams. It also takes some mice, bats and small birds. It nests in a hole in a rotten tree.

**Distribution:** Southeast Asia. Within the region, a generally scarce resident in southern parts of the mainland; locally fairly common in East Malaysia; rare in Singapore; vagrant in Brunei.

## COLLARED OWLET
*Glaucidium brodiei* 16 cm  F: Strigidae

**Description**: Small size and barred (not spotted) plumage are diagnostic.

**Voice**: A mellow whistle *poop poo-poop poop*.

**Habits**: This tiny owl is found mainly in closed forest, but can be found in nearby disturbed woodlands and scrub, mainly in elevated areas from low foothills to the upper montane zone. Restricted in Malaysia to forest above 900 metres. Is sometimes active during the day, hunting and calling. Like other owls, it has the ability to turn its head 180 degrees, looking down its back, as the bird in the photo demonstrates.

**Distribution**: Oriental region. Within the region, a widespread and locally fairly common resident throughout most of the mainland; a montane resident in Malaysia; heard only in Hong Kong.

## BROWN HAWK-OWL
*Ninox scutulata* 30 cm  F: Strigidae

**Description**: Unmistakable; apart from the smaller endemic Philippine Hawk-owl, *N. philippensis,* the only *Ninox* owl in the region.

**Voice**: A double hoot *hu-oop* repeated incessantly at dawn and dusk.

**Habits**: Breeds in closed forest and more open woodlands. During migration it can turn up in mangroves, gardens and other wooded areas to 1,500 metres elevation. Becomes active just after dark, feeding mainly on insects at the edge of the forest. Nests in a cavity in a tree.

**Distribution**: East Asia, Oriental region; northern populations migrate south. A widespread and locally fairly common resident and migrant in all countries and territories within the region.

# SPOTTED OWLET
### *Athene brama* 20 cm  F: Strigidae

**Description**: Small size and spotted plumage are diagnostic.

**Voice**: A variety of high-pitched cackling and chuckling notes.

**Habits**: An adaptable species that avoids closed forest; instead it settles in open woodlands, cultivated areas and parks, often nesting in buildings in villages. It even occurs in Lumpini Park in the centre of Bangkok, Thailand. Sometimes active during the day; if disturbed it quickly flies onto a large branch bobbing its head and staring down, as the photo shows. Feeds on insects and small vertebrates.

**Distribution**: Oriental region. Within the region, a locally fairly common resident in Myanmar, Thailand and parts of Indochina.

# SPOTTED WOOD-OWL
### *Strix seloputo* 48 cm  F: Strigidae

**Description**: Distinguished from the similar and sympatric Brown Wood-owl, *S. leptogrammica,* of the Oriental region, by wide (not narrow) barring on underparts and spots on wings.

**Voice**: A deep, rapid *who-ow* similar to a distant dog's bark.

**Habits**: Occurs in lowland forest, especially in forest edges, secondary growth, in nearby cultivated areas and parks with large trees. Starts calling at dusk and can sometimes be located by its call and spotted perched high in a tree, as this rare photograph shows.

**Distribution**: Southeast Asia into Sumatra and Java (Indonesia). Within the region: an uncommon resident in Myanmar, Thailand, Cambodia, south Vietnam and Peninsular Malaysia; rare in Singapore; fairly common in Palawan (Philippines).

## SHORT-EARED OWL
*Asio flammeus* 38 cm  F: Strigidae

**Description:** Note pale brown plumage and black carpal patch in wing.

**Voice:** Sometimes short *kee-aw* in flight.

**Habits:** Found in open country, grasslands and marshes. Perches horizontally on the ground or a low pole. Flies mainly by day, low across the ground, searching for small prey.

**Distribution:** Breeds worldwide in temperate and sub-arctic climate zones; winters in the south. A rare winter visitor in northern parts of the region; vagrant in Hong Kong, Malaysia, Singapore and Brunei.

## LARGE FROGMOUTH
*Batrachostomus auritus* 41 cm  F: Batrachostomidae

**Description:** Unmistakable; much larger than other frogmouths, also note prominent tufts on head.

**Voice:** A deep resonant *ooerrr*.

**Habits:** Found in primary forest and mature secondary forest, only in the extreme lowlands. A low density species seldom seen or heard within its small range. Comes out at night feeding on cicadas and grasshoppers. The single egg is laid on a flat round pad of compressed down, placed off the ground in a low bush. The brooding bird sits along (not across) the thin branch to incubate.

**Distribution:** Sunda subregion. Within the region, a rare resident in south Thailand and Malaysia.

## PHILIPPINE FROGMOUTH
*Batrachostomus septimus* 25 cm  F: Batrachostomidae

**Description**: Unmistakable; the only member of its family within this range; note the large bill typical of this family, seen well in this rare photograph.

**Voice**: A mournful, descending call with an abrupt beginning.

**Habits**: Found in primary forest and forest edges, from the lowlands to 2,500 metres elevation. Nesting has been recorded. Sometimes heard, but not often seen by observers.

**Distribution**: Philippine endemic. An uncommon resident in Luzon, Panay, Negros, Bohol, Layte, Samar, Mindanao and the Basilan islands.

## GOULD'S FROGMOUTH
*Batrachostomus stellatus* 25 cm  F: Batrachostomidae

**Description**: Distinguished from the next species by prominent scales on underparts; note also fairly long, barred tail and white greater wing coverts.

**Voice**: A distinctive, rising *oooh-wheeow* repeated at 7-second intervals.

**Habits**: A lowland species, usually found below 200 metres elevation in primary rainforest and mature secondary forest. A nocturnal, low density species difficult to observe, but regularly recorded with some effort during forest reserve surveys. Sometimes seen during the day roosting in the lower middle storey near a forest trail.

**Distribution**: Sunda endemic. Within the region, a rare resident in south Thailand; uncommon in Malaysia; extinct in Singapore.

## JAVAN FROGMOUTH
*Batrachostomus javensis* 24 cm  F: Batrachostomidae

**Description:** Distinguished with difficulty from previous species by small bill and wide mouth; male (photo) is greyer than female, but plumage features are difficult to distinguish under field conditions; Southeast Asian population sometimes treated as a separate species, Blyth's Frogmouth, *B. affinis*.

**Voice:** A variety of croaking and whistling notes.

**Habits:** Found in primary rainforest, closed secondary forest and along edges of clearings, mainly in the lowlands, occasionally to 800 metres elevation. Like other members of this cryptic family, it comes out at night and feeds by gleaning insects from the middle storey of the forest.

**Distribution:** Southeast Asia. Within the region, an uncommon resident in Myanmar, Thailand and Peninsular Malaysia; rare in East Malaysia.

## PALAWAN FROGMOUTH
*Batrachostomus chaseni* 25 cm  F: Batrachostomidae

**Description:** Unmistakable; the only member of its family within its range; taxonomy disputed; sometimes placed under *B. javensis*, *B. affinis* or Sunda Frogmouth, *B. cornutus*, endemic to Sumatra and Borneo.

**Voice:** Main call is an eerie, tapering *waaa-wooo;* also a ventriloquial soft whistle and a maniacal, laughing call.

**Habits:** Occurs in lowland forest reserves on Palawan, e.g. the Balsahan Trail near Puerto Princesa and St. Paul's National Park near Sabang. Sometimes heard, but rarely observed and little studied. Habits presumably as other members of its family.

**Distribution:** Philippine endemic. A rare resident on Palawan and Culion islands.

## GREY NIGHTJAR
*Caprimulgus indicus* 28 cm   F: Caprimulgidae

**Description**: Distinguished from other nightjars (with some difficulty) by its greyish plumage with bold black spots; note the small bill typical of this family.

**Voice**: A long run of rapid notes, *chuckoo-chuckoo-chockoo,* much faster than following species.

**Habits**: Breeds in forest and open woodlands, from 600 metres elevation to the tree limit. During migration it is found in cultivated areas, scrub and open country with some trees. Catches insects on the wing during the dark, swerving among the trees. Rests during the day in low trees or on the ground; sometimes flushed from rural road surfaces.

**Distribution**: Breeds in temperate East Asia, south into Thailand; winters in the Oriental region. A generally uncommon passage migrant and winter visitor throughout the region, including Hong Kong, Singapore and Brunei.

## LARGE-TAILED NIGHTJAR
*Caprimulgus macrurus* 30 cm   F: Caprimulgidae

**Description**: Dark brown plumage with some paler spots. Philippine subspecies treated by some authors as a separate species, the Philippine Nightjar, *C. manillensis*.

**Voice**: A hollow, penetrating *chonk* uttered repeatedly through the evening.

**Habits**: Found in forest edges, cultivation and often parks and villages. Rests on the ground or a low perch during the day and flies out at dusk, to hawk for insects in the air, often near street lights. Very vocal during breeding season, calling from a pole or branch. Nests on the bare ground under a tree.

**Distribution**: Oriental region, Austalasia. A widespread and locally common resident in much of region, including Singapore and Brunei.

## INDIAN NIGHTJAR
*Caprimulgus asiaticus* 23 cm  F: Caprimulgidae

**Description**: Small size with pale buff plumage.

**Voice**: Its call of accelerating *chook* notes speeds up to a roll and has been compared to a ping-pong ball dropping onto a table top.

**Habits**: Mostly an open country species found in cultivation and scrub as well as open plains with some trees. Prefers a low and dry terrain to 900 metres elevation. Rests during the day and flies out to hawk for insects at dusk, swerving low with pointed wings and a long tail like a small falcon.

**Distribution**: Oriental region. Within the region, a locally fairly common resident in Myanmar, Thailand and parts of Indochina.

## SAVANNA NIGHTJAR
*Caprimulgus affinis* 26 cm  F: Caprimulgidae

**Description**: Note greyish-brown plumage, much more finely spotted than other nightjars, and lacking bold black markings.

**Voice**: A raspy *chew-eep* often uttered at dusk while flying low across territory.

**Habits**: Prefers open woodlands with scattered scrub and dry plains, from the lowlands to 900 metres elevation. In the wet Sunda subregion, this habitat is found mainly behind the beach, near villages and on newly cleared land awaiting development. Rests on the ground during the day and comes out at dusk to perch in the open and hawk low for flying insects. It is doing well and numbers seem to be increasing.

**Distribution**: Oriental region. Within the region: a locally fairly common resident throughout much of the mainland, including Hong Kong and Singapore; locally common in the Philippines; recorded in Sabah (East Malaysia).

## EDIBLE-NEST SWIFTLET
*Aerodramus fuciphagus* 13 cm (*Collicalia fuciphaga*) F: Apodidae

**Description**: Usually indistinguishable in the field from other *Aerodramus* swiftlets. Note slender build and notch in tail. Its nest is diagnostic, a translucent cup made up of hardened saliva only. The Philippine subspecies is treated by some authors as a separate species.

**Voice**: A high-pitched *tscheerr*.

**Habits**: Found in all kinds of open country, especially near the coast and offshore islands; locally abundant. Also seen flying over forest, catching small insects. Nests inside deep limestone caves or man-made bunkers and navigates by an audible echolocation rattle. Its nests, fixed to cave walls, are collected by local people and traded commercially for consumption.

**Distribution**: Southeast Asia. A common resident in most of region, including Singapore and Borneo; uncommon on Palawan (Philippines); not recorded in Brunei.

## BLACK-NEST SWIFTLET
*Aerodramus maximus* 14 cm (*Collocalia maxima*) F: Apodidae

**Description**: Distinguished (in the breeding colony) from the Edible-nest Swiftlet by nest built with black feathers, held together with saliva.

**Voice**: Shrill calls in flight.

**Habits**: Similar to the Edible-nest Swiftlet; also echolocates. Spends most of its time on the wing. Since it never perches in trees or comes to the ground, it must build its nest in total darkness from materials from its own body. In Borneo, nesting colonies number millions of birds and nests are collected for consumption, although these are less valuable than the clean nests from the Edible-nest Swiftlet.

**Distribution**: Sunda subregion. Within the region, a common resident in south Thailand, Myanmar, Malaysia, Singapore and Brunei; locally abundant.

## WHITE-BELLIED SWIFTLET (Glossy Swiftlet)
*Collocalia esculenta* 9 cm  F: Apodidae

**Description**: A very small swiftlet with fast wing beats; shown here at nest; note very long wings; belly shows whitish in flight.

**Voice**: High-pitched, twitting sounds.

**Habits**: Feeds over all terrain from lowland open country to forests and highest montane peaks. Since it cannot echolocate, it builds its nest near the entrance to caves or in man-made structures where light can penetrate.

**Distribution**: Oriental region, Australasia. Within the region, a fairly common resident in Malaysia, Brunei and the Philippines; rare in south Thailand, Myanmar and Singapore.

## BROWN NEEDLETAIL (Brown-backed Needletail)
*Hirundapus giganteus* 25 cm  F: Apodidae

**Description**: Distinguished from other *Hirundapus* swifts by its uniformly dark brown plumage, except for small white patch under tail; note diagnostic white lores.

**Voice**: A squeaky *cheek*.

**Habits**: Flies over closed forest, from lowlands to montane altitudes; sometimes seen in more open woodlands, catching insects in the air, usually in pairs or a few together. Covers great distances fast, moving extremely quickly; regarded as the fastest of all birds in level flight; generates an audible whooshing sound as it passes. Rarely seen perched; nests in tree-holes but few recorded.

**Distribution**: Oriental region; partly migratory. Within the region: A widespread and fairly common resident and probably also winter visitor on much of mainland; uncommon in Singapore and Borneo, including Brunei and Palawan, the Philippines.

# SILVER-RUMPED SWIFT
## *Rhaphidura leucopygialis* 11 cm  F: Apodidae

**Description**: Small swift related to the needletails, but behaves like a swiftlet; note diagnostic broad wings; from behind white rump shows prominently.

**Voice**: A high-pitched *tirr-tirr*.

**Habits**: Mainly a forest bird; flies low over primary rainforest as well as secondary forest; found along forest edges and streams in forest, but seldom in open country and never around villages. Usually a few are seen together; sometimes they fly low to the ground, flapping somewhat like swallows. Doesn't perch. Reported to nest in cavities in trees but few recorded.

**Distribution**: Sunda subregion. Within the region, a locally fairly common resident in south Thailand, Myanmar, Malaysia and Brunei.

# HOUSE SWIFT (Little Swift)
## *Apus affinis* 15 cm  F: Apodidae

**Description**: Shown perched at nesting site; in flight white rump shows clearly; also look for square (not forked) tail.

**Voice**: Penetrating screams; very vocal at roosting sites in the evening.

**Habits**: Hunts insects on the wing, over open country and marshy areas, high during sunny weather, close to the ground during periods of low pressure. True to its name, it roosts near houses, flying about and calling conspicuously. Also perches under bridges and dams as well as on coastal cliffs and at inland cave entrances. Perches vertically on the wall; nests in similar places.

**Distribution**: Africa, tropical and subtropical Eurasia and the Oriental region. Within the region, a widespread and common resident on the mainland, including Hong Kong and Singapore; fairly common in Borneo, including Brunei; vagrant in the Philippines.

## ASIAN PALM-SWIFT
*Cypsiurus balasiensis* 12 cm  F: Apodidae

**Description:** Note the narrow, forked tail and narrow, pointed wings; also distinguished from swiftlets by a more direct flight pattern.

**Voice:** A shrill high-pitched trill.

**Habits:** Appears to be superficially similar to other small swifts, but is in fact quite unique and is the only member of its genus in Asia. Exclusively associated with tall, broad-leafed palm trees, often free-standing palms in open country or near cultivation. Swerves in large circles among the palm canopies, catching insects in the air. Roosts underneath the large leaves where it builds its tiny cup nest.

**Distribution:** Oriental region. A widespread and common resident throughout much of the region, including Singapore and Brunei; fairly common in parts of the Philippines.

## GREY-RUMPED TREESWIFT
*Hemiprocne longipennis* 20 cm  F: Hemiprocnidae

**Description:** Note pale rump, long forked tail and even longer wings; photo shows male; female lacks chestnut ear coverts.

**Voice:** A high-pitched *fee-fee-few* when flying.

**Habits:** Found in open woodlands, from secondary forest and forest edges to parks with large trees. Unlike Apodidae swifts, perches readily, usually high on open or dead branches sallying forth for insects during long raids, flapping and gliding somewhat like a bee-eater. The single egg is laid in a tiny cup nest built on a thick branch.

**Distribution:** Sunda subregion. Within the region, a widespread and fairly common (although never numerous) resident in South Thailand, Myanmar, Malaysia, Singapore and Brunei; vagrant in the Philippines.

## WHISKERED TREESWIFT
*Hemiprocne comata* 15 cm  F: Hemiprocnidae

**Description:** Small size; note long wings reaching beyond tail; photo shows male; female lacks chestnut ear coverts.

**Voice:** High-pitched *squeawk* in flight.

**Habits:** Found in lowland rainforest, along forest edges as well as nearby clearings, rivers and trails. Seen usually in pairs. Perches high on open branches flying out to catch small insects in the air nearby. Fairly tame and enjoyable to observe.

**Distribution:** Southeast Asia. Within the region, a fairly common resident in south Thailand, Myanmar, Malaysia, Brunei and Philippines; vagrant in Singapore.

## RED-NAPED TROGON
*Harpactes kasumba* 33 cm  F: Trogonidae

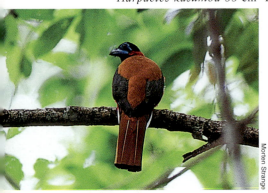

**Description:** Photo shows male; diagnostic red nape, contrasting with black head, barely visible; female has brown head with orange, not red underparts.

**Voice:** Six melancholy notes, *kaup, kaup, kaup*.

**Habits:** Found in primary and mature secondary rainforest; restricted to the lowlands below 600 metres elevation. Sometimes seen sitting quietly at mid-storey level in the forest or located by call. Presumably flies out to hawk for insects, but this is rarely observed. Little is known of this bird and its nest has never been described.

**Distribution:** Sunda subregion. Within the region: an uncommon and scarce resident in Malaysia; rare in south Thailand and Brunei; extinct in Singapore.

## DIARD'S TROGON
*Harpactes diardii* 30 cm  F: Trogonidae

**Description**: Photo shows female; male has blackish face and throat, separated from red underparts by white band across chest.

**Voice**: 10 to 12 *kaup* notes, more rapid and higher pitched than Red-naped Trogon.

**Habits**: Similar to Red-naped. Sits motionless below the canopy in lowland rainforest and in spite of its red colours is easy to miss. Flies off and disappears abruptly, flapping audibly on short, rounded wings. Little studied. Nests in tree cavities; nesting records are few. Trogons do poorly in captivity.

**Distribution**: Sunda subregion. Within the region, an uncommon resident in Malaysia, south Thailand and Brunei, and possibly Myanmar; extinct in Singapore.

## PHILIPPINE TROGON
*Harpactes ardens* 33 cm  F: Trogonidae

**Description**: Unmistakable; the only trogon within its range; photo shows male; female duller.

**Voice**: A descending series of soft notes.

**Habits**: Found mainly in primary rainforest, from the lowlands to lower montane elevations; also moves into nearby mature secondary growth to feed. Sits motionless in the middle storey as the photo shows. It feeds by hawking for insects, but this is rarely seen. This shy bird is heard more often than seen; it moves quietly into the forest beating its rounded wings softly as soon as it is disturbed. Its nest has never been located.

**Distribution**: Philippine endemic. A scarce resident on Luzon, Bohol, Leyte, Samar, Basilan, Mindanao and some smaller islands.

## WHITEHEAD'S TROGON
*Harpactes whiteheadi* 33 cm  F: Trogonidae

**Description:** Photo shows male; the only trogon on Borneo with a red head; note pale, almost white, lower breast usually poorly illustrated in field guides; female has red replaced with dull cinnamon.

**Voice:** A growling note; sways its tail while calling.

**Habits:** Restricted to primary forest above 1,000 metres elevation. A low density species sometimes seen sitting motionless in the shaded middle storey. Mt. Mulu and Kinabalu National Park are good locations to observe this restricted range species. It feeds on grasshoppers, ants and leaf insects that it gleans from the foliage or catches in the air. Its nest has never been found.

**Distribution:** Borneo endemic. Within the region, an uncommon resident in the mountains of Sabah and Sarawak.

## SCARLET-RUMPED TROGON
*Harpactes duvaucelii* 25 cm  F: Trogonidae

**Description:** Small size; distinguished from similar Cinnamon-rumped Trogon, *H. orrhophaeus,* by scarlet rump (male, photo) and brown head (female).

**Voice:** A descending and accelerating 10 to 15 notes, *ti-ti-ti-ti.*

**Habits:** Found in primary and mature secondary lowland rainforest. Typically perches a bit lower than the larger trogons. Although fairly often spotted on good forest birdwatching trails, the behaviour of this species is little studied and its nest has never been described.

**Distribution:** Sunda subregion. Within the region, an uncommon resident in south Thailand and Myanmar; locally fairly common in Malaysia and Brunei.

# RED-HEADED TROGON
### *Harpactes erythrocephalus* 34 cm  F: Trogonidae

**Description**: Note the diagnostic red head of the male (photo); female has brown head.

**Voice**: Five or more mellow notes *tiaup, tiaup*.

**Habits**: The only montane trogon in its range. Found exclusively at montane and lower montane elevations between 700 and 2,000 metres. Sits quietly at mid-storey level or slightly lower in the rainforest; shifts quickly to another perch when disturbed. Nests in a dead tree stump or tree cavity.

**Distribution**: Oriental region. Within the region, an uncommon resident in Peninsular Malaysia; a locally fairly common resident on the rest of the mainland, excluding Hong Kong.

# CRESTED KINGFISHER
### *Ceryle lugubris* 43 cm  F: Alcedinidae

**Description**: Distinguished from following species by its large size, crest and fine barring across its upperparts; in flight appears slaty grey.

**Voice**: A harsh, shrill call when taking off.

**Habits**: Frequents rivers and large streams with wide, stone-covered banks and tall vegetation. Less often at stagnent ponds from the lowlands into foothills and lower montane elevations at 1,800 m. Dives into the water for fish and also takes some tadpoles and water insects. When disturbed, it flies off with a purposeful, direct flight to the next perch on a stone or in a tree.

**Distribution**: East Asia, Oriental region. A generally uncommon resident in northern parts of the region, including Hong Kong; not recorded in Cambodia.

## PIED KINGFISHER
*Ceryle rudis* 30 cm  F: Alcedinidae

**Description**: Note characteristic pied plumage; in flight a white wing patch shows clearly.

**Voice**: A squeaky, sharp, twittering *chirruk*.

**Habits**: Occurs in lowland wetlands, often along rivers and canals, but near lakes and flooded fields as well. Requires steep earth banks nearby, where it digs a hollow for nesting. Perches on a branch, pole or rock near the water, then flies out and catches fish in a characteristic fashion by hovering over the water, looking down before plunging in.

**Distribution**: Oriental region. Within the region, a locally fairly common resident throughout most of the mainland, including Hong Kong.

## COMMON KINGFISHER
*Alcedo atthis* 17 cm  F: Alcedinidae

**Description**: Note small size and diagnostic rufous ear coverts.

**Voice**: A high-pitched *zeep* when taking off.

**Habits**: During migration, found in all types of open country wetlands, from freshwater ponds, rivers and canals to tidal mangroves; often seen in developed areas such as fish ponds and harbours. Avoids densely forested streams. Drops into the water from a low perch, diving for small fish. Breeds along up country streams.

**Distribution**: Eurasia, Oriental east to New Guinea; northern populations migrate south. A widespread and common winter visitor throughout the region; also resident in northern parts, including Hong Kong and possibly south into Peninsular Malaysia.

## BLUE-EARED KINGFISHER
*Alcedo meninting* 16 cm  F: Alcedinidae

**Description**: Distinguished with some difficulty from the previous species by its lack of rufous ear coverts, darker blue head and wings and darker rufous underparts.

**Voice**: Similar to previous species, but shorter and even more high-pitched.

**Habits**: Prefers a more wooded habitat than the previous species. Is usually seen at rivers and pools inside the forest and sometimes near cultivation, but never in open country. A low density species not numerous anywhere. Sits on a low perch near the water and flies down to catch small fish and invertebrates. Quite shy; it takes off in rapid flight low across the water when disturbed.

**Distribution**: Oriental region. A widespread but generally scarce resident in southern parts of the region, including Singapore, Brunei and parts of the Philippines.

## BLACK-BACKED KINGFISHER (Oriental Dwarf Kingfisher)
*Ceyx erithacus* 14 cm  F: Alcedinidae

**Description**: Distinguished from following species by darker, almost black wings and mantle, seen well from this angle; also note black ear patch.

**Voice**: A soft but penetrating whistle, somewhat like the Common Kingfisher, but higher pitched.

**Habits**: Breeds inside closed forest in the lowlands. During migration it moves into disturbed habitats and mangroves and has been known to turn up in gardens and at lower montane elevations. Often, but not always, settles near water. It feeds on small insects, spiders and maybe fish.

**Distribution**: Oriental region; migratory. An uncommon resident and passage migrant in northern parts of the region; winter visitor only in Malaysia; rare visitor to Brunei and Singapore.

## RUFOUS-BACKED KINGFISHER
*Ceyx rufidorsa* 14 cm  F: Alcedinidae

**Description**: Distinguished from the previous species by its paler wings; also note lack of black spot behind ear. Sometimes included in previous species as hybridization does occur, but this guide follows King et al (1975), MacKinnon & Phillipps (1993) and Lim & Gardner (1997).

**Voice**: Like previous species.

**Habits**: Strictly a forest bird, only occurring within primary and mature secondary rainforest in the lowlands. Shy; perches low. Usually seen flying low across the forest trail, like a tiny orange projectile, often near a small stream. The nest is built in a cavity in a low earth embankment.

**Distribution:** Sunda subregion; sedentary. Within the region, a scarce resident in south Thailand, Malaysia and Brunei; extinct in Singapore.

## BROWN-WINGED KINGFISHER
*Pelargopsis amauroptera* 36 cm  F: Alcedinidae

**Description**: Distinguished from following species by brown (not turquoise) wings and mantle; also note less distinctive cap.

**Voice**: A descending whistle, *tree treew-treew*.

**Habits**: A strictly coastal kingfisher found in mangroves, coastal forest and some distance up tidal rivers. The northern island of Langkawi, Malaysia, is a well-known location for this species. It perches in the open in a large tree near the water and flies down to the mud to look for prey.

**Distribution:** Oriental region. Within the region, an uncommon resident along the mainland west coast.

## STORK-BILLED KINGFISHER
### *Pelargopsis capensis* 37 cm  F: Alcedinidae

**Description**: Massive size, brown cap and turquoise upperparts are diagnostic.

**Voice**: A fluty *fuey-fuey* whistle; also a piercing alarm scream on take-off.

**Habits**: A conspicuous bird that perches out in the open near water that is surrounded by some vegetation, usually freshwater marshes, ponds and rivers, but also tidal mangroves. Drops onto the surface of the water below, mainly to catch fish, but also takes crustaceans, frogs, lizards and insects.

**Distribution:** Oriental region. A widespread resident throughout the region, including Singapore, Brunei and parts of the Philippines, although generally uncommon; locally abundant along Borneo's rivers.

## BANDED KINGFISHER
### *Lacedo pulchella* 23 cm  F: Alcedinidae

**Description**: Unmistakable; photo shows male; female has brown upperparts barred with black. A monotypic genus.

**Voice**: A long series of whistled *chi-wiu*.

**Habits**: Found in primary and mature secondary rainforest, both in the lowlands and at lower montane elevations, usually in dry patches distant from any source of water. Sits lethargically, somewhat like a trogon, in the middle storey below the canopy for long periods at a time. Hunts for insects in the forest. Nests in a tree cavity.

**Distribution:** Southeast Asia. A locally fairly common but generally scarce resident in southern parts of the region; not recorded in Brunei; extinct in Singapore.

## WHITE-THROATED KINGFISHER
*Halcyon smyrnensis* 27 cm  F: Alcidinidae

**Description**: Look for a dark chestnut head and lack of white collar.

**Voice**: A piercing, staccato laugh, often on take-off but also perched.

**Habits**: A very successful bird that has adapted well to disturbed habitats. Found in open woodlands and forest edges, but also grasslands with some trees, cultivated areas, parks and gardens. Sometimes seen near water, but more often sits over dry land, on a low perch, and pounces into the grass below for small prey. Noisy and conspicuous. Nests in burrows on steep ground.

**Distribution**: Subtropical and tropical Eurasia, Oriental region. A common resident throughout most of the region, including Hong Kong and Singapore; vagrant in Taiwan.

## BLACK-CAPPED KINGFISHER
*Halcyon pileata* 30 cm  F: Alcidinidae

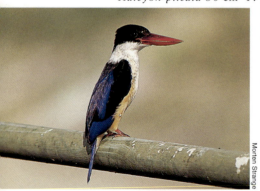

**Description**: Look for diagnostic black head.

**Voice**: Like White-throated Kingfisher; a piercing alarm call on take-off.

**Habits**: During migration frequents a variety of open country habitats, often coastal wetlands and freshwater marshes, sometimes dry fields with some scattered trees, as well as large parks. Drops down from a low perch to seize insects and small vertebrate prey. Nests in a burrow in the ground, often built in the bank of a woodland stream.

**Distribution**: East Asia, Oriental region; migratory. Within the region, a fairly common resident in the north, including Hong Kong; a passage migrant and winter visitor in the south, including Singapore, Brunei and parts of the Philippines.

## COLLARED KINGFISHER
*Halcyon chloris* 24 cm  F: Alcidinidae

Description: Note turquoise upperparts; also bright white underparts and collar.

Voice: A penetrating *krerk, krerk, krerk*.

Habits: A maritime kingfisher, found mainly in tidal areas, from mangroves and mudflats to sandy beaches and harbour areas. Locally it also moves inland to rivers near the sea, to open coastal woodlands and even parks and gardens. Catches mainly crustaceans in the mud or sand, but insects, worms, frogs, lizards and even small snakes are part of its diet. Nests in a tree cavity or burrow in a lobster mound.

**Distribution:** Oriental region, Australasia. A common resident in most of the region, including Singapore and Brunei. Also occurs in Laos; vagrant in south China.

## SPOTTED WOOD-KINGFISHER
*Actenoides lindsayi* 23 cm  F: Alcidinidae

Description: Unmistakable; the only member of this genus within its range.

Voice: A bubbling, musical trill breaking into fluty whistles; also a harsher, descending call.

Habits: Occurs in closed rainforest, in primary forest and mature secondary growth, from the lowlands into montane elevations. Not associated with water. Good views are difficult; best located by call. Sits passively on a branch in the middle storey, as shown in photo. Flies down to the ground to catch insects and snails.

**Distribution:** Philippine endemic. A generally scarce resident on Luzon, Negros and some smaller nearby islands. Regarded as near-threatened with global extinction.

## BLUE-CAPPED WOOD-KINGFISHER
*Actenoides hombroni* 27 cm  F: Alcidinidae

**Description**: Unmistakable; the only member of this genus within its range.

**Voice**: A series of loud *plew, plew;* calls briefly just before dawn.

**Habits**: Habits: Found in primary rainforest at montane elevations between 800 and 2,000 metres. Known locations include Mt. Katanglad, Lake Sebu and Mt. Apo. Little habitat remains for this low density species. It is difficult to find and rarely seen by observers.

**Distribution**: Philippine endemic. A rare resident on the island on Mindanao. Vulnerable to global extinction.

## CHESTNUT-HEADED BEE-EATER
*Merops leschenaulti* 20 cm  F: Meropidae

**Description**: Look for chestnut head combined with bright yellow throat.

**Voice**: A ringing trill, *pruuip, pruuip,* in flight.

**Habits**: Found in dry woodlands and open country with scattered trees, never in closed forest, from lowlands to lower montane elevations. An elegant bird that perches fairly low and flies out to seize insects in the air. The nest is a burrow in a steep earthen slope.

**Distribution**: Oriental region. Within the region, a fairly common resident on the mainland, south to northern Peninsular Malaysia only.

## BLUE-TAILED BEE-EATER
*Merops philippinus* 30 cm  F: Meropidae

**Description:** Look for diagnostic green head and neck.

**Voice:** A liquid ringing *be-rek, be-rek* in flight.

**Habits:** Found in open country with scattered trees, usually near freshwater marshes, rivers and coasts. Hawks for bees, wasps and butterflies from an open perch. Outside of breeding season it becomes locally abundant, congregating in large flocks, sometimes hundreds of birds roosting together in mangroves or marshes. Also nests in colonies, often digging burrows into riverbanks.

**Distribution:** Oriental region, east to New Guinea; partly migratory. Within the region, a widespread, common resident and passage migrant on the mainland and the Philippines; resident on Penang; a rare visitor to Hong Kong and East Malaysia; not recorded in Brunei.

## GREEN BEE-EATER
*Merops orientalis* 20 cm  F: Meropidae

**Description:** Note small size and very elongated tail-feathers; distinguished from Chestnut-headed Bee-eater by bluish throat.

**Voice:** Similar to the Blue-tailed Bee-eater, but more metallic and higher-pitched.

**Habits:** Found in dry open woodlands and forest edges, from the lowlands up to lower montane elevations. A gregarious bird usually seen in small flocks; perches lower than the larger bee-eaters. Hawks small insects in the air from an open branch. Nests in burrows on a slope and sometimes on level ground.

**Distribution:** Africa, subtropical Eurasia and the Oriental region. Within the region, a locally common resident in Myanmar, Thailand, south China and most of Indochina.

## BLUE-THROATED BEE-EATER

*Merops viridis* 28 cm  F: Meropidae

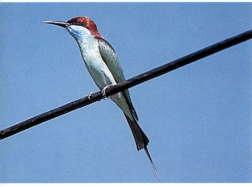

**Distribution:** Oriental region; nomadic; tropical populations disperse outside breeding season. A fairly common resident throughout the region, including Singapore and Brunei. Also a widespread non-breeding visitor to the region, including Hong Kong.

**Description:** Look for its plain blue throat and overall turquoise appearance; in flight its pale blue rump flashes brightly

**Voice:** Liquid notes in flight, like Blue-tailed Bee-eater.

**Habits:** Found in open, dry woodlands and coastal forests, and along forest edges. Perches quite high, making short sallies for flying insects. Breeds in small but dense colonies, digging burrows along riverbanks. Also, surprisingly, digs burrows in completely level soft ground, often on sandy shores, golf courses or air fields.

## RED-BEARDED BEE-EATER

*Nyctyornis amictus* 32 cm  F: Meropidae

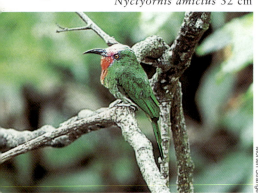

**Distribution:** Sunda subregion; sedentary. Within the region, resident in south Thailand, Myanmar, Malaysia and Brunei. Locally fairly common but generally scarce.

**Description:** Unmistakable; its massive build and red 'beard' are diagnostic. This and the following species form their own unique genus.

**Voice:** A characteristic croaking *aark, aark* plus a growling alarm call.

**Habits:** Strictly a forest bird found within primary and mature secondary rainforest, from the lowlands to lower montane elevations. Unlike *Merops* bee-eaters, this is an inconspicuous bird that perches at middle or upper storey level, often under cover. Hawks for insects and nests in burrows like other bee-eaters.

# BLUE-BEARDED BEE-EATER
## *Nyctyornis athertoni* 35 cm  F: Meropidae

**Description**: Unmistakable; massive build and blue 'beard' are diagnostic.

**Voice**: A variety of loud, croaking calls and a peculiar chuckle.

**Habits**: Found in deciduous forest and along forest edges, from the lowlands to 1,800 metres elevation. Sometimes this fairly shy bird it perches on wires along forested roads. When approached, it flies off with a heavy, undulating flight, to settle deeper inside the forest. Khao Yai in Thailand, where this photograph was taken, is a good location to view this species.

**Distribution**: Oriental region. Within the region, resident throughout most of the mainland, locally fairly common, but generally scarce.

# INDIAN ROLLER
## *Coracias benghalensis* 33 cm  F: Coraciidae

**Description**: Unmistakable; blue and turquoise wings flash brightly in flight.

**Voice**: A croaking *kyak*.

**Habits**: Found in open country, dry woodlands and along deciduous forest edges; avoids wet tropical forests. Often sits on a roadside telephone wire, pole or other open perch, sallying out to catch insects mid-air or on the ground. Flight pattern characteristically 'rolling' in the air, giving this family of birds its name.

**Distribution**: Subtropical Eurasia, Oriental region. Within the region, a widespread, common resident on much of the mainland; uncommon in northern Peninsular Malaysia.

## DOLLARBIRD
### *Eurystomus orientalis* 30 cm  F: Coraciidae

**Description**: Plumage appears all black; in sunlight it is a shiny, dark purple-greenish. Note white 'silver dollar' patch in wing.

**Voice**: A harsh chatter, *kack, kack*, in flight.

**Habits**: A successful bird that has benefited from forest clearance in the region. Found in open woodlands, along forest edges and in open country with large trees, where it flies out from a high perch and catches insects in the air. Displays during breeding season with air acrobatics and noisy calls. Nests in a tree cavity.

**Distribution**: Subtropical and tropical Eurasia into Australasia; northern populations migrate south. A fairly common resident throughout most of the region, including Singapore and Brunei; also a winter visitor to the region, including Hong Kong; vagrant in Taiwan.

## HOOPOE
### *Upupa epops* 30 cm  F: Upupidae

**Description**: Unmistakable and unique. The only member of its family, like the Osprey and a few other species.

**Voice**: As name indicates, a soft *hoop-hoop*.

**Habits**: Frequents open country with some tree cover, deciduous woodlands and forest edges. Is also seen around fields and plantations. Makes short flights on its rounded wings or hops about on the ground probing with its long bill for invertebrate prey. The nest is in a tree cavity or an earthen bank.

**Distribution**: Africa, Eurasia and the Oriental region; northern populations migrate south. Within the region, a fairly common resident south to the Malay Peninsula; stragglers reach Hong Kong, Taiwan, the Philippines and Borneo.

## WHITE-CROWNED HORNBILL
### *Berenicornis comatus* 90 cm  F: Bucerotidae

**Description**: Unmistakable; its white head is diagnostic. Photo shows male; female has black underparts.

**Voice**: A hooting *hoo...hu-hu-hu*.

**Habits**: Occurs in primary rainforest and occasionally in forest edges, from the lowlands to 1,000 metres elevation. This is a low density species throughout its range, but is sometimes recorded in suitable habitat - usually seen flying briefly and fairly low among the canopies. Recently several nests were located and studied in southern Thailand, where this picture was taken.

**Distribution:** Sunda subregion. Within the region, a scarce resident in south Thailand, Myanmar, Malaysia and Brunei; previously recorded in Vietnam.

Morten Strange

## BROWN HORNBILL
### *Ptilolaemus tickelli* 74 cm  F: Bucerotidae

**Description**: Distinguished from following species by brown (not blackish) plumage. A monotypic genus. Photo shows the male of the northern subspecies, which is sometimes treated as a full species, the White-throated Brown Hornbill, *P. austeni*. The Female has a brown throat.

**Voice**: A screaming *klee-ah*.

**Habits**: Mainly found in primary forest on slightly elevated hills, from low foothills to 1,500 metres elevation. Even in prime habitat, this species only occurs in low densities. It moves within the canopies of large trees, feeding predominantly on fruit. Shy and difficult to observe; sometimes seen flying across the forest trail.

**Distribution:** Oriental region. Within the region, an uncommon resident in northern parts of the mainland. Regarded as near-threatened with global extinction.

Atsuo Tsuji

## BUSHY-CRESTED HORNBILL
*Anorrhinus galeritus* 70 cm  F: Bucerotidae

**Description**: An all-dark hornbill. Look for diagnostic two-toned tail. A unique, monotypic genus.

**Voice**: Excited, chattering notes, *klee-klee-klee*.

**Habits**: Found in lowland and lower montane rainforest. Unlike most other hornbills, it moves below or within the canopies and makes short flights into the adjoining trees. Usually seen in small, noisy groups, moving restlessly along, calling incessantly. Seems gregarious, even in the breeding season, with several individuals observed feeding an entrapped female. Few nesting records.

**Distribution**: Sunda subregion. Within the region, locally fairly common, but a generally scarce resident in south Thailand, Myanmar, Malaysia and Brunei.

## RUFOUS-NECKED HORNBILL
*Aceros nipalensis* 116 cm  F: Bucerotidae

**Description**: Look for rufous head and underparts in male (photo, at nest); female is black with rufous throat. Tail and wing tips are white.

**Voice**: A soft *kup*.

**Habits**: Restricted to a narrow range of lower montane rainforest between 600 and 1,800 metres elevation. Found only in remote forested hills with drought deciduous types of vegetation. Like other hornbills, feeds mainly on fruit, and nests by encapsulating female inside cavity in a large, living, hardwood tree.

**Distribution**: Oriental region. Within the region, a rare resident in northern submontane parts of mainland. Regarded as vulnerable to global extinction due to deforestation and hunting.

# WRITHED HORNBILL
## *Aceros leucocephalus* 75 cm  F: Bucerotidae

**Description**: Distinguished from the partly sympatric Rufous Hornbill by its black (not dark rufous) body; also note characteristic tail pattern. Photo shows male at nest; female has black head and neck. Populations on Negros/Panay (photo) are sometimes treated as a full species, the Writhed-billed Hornbill, *A. waldeni*.

**Voice**: Has been desribed as a 'bleating, not very loud' (Gonzales & Rees 1988).

**Habits**: Occurs in primary and nearby secondary forest above 800 metres. Previously fairly common, but numbers are now much reduced due to hunting and habitat loss. Feeding and nesting habits much like other hornbills.

**Distribution:** Philippine endemic. A rare resident on Panay, Negros, Mindanao and some smaller nearby islands. Endangered with global extinction.

# WRINKLED HORNBILL
## *Rhyticeros corrugatus* 81 cm  F: Bucerotidae

**Description**: Look for small red casque and pale neck in male (photo); female distinguished with some difficulty from the Wreathed Hornbill by its white throat and black base of tail.

**Voice**: A short, loud *kak-kak*.

**Habits**: Strictly a lowland rainforest resident, found mainly in swamp forest and primary forest at low altitudes and nearby mature secondary forest. Sometimes encountered flying across the forest or visiting large fruiting trees. Rather shy; stays at canopy level. The only nesting records of this bird are an old record from Sumatra and one from southern Thailand.

**Distribution:** Sunda subregion. Within the region, a scarce resident in Malaysia; reported locally common in Brunei; possibly extinct in Thailand. Vulnerable to global extinction.

# WREATHED HORNBILL
*Rhyticeros undulatus* 100 cm  F: Bucerotidae

**Description**: Male (photo); note diagnostic yellow gular pouch with black stripe; also white tail. Female has blue pouch.

**Voice**: A short, harsh *kuk-kwehk*.

**Habits**: Found in lowland and lower montane rainforest; also roams into secondary forest and across forest edges in search of fruiting trees. Gregarious outside breeding season; large flocks numbering hundreds of birds are recorded annually at communal roosting sites in Thailand.

**Distribution**: Oriental region. A widespread and locally fairly common resident in parts of the region, including Brunei; locally abundant outside the breeding season.

# PLAIN-POUCHED HORNBILL
*Rhyticeros subruficollis* 90 cm  F: Bucerotidae

**Description**: Distinguished with difficulty from previous species by its smaller size and plain pouch; note lack of black stripe on yellow gular pouch on this male at its nest; also lacks corrugation on sides of bill.

**Voice**: Similar to the Wreathed Hornbill, although pitched slightly higher.

**Habits**: Distribution and habits of this little-known species is still under study. In northern Peninsular Malaysia, large flocks of hundreds of roosting hornbills have recently been confirmed to be this species. Believed to feed mainly on fruit. Its nest was recently located in Thailand, where this rare photograph was taken.

**Distribution**: Southeast Asia mainland, possibly also Sumatra. Within the region, a rare resident in Myanmar, Thailand and possibly northern Peninsular Malaysia. Regarded as vulnerable to global extinction.

# BLACK HORNBILL
## *Anthracoceros malayanus* 75 cm  F: Bucerotidae

**Description**: A fairly small, black hornbill; note white casque and nape in male (photo). Female has black bill and casque.

**Voice**: Harsh, growling cries.

**Habits**: Restricted to lowland altitudes, mainly swamp forest and other wet primary forest; also found in nearby mature, logged forest. Flies low across the forest, perching in the canopies or just below, often in small flocks of 2 to 5 birds. The nest is built in a cavity high in a hardwood tree.

**Distribution:** Sunda subregion. Within the region, a locally fairly common, although generally scarce, resident in Peninsular Malaysia and Brunei: rare in south Thailand. Near-threatened with global extinction.

# ORIENTAL PIED HORNBILL (Asian Pied Hornbill)
## *Anthracoceros albirostris* 70 cm  F: Bucerotidae

**Description**: Distinguished from other dark hornbills by its white belly, also by the white trailing edge on wings (in flight). Female's casque is smaller and darker than the male's.

**Voice**: A loud cackle, *yak-yak-yak*.

**Habits**: The only Asian member of this family to habitually venture into disturbed habitats. Often found along rivers, in open coastal woodlands, on islands and plantations. Also occurs in primary rainforest and must have large hardwood trees with cavities available for nesting. An active bird, flapping and gliding low from tree to tree, searching for fruit and invertebrate prey, often in pairs, or several individuals together.

**Distribution:** Oriental region. A widespread, fairly common resident throughout most of the region; rare resident in Singapore.

## RHINOCEROS HORNBILL
### *Buceros rhinoceros* 110 cm  F: Bucerotidae

**Description**: Unmistakable; its large size and red casque are always obvious; note black band in tail.

**Voice**: A characteristic goose-like honk, *ga-rk, ga-rk*, before and after take-off.

**Habits**: Found in lowland and lower montane rainforest, with primary as well as mature secondary growth nearby. Generally conspicuous; flies high over the forest, often in pairs, travelling great distances to reach fruiting fig trees. Perches high, feeding for long periods at a time. Also takes animal prey, especially during the breeding period.

**Distribution**: Sunda subregion. Within the region, resident in low densities in south Thailand, Malaysia and Brunei; extinct in Singapore.

## GREAT HORNBILL
### *Buceros bicornis* 122 cm  F: Bucerotidae

**Description**: Unmistakable; note massive size and yellow neck; yellow bar and white trailing edge in wing show clearly in flight. Photo shows female at nest; male has red eyes.

**Voice**: A far-reaching *ger-ok* during flight.

**Habits**: Found in large expanses of primary rainforest, at both lowland and lower montane elevations. A huge, conspicuous bird, often spotted in pairs, flying slowly high above the trees, calling loudly. Lands in the top of the tallest trees to feed on figs and other fruit. Feeding and nesting behaviour has been well documented by researchers in Thailand.

**Distribution**: Oriental region. Within the region, a widespread but generally scarce resident on most of the mainland.

## RUFOUS HORNBILL
*Buceros hydrocorax* 94 cm  F: Bucerotidae

**Description**: Note dark rufous plumage and white tail; in good light, its bill shines bright red.

**Voice**: A harsh, honking *kang-haw*, often when taking off.

**Habits**: Occurs in primary rainforest, from the lowlands to 1,500 metres elevation, a habitat almost totally obliterated in the Philippines, except for protected areas. Somewhat adaptable, it flies into nearby disturbed areas to feed; small flocks of 5 to 8 birds can still be seen daily at prime locations. A noisy and conspicuous bird that flies with heavy wingbeats to and from large fruiting trees, calling loudly.

**Distribution:** A Philippine endemic. A locally fairly common resident on Luzon, Bohol, Leyte, Samar, Mindanao, Basilan and some smaller nearby islands. Near-threatened with global extinction.

## HELMETED HORNBILL
*Rhinoplax vigil* 127 cm + tail  F: Bucerotidae

**Description**: Unmistakable; note elongated tail and red neck of male (photo). A monotypic genus.

**Voice**: A peculiar accelerating laughter that carries over a mile; heard often just before take-off.

**Habits**: Mainly a lower montane species found in foothills and elevations up to 1,500 metres. Also roams into lowland forests. Requires large expanses of primary forest with huge trees. Feeds in the canopies of fruiting trees, often with other hornbills. Nests in holes high in large, living hardwood trees, but few nests have been recorded.

**Distribution:** Sunda subregion. Within the region, an uncommon and scarce resident in south Thailand, Mynamar, Malaysia and Brunei; extinct in Singapore. Near-threatened with global extinction.

## FIRE-TUFTED BARBET
### *Psilopogon pyrolophus* 26 cm  F: Megalaimidae

**Description**: Unmistakable. Diagnostic yellow and black head pattern. Unique; the only member of its genus.

**Voice**: A loud, cicada-like buzz.

**Habits**: Strictly montane, this barbet is found only between 600 and 1,600 metres elevation. Can be seen well at Malaysian hill stations, where its buzzing call is a sure component in the backdrop of forest sounds. Feeds in fruiting trees or on insects (see photo) and is active during most of the day. Flies heavily with rapid wingbeats into the next tree.

**Distribution**: Sumatra and Peninsular Malaysia. Within the region, a locally fairly common resident in Peninsular Malaysia.

## LINEATED BARBET
### *Megalaima lineata* 29 cm  F: Megalaimidae

**Description**: Look for whitish streaks on head and a pale bill; shown at its nest.

**Voice**: A low-pitched, fluty *poo-poh, poo-poh*.

**Habits**: Frequents dry, open woodlands with scrub, long grass and some larger trees. Often found in coastal areas and around cultivation and plantations. Avoids closed forests. Feeds on fruits fairly low in the trees. Nests in a tree cavity.

**Distribution**: Oriental. Within the region, a widespread and fairly common resident on the mainland, south to northern Peninsular Malaysia.

## GREEN-EARED BARBET
*Megalaima faiostricta* 24 cm  F: Megalaimidae

**Description**: Distinguished from previous species fairly easily by its green ear coverts, less streaks on head and dark (not yellow) bill.

**Voice**: A resonant *too-er-rook* repeated over and over.

**Habits**: Prefers forest edges, mixed deciduous woodlands and nearby cultvation. Found mainly in the lowlands, locally to 900 metres elevation. Seen feeding in fruiting trees or flying somewhat laboriously with rapid wingbeats from one canopy to the next.

**Distribution**: Mainland Southeast Asia only. A widespread and generally common resident in Thailand and Indochina; an isolated population also exists in Guangdong, China.

## GOLD-WHISKERED BARBET
*Megalaima chrysopogon* 30 cm  F: Megalaimidae

**Description**: Distinguished from following species by a large yellow spot and lack of red on cheeks; also by its large size and chunky build.

**Voice**: A deep resonant *kootook, kootook* repeated quickly, over and over.

**Habits**: Found mainly in primary rainforest; occurs in the lowlands, but seems to prefer foothills and lower montane forest up to 1,500 metres. Probably fairly numerous, but not often seen in spite of its large size and bright plumage. Its call often aids in locating it. Sometimes spotted in tall fruiting trees with hornbills and other large birds and mammals.

**Distribution**: Sunda subregion. Within the region, a locally fairly common resident in south Thailand and Malaysia; rare in Brunei.

# RED-CROWNED BARBET
## *Megalaima rafflesii* 27  F: Megalaimidae

**Description**: Look for its full red crown; also its diagnostic blue throat and yellow cheek patch, more visible from below.

**Voice**: A resonant *took-took* (with bill closed), then a pause followed by a longer series.

**Habits**: A lowland rainforest bird that occurs both in primary forest and in regrown, logged forest and forest edges. Usually located by call, but is often seen high in fruiting fig trees, clambering about among the foliage, picking fruit. The flight is short and direct, with rapid beats of its rather small wings.

**Distribution**: Sunda subregion. Within the region, a locally fairly common resident in Malaysia and Brunei; uncommon in Singapore; rare in south Thailand and Myanmar. Near-threatened with global extinction.

# RED-THROATED BARBET
## *Megalaima mystacophanos* 23 cm  F: Megalaimidae

**Description**: Male (top) has diagnostic bright red throat; female has bluish-green head (bottom).

**Voice**: 1 to 4 slow *chok* notes at a rate of about 1 per second.

**Habits**: Found in lowland rainforest and also lower montane forest, up to 1,200 metres. Usually prefers closed primary forest or mature secondary forest, where it moves high in the trees, feeding on fruit and also some insects. The nest is built in a cavity in a dead tree.

**Distribution**: Sunda subregion. Within the region, a generally scarce resident in south Thailand, Myanmar, Malaysia and Brunei; extinct in Singapore.

## GOLDEN-THROATED BARBET
*Megalaima franklinii* 23 cm  F: Megalaimidae

**Description**: Distinguished from following species (which also has yellow throat) by its grey (not blue) cheeks and larger size.

**Voice**: A ringing *te-rhee-unk* repeated about once a second.

**Habits**: An upper montane specialist found mainly in the 1,500-2,400 metres range; in the northern part of its range, seen occasionally down to 900 metres. Prefers closed forest and usually stays inside cover in large trees where it is best located by its call. Although difficult to see well, it appears to be numerous in a suitable habitat. A frequent visitor to fruiting trees.

**Distribution:** Oriental region. Within the region, a locally common resident in upper montane parts of the mainland.

## BLACK-BROWED BARBET
*Megalaima oorti* 20 cm  F: Megalaimidae

**Description**: Note head features, with black brow and yellow throat.

**Voice**: Loud, staccato *took-took-trrook*.

**Habits**: Strictly montane, this barbet can be found in rainforest between 600 and 1,800 metres elevation. It frequents fruiting trees together with other frugivorous species. This small, green bird is not easy to see well, even in the lower trees typical of montane forest. However, the call is heard very often in the middle of the day, indicating that it is in fact a numerous bird.

**Distribution:** Oriental region. Within the region, a locally common resident with a patchy distribution covering parts of south China, Indochina and Peninsular Malaysia.

## BLUE-THROATED BARBET
### *Megalaima asiatica* 23 cm  F: Megalaimidae

**Description**: Distinguished from the Blue-eared Barbet by its larger size, plain blue cheeks and red forehead and nape.

**Voice**: A penetrating and typically barbet-like *took-arook*, repeated quickly for several minutes.

**Habits**: Mainly a lower montane specialist that seems to prefer that narrow band of productive primary forest between 600 and 1,800 metres elevation. Often heard in the right habitat, even late in the morning, but good views are difficult as it feeds on small fruits and various insects high inside the canopies.

**Distribution**: Oriental region. A locally fairly common resident in northwestern parts of the region.

## MOUSTACHED BARBET
### *Megalaima australis* 17 cm  F: Megalaimidae

**Description**: Note the two prominent and diagnostic black stripes above and below eye.

**Voice**: A repeated *took-a-rook*.

**Habits**: A forest barbet found in the lower montane range from 600 to 700 metres elevation and, at some locations, even lower. Lives in closed primary and secondary forest. Ventures out along the edges if there are large fig trees in fruit. The Khao Yai National Park in Thailand is probably the best place to see this limited-distribution barbet. The individual shown is excavating a nesting hole in a dead tree in that National Park.

**Distribution**: Mainland Southeast Asia only. A fairly common resident in parts of Myanmar, Thailand and Indochina.

## YELLOW-CROWNED BARBET
*Megalaima henricii* 22 cm  F: Megalaimidae

Description: Its yellow crown and blue throat are diagnostic.

Voice: A quick and distinctive *took-took-took-took-trrroook*, lasting about one second and repeated 10 to 20 times.

Habits: A lowland barbet occurring in primary and tall secondary forests, often in swampy areas in coastal lowlands, and in hills to 700 metres elevation. Rarely seen, but sometimes located by call. Little studied and few breeding sites have been recorded.

Distribution: Sunda subregion. A generally scarce resident in south Thailand and Malaysia; common in Brunei; extinct in Singapore.

## GOLDEN-NAPED BARBET
*Megalaima pulcherrima* 20 cm  F: Megalaimidae

Description: Its faint yellow nape is difficult to see in the field, but note diagnostic blue throat and forehead, and complete lack of red.

Voice: A rapid, repeated *took-took-trrook*.

Habits: A montane specialist found in primary rainforest, usually between 1,200 and 2,000 metres elevation, but has been recorded to 3,200 metres and down to 900 metres. The forest around the Kinabalu H.Q. (Sabah) is a good location to observe this endemic. It also occurs on Mt. Mulu (Sarawak). Feeds on fruits high in the stunted montane trees, but is little studied and its nest has never been found.

Distribution: Borneo endemic. Within the region, a locally fairly common resident on mountains in Sabah and Sarawak.

## BLUE-EARED BARBET
### *Megalaima australis* 17 cm  F: Megalaimidae

**Description:** Its red and blue head pattern and small size are diagnostic. Captive photo.

**Voice:** A rapid, high-pitched and monotonous *too-trrook, too-trrook*.

**Habits:** Found in lowland and lower montane primary rainforest and in forest edges, especially on Borneo where the Coppersmith Barbet is absent. Also seen in cultivated areas, parks and gardens. Mostly located by call; this small green bird is difficult to spot as it moves about in the dense canopies of 30-metre high fruiting trees.

**Distribution:** Oriental region. A widespread and fairly common resident throughout much of the region, including Brunei; extinct in Singapore.

## COPPERSMITH BARBET
### *Megalaima haemacephala* 15 cm  F: Megalaimidae

**Description:** Unmistakable; note yellow head pattern and streaked underparts; the smallest barbet; shown calling, in photo.

**Voice:** A resonant *tonk, tonk*, 1 to 2 times per second, for minutes at a time.

**Habits:** Found in open woodlands and forest edges, never in closed forest. Also seen in gardens and parks and occasionally in mangroves. Visits trees with small fruits and berries, comes quite low to the ground. Calls incessantly from a top branch, often late in the afternoon. The nest is built in a hole in a dead branch.

**Distribution:** Oriental region. Within the region, a widespread and common resident on the mainland, including Singapore. The only Megalaimidae in the Philippines.

## BROWN BARBET
*Calorhamphus fuliginosus* 18 cm  F: Megalaimidae

**Description:** Unmistakable, the only brown barbet; note paler underparts and strong bill.

**Voice:** A thin, screaming *pseeoo*, unlike any other barbet.

**Habits:** A forest bird found in primary lowland rainforest and mature secondary growth; also in big trees along forest edges. Usually moves high at canopy level but is sometimes seen lower, clambering through the branches like a parrot, looking for fruit and gleaning insects from the foliage, usually in small groups.

**Distribution:** Sunda subregion. Within the region, a locally fairly common resident in south Thailand, Myanmar, Malaysia and Brunei; extinct in Singapore.

## MALAYSIAN HONEYGUIDE
*Indicator archipelagicus* 16 cm  F: Indicatoridae

**Description:** Note the heavy bill and general finch-like appearance.

**Voice:** Similar to a cat's voice, followed by an ascending rattle, *miaw-krrruuu*.

**Habits:** A cryptic forest bird found mainly in primary forest, but also recorded in secondary growth, from the lowlands to 800 metres elevation. A low density species that many experienced ornithologists in the region have never observed. It feeds on insects and honeycombs. This small family is named after an African species, which guides humans to bee's nests and then eats the leftovers. Breeding habits have not been observed; may be nest parasitic on the Brown Barbet.

**Distribution:** Sunda subregion. Within the region, a rare resident in south Thailand and Malaysia; not recorded in Brunei. Near-threatened with global extinction.

## SPECKLED PICULET
### *Picumnus innominatus* 10 cm  F: Picidae

**Description**: A tiny woodpecker; unmistakable; note its distinctly barred underparts.

**Voice**: A sharp *tsick*; also makes a faint tapping noise while feeding.

**Habits**: Mainly a lower montane forest species found in the foothills and elevated areas up to 1,800 metres, in the northern part of its range and also the lowlands. Moves low in bamboo thickets, restlessly picking up tiny prey. Often found in the company of other insectivorous birds in so-called birdwaves. Quite tame; can be approached, but doesn't stay long in one place.

**Distribution**: Oriental region. Within the region, a locally fairly common, but generally scarce, resident in northern parts of the region, including montane Peninsular Malaysia, but excluding Hong Kong; rare in northern Borneo, including Brunei.

## RUFOUS PICULET
### *Sasia abnormis* 9 cm  F: Picidae

**Description**: Unmistakable within range; replaced in the rest of the Oriental region by the similar White-browed Piculet, *S. ochracea*; photo shows female; male has yellow forehead.

**Voice**: A sharp and high-pitched *kik-ik-ik*; also makes a faint tapping noise while feeding.

**Habits**: Occurs in primary rainforest, from the lowlands into lower hills at 800 metres, but is often seen in adjacent secondary growth and has a preference for moving into low scrub and bamboo as the photo shows. Sometimes participates in bird waves, but although it is fairly tame, good views are difficult, as it stays out of sight and hops continuously.

**Distribution**: Sunda subregion. Within the region, a generally scarce resident in south Thailand, Myanmar, Malaysia and Brunei.

## RUFOUS WOODPECKER
*Celeus brachyurus* 25 cm  F: Picidae

**Description**: Black bill and narrow black bars on upperparts are diagnostic; male (photo) has faint red spot behind eye.

**Voice**: A descending series of loud notes, *he, he, he.* Also drums on hollow tree branches.

**Habits**: An adaptable woodpecker found in lowland rainforest, forest edges and adjacent scrub. Moves from large branches at canopy level to thin bushes near the ground, in search of ants, its main food source. A hole to contain the nest is excavated in a dead tree or a nest of tree ants.

**Distribution**: Oriental region. A widespread and locally fairly common resident in most of the region, including Singapore; uncommon in Brunei; vagrant in Hong Kong.

## LACED WOODPECKER
*Picus vittatus* 30 cm  F: Picidae

**Description**: Note green wings with streaks on lower underparts and wing edges; photo shows female; male has red crown.

**Voice**: A shrill, explosive *kweeck*.

**Habits**: In the north it occurs in primary as well as secondary forest, from the lowlands to lower montane altitudes, and scrub. On the Malay Peninsula, mainly found in coastal forests, coconut groves and mangroves. Moves low and often hops on the ground to feed on ants and other invertebrates.

**Distribution**: Oriental region. Within the region, a widespread and fairly common resident on the mainland, including Singapore.

## BLACK-HEADED WOODPECKER
*Picus erythropygius* 33 cm F: Picidae

**Description**: Unmistakable; bright red rump prominent in flight; photo shows male; female lacks red crown patch.

**Voice**: A yelping laughter, *ka-tek-a-tek*.

**Habits**: Found in drought deciduous forests and forest edges from lowlands up to lower montane elevations. Flies in typical woodpecker style, with an undulating flight to the next tree, landing low and working its way up, picking out invertebrate prey from behind the bark.

**Distribution:** Mainland Southeast Asia only. A generally uncommon resident in Myanmar, Thailand and parts of Indochina.

## GREATER YELLOWNAPE
*Picus flavinucha* 34 cm F: Picidae

**Description**: Note large yellow nape; distinguished from the Lesser Yellownape by its larger size and plain grey underparts.

**Voice**: An explosive *kiyaep*.

**Habits**: Found in closed lowland forest and deciduous woodlands, and pine forests up to 2,000 metres elevation. In Malaysia found only in lower and upper montane forest. Flies conspicuously among the trees, often landing low to feed on ants and other invertebrate prey on or inside the bark, gradually moving higher. Easy to observe and quite approachable.

**Distribution:** Oriental region. Within the region, a widespread and fairly common resident on much of the mainland, excluding Hong Kong; also found in montane Peninsular Malaysia.

## CRIMSON-WINGED WOODPECKER
### *Picus puniceus* 25 cm  F: Picidae

**Description:** Note plain red wings and lack of barring except for faint white spots on flanks; photo shows female; male has red malar stripe.

**Voice:** A distinctive *tiuik*.

**Habits:** Found in lowland rainforest and forest edges; on Borneo resides at lower montane elevations. Often moves high in the trees, but comes out onto the thin branches searching for ants, termites and their eggs; also feeds on plant sap.

**Distribution:** Sunda subregion. Within the region, a locally fairly common resident in south Thailand, Myanmar and Malaysia; uncommon in Brunei; extinct in Singapore.

## LESSER YELLOWNAPE
### *Picus chlorolophus* 27 cm  F: Picidae

**Description:** Distinguished from Greater Yellownape by barred underparts and white cheek bar; photo shows female; male has full red crown and malar stripe.

**Voice:** A descending *peee-uu*.

**Habits:** Much like the Greater Yellownape, although not quite as large and conspicuous in behaviour. Often heard or seen flying low through the forest, from tree to tree. Devoted participant in the so-called birdwaves (moving flocks of various insectivorous forest birds).

**Distribution:** Oriental region. Within the region, a widespread and fairly common resident on much of the mainland, excluding Hong Kong and Cambodia; also resident in montane Peninsular Malaysia.

## CHECKER-THROATED WOODPECKER
*Picus mentalis* 28 cm  F: Picidae

**Description:** Distinguished with some difficulty from the Crimson-winged Woodpecker by its streaked throat, plain flanks (without white streaks) and a faint (sometimes visible) black pattern in the primary wing feathers.

**Voice:** An ascending *kiyee, kiyee*.

**Habits:** Occurs in primary rainforest, from the lowlands to 900 metres elevation. Seen less often in mature secondary forest. Although reported to be common on Borneo, it appears to be a low density species. Sometimes spotted feeding with other species on tree trunks in bird waves. Otherwise little studied and few breeding records exist.

**Distribution:** Sunda subregion. Within the region, a generally scarce resident in south Thailand, Myanmar and Malaysia; a single record from Brunei; extinct in Singapore.

## BANDED WOODPECKER
*Picus miniaceus* 25 cm  F: Picidae

**Description:** Distinguished from the Crimson-winged Woodpecker by the faint black barring on its back and underparts; female in photo; male has red malar patch and more distinct barring; note the strong legs and toes typical of all woodpeckers.

**Voice:** A penetrating, descending *peew*.

**Habits:** Found in primary and secondary rainforest, forest edges, nearby plantations and sometimes gardens. Often sits high on a branch, calling regularly throughout the morning. Feeds high on large branches and sometimes low in scrub, mainly on ants. The nest hole is excavated in a dead tree.

**Distribution:** Sunda subregion. Within the region, a fairly common resident in Malaysia and Brunei; locally common in Singapore; uncommon in south Thailand and Myanmar.

## COMMON GOLDENBACK (Common Flameback)
### *Dinopium javanense* 30 cm  F: Picidae

**Description**: Distinguished with difficulty from the Greater Goldenback by its single (not double) black malar stripe and 3 (not 4) toes; female shown in photo; male has red crest.

**Voice**: A sharp *churrrr* and *klek-klek* in flight.

**Habits**: Found in open coastal woodlands, mangroves and disturbed habitats such as plantations, scrub and mature gardens. A noisy and conspicuous woodpecker, it flies from tree to tree, searching the bark for invertebrates, starting from the bottom of the tree and working up. Often seen in pairs.

**Distribution:** Oriental region. Within the region, a widespread and common resident throughout much of the mainland and parts of the Philippines; fairly common in Borneo; uncommon in Brunei and Singapore.

## OLIVE-BACKED WOODPECKER
### *Dinopium rafflesii* 28 cm  F: Picidae

**Description**: Green upperparts and pied head pattern and crest are diagnostic; photo shows male; female has black crest.

**Voice**: A soft trilling *tiiiii*.

**Habits**: Found in lowland rainforest, mainly in primary forest; also seen in mature secondary growth. Seems to occur in low densities. It does not mix with other birds and is rarely recorded during forest surveys. It hops up tree trunks like other woodpeckers, feeding on ants, termites and ant pupae, then flying to the next tree with an undulating flight.

**Distribution:** Sunda subregion. Within the region, a rare resident in south Thailand, Myanmar, Malaysia and Brunei; extinct in Singapore.

## BUFF-RUMPED WOODPECKER
*Meiglyptes tristis* 15 cm  F: Picidae

**Description**: Distinguished from other small woodpeckers by its heavily barred upperparts contrasting with buff head and rump (visible in flight); male (photo) has a red malar stripe.

**Voice**: A trilling *kiiiii;* also a sharp flight-note, *chit.*

**Habits**: Found in lowland rainforest, especially in mature secondary growth, forest edges and clearings; also ventures into nearby scrub, sometimes coming down low to feed on ants in the thin branches. An active and vocal feeder, often seen in pairs, flying quickly from tree to tree with the undulating flight typical of the family.

**Distribution**: Sunda subregion. Within the region, a locally fairly common resident in south Thailand, Myanmar and Malaysia; uncommon in Brunei; extinct in Singapore.

## BLACK-AND-BUFF WOODPECKER
*Meiglyptes jugularis* 22 cm  F: Picidae

**Description**: Distinguished from the similar Heart-spotted Woodpecker by its white neck and black throat (not vice versa).

**Voice**: A sharp *keek-eek-eek.*

**Habits**: Occurs in primary forest from the lowlands to 900 metres elevation. A low density species that is not often encountered. Small and agile, it flies quickly through the forest and lands on tree trunks to search for invertebrates. Often ventures out onto the thin outer branches of trees while feeding. The individual shown is inspecting a potential nesting site.

**Distribution**: Mainland Southeast Asia only. A generally scarce resident in Myanmar, Thailand and parts of Indochina.

## GREAT SLATY WOODPECKER
### *Mulleripicus pulverulentus* 50 cm  F: Picidae

**Description**: Unmistakable; note huge size, grey plumage and buffy throat; only the male (photo) has a red malar stripe.

**Voice**: A characteristic quivering call of 4 to 5 notes; also a frequent *crronk* in flight.

**Habits**: Found in large forests, in rainforest and deciduous woodlands and sometimes mangroves. Mainly recorded in the lowlands, upwards to 1,000 metres. Generally in low densities, but in a suitable habitat, fairly numerous locally. Sometimes seen in small noisy flocks moving through the forest, often late in the day.

**Distribution:** Oriental region. Within the region, an uncommon resident throughout most of the mainland, East Malaysia and Palawan (Philippines); common in Brunei; vagrant in Singapore.

## WHITE-BELLIED WOODPECKER
### *Dryocopus javensis* 43 cm  F: Picidae

**Description**: Unmistakable; large size and white lower belly and rump visible in flight are diagnostic; male (bottom) has more red on head.

**Voice**: A characteristic loud single note *keer;* also a noisy *kek-ek-ek* in flight.

**Habits**: Occurs in a variety of woodlands, from closed lowland rainforest and mangroves to more open deciduous woodlands in the northern parts of its range. In the tropics, found only in lowlands; in the north also seen in hills to 1,500 metres elevation. Must have large trees in habitat for feeding and nesting. Often seen in pairs, pecking at invertebrates on dead branches, as the photo shows.

**Distribution:** Oriental region. Within the region, a generally scarce resident throughout most of the mainland; fairly common in Malaysia, Brunei and the Philippines; rare in Singapore.

## RUFOUS-BELLIED WOODPECKER
### *Picoides hyperythrus* 23 cm  F: Picidae

**Description**: Note diagnostic rufous underparts; photo shows male; female has black cap with white spots.

**Voice**: A trilling and soft *kiiii*.

**Habits**: Found in montane woodlands, mainly at lower montane elevations between 600 and 1,200 metres; in China recorded to the tree limit. Frequents open woodlands with oaks and pines typical to these areas. Hops up tree trunks, as shown in the photo, feeding on insects and larvae in the bark.

**Distribution**: Oriental region, partly migratory. Within the region, an uncommon resident in northern montane parts of the mainland; winter visitor to southeast China only; vagrant in Hong Kong.

## FULVOUS-BREASTED WOODPECKER
### *Picoides macei* 18 cm  F: Picidae

**Description**: Note broad barring on upperparts and tail; fulvous breast streaked with black; male (captive photo) has red forehead; female has all-black cap.

**Voice**: An explosive *tchick*.

**Habits**: Frequents dry open country with scattered small trees, drought deciduous woodlands and adjacent gardens. Flies from tree to tree, landing low and pecking ants and termites from the bark, while spiraling up the trunk.

**Distribution**: Oriental region. Within the region, an uncommon resident in parts of Myanmar, Thailand and Indochina.

## BROWN-CAPPED WOODPECKER (Sunda Woodpecker)
*Picoides moluccensis* 13 cm   F: Picidae

**Description**: A very small black and white woodpecker; distinguished from the similar Grey-capped Woodpecker, *Dendrocopus canicapillus*, by its brown cap. Female (photo) missing the male's thin red line behind the eye.

**Voice**: A short, penetrating trill, somewhat like a telephone ring.

**Habits**: Mainly a mangrove bird, but also occurs in open woodlands and nearby gardens. Adapts well to disturbed habitats and its expansion is possibly due to regional forest clearance. An active bird, always searching through the thin branches for minute invertebrate prey.

**Distribution**: Sunda subregion into east Indonesia. Within the region, a fairly common resident in Peninsular Malaysia; common in Singapore; uncommon in Borneo, including Brunei; unconfirmed in Thailand.

Morten Strange

## HEART-SPOTTED WOODPECKER
*Hemicircus canente* 15 cm   F: Picidae

**Description**: Distinguished from the similar Black and Buff Woodpecker by its white throat and black neck (not vice versa); note white forehead on this female; male has black forehead.

**Voice**: Similar to Black and Buff Woodpecker; a sharp *chirrick* in flight.

**Habits**: Found in dense primary forest and deciduous woodlands and edges, from the lowlands to 900 metres elevation. Moves high in large trees; climbs along thin, open branches in the canopy, gleaning insects from the bark, as the photo shows.

Atsuo Tsuji

**Distribution**: Oriental region. Within the region, an uncommon resident in parts of Myanmar, Thailand and Indochina.

## ORANGE-BACKED WOODPECKER
### *Reinwardtipicus validus* 30 cm  F: Picidae

**Description:** Female (photo) has pale back and grey-brown underparts. Male has reddish underparts and crown, and a striking orange back that flashes in flight. A unique, monotypic genus.

**Voice:** A sharp *kit, kit* and a trilling *ki-ik*.

**Habits:** Found in lowland rainforest, mainly in primary forest and less often in mature secondary growth. Never ventures out on the thin branches, as do some woodpeckers, preferring to feed high on the main trunks of large trees. Note the tubes of termites on this hardwood trunk, undoubtedly attracting the individual in the photograph. Frequently 'calls' by drumming on dead branches.

**Distribution:** Sunda subregion. Within the region, a generally scarce resident in south Thailand, Malaysia and Brunei; extinct in Singapore.

## GREATER GOLDENBACK
### *Chrysocolaptes lucidus* 33 cm  F: Picidae

**Description:** Distinguished with difficulty from the Common Goldenback by its size and double black malar stripe; also by white (not black) neck, seen well from this angle; photo shows female; male has red cap.

**Voice:** A sharp *di-d-di-di*.

**Habits:** Found in all types of wooded habitat, from coastal mangroves and disturbed woodlands, to primary forest; also seen in elevated areas up to 1,200 metres. A noisy and conspicuous woodpecker, calling out loudly and flying between large trees with a heavily undulating flight pattern typical of the family. Also drums on dead wood.

**Distribution:** Oriental region. Within the region, a widespread and generally fairly common resident in most of the mainland and the Philippines; on Borneo, found only in Sabah.

## DUSKY BROADBILL
*Corydon sumatranus* 27 cm  F: Eurylaimidae

**Description**: Unmistakable; the only member of this genus; note broad red bill, pink throat and white spot in wing that folds out like a distinct band in flight.

**Voice**: A series of eerie screams, *ky-ee, ky-ee*.

**Habits**: Found in closed forest, mainly lowland primary rainforest and mature secondary growth. Often seen near water in swampy areas or along small streams. Sits just below the canopy in the upper storey, gleaning insects from the foliage or making rather ungainly flights out from perch on its rapidly moving, short wings. Sometimes moves through the trees in small, noisy flocks.

**Distribution**: Southeast Asia. Within the region, a generally scarce resident in southern parts, including Brunei; extinct in Singapore.

## BLACK-AND-RED BROADBILL
*Cymbirhynchus macrorhynchos* 25 cm  F: Eurylaimidae

**Description**: Distinguished best from the following species by the white stripe in wing; the only member of its genus.

**Voice**: A low, clear whistle followed by some harsher notes.

**Habits**: Found in a variety of woodlands, from forest edges in lowland rainforest to cultivated areas and mangroves. Always seems to be associated with water; often seen near a stream or in a flooded part of the forest, although it does not fish. Catches insects in the middle storey or at eye level. The nest is a suspended pouch nest.

**Distribution**: Southeast Asia into Sumatra (Indonesia). Within the region, a locally fairly common resident in Malaysia and Brunei; rare further north; extinct in Singapore.

# BANDED BROADBILL
*Eurylaimus javanicus* 23 cm  F: Eurylaimidae

**Description:** Note yellow stripe in wing; from the back, distinct yellow blotches on lower back and rump are characteristic. Replaced in the Philippines by the endemic Wattled Broadbill, *E. steerii,* the only member of this family in that country.

**Voice:** A single whistle *yeow* followed by a cicada-like, buzzing trill.

**Habits:** Found in primary and mature secondary lowland rainforest. A low density forest specialist that is difficult to find. Sits passively below the canopy and moves back into the forest quickly if disturbed. Reported to fly out for insects in the air, although this is rarely observed. There are few nesting records of this elusive species.

**Distribution:** Southeast Asia into Java (Indonesia). A scarce resident in southern parts of the region, including Brunei; extinct in Singapore.

# BLACK-AND-YELLOW BROADBILL
*Eurylaimus ochromalus* 15 cm  F: Eurylaimidae

**Description:** Unmistakable. Note small size and yellow on wings and back; from the front, pinkish underparts show clearly.

**Voice:** An accelerating 7 to 11-second trill.

**Habits:** Found in primary and mature secondary lowland rainforest. Not easy to view well, as this small bird usually moves high at canopy level. Sometimes seen in the middle storey of the forest; can be located by call. Feeds on insects.

**Distribution:** Sunda subregion. Within the region, a fairly common resident in south Thailand, Myanmar, Malaysia and Brunei; extinct in Singapore.

# SILVER-BREASTED BROADBILL
## *Serilophus lunatus* 15 cm  F: Eurylaimidae

**Description**: Unmistakable; the only member of this genus; note small size; female has faint white band across grey breast.

**Voice**: A clear *pi-uu* which has been compared to a rusty hinge squeaking.

**Habits**: Mainly a lower montane forest species that seems to prefer the 600 to 1,200-metre range, although it has been recorded from 1,800 metres to 300 metres in its northern range. Frequents primary forest and forest edges, where it hawks for insects in the air or picks them from the middle storey foliage. Fairly tame and sometimes offers good views. The nest is a pouch with a side entrance typical of the family.

**Distribution**: Oriental region to Sumatra (Indonesia). Within the region, a locally fairly common resident throughout much of the mainland, including montane Peninsular Malaysia.

# LONG-TAILED BROADBILL
## *Psarisomus dalhousiae* 28 cm  F: Eurylaimidae

**Description**: Unmistakable; the only member of this genus; white patch in wing visible in flight. Captive photo.

**Voice**: A distinctive series of 5 to 8 shrill notes, *pseew, pseew*.

**Habits**: In its southern range, a montane specialist found only in forest between 700 and 2,000 metres elevation; in the north it is found also in the lowlands. Moves through closed forest, sometimes forming small flocks or mixing with other insectivorous species in bird-waves.

**Distribution**: Oriental region. Within the region, a widespread and locally fairly common, (but generally scarce) resident on the mainland and on mountains in Peninsular Malaysia and north Borneo.

## GREEN BROADBILL
*Calyptomena viridis* 18 cm   F: Eurylaimidae

**Description**: On Borneo, distinguished from two island endemic green broadbills by small size and plain plumage; unmistakable in rest of its range; female lacks black spots of male (photo).

**Voice**: A soft trill *tui, tui, trrrr*.

**Habits**: Frequents lowland and lower montane rainforest. Often overlooked, as it usually sits motionless inside the canopy or just below, flying quickly to a new position when disturbed. Its foliage-green plumage offers a perfect camouflage. Unlike other broadbills, it feeds mainly on fruits. The nest is a large, delicately constructed pouch with a side entrance, suspended in the air, often near a forest stream.

**Distribution**: Sunda subregion. Within the region, a fairly common resident in south Thailand, Myanmar, Malaysia and Brunei; extinct in Singapore.

## BLUE-HEADED PITTA
*Pitta baudii* 17 cm   F: Pittidae

**Description**: Unmistakable; photo shows male; female has buff underparts and dull rufous upperparts; note the small tail, typical of the family, showing well in this rare view.

**Voice**: No information.

**Habits**: Occurs in lowland primary rainforest, often along rivers but apparently not above 600 metres elevation. Hops along the forest floor and finds invertebrate prey by turning over leaves with a rapid jerk of the beak. Regularly sighted on trails in Danum Valley (Sabah) where this photograph was taken. A report from Mulu National Park (Sarawak) describes a nest containing two eggs.

**Distribution**: Borneo endemic. A scarce resident in Sabah and Sarawak (East Malaysia). Near-threatened with global extinction.

## WHISKERED PITTA (Koch's Pitta)
*Pitta kochi* 20 cm  F: Pittidae

**Description**: Distinguished from the sympatric Red-bellied Pitta, *P. erythrogaster,* by its much larger size, pale whiskers contrasting with dark ear coverts and lack of black band across chest.

**Voice**: Characteristic 5 to 9 pigeon-like *woo* notes, descending in pitch and accelerating.

**Habits**: Resident in montane forest, especially from 900 to 1,400 metres elevation. Recently recorded at 300 metres in the Angat forest north of Manila. In the Sierra Madre mountains of northern Luzon, it is locally fairly numerous, but generally a low density species, shy and retiring, mainly located by call and rarely seen. Hops on or near the ground, foraging for invertebrates on the damp forest floor.

**Distribution**: Philippine endemic. A rare resident in montane parts of Luzon island. Vulnerable to global extinction due to hunting and habitat loss.

## MANGROVE PITTA
*Pitta megarhyncha* 20 cm  F: Pittidae

**Description**: Distinguished from the following species by habitat, strong bill and dark crown.

**Voice**: Similar to following species, but more slurred; calls often during breeding season.

**Habits**: A mangrove specialist occurring mostly in tidal mangrove forest, although seen occasionally in nearby coastal woodlands. A low density species, but in a suitable habitat quite predictable, and can be lured out with a tape play-back. Calls from a low branch in the forest and perches on the ground and on lobster mounds.

**Distribution**: Southeast Asia's western coast, from Sunderbans to Sumatra (Indonesia). Within the region, a generally scarce resident on the west coast of the mainland; rare in Singapore.

## BLUE-WINGED PITTA
### *Pitta moluccensis* 20 cm  F: Pittidae

**Description**: Distinguished from the previous species by a pale coronal band and small bill; note short tail that creates a stocky appearance in flight.

**Voice**: A fluty *tu-teew*.

**Habits**: Resident in deciduous lowland forests and open woodlands. Avoids closed tropical rainforest. During migration often found in coastal scrub and gardens. Feeds on invertebrate prey while hopping along on the ground and perching on low branches. Moves higher up when calling. Makes short flights along the ground with rapid wingbeats.

**Distribution**: Oriental region. A widespread and fairly common resident within the region; a passage migrant and winter visitor in much of the region, including Brunei; an uncommon visitor to Singapore; vagrant in the Philippines.

## GARNET PITTA
### *Pitta granatina* 18 cm  F: Pittidae

**Description**: Unmistakable; the red belly and purple back are diagnostic; East Malaysia birds have less or no red on crown.

**Voice**: A monotone whistle, lasting 1 to 2 seconds.

**Habits**: A lowland primary forest specialist, often seen on wet ground. It prefers to hop along in the leaf litter on the forest floor, frequently jumping up to perch on fallen logs, as the photo shows. It does not adapt well to disturbed habitats, where more light penetrates and the undergrowth is denser. Feeds on invertebrates and also some seeds. Shy and elusive; good views of this small forest jewel are rare.

**Distribution**: Sunda subregion. Within the region, a scarce resident in Malaysia; rare in south Thailand and Myanmar; extinct in Singapore.

# HOODED PITTA
*Pitta sordida* 18 cm  F: Pittidae

**Description**: Note its all-green plumage, with black head and short tail; white spot in wing distinct in flight. Captive photo.

**Voice**: A monosyllabic whistle *pih-pih*.

**Habits**: Mainly a forest bird found in closed forests, mature secondary growth and, during migration, in scrub. Hops on the ground turning over fallen leaves to prey on worms, insects and other invertebrates. Sometimes perches on a branch near the ground. Flies off low and fast.

**Distribution**: Oriental region, Australasia. Within the region, a locally fairly common resident throughout much of mainland, Philippines and Borneo, excluding Brunei; an uncommon winter visitor in Peninsular Malaysia and Singapore.

# AZURE-BREASTED PITTA (Steere's Pitta)
*Pitta steerii* 18 cm  F: Pittidae

**Description**: Distinguished from previous species by purple spot on breast and head pattern.

**Voice**: A very distinctive series of 5 or 6 yelps.

**Habits**: Found in rainforest below 750 metres elevation, a habitat fast disappearing within its range. Regularly reported from Raja Sikatuna National Park on Bohol, otherwise very scarce. Calls mainly in late Philippine breeding season (Apr-Jun) or after rain. Hops on the ground, but flies up to perch several metres off the ground. Otherwise little studied.

**Distribution**: Philippine endemic. A rare resident on the islands of Bohol, Samar, Leyte and Mindanao. Vulnerable to global extinction.

## BAR-BELLIED PITTA
*Pitta ellioti* 23 cm  F: Pittidae

**Description:** Distinguished from Hooded Pitta by its green crown and barred underparts; photo shows captive male; female has green replaced with buff.

**Voice:** A trisyllabic whistle *tu-wi-whii*.

**Habits:** A lowland rainforest specialist found in closed forest below 400 metres elevation. Not much studied; habits presumably like other members of this family.

**Distribution:** Mainland Southeast Asia only. A scarce resident in Vietnam, Cambodia and Laos; rare in eastern Thailand.

## GURNEY'S PITTA
*Pitta gurneyi* 22 cm  F: Pittidae

**Description:** Unmistakable; photo shows male; female is duller with finely barred underparts and ochraceous (not blue) crown.

**Voice:** A short, explosive *lilip*; also a falling *skyeew*.

**Habits:** Found in primary lowland rainforest and adjacent mature secondary growth. At present the area around the Khao Nor Chuchi forest reserve near Krabi (Thailand) is the only known location for this species and even here it is rarely observed. It is on the brink of extinction. Teams of Thai and foreign ornithologists have studied it thoroughly and comprehensive reports are available from the Mahidol University in Bangkok.

**Distribution:** Mainland Southeast Asia only. A rare resident in south Thailand and possibly Myanmar.

## EARED PITTA
### *Pitta phayrei* 23 cm  F: Pittidae

**Description**: Distinguished from other pittas by its warm golden-brown plumage; photo shows male; female is duller with black on head replaced by dark brown and more scales on underparts.

**Voice**: A whistling *wheeow-whit;* also a whining alarm call.

**Habits**: Found in closed rainforest and deciduous forest, as well as in secondary growth and dry bamboo. Although found mainly in the lowlands, it has been recorded to 1,500 metres elevation. Feeds on the ground and on fallen logs and flies up briefly to perch on branches as this rare photograph shows.

**Distribution:** Mainland Southeast Asia only. A generally scarce resident in parts of Myanmar, Thailand, Indochina and south China.

## SINGING BUSH-LARK (Australasian Bushlark)
### *Mirafra javanica* 15 cm  F: Alaudidae

**Description**: Distinguished with difficulty from other larks by stout bill and weak brown streaks on tawny chest.

**Voice**: A melodic, whistling song.

**Habits**: An open country bird found on dry fields, rice stubble and dry mudflats near marshes. Sings from the ground or while fluttering in the air. Flies off when disturbed, but quickly drops back onto the ground. Feeds on insects and also some seeds. The nest is built in a small depression on the ground.

**Distribution:** Africa, the Oriental region and Australasia. Partly migratory. Within the region, an uncommon resident in parts of the mainland and the Philippines.

## PLAIN MARTIN
### *Riparia paludicola* 11 cm  F: Hirundinidae

**b Distribution:** Africa and the Oriental region; sedentary. Within the region, an uncommon resident in north-western parts of the mainland and on Taiwan; locally common on Luzon (Philippines).

**Description:** Distinguished from the more widespread migratory Sand Martin, *R. riparia*, by lack of distinct band across breast. The Dusky Crag-martin, *R. concolor*, which breeds on limestone cliffs, has all-dark plumage.

**Voice:** A subdued, harsh chatter and a short *brret,* while flying around its nesting site.

**Habits:** Frequents open country, usually near river valleys, where it nests in colonies. It nests inside a burrow in a steep sandy embankment. Always seen in flocks, flying high and low, catching minute insects in the air. Often rests on wires, as shown in the photo.

## BARN SWALLOW
### *Hirundo rustica* 15 cm  F: Hirundinidae

**Distribution:** Breeds worldwide in northern hemisphere; winters in south. Within the region, resident in south China, including Hong Kong and in north Vietnam; an abundant passage migrant and winter visitor throughout.

**Description:** Distinguished from the Pacific Swallow by black band across chest, contrasting with white belly and longer, very forked tail.

**Voice:** A high-pitched chattering *twit, twit*.

**Habits:** Frequents open country at all elevations. Flies with a fluttering pattern, catching small insects on the wing, high in sunny weather, low in wet. Perches readily on poles and wires. During peak migration flocks numbering thousands will gather at evening roosts in marshes or on buildings in cities.

## PACIFIC SWALLOW
*Hirundo tahitica* 14 cm  F: Hirundinidae

**Description:** Distinguished from the Barn Swallow by its uniformly dusky underparts and shorter, less forked tail.

**Voice:** Like Barn Swallow.

**Habits:** Found mainly near the coast and around nearby marshes; in the wet tropics also found far inland and in the mountains. During winter it mixes with migratory Barn Swallows when feeding, but not at communal roosting sites. The nest is built with mud pellets, under a cliff overhang or man-made structure, often a bridge or dam.

**Distribution:** Oriental region, Australasia; sedentary. A common resident in much of the region, including Singapore and Brunei.

## WIRE-TAILED SWALLOW
*Hirundo smithii* 13 cm (+ tail)  F: Hirundinidae

**Description:** Greatly elongated tail (difficult to see when flying) is diagnostic; note instead bright white underparts and chestnut crown.

**Voice:** A soft twittering.

**Habits:** An open country swallow, found in the lowlands to 1,500 metres elevation, usually near water such as lakes, rivers and canals. Usually solitary or just a few together. Catches insects in the air, flying low with an acrobatic twisting and turning. Rests on a wire or an open branch between sorties.

**Distribution:** Africa and the Oriental region. Within the region, a generally scarce resident in parts of Myanmar, Thailand, Laos, Vietnam and possibly Cambodia.

## RED-RUMPED SWALLOW
*Hirundo daurica* 18 cm  F: Hirundinidae

**Distribution:** Eurasia, the Oriental region. Northern populations migrate south, reaching Africa. A widespread and locally common resident throughout the region; migrant only in Hong Kong, Singapore and Borneo, including Brunei.

**Description:** A large, heavy swallow; prominent red rump is diagnostic in all plumages; photo shows subspecies, *H. d. badia*, resident on the Malay Peninsula. Northern populations have heavy black streaks on underparts; some of these subspecies are sometimes treated as the full species, the Striated Swallow, *H. striolata*.

**Voice:** Sometimes a metallic *cheenk*.

**Habits:** Found in a more wooded habitat than most other swallows, often in forest edges and deciduous woodlands extending into montane elevations. During migration also found in open country and coastal areas. The nest is constructed of mud pellets under a cliff or building overhang.

## BAR-WINGED FLYCATCHER-SHRIKE
*Hemipus picatus* 15 cm  F: Campephagidae

**Distribution:** Oriental region. Within the region, a widespread and fairly common resident on most of the mainland, in East Malaysia mainly in montane regions; single recording from Brunei.

**Description:** Distinguished from the Pied Triller by its smaller size, lack of white supercilium and more narrow wing bar; photo shows male, with juvenile Emerald Cuckoo. Female has a slaty-grey (not black) back.

**Voice:** A clear *chir-up, chir-rup*.

**Habits:** An arboreal bird found in a variety of wooded habitats, from closed forest to forest edges and bamboo, in both lowlands and montane areas to 2,000 metres elevation. A lively bird that flies about at canopy level and lower levels, mainly hunting for insects, larvae and spiders on the foliage. Also flies out to catch small flying prey. Often spotted with other insectivorous species in bird waves.

# BLACK-WINGED FLYCATCHER-SHRIKE
## *Hemipus hirundinaceus* 15 cm  F: Campephagidae

**Description:** Much like previous species in appearance, but lacks white in wing; photo shows male; female is duller.

**Voice:** Like previous species.

**Habits:** Found in primary rainforest, mature secondary forest and mangroves, mainly in the extreme lowlands below 300 metres. In other parts of range (Sumatra and Java, Indonesia) it has been reported at lower montane elevations. Often comes out on logging trails and clearings, from the outside of canopies or lower, hawking for insects as shown in this photo. Also seen with other birds in bird waves.

**Distribution:** Sunda subregion. Within the region, an uncommon resident in south Thailand, Myanmar and Peninsular Malaysia; more numerous in East Malaysia and Brunei.

# LARGE WOOD-SHRIKE
## *Tephrodornis virgatus* 23 cm  F: Campephagidae

**Description:** Distinguished from the sympatric Common Woodshrike, *T. pondicerianus* (18 cm), by its larger size, lack of pale supercilium and white (not black) base of tail visible when wings are opened.

**Voice:** A loud, ringing *kee-a, kee-a;* also a harsher *chreek.*

**Habits:** Found in closed rainforest and deciduous forest in northern range, from the lowlands to 1,400 metres. Feeds on invertebrates such as flying insects and lavae, at canopy or mid-storey level. The individual in the photo is carrying food for its fledged young nearby; observed at Taman Negara National Park (Malaysia).

**Distribution:** Oriental region. Within the region, a generally fairly common resident on the mainland and East Malaysia; vagrant in Brunei; not recorded in Hong Kong; extinct in Singapore.

# LARGE CUCKOO-SHRIKE (Black-faced Cuckoo-shrike)
## *Coracina novaehollandiae* 30 cm  F: Campephagidae

**Description**: Distinguished from other cuckoo-shrikes by its large size and diffuse black mask. The Peninsular Malaysia subspecies also occurs on Java and Bali; sometimes treated as the separate species, the Malaysian Cuckoo-shrike, *C. javensis*.

**Voice**: A far-carrying, ringing *kle-eeep,* when flying high across the trees.

**Habits**: Found in open woodlands with scattered tall trees and pines. In Peninsular Malaysia, restricted to a montane habitat where much the same vegetation predominates. Usually moves high in the foliage, displaying in a conspicuous fashion in early morning and late evening.

**Distribution**: Oriental region, Australasia. Within the region, a fairly common resident on the mainland and montane Peninsular Malaysia; vagrant in Hong Kong.

# PIED TRILLER
## *Lalage nigra* 18 cm  F: Campephagidae

**Description**: Distinguished from the similar Ashy Minivet, *Pericrocotus divaricatus*, by its white wing-bar and supercilium; photo shows female; male has black upperparts and uniform white underparts.

**Voice**: A slurred trill and a harsher *chack*.

**Habits**: Frequents coastal woodlands, from tidal mangroves to casuarina groves and adjacent cultivation. Has adapted to the park and garden habitat. Makes short flights from tree to tree, calling softly. Hops along inside the canopy, calling softly, never staying long in one place. Gleans invertebrates from the leaves and stems. The nest is a small cup built on a thin branch, high in a tree.

**Distribution**: Southeast Asia into Java (Indonesia). Within the region, an uncommon resident in south Thailand; common in Malaysia, Singapore, Brunei and the Philippines.

## SMALL MINIVET
*Pericrocotus cinnamomeus* 15 cm  F: Campephagidae

**Description**: A small bird, distinguished with difficulty from the Fiery Minivet, *P. igneus,* (Sunda sub-region) by its orange (not red) underparts (male, top), and grey (not yellow) underparts (female, bottom).

**Voice**: A thin whistle *tsee-tsee*.

**Habits**: Travels through open woodlands, mangroves and plantations in small flocks; sometimes seen near villages. An active bird that flutters restlessly among the thin branches of small trees, catching insects and calling softly.

**Distribution:** Oriental region. Within the region, a fairly common resident in parts of Myanmar, Thailand and Indochina.

## GREY-CHINNED MINIVET
*Pericrocotus solaris* 17 cm  F: Campephagidae

**Description**: Distinguished with difficulty from Scarlet Minivet by size and slaty (not black) head (male, top), and by grey (not yellowish) head (female, bottom).

**Voice**: A diagnostic thin *tsee-sip*.

**Habits**: A montane resident usually found in forest between 1,000 and 2,000 metres elevation; in its northern range; also seen sometimes at lower altitudes. Frequents closed forest as well as forest edges. It is a sociable bird; one or several pairs travel together, always on the move, fluttering around the thin branches of the canopies, calling incessantly, chasing insects at clearings, also briefly at eye level.

**Distribution:** Oriental region. Within the region, a widespread and locally common resident in much of the region, including Hong Kong and the mountains in Malaysia.

## SCARLET MINIVET
*Pericrocotus flammeus* 20 cm  F: Campephagidae

**Description:** Note scarlet-red underparts and black head of male (photo); female has red replaced with yellow, and a yellow face.

**Voice:** A soft, penetrating, high-pitched *tweep, tweep*.

**Habits:** A forest bird found mainly in primary lowland rainforest in the tropics; in its northern, range found in disturbed woodlands and at higher altitudes. An attractive and pretty bird, but frustratingly difficult to see well, as it moves high in the thin branches of the tall canopy. Usually a few pairs move about together, perching briefly and flying from tree to tree, calling to each other in a constant search for insects.

**Distribution:** Oriental region; the northern populations are somewhat nomadic. A widespread and fairly common resident in most of the region, including Hong Kong; uncommon in Borneo, including Brunei; rare in Singapore.

## GREEN IORA
*Aegithina viridissima* 14 cm  F: Chloropseidae

**Description:** Distinguished from the following species by its green head and prominent eye-ring; photo shows male; female has more yellowish underparts.

**Voice:** A soft, whistling chatter.

**Habits:** Occurs in lowland rainforest, both in primary forest and secondary forest and edges. Creeps about at the edge of the foliage, as shown in the photograph, at the canopy and occasionally down to eye level. Doesn't perch for long and good views are difficult. Often moves along with other birds in waves.

**Distribution:** Sunda subregion. A generally scarce resident in south Thailand, Myanmar and Brunei; extinct in Singapore.

## COMMON IORA
### *Aegithina tiphia* 15 cm  F: Chloropseidae

**Description**: Some variations in plumage with this species, but always more yellowish than the Green Iora; photo shows female; male has darker upperparts, contrasting more strongly with yellow underparts.

**Voice**: Like previous species.

**Habits**: Found in open woodlands, mangroves and coastal scrub, never in closed forest. Has adapted well to disturbed habitats. Often seen in gardens. Moves restlessly around in trees and bushes, picking invertebrates from the leaves. The nest is a tiny cup carefully built on a forked branch.

**Distribution**: Oriental region. A widespread and common resident in most of the region, including Singapore and Brunei.

## LESSER GREEN LEAFBIRD
### *Chloropsis cyanopogon* 18 cm  F: Chloropseidae

**Description**: Distinguished with difficulty from the following species by its thinner bill and yellow border along black throat patch (male, photo).

**Voice**: A frequent and high-pitched whistle, *see-to-see*.

**Habits**: Occurs in rainforest, mainly in the lowlands; recorded to 700 metres elevation only. Prefers closed primary forest, but sometimes moves into tall secondary growth and edges. Usually seen high at canopy level where it feeds on small fruits and caterpillars. Although fairly numerous at prime locations, good views are difficult and no nests have been found.

**Distribution**: Sunda subregion. Within the region, a locally fairly common resident in south Thailand, Myanmar, Malaysia and Brunei; uncommon in Singapore.

## GREATER GREEN LEAFBIRD
*Chloropsis sonnerati* 21 cm  F: Chloropseidae

**Description**: Distinguished with difficulty from the previous species by its powerful bill, yellow throat and eye-ring (female, bottom); and lack of yellow border along black throat patch (male, photo top).

**Voice**: A loud, ascending whistle *chee-zi-chee*.

**Habits**: Found in rainforest, from the lowlands to lower montane elevations, mainly closed primary forest but also tall secondary growth and edges. Moves quite conspicuously at canopy level, jumping about in the thin branches, calling out and flying from tree to tree. Often visits fruiting fig trees, but also takes invertebrate prey. Few nesting records.

**Distribution**: Sunda subregion. Within the region, a locally fairly common resident in south Thailand, Myanmar, Malaysia and Brunei; rare in Singapore.

## GOLDEN-FRONTED LEAFBIRD
*Chloropsis aurifrons* 20 cm  F: Chloropseidae

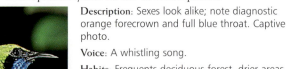

**Description**: Sexes look alike; note diagnostic orange forecrown and full blue throat. Captive photo.

**Voice**: A whistling song.

**Habits**: Frequents deciduous forest, drier areas of rainforest, forest edges and cultivated areas, from the lowlands to lower montane elevations. An active and vocal bird that moves about in the thin branches, searching for small insects and larvae.

**Distribution**: Oriental region. Within the region, a common resident throughout much of the mainland.

## BLUE-WINGED LEAFBIRD
*Chloropsis cochinchinensis* 19 cm   F: Chloropseidae

**Description**: Note diagnostic blue stripe in wing; photo shows male; female lacks black throat.

**Voice**: A liquid whistle *chee-cheerup*.

**Habits**: An arboreal bird found in all types of forest, from deciduous woodlands to closed rainforest and forest edges. Prefers to move high in the canopies of large trees, but is sometimes seen at lower levels along clearings and trails. An attractive and active bird that clambers along thin branches, picking out fruit and small insects.

**Distribution**: Oriental region. A common resident throughout much of the region, including Singapore; uncommon in Brunei.

## ORANGE-BELLIED LEAFBIRD
*Chloropsis hardwickii* 20 cm   F: Chloropseidae

**Description**: The only leafbird with an orange belly; male shown in photo; female lacks black throat and chest.

**Voice**: A melodious rippling song and a single *chip*.

**Habits**: Mainly a montane forest bird found from the foothills up to 2,000 metres elevation. Often seen perched high, singing in the forest early in the morning or in the evening before dusk. Flies conspicuously from tree to tree at canopy level, picking invertebrates from the thin branches or small fruits from fig trees.

**Distribution**: Oriental region. A fairly common resident in much of the region, including Hong Kong and montane Peninsular Malaysia.

## COLLARED FINCHBILL
*Spixixos semitorques* 22 cm  F: Pycnonotidae

**Description**: Unmistakable; note short pale bill and white collar. Captive photo.

**Voice**: Fluty calls and typical bulbul whistles.

**Habits**: Found in scrub, forest edges, cultivated areas and gardens where it moves about, low in the vegetation. Crushes seeds and beans with its powerful beak and takes some fruit and insects like other bulbuls.

**Distribution**: Oriental region. Resident in south China, Taiwan and northern Vietnam; vagrant in Hong Kong.

## STRAW-HEADED BULBUL
*Pycnonotus zeylanicus* 28 cm  F: Pycnonotidae

**Description**: Unmistakable; large size and orange cap are diagnostic.

**Voice**: A loud and bubbling song, more like a thrush than a bulbul, sometimes in duet.

**Habits**: Prefers extreme lowland forest edges near waterways such as streams, large rivers and tidal mangroves. Also found in disturbed forest adjacent to, but never in, primary rainforest. Shy and retiring; usually detected by its powerful song. Flies low from tree to tree, but rarely perches in the open. Much reduced in numbers due to trapping for the bird trade.

**Distribution**: Sunda subregion. Within the region, an uncommon resident in Malaysia; rare in Singapore and Brunei; previously recorded in south Thailand and Myanmar. Vulnerable to global extinction.

## BLACK-AND-WHITE BULBUL

*Pycnonotus melanoleucos* 18 cm  F: Pycnonotidae

**Description**: Unmistakable; the only pied bulbul.

**Voice**: A tuneless *cher-leet*.

**Habits**: An enigmatic bird found in lowland rainforest and mangroves, but has also been sighted at lower montane elevations and in gardens. Seems to occur in low densities and is possibly somewhat nomadic. Rarely seen. Usually spotted moving fairly low along the forest edges, as shown in the photo, but has also been recorded at canopy level.

**Distribution:** Sunda subregion. A generally uncommon resident in south Thailand and Malaysia; locally fairly common in Brunei; extinct in Singapore.

Edward Vercruysse

## BLACK-HEADED BULBUL

*Pycnonotus atriceps* 18 cm  F: Pycnonotidae

**Description**: Wings bright yellow-olive; note lack of crest.

**Voice**: Weak, tuneless, sharp chirps.

**Habits**: Found in rainforest and especially in mature secondary forest and forest edges, from the lowlands to lower montane altitudes. Moves about in the middle storey and sometimes down to eye level, feeding on fruit and some invertebrates.

**Distribution:** Oriental region; somewhat nomadic outside breeding season. A locally fairly common resident in much of the region, including Brunei; rare in Singapore.

Morten Strange

## BLACK-CRESTED BULBUL
*Pycnonotus melanicterus* 19 cm  F: Pycnonotidae

**Description**: Distinguished from the previous species by its long crest, white eye and black tail; throat also black or yellow depending on subspecies.

**Voice**: A slurred whistle.

**Habits**: A forest bird found in rainforest and deciduous woodlands, mainly at montane elevations. In its northern range, also found in the lowlands. Often seen in large trees at the edge of the forest, calling out and feeding actively on small fruits; it also takes some insects.

**Distribution**: Oriental region. A fairly common resident in most of the region; in the south, mainly montane; on Borneo restricted to the mountains; introduced in Singapore.

## SCALY-BREASTED BULBUL
*Pycnonotus squamatus* 16 cm  F: Pycnonotidae

**Description**: A small bird; unmistakable; note scaly underparts and white throat.

**Voice**: A series of sharp notes, *wit-wit*.

**Habits**: Found in primary rainforest, usually at lower montane elevations, but sometimes in lowlands, not above 1,000 metres. Moves about high in the forest at canopy or mid-storey level, feeding on fruits.

**Distribution**: Sunda subregion. Within the region, a generally scarce resident in South Thailand, Myanmar and Malaysia; on Borneo restricted to lower montane elevations.

## GREY-BELLIED BULBUL
*Pycnonotus cyaniventris* 16 cm  F: Pycnonotidae

**Description**: Look for diagnostic dark grey head and underparts.

**Voice**: A typical, bulbul-like whistle *pi-pi-pi-pi*.

**Habits**: A rainforest species occurring from the lowlands to lower montane elevations, mainly in closed primary forest, but also in tall secondary growth and edges. Moves about in the canopies, sometimes lower, most often seen visiting fruiting trees. Few nesting records.

**Distribution**: Sunda subregion. Within the region, a generally scarce resident in south Thailand, Myanmar, Malaysia and Brunei; extinct in Singapore.

## RED-WHISKERED BULBUL
*Pycnonotus jocosus* 20 cm  F: Pycnonotidae

**Description**: Unmistakable; note red spot behind eye and crest; underparts whitish.

**Voice**: A varied whistling song; a short, repeated *wit-ti-waet*.

**Habits**: An adaptable and successful species found mainly in open woodlands, forest edges and cultivated areas. Often seen near villages, where it perches in the top of small trees chattering incessantly and flying out to catch insects in the air.

**Distribution**: Oriental region. Within the region, a widespread and common resident throughout most of the mainland, including Hong Kong; uncommon in northern Peninsular Malaysia; introduced in Singapore; recently recorded in the Philippines.

## LIGHT-VENTED BULBUL (Chinese Bulbul)
*Pycnonotus sinensis* 19 cm   F: Pycnonotidae

**Description**: Note diagnostic head pattern; also look for olive streak in wing, and pale lower belly and vent.

**Voice**: Vocal, a whistling chatter, less tuneful than previous species.

**Habits**: This is one of the most widespread and common birds within its range. Very adaptable; it lives in scrubby forest as well as mangroves, cultivated areas, parks, gardens and open country with some trees. Found from the lowlands to hills at 600 metres. Opportunistic; it feeds on both berries and insects. The cup-shaped nest is placed low in a bush.

**Distribution**: Oriental region. Within the region, a common resident in southeast China, including Hong Kong and in northern Laos and Vietnam.

## SOOTY-HEADED BULBUL
*Pycnonotus aurigaster* 20 cm   F: Pycnonotidae

**Description**: Note black head contrasting with pale cheeks; underparts light grey; vent either red or yellow. Captive photo.

**Voice**: A soft chatter with whistling and harsher notes.

**Habits**: Mainly an open woodland species found in open country with scattered trees, cultivated areas and gardens; often seen near rural villages, but not in towns. A vocal and conspicuous bird; always moves about in small flocks, flying restless between the small trees and bushes, perching low.

**Distribution**: Oriental region. Within the region, a common resident throughout much of the mainland, including Hong Kong.

## PUFF-BACKED BULBUL
### *Pycnonotus eutilotus* 23 cm  F: Pycnonotidae

**Description**: Distinguished with difficulty from other bulbuls by a tufty crest and dark brown (not olive or greyish) wings.

**Voice**: A typical, bulbul-like whistle *tju-lip*.

**Habits**: Found in lowland rainforest, in primary and nearby secondary forest and along edges. Moves about in the middle storey of the forest. A low density species sometimes seen with other bulbuls in fruiting trees. No nesting records.

**Distribution**: Sunda subregion. Within the region, a scarce resident in south Thailand, Myanmar, Malaysia and Brunei; extinct in Singapore.

## STRIPE-THROATED BULBUL
### *Pycnonotus finlaysoni* 20 cm  F: Pycnonotidae

**Description**: Look for diagnostic yellow streaks on forehead and throat.

**Voice**: A squawking *whic-ic*.

**Habits**: A fairly adaptable forest bird that occurs both in closed rainforest in its tropical range, and in open deciduous forest and nearby scrub further north. In Peninsular Malaysia, most predominant in submontane forest and forest edges, from the low hills to 1,000 metres elevation. An easy bird to observe, as it often appears in fruiting trees and along trails, moving low in the trees, sometimes landing briefly near the ground in open clearings.

**Distribution**: Mainland Southeast Asia only. A fairly common resident in Myanmar, south China, Thailand, Indochina and Peninsular Malaysia.

## FLAVESCENT BULBUL
### *Pycnonotus flavescens* 22 cm  F: Pycnonotidae

**Description**: Distinguished from other montane bulbuls by its yellowish wings, lower belly and vent.

**Voice**: A soft song and a harsher chatter *tcherrp*.

**Habits**: A strictly upper montane species found only in forest, forest edges and nearby scrub. Occurs from 900 metres to the highest summits in Thailand; to 2,750 metres in China; and to the tree limit (3,400 metres) in Sabah. Often the only member of its family at these elevations, it can become numerous. Quite inquisitive, often seen along roads and trails, moving from the highest tree tops down to eye level, picking up small fruits and invertebrate prey.

**Distribution:** Oriental region. A locally common resident in montane areas of the mainland and East Malaysia.

## YELLOW-VENTED BULBUL
### *Pycnonotus goiavier* 20 cm  F: Pycnonotidae

**Description**: Look for prominent white supercilium contrasting with a dark crown; vent is yellow.

**Voice**: A bubbling, chattering song; also a harsh alarm call, *tweit-tweit*.

**Habits**: An adaptable and successful species that has invaded disturbed habitats, from its original haunts of forest edges, open woodlands and mangroves. The predominant garden bird within its range, now expanding into cities and montane hill stations. An active feeder on small fruits and insects. Unlike other bulbuls, it lands on the ground. Very vocal, especially at daybreak.

**Distribution:** Southeast Asia into Bali (Indonesia). A common resident in southern parts of region, including Singapore and Brunei; locally abundant.

# OLIVE-WINGED BULBUL

*Pycnonotus plumosus* 20 cm  F: Pycnonotidae

**Description**: Distinguished with difficulty from other bulbuls by the olive streak in its wings.

**Voice**: A subdued, chattering song, more squeaky than the Yellow-vented.

**Habits**: A forest bird, although it seems to prefer forest edges, secondary growth, mangroves, and nearby scrub, but not gardens or villages. Moves about fairly low at the edge of the vegetation, but prefers to stay under cover and sings from a concealed location. Takes a variety of small fruits, berries and invertebrate prey.

**Distribution:** Sunda subregion. Within the region, a fairly common resident in south Thailand, Myanmar, Malaysia, Singapore, Brunei and Palawan (Philippines).

# STREAK-EARED BULBUL

*Pycnonotus blanfordi* 20 cm  F: Pycnonotidae

**Description**: Appears plain, but is in fact easy to recognise by its pale bill and streaks below eye.

**Voice**: A harsh chatter.

**Habits**: An adaptable arboreal bird that avoids closed forest and proliferates in open woodland and cultivated areas in the lowlands. It has taken over the garden niche and in some Asian urban areas is the dominant bulbul in city parks. Feeds in fruiting trees from the canopy down to eye level. An active and lively element of urban wildlife; sometimes becomes quite bold.

**Distribution:** Mainland Southeast Asia only. A locally common resident in Myanmar, Thailand and Indochina; uncommon in northern Peninsular Malaysia.

## CREAM-VENTED BULBUL
*Pycnonotus simplex* 17 cm  F: Pycnonotidae

**Description**: Look for its prominent white eye-ring; also note small and slender build; on Borneo (where local race has red eye) look for pale belly and vent.

**Voice**: A short *clip-clip*.

**Habits**: Found in primary rainforest, mature secondary growth and forest edges. A small, quick-moving bulbul that flutters about at the canopy or mid-storey level, often with other bulbuls, picking up small fruits; also takes insects.

**Distribution**: Sunda subregion. A locally fairly common resident in south Thailand and Malaysia; uncommon in Singapore and Brunei.

## RED-EYED BULBUL
*Pycnonotus brunneus* 18 cm  F: Pycnonotidae

**Description**: Apart from its red eye, look for general dark appearance, including brownish underparts.

**Voice**: A high-pitched, trilling whistle.

**Habits**: A forest bird found in lowland primary and mature secondary forest, and along forest edges. A predictable visitor to fruiting trees, often with other bulbuls, feeding actively at canopy and middle-storey levels. Otherwise little studied; few nesting records.

**Distribution**: Sunda subregion. Within the region, a fairly common resident in south Thailand, Myanmar, Malaysia and Brunei; locally numerous; rare in Singapore.

# SPECTACLED BULBUL
*Pycnonotus erythropthalmos* 17 cm  F: Pycnonotidae

**Description**: Distinguished with difficulty from the Red-eyed Bulbul by orange orbital ring; slender build and generally paler appearance.

**Voice**: A varied and chattering song.

**Habits**: Found in primary and secondary lowland rainforest; visits fruiting trees with other bulbuls, but in smaller numbers. Difficult to get good views of this species, as it moves about in the canopy or middle storey; sometimes moves lower to reach fruit.

**Distribution**: A generally scarce resident in south Thailand, Myanmar, Malaysia and Brunei; extinct in Singapore.

# FINSCH'S BULBUL
*Criniger finschii* 17 cm  F: Pycnonotidae

**Description**: Distinguished with difficulty from other bulbuls by its yellow throat, center of belly and vent.

**Voice**: Musical chatter and a loud *choi-choi-chong-choi*.

**Habits**: Restricted to primary lowland rainforest and forest edges below 600 metres elevation. A low-density species often missed during surveys. Taman Negara National Park is one of its regular haunts, where this rare photograph was taken. Here it occasionally turns up in fruiting trees.

**Distribution**: Sunda subregion. Within the region, a rare resident in south Thailand and Malaysia; recorded once in Brunei.

## PUFF-THROATED BULBUL
### *Criniger pallidus* 24 cm  F: Pycnonotidae

**Description:** Distinguished with some difficulty from the following species by its buff and yellow (not pale grey) underparts; also note different voice and range; distinguished from other bulbuls by its white throat and crest.

**Voice:** A resonant and scolding *churrk-churrk*.

**Habits:** Found in forested areas, often inside dense primary forest but also near the edges, from the lowlands to 1,200 metres in Thailand and Indochina; and in China to 1,600 metres elevation. Moves about in the middle storey or higher, often staying under cover, but its noisy call gives it away. Best seen when it comes out to feed in fruiting trees.

**Distribution:** Mainland Southeast Asia only. A locally fairly common resident in Myanmar, south China (excluding Hong Kong), Thailand and Indochina.

## OCHRACEOUS BULBUL
### *Criniger ochraceus* 23 cm  (*Alophoixus ochraceous*)  F: Pycnonotidae

**Description:** Look for a bright white throat, contrasting with brown upperparts; also notice crest.

**Voice:** Whistling calls and a noisy chatter, *chi-wau*.

**Habits:** A rainforest species occurring mainly in primary forest, from the foothills (300 metres) to lower montane elevations at 1,000 metres; and on Borneo up to 1,600 metres. Within its northern range, it is found in the lowlands. Stays under cover more than other bulbuls, moving about low branches, somewhat like a babbler. Calls often. Feeds on small berries and insects.

**Distribution:** Southeast Asia into Sumatra (Indonesia). A locally fairly common resident in the southern part of the region; on Borneo restricted to lower montane habitat.

## YELLOW-BELLIED BULBUL

*Griniger phaeocephalus* 20 cm (*Alophoixus phaeocephalus*)  F: Pycnonotidae

**Description**: Yellow underparts, white throat and lack of crest together are diagnostic.

**Voice**: A harsh alarm call *cree-cree*.

**Habits**: Mainly found in primary lowland rainforest, where it moves about below the canopy, in the middle storey or down at eye level. Seen less often in nearby secondary forest and edges. Flies conspicuously among the trees, searching for small berries and insects.

**Distribution**: Sunda subregion. A locally fairly common resident in south Thailand, Myanmar, Malaysia and Brunei; extinct in Singapore.

## HAIRY-BACKED BULBUL

*Hypsipetes criniger* 17 cm  (*Tricholestes criniger*)  F: Pycnonotidae

**Description**: Note the diagnostic yellow patch around eye contrasting with olive-brown crown; small and stocky build.

**Voice**: A short chatter with whistling notes.

**Habits**: Found in lowland rainforest, both primary and nearby secondary growth. Often seen along forest edges and clearings where it comes down to the middle storey, occasionally at eye level, feeding on small berries and insects. Its nest has not been described.

**Distribution**: Sunda subregion. A locally fairly common resident in south Thailand, Myanmar and Malaysia; rare in Brunei.

## GREY-EYED BULBUL
*Hypsipetes propinquus* 19 cm  F: Pycnonotidae

**Distribution:** Mainland Southeast Asia only. A locally fairly common resident in Myanmar, south China (excluding Hong Kong), Thailand and Indochina.

**Description:** In south Thailand, distinguished with difficulty from the following species by its lack of brown crown and tawny brown vent.

**Voice:** A distinctive, mewing *cheer-y*.

**Habits:** A forest bird found in primary forest, but just as often in forest edges, secondary growth and nearby scrub. In Khao Yai National Park in Thailand this appears to be the most numerous bulbul along the roads. Found mainly in the lowlands and recorded to 1,100 metres elevation. Feeds in fruiting trees, often together with other bulbuls.

## BUFF-VENTED BULBUL
*Hypsipetes charlottae* 20 cm (*Iole olivacea*)  F: Pycnonotidae

**Distribution:** Sunda subregion. A locally fairly common resident in south Thailand, Myanmar and Malaysia; uncommon in Brunei; very rare in Singapore.

**Description:** Distinguished with difficulty from other bulbuls by brown crown contrasting with buff face; note also its slender build and buff belly and vent.

**Voice:** A typical, bulbul-like *whee-it*.

**Habits:** Found in lowland rainforest, in primary forest and nearby secondary growth and edges. Usually seen moving about high in large trees at canopy or mid-storey level. An active feeder often observed in fruiting trees with other bulbuls. Few nesting records.

## MOUNTAIN BULBUL
*Hypsipetes mcclellandii* 24 cm  F: Pycnonotidae

**Description**: Unmistakable; note olive upperparts and white streaks on head, extending down onto chest.

**Voice**: A metallic *tsiuc-tsiuc.*

**Habits**: A strictly montane species found above 900 metres and to the tree limit above 2,000 metres. Often the only member of its family at these elevations. A successful species occurring both in primary forest and in disturbed habitats such as forest edges and gardens. Moves in the tops of the relatively low montane trees, feeding on fruit and some insects.

**Distribution:** Oriental region. A common resident in northern parts of the region, excluding Hong Kong, and in montane Peninsular Malaysia; locally abundant.

## STREAKED BULBUL
*Hypsipetes malaccensis* 23 cm (*Ixos malaccensis*)  F: Pycnonotidae

**Description**: Grey streaks on pale chest are diagnostic; rest of underparts are bright white; large and slender.

**Voice**: A loud, metallic rattle.

**Habits**: A low density species restricted to lowland primary rainforest or mature secondary growth with large trees. Strictly a canopy bird that does not descend to the lower storeys, even in fruiting trees. Otherwise quite conspicuous, often calling loudly and displaying by raising one wing at a time.

**Distribution:** Sunda subregion. An uncommon resident in south Thailand, Myanmar, Malaysia and Brunei.

## ASHY BULBUL
*Hypsipetes flavala* 20 cm  F: Pycnonotidae

**Description**: Note diagnostic black crest and generally ashy grey plumage; Malay Peninsula subspecies *H. f. cinerea* lacks the yellow-greenish patch in wing.

**Voice**: A loud, ringing call and a quiet *hi-yeah*.

**Habits**: A forest bird found mainly at lower montane elevations between 600 and 1,800 metres; recorded to 2,100 metres elevation and sometimes down to 200 metres or below. It prefers closed forest and forest edges, moving high in the upper or middle storey of large trees. Visits fruiting trees in pairs or a small group, often with other bulbuls; also takes small invertebrate prey.

**Distribution**: Oriental region. A locally fairly common resident in parts of the mainland; in Malaysia mainly montane; an uncommon visitor to Singapore.

## CHESTNUT BULBUL
*Hypsipetes castanotus* 20 cm (*Hemixos castanonotus*)  F: Pycnonotidae

**Description**: White throat contrasting with chestnut face and black crown are diagnostic. Closely related to Ashy Bulbul and sometimes considered conspecific. Captive photo.

**Voice**: Various harsh notes and a loud, ringing call.

**Habits**: Found in wooded areas and dense scrub, from the lowlands up to 900 metres elevation. An adaptable species that has recently spread into Hong Kong, where it is doing well.

**Distribution**: Oriental region. A locally fairly common resident in southeast China, Hong Kong and northern Vietnam.

## BLACK BULBUL

*Hypsipetes madagascariensis* 25 cm (*Hypsipetes leucocephalus*)  F: Pycnonotidae

**Description**: Red bill and overall black plumage are diagnostic; two white-headed subspecies are found during winter. Captive photo.

**Voice**: A 4-note ringing call; also mewing and squawking notes.

**Habits**: Found in closed forest as well as secondary growth and along edges. Breeds at montane elevations between 500 metres and the tree limit. Outside the breeding season it disperses widely, also into lowlands. Moves about in noisy and active flocks, feeding on fruit and insects.

**Distribution**: Oriental region; northern populations migrate south. A fairly common resident in the north; mainly a winter visitor in the south, including Hong Kong.

## BLACK DRONGO

*Dicrurus macrocercus* 29 cm  F: Dicruridae

**Description**: Note its slender build and very long, deeply forked tail.

**Voice**: A variety of ringing calls.

**Habits**: The only exclusively open country drongo. Found in clearings, areas with long grass, cultivated fields and marshes. Sits on an open perch, often on a fence pole, telephone wire, exposed branch or the back of a domestic cow. Sallies out from its perch like a large flycatcher, to catch insects in the air.

**Distribution**: Oriental region, East Asia; migratory. A widespread and common resident and migrant on the mainland, including Hong Kong; winter visitor only on the Malay Peninsula, including Singapore.

## ASHY DRONGO
*Dicrurus leucophaeus* 29 cm  F: Dicruridae

**Description:** Shape much like the Black Drongo, but note its somewhat shorter tail; plumage variable with subspecies but never as shining black.

**Voice:** A mewing call.

**Habits:** Found in a variety of wooded habitats, from montane forests (as high as 3,900 metres), to coastal mangroves and open woodlands, especially during migration. A conspicuous bird often seen sitting high on an open branch at the edge of the forest. Flies out to catch insects in the air.

**Distribution:** Oriental region; migratory. A widespread, common resident; passage migrant and winter visitor throughout most of the region; an uncommon visitor in Hong Kong and Singapore; and a montane resident on Borneo.

## CROW-BILLED DRONGO
*Dicrurus annectans* 27 cm  F: Dicruridae

**Description:** Distinguished from other drongos by its stocky build and straight, slightly forked tail; immature bird (photo) has white streaks in underpart plumage.

**Voice:** A typical drongo call, with a loud whistle and harsh *churs*.

**Habits:** During migration, this bird is usually found in a variety of wooded habitats, from closed forest to coastal scrub and mangroves. Can turn up at any wooded location but is usually seen sitting alone in the middle storey, often concealed and generally less conspicuous than other drongos.

**Distribution:** Oriental region; breeds in Myanmar. Otherwise an uncommon migrant and winter visitor in parts of the region, including Singapore and northern Borneo; vagrant in Brunei and the Philippines.

# BRONZED DRONGO
### *Dicrurus aeneus* 23 cm  F: Dicruridae

**Description**: Small size and glossy sheen in plumage are diagnostic.

**Voice**: A variety of clear whistles and harsh notes.

**Habits**: A forest bird found in closed forest, from the lowlands to lower and occasionally upper montane elevations. Prefers clearings near primary forest, also river edges where it sits high on an exposed branch hawking for insects. A vocal, conspicuous and highly territorial species. The pair performs noisy displays at their favourite site.

**Distribution**: Oriental region; sedentary. A widespread and locally fairly common resident on the mainland and on Borneo; scarce in Brunei; extinct in Singapore.

# LESSER RACKET-TAILED DRONGO
### *Dicrurus remifer* 25 cm + tail  F: Dicruridae

**Description**: Look for diagnostic thin 'rackets' in tail.

**Voice**: Like other drongos, a variety of whistles; also mimics other birds' calls.

**Habits**: A montane species that begins to appear where the Greater disappears, i.e. from 800 metres and upwards to the tree limit; in the northern part of its range, also reported in the lowlands. Usually seen sitting passively in the middle storey of dark primary forest. Also joins mixed feeding flocks, the so-called bird waves.

**Distribution**: Oriental region. A locally fairly common resident in parts of the mainland and montane Peninsular Malaysia.

## SPANGLED DRONGO (Hair-crested Drongo)
*Dicrurus hottentottus* 32 cm   F: Dicruridae

**Distribution:** Oriental region, East Asia; northern populations migrate south. A fairly common resident and winter visitor on mainland, including Hong Kong and parts of Philippines; a mainly lower montane resident on Borneo; rare in Brunei.

**Description:** A large drongo with diagnostic, backward-turned tip of tail; one subspecies has thin, hair-like feathers on crown.

**Voice:** Typical for the family; melodious whistles mixed with harsh calls.

**Habits:** A forest bird that prefers secondary forest, clearings and woodlands at the edge of denser growth, from the lowlands up to 1,600 metres elevation. Hawks for insects from an open perch but also searches tree trunks for insects and termites and visits flowering trees for nectar. During migration will congregate in small flocks at prime feeding sites.

## GREATER RACKET-TAILED DRONGO
*Dicrurus paradiseus* 32 cm + tail   F: Dicruridae

**Distribution:** Oriental region. A common resident in most of the region, including Singapore and Brunei.

**Description:** Distinguished from the Lesser Drongo by its larger size and wider 'rackets' in its elongated tail feathers.

**Voice:** A confusing variety of melodious and very harsh calls; mimics other forest birds frustratingly well.

**Habits:** An adaptable forest bird found in primary rainforest, deciduous woodlands as well as forest edges and nearby scrub. Perches in the middle storey below the canopy, sallying for insects in the open space among the trees. Also joins bird waves and often follows monkeys around, catching prey they stir up. The breeding couple aggressively attacks intruders (including humans) near the nest.

# DARK-THROATED ORIOLE
## *Oriolus xanthonotus* 20 cm  F: Oriolidae

**Description**: A small bird; look for diagnostic black streaks on a white belly; female lacks black patterns of male (left) on head, chest, wings and tail. Note its undulating flight, with wings intermittently closed (right).

**Voice**: A characteristic, fluty song, like the Black-naped Oriole, but somewhat weaker.

**Habits**: Found in low densities in extreme lowland rainforest, in primary forest and mature secondary growth with large trees, not above 350 metres elevation. Usually located by call. Sometimes seen high in the canopy, or just below, feeding on insects or small fruit.

**Distribution:** Sunda subregion. An uncommon resident in south Thailand, Myanmar, Malaysia, Brunei and Palawan (Philippines); extinct in Singapore.

# BLACK-NAPED ORIOLE
## *Oriolus chinensis* 27 cm  F: Oriolidae

**Description**: Unmistakable, apart from its close relative the Slender-billed Oriole, *O. tenuirostris*, of the northern Oriental region; sometimes considered conspecific. Female somewhat duller than male (photo).

**Voice**: A loud, fluty whistle and a low hissing sound.

**Habits**: With a peculiar distribution (doesn't breed in Thailand and is absent from Borneo) this handsome bird is locally abundant in forest edges, mangroves, open coastal woodlands and even urban parks. A pair or small flock are usually seen, often late in the afternoon, flying from tree to tree, calling loudly. Feeds on fruit and large insects.

**Distribution:** Oriental region; northern populations migrate south. A common resident in the north, including Hong Kong, also in Peninsular Malaysia and Singapore; a common migrant elsewhere; vagrant in Borneo.

## BLACK-HOODED ORIOLE
### *Oriolus xanthornus* 25 cm  F: Oriolidae

**Description**: Distinguished from the Dark-throated Oriole by its bright yellow belly.

**Voice**: A fluty whistle, somewhat clearer than previous species.

**Habits**: Prefers dry deciduous forest and open woodlands; on the Malay Peninsula, lives in coastal mangroves only. Will move from the forest into nearby cultivation. A conspicuous bird, often seen high in the trees in the company of other birds, feeding on insects, fruit or nectar (as shown in this photograph). A few birds will sometimes move about together, calling out and chasing each other from tree to tree.

**Distribution**: Oriental region. A fairly common resident throughout the mainland, from Yunnan (south China) to Langkawi island (Malaysia); recorded from East Malaysia.

B. Van Elegem

## BLACK-AND-CRIMSON ORIOLE
### *Oriolus cruentus* 22 cm  F: Oriolidae

**Description**: Note bluish bill and red patch on breast (male, photo); female has red replaced with faint streaks of chestnut.

**Voice**: A short, melodious whistle; also a nasal *mew*.

**Habits**: A strictly montane species mostly found in a narrow range of 1,200 to 1,800 metres above sea level; locally between 500 and 2,400 metres. Stays in the forest, in the canopy or just below, feeding mainly on caterpillars and other invertebrates. Often participates in bird waves. Although this species is quite numerous, its nest has never been found.

**Distribution**: Sunda subregion. A locally fairly common resident in montane Peninsular Malaysia and Borneo.

Morten Strange

## ASIAN FAIRY BLUEBIRD
*Irena puella* 25 cm  F: Irenidae

**Description**: Unmistakable; photo shows male; female a uniform dull turquoise blue; some authors place it with the orioles in Oriolidae, or with leafbirds in either Irenidae or Chloropseidae.

**Voice**: A loud, liquid whistle *whee-eet*.

**Habits**: A forest bird found mainly in primary rainforest and adjacent secondary growth with large trees, from the lowlands into lower montane elevations. Usually moves at canopy level, only coming down briefly to pick fruit in the lower branches of fruiting fig trees, where several individuals sometimes congregate.

**Distribution**: Oriental region. A locally common resident in much of the region, including Singapore, Brunei and Palawan (Philippines).

## CRESTED JAY
*Platylophus galericulatus* 33 cm  F: Corvidae

**Description**: Distinguished from the Black Magpie, *Platysmurus leucopterus*, (of similar distribution, habitat, colour and behaviour) by its very long crest and white on neck (not in wing); both form their own genus. Captive photo.

**Voice**: A loud, harsh rattle.

**Habits**: A rainforest specialist found only in closed forest, occasionally near forest edges but always inside cover. Occurs mainly in the lowlands and sometimes in foothills to 750 metres elevation. Both of these forest Corvidae are noisy and rowdy. Often a resident pair are seen together, flying about in the dark middle storey below the canopy. The nest of this species has not been found.

**Distribution**: Sunda subregion. A generally uncommon resident in south Thailand, Myanmar and Malaysia; rare in Brunei.

# EURASIAN JAY
## *Garrulus glandarius* 33 cm  F: Corvidae

**Description**: Unmistakable; its white rump flashes brightly on take-off; northern race has white cheeks and black cap replaced with light chestnut head.

**Voice**: Mainly a loud, rasping *cha-ak*.

**Habits**: An arboreal bird found in deciduous forest, oak woodlands, pine forest and edges. Usually seen in pairs during breeding season, otherwise in small groups. Flies from tree to tree on rounded wings; drops to the ground to search for acorns, pine cones or invertebrate prey.

**Distribution**: Eurasia, the Oriental region; somewhat nomadic outside breeding season. A locally fairly common resident in China, including Hong Kong, Myanmar, Thailand and parts of Indochina.

# SHORT-TAILED MAGPIE (Indo-Chinese Green Magpie)
## *Cissa thalassina* 36 cm  F: Corvidae

**Description**: Distinguished (with difficulty) from following species, where ranges overlap, by its shorter tail and white edge of primaries. Also note the deeper green colour and dark red bill and feet.

**Voice**: A loud *keek-a-wee*.

**Habits**: Keeps to the lower montane forest on the mainland, from the foothills to 1,500 metres elevation. Recorded at 900 metres in China. On Mt. Kinabalu (Sabah) this species replaces the following at 1,000 metres elevation, extending much higher to 2,400 metres. Can sometimes be seen around the park headquarters. It keeps to closed forest where it feeds on large insects, caterpillars, frogs and snails.

**Distribution**: Southeast Asia, from south China into Java (Indonesia). An uncommon resident in parts of the mainland (excluding Cambodia) and East Malaysia.

## GREEN MAGPIE (Common Green Magpie)
### *Cissa chinensis* 38 cm  F: Corvidae

**Description**: Where ranges overlap, this bird is distinguished from the previous species (with difficulty) by its longer tail.

**Voice**: A peculiar variety of explosive whistles and chattering.

**Habits**: A mainly montane bird found between 300 and 1,600 metres elevation in Malaysia. In its northern range, found also in the lowlands. This shy bird prefers closed forest, often travels in pairs or as part of a bird wave, in the middle and lower storeys. Clambers about trees and creeper plants like a malkoha (Cuculidae) looking for small prey. Shuns open spaces and only flies briefly into next cover.

**Distribution:** Oriental region. A locally fairly common resident in the north and on low mountains in Malaysia.

## BLACK-BILLED MAGPIE
### *Pica pica* 45 cm  F: Corvidae

**Description**: Unmistakable. Note black-and-white plumage, long tail and white lower belly.

**Voice**: A loud, explosive rattle.

**Habits**: Found in deciduous forest edges, open country with scattered trees and cultivated areas. Often seen near villages, but not really tame. Omnivorous; often walks along on the ground looking for food. Has benefited from forest clearance within the region. The nest is a large, domed structure built of sticks inside a dense tree.

**Distribution:** Worldwide, Northern Hemisphere. A common resident in the north, including Hong Kong; rarer in the south, possibly expanding; recently recorded in Thailand.

## RUFOUS TREEPIE
### *Dendrocitta vagabunda* 43 cm  F: Corvidae

**Description**: Distinguished from the Grey Treepie, *D. formosae*, (which replaces this species in the northeastern parts of the mainland) by its rufous back and breast and pale wings.

**Voice**: A variety of rattling and raucous calls, mixed with some clear notes.

**Habits**: Found in a variety of wooded habitats, from deciduous forest to cultivated areas and edges of villages. Moves about high in the trees or briefly lower to feed, often in pairs. Omnivorous; at the center of its range in India, it is reported to approach houses to scavenge kitchen scraps.

**Distribution**: Oriental region. A generally uncommon resident in Myanmar, Thailand, and parts of Indochina and extreme southwest China.

## SUNDA TREEPIE
### *Dendrocitta occipitalis* 40 cm  F: Corvidae

**Description**: Unmistakable; photo shows Borneo subspecies by MacKinnon & Phillipps (1993) considered a separate species, *D. cinerascens*. Previously considered conspecific with the Grey Treepie, *D. formosae*, of the Oriental region.

**Voice**: A clear, bell-like whistle and rattling chattering.

**Habits**: An arboreal bird found in primary rainforest and in adjacent scrub and plantations. Often seen at the Kinabalu National Park Headquarters. A vocal and conspicuous bird, it moves through the canopy and the middle storey of the forest early in the morning on the lookout for large insects. It also takes some small fruits.

**Distribution**: Borneo and Sumatra. A fairly common resident in the mountains of Sabah and Sarawak.

# RACKET-TAILED TREEPIE
## *Crypsirina temia* 33 cm  F: Corvidae

**Description**: Combination of plumage, habitat, skulking, arboreal behavior are characteristic.

**Voice**: A soft mewing and a harsh *craak-craak*.

**Habits**: This treepie avoids the humid tropical parts of the Sunda subregion and can only be found in areas described here and in Java and Bali, Indonesia. It prefers the dry deciduous woodlands and coastal scrub adjacent to tidal mangroves; found from the beach inland to 900 metres elevation. In a suitable habitat it can be quite predictable, but is generally inconspicuous, creeping about among the low vegetation, seldom perching in the open. Best seen flying briefly from tree to tree.

**Distribution:** Southeast Asia into Bali (Indonesia). A widespread and fairly common resident throughout much of the mainland; uncommon in northern Peninsular Malaysia only.

# HOUSE CROW
## *Corvus splendens* 43 cm  F: Covidae

**Description**: Distinguished from other crows in the region by its grey back and chest.

**Voice**: A rasping *khaaak*.

**Habits**: Mainly an open country bird found in plains, fields with scattered trees, cultivated areas, sea coasts and villages, even in busy cities. Omnivorous; feeds on all edible matter, including human garbage. An intelligent, bold and opportunistic species that has settled far from its natural range (e.g. East Africa and Western Australia).

**Distribution:** Oriental region and west into Iran. Resident in southwest China and Myanmar; introduced into Peninsular Malaysia and Singapore where locally abundant; vagrant in Thailand and Cambodia.

## LARGE-BILLED CROW
*Corvus macrorhynchos* 51 cm  F: Corvidae

**Description:** Look for all-black plumage and large bill; Slender-billed Crow, *Corvus enca*, of the Sunda subregion (with Borneo) has a narrow bill and shallow wing beats.

**Voice:** Like House Crow, but deeper.

**Habits:** Found in forest edges and open country with large trees and coasts. Often seen near villages, but not really tame and does not usually enter populated areas (except in downtown Bangkok!). Omnivorous. Usually seen in pairs at evening roosts in mangroves; flocks will also congregate in large trees. The nest is a platform of sticks high in a tree.

**Distribution:** Oriental region. A widespread and common resident on the mainland, including Hong Kong and Singapore; the only Corvidae found throughout the Philippines; vagrant in Borneo.

## GREAT TIT
*Parus major* 13 cm  F: Paridae

**Description:** Note white cheeks contrasting with black head and chest.

**Voice:** A high-pitched, penetrating *chee-wit*.

**Habits:** Frequents a peculiar variety of habitats. In Europe this is a common garden bird at feeding tables and nesting boxes. In China it is mainly a forest bird; in Myanmar and Thailand it is restricted to montane forest above 800 metres; in Peninsular Malaysia it is found only in large, tidal mangrove forests on the western coast. An active feeder, it constantly flutters about, picking insects from the thin branches of small trees.

**Distribution:** Eurasia, Oriental region. A common resident in the north, including Hong Kong; further south it is mainly montane; an uncommon resident in mangroves on the Malay Peninsula; vagrant in Borneo.

## YELLOW-CHEEKED TIT
*Parus spilonotus* 14 cm  F: Paridae

**Description**: Unmistakable; photo shows male; female has the same pattern, but somewhat duller.

**Voice**: A frequent and loud *tee-cher*.

**Habits**: A montane resident found between 900 and 2,600 metres elevation. Occurs in forest and forest edges, and often in open and somewhat stunted mixed woodlands and pines. Typical of the family, it is an active and lively bird, moving quickly around the outside of the trees, from canopy level to near the ground, in constant search of tiny insects and larvae.

**Distribution**: Oriental region. A locally fairly common resident in the northern montane parts of the mainland; rare in Hong Kong.

## WHITE-FRONTED TIT
*Parus semilarvatus* 14 cm  F: Paridae

**Description**: Unmistakable; note dark plumage and distinct white forehead; Mindanao subspecies has a white patch in wing.

**Voice**: No information.

**Habits**: This distinct Philippine endemic occurs from lowland forest to 1,000 metres elevation. Found in forest and forest edges it can sometimes be seen perched in the open on a dead branch, often in pairs. Participates in mixed species bird waves. Otherwise little studied; feeding and breeding habits are unknown.

**Distribution**: Philippine endemic. An uncommon resident on the islands of Luzon and Mindanao only. Near-threatened with global extinction.

## SULTAN TIT
*Melanochlora sultanea* 20 cm  F: Paridae

**Description**: Unmistakable; the only member of its genus. Upperparts all-black in male; female somewhat duller; note yellow crest visible on the top bird.

**Voice**: A loud whistle *cheerie-cheerie* and other chipping and chattering notes.

**Habits**: A forest bird found in closed rainforest and deciduous forest, from the lowlands to the foothills, locally to 1,500 metres elevation. Unlike other tits, it travels high throughout the canopy and middle storey of the forest and is never observed at eye level. Often seen in pairs. An active and restless feeder, it searches through the outer foliage for insects and small fruits.

**Distribution**: Oriental region. A generally scarce resident in parts of the mainland, excluding Cambodia and Hong Kong.

## YELLOW-BROWED TIT
*Sylviparus modestus* 10 cm  F: Paridae

**Description**: A non-descript, warbler-like tit. Distinguished from similar leaf-warblers by its lack of pale supercilium and wing bars; yellow eyebrow not visible. Unique; the only member of its genus.

**Voice**: A thin *si-si-si-si*.

**Habits**: This upper montane specialist is resident only in the high mountains from 1,400 to 3,600 metres; disperses to somewhat lower elevations during the northern winter. A low density species and easily overlooked. It looks and behaves more like a leaf-warbler than a tit, moving quietly inside closed forests, often low in the trees and in the company of other species during bird waves.

**Distribution**: Oriental region. A scarce resident in the northern upper montane parts of the region.

## VELVET-FRONTED NUTHATCH
*Sitta frontalis* 12 cm  F: Sittidae

**Description**: Look for diagnostic red bill and black forehead; male has black eyebrow; missing in female (photo).

**Voice**: A sharp, ringing *chih-chih*.

**Habits**: An arboreal bird found in deciduous forest and rainforest, from the lowlands to lower montane elevations. The nuthatch pries insects and ants from the bark of trees like woodpeckers, but does not use its tail for support and therefore is a very agile climber. Runs up and down branches and trunks with amazing speed and ease, often with other insectivorous birds in bird waves.

**Distribution**: Oriental region. A widespread and locally fairly common resident in much of the region, including Brunei and Hong Kong (where possibly introduced); vagrant in Singapore.

## BLUE NUTHATCH
*Sitta azurea* 13 cm  F: Sittidae

**Description**: Unmistakable; dark blue upperparts appear black in poor light.

**Voice**: A high-pitched, squeaky *chee-chee*.

**Habits**: Restricted to montane forest above 900 metres. In Peninsular Malaysia, often seen at the hill stations, usually during bird waves when one or more waves move restlessly through the middle storey of the forest. This active bird runs in quick jerks up and down branches, probing for tiny invertebrates and quickly disappearing from sight. Although this species is quite numerous, its nest has never been found.

**Distribution**: Found only in Malaysia, Sumatra and Java (Indonesia). A locally common resident in montane Peninsular Malaysia.

## BROWN-THROATED TREECREEPER
*Certhia discolor* 16 cm  F: Certhiidae

**Description**: Unmistakable in Thailand and Indochina, where it is the only member of this family. Distinguished with difficulty in Myanmar and south China by it greyish-brown throat and belly.

**Voice**: A high-pitched *tchi-chip*.

**Habits**: A montane forest specialist found from 1,400 metres to the highest elevations; in China from 1,200 to 3,000 metres. Prefers primary forest with large shady trees. This is a passerine and not remotely related to woodpeckers, although it feeds like one. It runs up (never down) tree trunks prying tiny invertebrates from the bark. When it reaches the top branches it quickly flies down.

**Distribution**: Oriental region. A local and uncommon resident in montane parts of Myanmar, south China, northern Thailand, Laos and Vietnam.

## STRIPE-HEADED RHABDORNIS (Stripe-headed Creeper)
*Rhabdornis mystacalis* 16 cm  F: Rhabdornithidae

**Description**: Note prominent streaks on flanks; upperparts are brownish grey; photo shows male; female is paler.

**Voice**: A single, high note.

**Habits**: This is the most widespread and common member of a family with 3 members only, all in the same genus and endemic to the Philippines. It occurs in forest and forest edges from the lowlands to 1,200 metres elevation; also found in nearby clearings with scattered trees and in coconut groves. It hops along branches and the trunks of large trees picking invertebrates from the bark with its long, decurved bill; it also sometimes sits passively, high on a dead branch.

**Distribution**: A Philippine endemic. A locally fairly common resident on most major islands.

# BLACK-CAPPED BABBLER
## *Pellorneum capistratum* 18 cm  F: Timaliidae

**Description**: Note warm rufous underparts and black cap, contrasting with white throat.

**Voice**: An ascending whistle *pi-uu*.

**Habits**: Found in rainforest, mainly from primary lowland forest, to foothills at 750 metres elevation. A terrestrial bird that walks on the ground and makes a short low flight when disturbed. Feeds on small invertebrates in the leaf litter, only occasionally flying up to perch on a low branch as shown in the photo. Good views of this low density skulker are rare.

**Distribution:** Sunda subregion. A scarce resident in south Thailand, Myanmar, Malaysia and Brunei; extinct in Singapore.

# BUFF-BREASTED BABBLER
## *Trichastoma tickelli* 15 cm (*Pellorneum tickelli*)  F: Timaliidae

**Description**: Distinguished with difficulty from other babblers by its nondescript plumage, buffy-brown sides of its head and small bill.

**Voice**: A distinctive *pi-chew*.

**Habits**: Occurs in forest, often near the edges or in nearby bamboo thickets, from the lowlands to 2,100 metres; in Malaysia, found only in the lower montane range of 600 to 1,500 metres. A real skulker, typical of its genus, that hops around inside low cover, just off the ground, feeding on insects. Best located by call.

**Distribution:** Oriental region. A locally fairly common resident throughout most of the mainland; in Peninsular Malaysia, restricted to montane elevations.

## SHORT-TAILED BABBLER
*Trichastoma malaccense* 14 cm (*Malacocincla malaccensis*) F: Timaliidae

**Description**: Distinguished with difficulty from other babblers by its short tail and white throat and chest that contrast with its grey head and brown crown. Its call is diagnostic.

**Voice**: 4 to 5 clear, slow, descending notes.

**Habits**: Often calls at dawn. A lowland rainforest bird found in primary and mature secondary forest. It never leaves cover and never flies far. Hops about on the ground or on low sticks and fallen logs like a small mammal. Can be attracted by mimicking its call.

**Distribution**: Sunda subregion. A locally fairly common resident in south Thailand, Myanmar, Malaysia, Singapore and possibly Brunei.

## WHITE-CHESTED BABBLER
*Trichastoma rostratum* 15 cm  F: Timaliidae

**Description**: Distinguished with difficulty from other babblers by its bright white underparts that contrast with its uniformly brown upperparts. Its call is diagnostic.

**Voice**: A powerful whistle, *chee-swee-phew*.

**Habits**: Mainly found near water in wet lowland rainforest, peat swamps, near streams and also sometimes behind tidal mangroves. Secretive and shy, it moves low on or near the ground, often in pairs. Calls early in the morning from a hidden perch.

**Distribution**: Sunda subregion. A scarce resident in south Thailand, Myanmar, Malaysia, Brunei and Singapore. Regarded as near-threatened with global extinction.

## HORSFIELD'S BABBLER
*Trichastoma sepiarium* 15 cm (*Malacocincla sepiarium*) F: Timaliidae

**Description**: Distinguished with difficulty from other babblers by its thick bill and buff underparts, combined with grey face. Its call is diagnostic.

**Voice**: A loud *pee-oo-weet,* at early dawn.

**Habits**: Found in primary forest and forest edges, often near rivers and streams, from the lowlands to lower montane elevations. Seems to move a little higher in the vegetation than other *Trichastoma* babblers, hopping along low branches and creepers, inspecting the foliage for insects and ants.

**Distribution**: Sunda subregion. A scarce resident in south Thailand, Malaysia and Brunei.

## ABBOTT'S BABBLER
*Trichastoma abbotti* 16 cm (*Malacocincla abbotti*) F: Timaliidae

**Description**: Distinguished with difficulty from other babblers by its pale throat, buff belly and fairly long tail. Its call is diagnostic.

**Voice**: A clear, 3- to 4-note whistle, the last note always sharply higher.

**Habits**: A fairly adaptable bird, on Borneo restricted to primary lowland rainforest, but elsewhere found also in secondary forest, mangroves and nearby scrub and, in Singapore, even in some gardens. Moves near the ground, clambering through the dense undergrowth. Calls in the dim light of dusk and dawn and will come out to investigate if its call is mimicked.

**Distribution**: Oriental region. A widespread and fairly common resident in the south of mainland, including Singapore; uncommon in Borneo, including Brunei.

## MOUSTACHED BABBLER
*Malacopteron magnirostre* 18 cm  F: Timaliidae

**Description**: Distinguished with difficulty from following species by a faint black stripe that separates its white throat and grey head.

**Voice**: A rich whistle of 4 to 5 descending notes.

**Habits**: Occurs deep inside primary forest, in forest edges and closed secondary growth. Found mainly in the lowlands; locally to 900 metres elevation. Numerous in favourable habitats in southern Thailand and Taman Negara (Malaysia); in other areas less so. It moves through the forest at eye level or slightly higher, flying restlessly from branch to branch.

**Distribution**: Sunda subregion. A locally fairly common resident in south Thailand, Myanmar and Malaysia; uncommon in Brunei; rare in Singapore.

## SOOTY-CAPPED BABBLER
*Malacopteron affine* 17 cm  F: Timaliidae

**Description**: Look for a dark slaty crown and greyish (not brown) upperparts.

**Voice**: A pretty song of about 8 whistling tones on an undulating scale.

**Habits**: A lowland rainforest bird found in primary forest and nearby secondary growth and edges. Typical of *Malacopteron* babblers, it moves within the lower and middle storeys in the forest, never on the ground itself. Gleans invertebrates from the foliage. The nest is a small cup placed above the ground, inside a densely leafed tree.

**Distribution**: Sunda subregion. A locally fairly common resident in Malaysia and Brunei; rare in south Thailand.

## SCALY-CROWNED BABBLER
*Malacopteron cinereum* 17 cm   F: Timaliidae

**Description**: Look for pink legs and pale chest; scales on rufous crown are sometimes visible.

**Voice**: 5 to 6 whistling notes, ascending slowly.

**Habits**: A forest bird found in primary rainforest and mature secondary forest, mainly in the lowlands; locally also found at lower montane elevations. Moves in the lower storey of the forest, hopping along inside the undergrowth, occasionally up into the middle storey. Calls all through the morning, but never stays long in one place.

**Distribution**: Southeast Asia into Java (Indonesia). A locally fairly common resident in southern Indochina, south Thailand, Malaysia and Brunei.

## RUFOUS-CROWNED BABBLER
*Malacopteron magnum* 18 cm   F: Timaliidae

**Description**: A fairly chunky babbler; distinguished from the similar Scaly-crowned Babbler by size, grey (not pink) legs, grey streaks on chest and 'clean' rufous-black crown.

**Voice**: Like Sooty-capped Babbler, but more varied; up to 12 clear, undulating whistles rising at the end.

**Habits**: Much like the Scaly-crowned Babbler, except it does not venture into montane forest. Seen moving at eye-level through the forest, sometimes up into the middle storey, never onto the ground itself. A vocal and active bird that hops along slowly, never resting for long. Also participates in bird waves.

**Distribution**: Sunda subregion. A scarce resident in south Thailand and Myanmar; locally common in Malaysia and Brunei.

## CHESTNUT-BACKED SCIMITAR-BABBLER
### *Pomatorhinus montanus* 20 cm  F: Timaliidae

**Distribution**: Sunda subregion. A scarce resident in Malaysia and Brunei.

**Description**: Unmistakable within its range; in south Thailand and the northern mainland it is replaced by the White-browed Scimitar-babbler, *P. schisticeps*, which appears to be identical except for a rufous (not black) crown. Captive photo.

**Voice**: A loud, mellow *hoot-hoot-hoot*.

**Habits**: Occurs in primary and mature secondary rainforest, mainly inside closed forest; occasionally seen around the edges. Moves through the middle storey below the canopy and sometimes down to eye level. Feeds on insects, grubs and sometimes fruit and nectar. The nest is a ball of vegetation made of leaves and grasses, placed low in the undergrowth.

## STRIPED WREN-BABBLER
### *Kenopia striata* 14 cm  F: Timaliidae

**Distribution**: Sunda subregion. A generally scarce resident in south Thailand and Malaysia; not recorded from Brunei; extinct in Singapore.

**Description**: Distinguished from other babblers by its small, chunky size combined with a distinct head pattern and white underparts streaked with black. A unique bird, the only member of its genus.

**Voice**: A clear whistle, *ti-ki-tii*.

**Habits**: A rainforest bird restricted to lowland forest and often somewhat swampy alluvial areas from sea level to 300 metres elevation. Moves low inside primary forest; also in secondary forest with undergrowth of palms or creepers. Can be lured out with a tape playback, to sing from a low perch, as this striking photograph demonstrates.

## MOUNTAIN WREN-BABBLER
### *Napothera crassa* 15 cm  F: Timaliidae

**Description**: Sometimes overlaps at lower elevations with the following species. Look for a general dark appearance and lack of white eyebrow. Sometimes treated as subspecies of Streaked Wren-babbler, *N. brevicaudata,* of mainland Southeast Asia.

**Voice**: Low churring and chattering notes; also a shrill whistle.

**Habits**: A strictly montane species found in primary forest from 1,300 to 2,500 metres elevation. Prefers the darker areas around wet gullies, steep hills with small streams and rocky ravines with dense bamboo and undergrowth. Here it moves about, staying inside cover, as this rare photograph shows. Its nest has never been found.

**Distribution:** A Borneo endemic. A scarce resident in the mountains of Sabah and Sarawak.

## EYE-BROWED WREN-BABBLER
### *Napothera epilepidota* 11 cm  F: Timaliidae

**Description**: Distinguished from other wren-babblers by its pale throat, sides of head and supercilium; also note its short tail.

**Voice**: A loud *peeeow* and some chattering and churring notes.

**Habits**: A forest bird found mainly in primary forest from 900 to 2,100 metres elevation. In East Malaysia, occurs to 1,700 metres elevation; in parts of its range, notably in Peninsular Malaysia, also in lowland forest. Locally probably fairly numerous in a favourable habitat, but keeps low inside the undergrowth so good views of this shy bird are rare.

**Distribution:** Oriental. A locally fairly common resident in montane parts of the mainland; uncommon in Malaysia.

## PYGMY WREN-BABBLER
### *Pnoepyga pusilla* 9 cm  F: Timaliidae

**Description**: Distinguished from other wren-babblers by its small size; note complete lack of tail. Photo shows individual carrying nesting material.

**Voice**: A sharp 2- to 3-note whistle, descending slowly.

**Habits**: Strictly montane; found only in closed forest above 1,200 metres elevation; in Taiwan found between 2,000 and 2,500 metres. Hops along the forest floor, appearing more like a mouse than a bird. Flies quickly up on roots and fallen logs. Good views are difficult, but the species is often located by its penetrating call.

**Distribution**: Oriental region. A widespread and locally fairly common resident in montane parts of the mainland, excluding Hong Kong.

## GOLDEN BABBLER
### *Stachyris chrysaea* 13 cm  F: Timaliidae

**Description**: Unmistakable; bright yellow underparts with slightly darker upperparts and some faint black streaks on head are diagnostic.

**Voice**: A soft whistle *pi-pi-pi-pi*, trailing off.

**Habits**: Restricted to montane forest from 900 to 2,000 metres elevation. Never seen alone; always in small flocks or with other species in waves. Doesn't perch for long, is always on the move. Flutters through thickets, just off the ground or at eye level, hunting the abundance of small invertebrates found in this habitat.

**Distribution**: Oriental region. A locally fairly common resident in montane parts of the mainland.

## GREY-THROATED BABBLER
*Stachyris nigriceps* 15 cm F: Timaliidae

**Description**: Distinguished with difficulty from other babblers by its pale malar stripe, contrasting with its grey throat.

**Voice**: A high-pitched, rattling whistle *pree-pree-eee*.

**Habits**: Mainly a lower montane species found in rainforest from 300 to 1,800 metres elevation; found also in the lowlands, in its northern range. A typical shy babbler, staying within cover. Moves through the lower storey in primary forest or forest edges, usually just off the ground. Often spotted together with other birds in bird waves, but good views are difficult.

**Distribution:** Oriental region. A locally fairly common resident mainly in montane parts of the region.

## GREY-HEADED BABBLER
*Stachyris poliocephala* 15 cm F: Timaliidae

**Description**: Distinguished with difficulty from other babblers by its warm chestnut plumage contrasting with its uniformly grey head.

**Voice**: A song of 2 to 4 wavering notes.

**Habits**: A lowland rainforest bird found in primary and mature secondary forest. A typical skulker, staying inside cover, shy and rarely seen well. Moves low through the undergrowth, chattering softly, often in the company of other birds during bird waves.

**Distribution:** Sunda subregion. A scarce resident in south Thailand, Malaysia and Brunei.

## CHESTNUT-RUMPED BABBLER
*Stachyris maculata* 17 cm  F: Timaliidae

**Description:** Look for chunky size and scaly underparts; chestnut rump noticeable from behind.

**Voice:** A loud series of hooting notes, *who-hoop who-hoop*.

**Habits:** Found in primary rainforest and mature secondary forest and edges; restricted to lowland forest and forested swamps. A shy bird. Although generally a low density species, it will sometimes suddenly appear in noisy groups, moving conspicuously through the lower and middle storeys, calling and displaying agitatedly to each other.

**Distribution:** Sunda subregion. An uncommon resident in south Thailand, Malaysia and Brunei; extinct in Singapore.

## CHESTNUT-WINGED BABBLER
*Stachyris erythroptera* 14 cm  F: Timaliidae

**Description:** Distinguished with difficulty from other babblers by its blue orbital ring and malar stripe; note also chestnut wings contrasting with grey underparts.

**Voice:** A rapid series of low, hooting whistles, *hoop-hoop-hoop*.

**Habits:** A lowland rainforest bird found in primary and mature secondary forest and edges. Moves constantly through the lower storey, rarely above eye-level, usually just off the ground, gleaning tiny invertebrates from the foliage as shown in the photo. A skulking species, but not shy. Can be attracted by mimicking its call; however it rarely emerges from cover so good views are difficult.

**Distribution:** Sunda subregion. A locally fairly common resident in south Thailand, Myanmar, Malaysia and Brunei; uncommon in Singapore.

## STRIPED TIT-BABBLER
*Macronous gularis* 13 cm  F: Timaliidae

**Description**: Notice the diagnostic broad streaks on yellowish throat and chest.

**Voice**: A resonant, monotonous *chuck chuck chuck* repeated incessantly; also a harsh churring rattle while feeding.

**Habits**: Not really arboreal, although associated with forest; prefers forest edges, nearby low scrub and overgrown cultivation, and dense gardens. Always seen in small groups, jumping about inside cover. Flies only briefly, low across the ground, to reach the next bush quickly. Picks invertebrate prey from the leaves and stems. The nest is a domed ball of vegetation with a side entrance, built in a dense bush near the ground.

**Distribution**: Oriental region. A widespread and common resident through much of the region, including Brunei, Singapore and Palawan (Philippines).

## FLUFFY-BACKED TIT-BABBLER
*Macronous ptilosus* 15 cm  F: Timaliidae

**Description**: Notice the very dark brown plumage; black throat contrasting with chestnut cap and blue orbital ring are diagnostic.

**Voice**: A loud, hollow *poop-poop-poop*.

**Habits**: Although found near primary forest, this species has a tendency to venture outside the forest into nearby edges and clearings with thick re-growth. Restricted to lowland rainforest, often near swampy areas. It always moves near the ground, often in pairs, sometimes performing noisy displays.

**Distribution**: Sunda subregion. A locally fairly common resident in south Thailand, Malaysia and Brunei; extinct in Singapore.

## MASKED LAUGHINGTHRUSH (Black-faced Laughingthrush)
### *Garrulax perspicillatus* 30 cm  F: Timaliidae

**Description:** Broad black mask and a grey head are diagnostic.

**Voice:** A variety of loud, laughing calls, especially a strident *piew, piew.*

**Habits:** One of the most numerous members of this large family within its range; occurs in all wooded habitats and cultivated areas, also near villages where dense cover is available. Moves in small groups, low through the thickets. It breeds from March to August, building a large cup-shaped nest inside thick undergrowth.

**Distribution:** Oriental region. A widespread and locally common resident in south-east China, including Hong Kong, and south into northern Vietnam.

## SUNDA LAUGHINGTHRUSH
### *Garrulax palliatus* 30 cm  F: Timaliidae

**Description:** Unmistakable; underparts a warm grey; note pale blue orbital skin.

**Voice:** A variety of whistling and harsher notes.

**Habits:** This babbler occurs in primary rainforest and forest edges from 850 to 2,200 metres elevation. Regularly seen at the Mount Kinabalu Park Headquarters in Sabah, this bird moves low through the undergrowth early in the morning, often emerging near the roads. A few are always on the move together, calling to each other, and during the day can be seen in bird waves.

**Distribution:** Endemic to Sumatra and Borneo. A locally fairly common resident in montane parts of East Malaysia.

## WHITE-THROATED LAUGHINGTHRUSH
*Garrulax albogularis* 30 cm  F: Timaliidae

**Description**: A bright white throat contrasting with an olive-brown breast band are diagnostic; belly light brown. Captive photo.

**Voice**: A harsh call, often in chorus; also low chattering.

**Habits**: A strictly montane laughingthrush found from 600 to 4,500 metres; on the mainland, usually above 2,700 metres; on Taiwan from 850 to 1,500 metres. Moves through conifers and other montane vegetation in noisy groups.

**Distribution**: Oriental region. A locally fairly common resident in montane parts of south China, north Vietnam and Taiwan.

## WHITE-CRESTED LAUGHINGTHRUSH
*Garrulax leucolophus* 30 cm  F: Timaliidae

**Description**: Unmistakable; no other *Garrulax* babbler has a similar striking head pattern. Captive photo.

**Voice**: A noisy, melodious, laughing call.

**Habits**: Found in a variety of wooded habitats, from forest to secondary growth and bamboo thickets in lowlands, up to lower montane elevations at 1,200 metres. Always moves around in small flocks, jumping and flying with long glides through the lower and middle storeys. Often drops down to the ground to feed. When several birds start calling in chorus, the racket is deafening.

**Distribution**: Oriental region. A widespread and locally common resident on much of the mainland; fairly common in Singapore (introduced).

## GREATER NECKLACED LAUGHINGTHRUSH
### *Garrulax pectoralis* 33 cm  F: Timaliidae

**Description**: Distinguished from the sympatric and similar Lesser Necklaced Laughingthrush, *G. monileger*, by its black moustache and streaks on cheeks, clearly visible in the photo.

**Voice**: A descending laughter, *kow-ow-ow*.

**Habits**: A conspicuous denizen of deciduous woodlands, from the lowlands to 1,200 metres elevation. Often found in teak and oak forests and also nearby cultivation. Like other Garrulax babblers, small groups move through low trees, calling out loudly and frequently dropping to the ground to feed.

**Distribution**: Oriental region. A locally fairly common resident in northern and western parts of the mainland, including Hong Kong; escapees occur in Singapore.

## BLACK LAUGHINGTHRUSH
### *Garrulax lugubris* 26 cm  F: Timaliidae

**Description**: Unmistakable; note all-black plumage and reddish bill, contrasting with blue orbital skin.

**Voice**: A variety of clear *hoopoop* notes mixed with a harsher 'laughing' call.

**Habits**: Occurs in primary rainforest and occasionally forest edges in the lower montane range from 900 to 1,800 metres elevation. It moves in small groups through the lower and middle storeys of the forest, sometimes with other species during bird waves. This low density species, not numerous anywhere has been little studied; its nest has never been found. Usually shy and rarely seen well, this individual stopped briefly to sun itself in the open.

**Distribution**: Sunda subregion. A generally scarce resident in montane parts of Malaysia; one sighting from Brunei.

# BLACK-THROATED LAUGHINGTHRUSH
## *Garrulax chinensis* 30 cm  F: Timaliidae

**Description**: The combination of white cheek patch with black throat and slaty-grey head are diagnostic. Captive photo.

**Voice**: A thrush-like song, combining musical whistles with harsher notes.

**Habits**: Mainly found in mixed forest, deciduous woodlands, in secondary growth and nearby scrub, from the lowlands to lower montane elevations. Often mixes with other laughingthrushes in feeding parties moving through the forest.

**Distribution**: Mainland Southeast Asia only. A locally fairly common resident in parts of the mainland, including Hong Kong.

# GREY-SIDED LAUGHINGTHRUSH
## *Gallulax caerulatus* 28 cm  F: Timaliidae

**Description**: Note black lores and ocular region, also ochraceous throat and chest contrasting with pale grey belly; wings and tail are rufous. Captive photo. The Taiwan subspecies, *G. poecilorhynchus,* is sometimes treated as the full species, the Rufous, Rusty or Scaly-headed Laughingthrush.

**Voice**: A loud, human-like whistle.

**Habits**: A montane forest species found in closed forest and bamboo thickets from 1,100 metres up to the tree limit. It moves low through the vegetation in small groups.

**Distribution**: Oriental region. Resident in mountains in south China and north Myanmar; locally common in Taiwan; recorded as an escapee in Hong Kong.

# CHESTNUT-CAPPED LAUGHINGTHRUSH
## *Garrulax mitratus* 25 cm  F: Timaliidae

**Description**: Note diagnostic white patch in wing, visible when perched and flying.

**Voice**: A varied song of slurred whistles.

**Habits**: A montane rainforest bird found mainly between 800 and 2,000 metres elevation; on Borneo between 300 and 3,000 metres. A successful species found in primary forest and disturbed edges and in gardens. Perhaps the most numerous bird at Malaysian hill stations and popular resorts like Kinabalu National Park. Moves through the middle and lower storeys of the vegetation. An omnivorous bird, it can become quite tame locally and picks up rice at garden feeding tables.

**Distribution**: Sunda subregion. A common resident in montane parts of Malaysia; locally abundant.

# HWAMEI
## *Garrulax canorus* 25 cm  F: Timaliidae

**Description**: Distinguished from other laughingthrushes by faint dark streaks in tawny brown plumage and conspicuous eye-ring; its chinese name means 'painted eyebrow'. Captive photo.

**Voice**: A loud, varied song more like a thrush than a babbler.

**Habits**: Found in forest edges, dense woodlands, scrub and nearby gardens. Stays inside cover and regularly jumps down to the ground. Often located by call; its attractive voice has made it a popular cage bird.

**Distribution**: Oriental region. A widespread and fairly common resident in south China, including Hong Kong, northern Vietnam and Laos; introduced in Singapore.

## WHITE-BROWED LAUGHINGTHRUSH
*Garrulax sannio* 25 cm  F: Timaliidae

Description: Note distinct white eyebrow and cheeks; also warm chestnut-brown body and tail.

Voice: A variety of musical calls, especially a ringing *piow, piow.*

Habits: Found in open woodlands and cultivation; also moves into grasslands with scrub and villages; mainly found in the mountains above 600 metres elevation, rarely lower. Moves low through the thickets in small groups and can be quite approachable. The nest is placed low inside a bush.

**Distribution:** Oriental region. A locally fairly common resident in northern parts of the mainland, south to northern Thailand; uncommon in Hong Kong.

## MOUNTAIN MORRISON LAUGHINGTHRUSH
*Garrulax morrisonianus* 28 cm  F: Timaliidae

Description: Note chestnut-brown sides of head and golden-olive streak in wing. Treated by De Schauensee (1984) as a subspecies of the Black-faced Laughingthrush, *G. affinis,* in the Himalayas.

Voice: A variety of high-pitched, rolling and whistling notes.

Habits: This is a strictly montane babbler found only in the upper montane zone between 2,000 and 3,300 metres elevation. Moves low in the stunted alpine woodlands, often dropping to the ground to feed on insects and berries, as shown in the photograph.

**Distribution:** A Taiwan endemic. A locally fairly common resident in montane parts of the island.

# CHESTNUT-CROWNED LAUGHINGTHRUSH
## *Garrulax erythrocephalus* 27 cm  F: Timaliidae

**Description:** Note chestnut-brown crown as well as bright golden-olive primaries in wing.

**Voice:** A fluty whistle, also a high-pitched *hee-hee-hee*.

**Habits:** Mainly an upper montane species found from 1,300 metres to the tree limit. Occurs in closed forest and occasionally overgrown edges. In spite of its size and colour, not an easy bird to see well. Stays inside cover in the middle or lower storeys and glides off further into the forest as soon as disturbed.

**Distribution:** Oriental region. A fairly common resident in montane parts of the mainland including Peninsular Malaysia.

# RED-TAILED LAUGHINGTHRUSH
## *Garrulax milnei* 27 cm  F: Timaliidae

**Description:** Several northern babblers have red wings, but notice the combination of rufous crown and grey face with the wings; upperside of tail red. Captive photo.

**Voice:** Loud strident whistles and chattering contact calls.

**Habits:** Strictly montane, usually found at upper montane elevations above 1,800 metres, locally sometimes down to 1,000 metres. A shy bird that moves through the dense undergrowth of closed forest in small groups. Good views are difficult. Sometimes displays agitatedly by lifting tail and wings.

**Distribution:** Oriental region. An uncommon resident in the mountains in the northern part of the mainland; rare in Thailand. Near-threatened with global extinction.

## RED-FACED LIOCICHLA
*Liocichla phoenicea* 24 cm  F: Timaliidae

**Description**: Note the diagnostic red orbital area and cheeks. Captive photo.

**Voice**: A loud musical song *chi-chweew tu-reew-ri;* also low chattering and a rattling alarm call.

**Habits**: A strictly montane species usually found at upper montane elevations between 1,400 and 2,200 metres; during winter down to 1,000 metres. This shy bird stays low inside cover in forest and dense forest edges; prefers damp and dark areas.

**Distribution**: Oriental region. A rare resident in northern montane parts of the mainland; uncommon in Thailand.

## SILVER-EARED MESIA
*Leiothrix argentauris* 18 cm  F: Timaliidae

**Description**: Unmistakable; male (photo) has maroon red rump.

**Voice**: A slurred song mixed with clear whistles; also a low chattering while feeding.

**Habits**: A montane bird found in rainforest from 1,300 to 2,000 metres elevation; seen locally down to 900 metres. Always in small vocal feeding parties, moving low through primary forest, nearby scrub and bamboo thickets. Skulking and restless, but tame. A bird wave that includes a large flock of this delightful species constitutes the highlight of birdwatching in the region.

**Distribution**: Oriental region. A locally fairly common resident in montane parts of the mainland; locally numerous in Peninsular Malaysia; introduced in Hong Kong.

## RED-BILLED LEIOTHRIX (Peking Robin)
*Leiothrix lutea* 16 cm  F: Timaliidae

**Description:** Unmistakable; note red bill and bright yellow throat. Captive photo.

**Voice:** A fine melodious song, like a weak version of the Hwamei's.

**Habits:** A montane bird found in closed forest from 900 to 2,700 metres elevation; outside the breeding season also found lower, often in nearby scrub, bamboo and cultivated areas. Moves through the vegetation in small groups, keeping to the low undergrowth. A popular cage bird, escapees can turn up outside its natural range.

**Distribution:** Oriental region. A locally fairly common resident in south China, including Hong Kong; uncommon in northern Vietnam and Myanmar.

## CUTIA
*Cutia nipalensis* 20 cm  F: Timaliidae

**Description:** Unmistakable, the only member of its genus; both build and coloration unlike any other babbler. Photo shows female; male has uniformly rufous mantle and rump.

**Voice:** A rising *hweeet*.

**Habits:** A montane bird found in primary forest between 1,200 and 2,700 metres elevation. Occasionally ventures out to trailedges and roadsides. Moves somewhat heavily through the middle storey of the forest, flying briefly from branch to branch. It clambers about in creepers and epiphytes looking for invertebrate prey, as shown in this rare photograph from Fraser's Hill in Malaysia.

**Distribution:** Oriental region. A generally scarce resident in northwestern parts of the mainland and in montane Peninsular Malaysia; rare in Thailand.

## WHITE-BROWED SHRIKE-BABBLER
*Pteruthius flaviscapis* 13 cm   F: Timaliidae

**Description**: Unmistakable; note prominent, white eyebrow and chestnut-brown patch in wing, partly obstructed here; female is duller.

**Voice**: A 4-note whistle, *chi-chewp, chi-chewp*.

**Habits**: Strictly a montane bird, found exclusively in closed forest between 800 and 2,200 metres elevation. Unlike other small babblers, this one moves fairly high in the trees, often seen on large branches in the middle storey, hunting for insects. Often seen in resident pairs. It also participates in bird waves.

**Distribution:** Oriental region. A locally fairly common resident throughout montane parts of the mainland and East Malaysia; vagrant in Hong Kong.

## BLACK-EARED SHRIKE-BABBLER
*Pteruthius melanotis* 11 cm   F: Timaliidae

**Description**: Distinguished from the following species by the dark patch behind ear. Photo shows female; male is brighter, with white wing stripes.

**Voice**: A thin, high-pitched *si-si-see* and *too-weet*.

**Habits**: A strictly upper montane babbler found in low densities inside forest between 1,400 and 2,200 metres elevation in Thailand; in China between 1,200 and 2,400 metres. Like other members of this genus it moves fairly high inside the middle storey of primary forest and into forest edges, but rarely comes into the open and good views are difficult.

**Distribution:** Oriental region. A locally fairly common resident throughout montane parts of the mainland and East Malaysia; vagrant in Hong Kong.

# CHESTNUT-FRONTED SHRIKE-BABBLER
## *Pteruthius aenobarbus* 11 cm  F: Timaliidae

**Description:** Male (photo) has distinct chestnut-brown forehead and throat, showing well from this angle; female distinguished (with difficulty) from previous species by lack of black 'ear'.

**Voice:** Chattering and whistling notes and a warbler-like song, *ka-chip, ka-chip*.

**Habits:** Mainly a lower montane species found in forest and forest edges between 900 and 1,700 metres elevation; occasionally seen higher, recorded to 2,500 metres. Often seen briefly as it moves high through the trees with other species in a bird wave, often in pairs. Since appearance and habits are similar to the previous species, care should be taken to tell them apart.

**Distribution:** Oriental region south to Java (Indonesia). A generally uncommon resident in montane parts of the mainland, excluding Malaysia.

# WHITE-HOODED BABBLER
## *Gampsorhynchus rufulus* 24 cm  F: Timaliidae

**Description:** Distinguished from the White-headed Bulbul, *Hypsipetes thompsoni*, (Family: Pycnonotidae) by its rufous (not grey) plumage, pink (not red) bill and longer tail. Unique among babblers and the only member of its genus.

**Voice:** A distinctive, harsh *kaw-ke-yawk*.

**Habits:** A lower montane specialist occurring in forested areas between 500 and 1,800 metres elevation. It depends on closed primary forest, but often ventures out to the edges, perching low in nearby bamboo and dense scrub. Also participates in bird waves. A low density species that is rarely seen; does not appear to be numerous anywhere.

**Distribution:** Oriental region. A scarce resident in montane parts of the mainland.

## SPECTACLED BARWING
*Actinodura ramsayi* 24 cm  F: Timaliidae

**Description**: Look for distinct eye-ring and fine black barring on wings and tail.

**Voice**: A series of clear, descending notes *tu-tui-tui-tui-tuuu*.

**Habits**: Occurs in montane forest from 1,000 to 2,100 metres. Moves through the upper or middle storey of the forest, flying from branch to branch, often appearing briefly near edges of forest and roadsides. Sometimes moves low into nearby scrub. Fairly numerous within its small world range and is often spotted at Doi Inthanon in Thailand.

**Distribution**: Mainland Southeast Asia only. A locally fairly common resident in montane parts of Myanmar, south China, Thailand, Laos and Vietnam.

## FORMOSAN BARWING
*Actinodura morrisoniana* 18 cm  F: Timaliidae

**Description**: Note the chestnut-brown head and streaked breast and neck.

**Voice**: No information.

**Habits**: This is an upper montane specialist found only from 1,400 to 2,800 metres. Moves fairly low through the deciduous montane forest, preferring to stay inside cover, as the photograph shows. Can be seen at the island's major montane birding spots: the forest north of Wushe and the Hsitou Forest Recreation Area further south.

**Distribution**: Taiwan endemic. A resident in the montane parts of the island.

## BLUE-WINGED MINLA
### *Minla cyanouroptera* 16 cm  F: Timaliidae

**Description:** Quite distinctive, with a long tail and pale grey plumage. Photo shows the Malay Peninsula race, *M. c. sordidior;* the northern race has more blue in its wing and a blue crown.

**Voice:** A clear, 2-tone whistle, *pi-piu.*

**Habits:** A montane species found mainly from 900 to 2,000 metres; during summer, in its northern range, up to 3,000 metres. Moves restlessly through the middle and upper storey of montane rainforest, in small vocal groups, often with other species in bird waves.

**Distribution:** Oriental region. A locally common resident in montane parts of the mainland.

## CHESTNUT-TAILED MINLA
### *Minla strigula* 17 cm  F: Timaliidae

**Description:** Unmistakable; note its diagnostic checkered throat.

**Voice:** A slurred whistle.

**Habits:** This is an upper montane specialist found only from 1,800 to 3,700 metres. In Peninsular Malaysia, only found in the Cameron Highlands region (peak: 2,032 metres). Doi Inthanon (the highest mountain in Thailand at 2,565 metres) is a good location for this species. This forest bird often moves in chattering flocks, low through the undergrowth and emerges near trails, roads and gardens where it can be virtually tame.

**Distribution:** Oriental region. A locally fairly common resident in montane parts of the mainland.

## RUFOUS-WINGED FULVETTA
*Alcippe castaneceps* 11 cm  F: Timaliidae

**Description**: Its small size, a distinctive head pattern and rufous streak in wing are diagnostic.

**Voice**: A quiet warbling song and a frequent contact call, *tsi-tsi-tsirr*.

**Habits**: Found in montane forest from 900 to 2,700 metres, usually in the higher parts of this range; in China, recorded down to 300 metres. Moves quickly through the lower storey of the forest, often just off the ground. Mobile and restless, it never flies far. Has a peculiar habit of clinging briefly to vertical, moss-covered tree trunks, as shown in the photo. Always seen in small groups and a certain participant in montane bird waves.

**Distribution:** Oriental region. A locally fairly common resident in upper montane parts of the mainland.

Morten Strange

## STREAK-THROATED FULVETTA
*Alcippe cinereiceps* 11 cm  F: Timaliidae

**Description**: Note the diagnostic combination of a uniformly greyish head and throat, with distinct pale and black streaks in wing.

**Voice**: A rattling song of 3 to 4 notes.

**Habits**: A montane fulvetta that occurs in forest between 1,400 and 2,700 metres; outside this area, recorded down to 650 metres and to the highest vegetation limit at 4,600 metres. Moves low, concealed in the undergrowth inside closed forest, feeding on insects.

**Distribution:** Oriental region. A locally fairly common resident in northern montane parts of the mainland, excluding Thailand and Hong Kong.

Samson So

## BROWN FULVETTA
*Alcippe brunneicauda* 15 cm  F: Timaliidae

**Description:** Lacks distinctive features; distinguished from other babblers by its pale underparts and lack of markings on greyish head.

**Voice:** A series of descending, high-pitched whistles, *pi-pi-pi-pi*.

**Habits:** A rainforest bird found in primary and mature secondary forest, from the lowlands and occasionally into lower montane elevations. Moves between the lower and middle storeys of the forest, feeding mainly on invertebrates, often as part of mixed species flocks; also takes some fruit.

**Distribution:** Sunda sub-region. A generally scarce resident in south Thailand, Malaysia and Brunei.

## MOUNTAIN FULVETTA
*Alcippe peracensis* 16 cm  F: Timaliidae

**Description:** Note prominent black head stripe; distinguished from the following species by its pale grey (not buff) underparts.

**Voice:** A somewhat faint whistling song, ascending on the last note.

**Habits:** A montane rainforest bird found from the foothills up into the upper montane habitat. Moves through the lower storey of primary forest and forest edges, always part of mixed species bird waves within its range. Skulking and restless behavior, but very tame and fairly easy to observe.

**Distribution:** Mainland Southeast Asia only. A locally common resident in montane parts of Peninsular Malaysia and Indochina; uncommon in Thailand.

## GREY-CHEEKED FULVETTA
*Alcippe morrisonia* 15 cm  F: Timaliidae

**Description:** Unmistakable within its range and altitude; the similar Brown-cheeked Fulvetta, *A. poioicephala*, of the lowlands, has pale brown cheeks, throat and eye.

**Voice:** A soft whistle, alternating with squeaking and buzzing notes.

**Habits:** A montane babbler found in primary forest and edges from 900 to 3,000 metres. During the northern winter, it moves lower. Abundant in a suitable habitat; seems to participate in all the montane bird waves. Moves inside the vegetation, from the middle storey down to just off the ground, in a constant, frantic search for invertebrates.

**Distribution:** Oriental region. A locally common resident in montane parts of the mainland and on Taiwan; an uncommon visitor to Hong Kong.

## RUFOUS-BACKED SIBIA
*Heterophasia annectens* 20 cm  F: Timaliidae

**Description:** Distinguished from the following species by rufous wing coverts and lower back; also note faint rufous hues on lower belly.

**Voice:** Four clear, whistling notes; also a harsh chatter.

**Habits:** A montane species found in primary forest from 1,000 to 2,000 metres; in its northern range, down to 600 metres. Also emerges at forest edges to catch insects, but generally stays high in the middle storey and inside denser cover than the following species.

**Distribution:** Oriental region. A locally fairly common resident in northwestern montane parts of the mainland.

## BLACK-HEADED SIBIA
*Heterophasia melanoleuca* 23 cm  F: Timaliidae

**Distribution:** Mainland Southeast Asia only. A locally common resident in northern montane regions of the mainland.

**Description:** Unmistakable; distinguished from the previous species by its black back and rump.

**Voice:** A ringing musical whistle of 5 clear notes; also a rattling alarm call.

**Habits:** An upper montane specialist found only in forest above 1,000 metres elevation to the tree limit. A conspicuous and confident babbler that moves from the highest tree tops to the ground; often seen at forest edges and clearings. At montane picnic areas it feeds in the open on dead insects and crumbs.

## LONG-TAILED SIBIA
*Heterophasia picaoides* 30 cm  F: Timaliidae

**Distribution:** Oriental region. A locally fairly common resident in montane regions of the mainland; locally numerous in montane Peninsular Malaysia.

**Description:** Unmistakable; as its Latin species name indicates, this bird seems more like a magpie (Corvidae) than a babbler.

**Voice:** A single, ringing note repeated incessantly, *tsiip-tsiip-tsiip*.

**Habits:** A montane species occurring mainly between 900 and 1,800 metres; found locally to 3,000 metres. Always seen in vocal flocks, fluttering through the trees at canopy or mid-storey level in primary forest or forest edges and even gardens. Not shy, but always on the move. Doesn't seem to mix with other species.

## STRIPE-THROATED YUHINA
*Yuhina gularis* 15 cm  F: Timaliidae

**Description**: Note distinct crest, wing pattern and striped throat, best seen on bird at left.

**Voice**: A distinct, nasal mewing.

**Habits**: An upper montane species found in the 1,200 to 3,000 metre zone; found somewhat lower in winter. Moves in the middle and lower storeys of closed forest and forest edges, visiting flowering trees and often mixing with other birds in bird waves.

Tim Loseby

**Distribution**: Oriental region. A locally fairly common resident in northwestern montane parts of the mainland.

## CHESTNUT-CRESTED YUHINA
*Yuhina everetti* 14 cm  F: Timaliidae

**Description**: Unmistakable; note white underparts contrasting with grey upperparts and chestnut cap sometimes raised into a crest.

**Voice**: A low *chit-chit*.

**Habits**: A montane species found mainly in the lower montane habitat, from the foothills up to 1,800 metres. Behaves more like a warbler (Sylviidae) than a babbler. Always in small chattering flocks. It moves through the forest at the middle storey or canopy level fluttering from one tree to the next, searching among the thin branches for tiny invertebrates.

Morten Strange

**Distribution**: Borneo endemic. A locally common resident in the mountains of Sabah and Sarawak.

## WHITE-BELLIED YUHINA
*Yuhina zantholeuca* 12 cm  F: Timaliidae

**Description**: Its size, plumage (white/olive-green) and behavior all appear warbler-like (Sylviidae), but note distinct crest and lack of features in wing and head.

**Voice**: A high-pitched *si-si-si*.

**Habits**: A successful forest bird in the deciduous and seasonal forests of the subtropics; less numerous in the wet rainforest in the tropical Sunda subregion. Occurs at lowland as well as lower montane altitudes; found locally up to 1,800 metres. Moves restlessly through the middle storey and canopy, often in bird waves with other species.

**Distribution:** Oriental region. A widespread and locally common resident in the northern part of the mainland, including Hong Kong; uncommon in Malaysia; rare in Brunei.

## WHITE-BROWED SHORTWING
*Brachypteryx montana* 15 cm  F: Turdidae

**Description**: Male (photo) unmistakable; female is dark brown.

**Voice**: A short, warbling song; also an abrupt alarm call, *tack*.

**Habits**: A strictly upper montane species found above 1,400 metres and mostly from 2,000 to 3,000 metres. Moves on or near the ground much like a wren-babbler, often near a small stream. A shy skulker that sometimes ventures out in the open, near a trail or clearing.

**Distribution:** Oriental region. A locally fairly common but generally scarce resident in high mountains on the mainland as well as Taiwan, Borneo and the larger Philippine islands.

## SIBERIAN RUBYTHROAT
*Luscinia calliope* 17 cm  F: Turdidae

**Description:** Distinguished from the much rarer White-tailed Rubythroat, *L. pectoralis*, by its brown (not greyish-black) plumage. Photo shows male; female has white (not red) throat.

**Voice:** A musical whistle, *chee-wee*.

**Habits:** Found during the northern winter, from Nov to April. In winter quarters it can turn up in a variety of habitats, from forest edges and secondary growth, to scrub and grasslands. Often seen near water, from the lowlands to 1,200 metres. A skulker which moves about low inside thickets and bushes; during the day it sometimes (but not often) flies across open ground.

**Distribution:** Breeds in northern East Asia; winters in the Oriental region. A common winter visitor throughout the mainland, including Hong Kong; rare in the Philippines and Peninsular Malaysia; a single record from Brunei.

## SIBERIAN BLUE ROBIN
*Luscinia cyane* 15 cm  F: Turdidae

**Description:** Photo shows female; note upright, flycatcher-like posture; male has dark blue upperparts contrasting sharply with bright white underparts.

**Voice:** A thin, ascending *see-ik* and a quiet, hard *tuck*.

**Habits:** Like the previous species, is widespread during migration, but usually flies further south where it seeks closed forest for winter quarters. Found in a variety of wooded habitats, from primary lowland rainforest to drier forests and occasionally gardens. Often hops on the ground, in a clearing or along a forest trail, feeding on insects; also flies up quickly to perch inside a low bush.

**Distribution:** Breeds in northeast Asia; winters in the Oriental region, south to Sumatra. A fairly common passage migrant and winter visitor on the mainland, including Singapore; rare in Hong Kong; vagrant in the Philippines and Brunei.

## MAGPIE ROBIN (Oriental Magpie Robin)
*Copsychus saularis* 23 cm  F: Turdidae

**Description:** Unmistakable; photo shows male; in the female black parts are replaced by slaty grey.

**Voice:** A clear, melodious song; also a rasping alarm call.

**Habits:** Found in forest edges, mangroves, cultivated areas, villages and gardens throughout the lowlands into lower montane elevations. Has benefited from forest clearance, but has suffered from capture for the bird trade. Sings from an open perch in the morning and can become quite tame in parks and gardens, often hopping on the lawn looking for invertebrate prey.

**Distribution:** Oriental region. A widespread and common resident in most of the region, including Hong Kong; uncommon in the Philippines; rare in Singapore.

## WHITE-RUMPED SHAMA
*Copsychus malabaricus* 28 cm  F: Turdidae

**Description:** Note white rump and long tail; rufous belly provides sharp contrast to black chest. Male shown in photo; female is a duller colour.

**Voice:** A rich and melodious song of nightingale-like quality; also a harsh alarm call.

**Habits:** Found in a variety of forested habitats, from lowland rainforest to secondary growth and deciduous woodlands. Very shy and difficult to view well, but its powerful song is often heard. Sometimes spotted flying away into the forest, white rump flashing brightly. A popular cage bird.

**Distribution:** Oriental region. A widespread and locally fairly common resident in much of the region, including Brunei; rare in Singapore.

# WHITE-VENTED SHAMA (Palawan Shama)
## *Copsychus niger* 20 cm  F: Turdidae

**Description**: Unmistakable within its range. Note white vent. One of the 3 shamas endemic to the Philippines, in addition to the following species and the White-browed Shama, *C. luzoniensis*, of Luzon and some smaller islands.

**Voice**: A rich, melodious song similar to the Common Blackbird's.

**Habits**: A forest bird that can be found at the islands' main forest reserves, the Balsahan Trail and St. Paul's National Park, where this rare photograph was taken. Like other Shamas, it is shy and good views are rare. However, it will respond to a taped play-back of its call. Please use this method with restraint, as it does stress the bird.

**Distribution**: Philippine endemic. A locally fairly common resident on Palawan and some smaller nearby islands.

# BLACK SHAMA
## *Copsychus cebuensis* 20 cm  F: Turdidae

**Description**: Unmistakable within its tiny range. Entirely glossy black, including bill and feet.

**Voice**: The song is a melodious vibrato.

**Habits**: Survives in small numbers in secondary forest, scrub and nearby cultivation on Cebu. Little of its authentic habitat is left on the island. Scrub near Casili is believed to hold 50 birds and it also occurs within the Central Cebu National Park at Tabunan, where this photograph was taken. Shy, skulking and mostly only heard; it does respond to a taped play-back.

**Distribution**: Philippine endemic. Found only on the island of Cebu, where it is local and scarce. Endangered with global extinction.

## PLUMBEOUS REDSTART
### *Rhyacornis fuliginosus* 14 cm  F: Turdidae

**Description**: Unmistakable. Photo shows male; female is greyish with scaled white underparts and distinct white rump.

**Voice**: A short, sharp, whistle, *kree*.

**Habits**: Habitat and habits similar to River Chat. A specialized riverside species occurring around clear, fast-flowing rivers in forested areas. It is resident from 800 metres to the highest summits; during winter it descends to lower elevations. Often seen in pairs, feeding in the river valley, never far from the water. Often seen flying low across the water and perching on boulders along the stony banks, as shown in the photo.

**Distribution:** Oriental region; somewhat nomadic. An uncommon resident and winter visitor in northern parts of the mainland, including Hong Kong.

## LUZON WATER-REDSTART
### *Rhyacornis bicolor* 14 cm  F: Turdidae

**Description**: Unmistakable within its range. The only riverine thrush in the Philippines.

**Voice**: No information.

**Habits**: Found along clear, fast-flowing rivers in forested areas from 300 metres upwards. Still a regular sighting along rivers in areas like Mt Pulog and Mt Polis, but pollution and siltation of streams by logging and mining operations has caused a decline of this species. Habits reported to be very similar to previous species; no nesting records to date.

**Distribution:** Philippine endemic. An uncommon resident in the northern part of Luzon island. Endangered with global extinction.

# WHITE-TAILED ROBIN
## *Cinclidium leucurum* 18 cm  F: Turdidae

**Description**: Note the diagnostic tail pattern showing well in this photo of a male. The female is brown, but has the same tail feature.

**Voice**: A powerful, whistling song of 7 to 8 notes.

**Habits**: Strictly a montane forest bird found in closed forest from 1,000 to 2,400 metres. In the northern part of its range, it tends to move lower during the winter months before the breeding season. It is a low density, secretive bird that shuns human habitation. Occasionally it can be seen briefly on the ground along forest edges or trails, as this rare photograph shows.

**Distribution:** Oriental region. A scarce resident in montane parts of the mainland.

# CHESTNUT-NAPED FORKTAIL
## *Enicurus ruficapillus* 20 cm  F: Turdidae

**Description**: Distinguished from other forktails by chestnut cap and scaly breast. Photo shows female; male has chestnut cap only (not full mantle and back).

**Voice**: Piercing, shrill whistles.

**Habits**: A specialized forest bird found in low densities along small, forested rivers and streams. Flies out to perch on the forest floor, trails and low vegetation nearby, but always returns to the water. Runs and flies along the vegetated banks and picks up insects, somewhat like a Grey Wagtail. Generally extremely shy and restless; often located by its high-pitched call, but difficult to approach and view well.

**Distribution:** Sunda subregion. A scarce resident in south Thailand, Myanmar, Malaysia and Brunei.

## SLATY-BACKED FORKTAIL
### *Enicurus schistaceus* 25 cm  F: Turdidae

**Distribution**: Oriental region. A locally fairly common resident in montane parts of the mainland; an uncommon visitor to Hong Kong.

**Description**: Distinguished from the similar Black-backed Forktail, *E. immaculatus,* overlapping in range in Myanmar and northwest Thailand by slaty (not black) crown and mantle.

**Voice**: A penetrating *chick.*

**Habits**: Like other members of this genus, it frequents forested streams and rivers. This species is a lower montane specialist found between 400 and 1,800 metres; in its northern range found at lower elevations in winter; in Peninsular Malaysia found above 900 metres elevation. Runs in flowing water picking up insects; also sometimes flies out with a heavily undulating flight to perch on nearby rocks and roadsides.

## WHITE-CROWNED FORKTAIL
### *Enicurus leschenaulti* 28 cm  F: Turdidae

**Distribution**: Oriental region. A widespread but generally scarce resident on the mainland and on Borneo including Brunei; not recorded in Singapore or Hong Kong.

**Description**: Distinguished from the Spotted Forktail, *E. maculatus* by its smooth, black (not white-spotted) mantle; note prominent white forehead. Overlaps with *E. maculatus* in extreme northern range.

**Voice**: A sharp, high-pitched screech.

**Habits**: Found along forested streams, usually slow narrow creeks inside dense vegetation. In its northern range, often seen in elevated areas to 2,000 metres. In the Sunda subregion, found mainly in lowland rainforest. Feeds on the ground near water or in nearby open areas, but is very shy, so good views are difficult. Usually seen in a glimpse as it flushes and flies deeper into the forest.

# BLACK-BREASTED FRUIT-HUNTER (Black-breasted Triller/Jeffery)
## *Chlamydochaera jefferyi* 21 cm  F: Turdidae

**Description**: Unmistakable; the only member of its genus. Photo shows male; female has grey on belly and mantle replaced with brown. Smythies (1981) places it with Campephagidae.

**Voice**: No information.

**Habits**: Found in closed forest at montane elevations. It has been reported from Mt Kinabalu (where this rare photograph was taken), Mt Mulu and some nearby less visited peaks. Feeds on fruit and can be spotted in fruiting trees where it behaves like a pigeon. Otherwise rarely seen and little studied; its nest has never been described.

**Distribution**: A Borneo endemic. A rare resident on mountains in Sabah and Sarawak.

# GREEN COCHOA
## *Cochoa viridis* 28 cm  F: Turdidae

**Description**: Distinguished from the sympatric but rarer Purple Cochoa, *C. purpurea,* by white patches in its wings, seen well here on this male. Female has white wing patches mixed with green.

**Voice**: A pure, short whistle.

**Habits**: A strictly montane thrush with quiet and sluggish behaviour. Found in primary forest from 900 to 2,700 metres, usually in the upper parts of this range. Often spotted in the tall branches of fruiting trees, tries to stay within the canopy. Also can come lower, even landing on the ground. Feeds on insects.

**Distribution**: Oriental region. A scarce resident in northern montane parts of the mainland.

## STONECHAT
*Saxicola torquata* 14 cm  F: Turdidae

**Description:** Female (photo). Distinguished from following species by its paler brown plumage. Male has black head and mantle separated by white neck. Eastern Palearctic populations sometimes treated as the Siberian Stonechat, *S. maura*.

**Voice:** A subdued alarm call, *chack chack,* like two stones struck together.

**Habits:** Occurs in open country. During migration this successful bird spreads out widely and can turn up in patches of cleared grassland from coastal lowlands near the beach to mountains at 2,000 metres. Perches low, in open terrain, on a grass stem, a small bush or a wire; flies quickly from there to catch insects and larvae.

**Distribution:** Breeds in temperate and subtropical Eurasia, winters in Africa; Oriental region. A common winter visitor in northern parts of mainland, including Hong Kong; uncommon further south, including Singapore; rare in north Borneo, including Brunei.

## PIED BUSHCHAT
*Saxicola caprata* 13 cm  F: Turdidae

**Description:** Male (right) all black with distinct white rump and wing patch; female (left) dark brown with rusty rump.

**Voice:** A short, weak song; also faint alarm call, *chack chack*.

**Habits:** An open country species found in grasslands with scattered trees, scrub, fields and other cultivation, from the lowlands to lower montane elevations. Sits on a low, exposed perch, calling softly, sometimes flicking its tail upwards. Flies out to grab insects on the ground.

**Distribution:** Middle East through the Oriental region, east to New Guinea. A locally common resident in parts of the mainland and the Philippines; vagrant in Borneo, including a single record in Brunei.

# GREY BUSHCHAT
## *Saxicola ferrea* 16 cm  F: Turdidae

**Description**: Note grey plumage and black face mask of male (left). Female like immature (right) but without buffy streaks.

**Voice**: A short warbling song, also a soft *churr* and a harsher *bzech*.

**Habits**: Resident mainly in hills and at higher altitudes to 2,500 metres. During winter, disperses more widely to low-lying areas. Frequents forest edges and scrub. During migration is found in more open terrain. Fairly conspicuous and vocal. Sits low on an open perch and flies out to catch insects.

**Distribution:** Oriental region; partly migratory. A widespread and fairly common resident and winter visitor in northern parts of the mainland; uncommon winter visitor in Hong Kong and Taiwan.

# RIVER CHAT
## *Thamnolaea leucocephala* 19 cm  F: Turdidae

**Description**: Unmistakable. Sexes are alike with maroon rump and tail, and black terminal band.

**Voice**: A sharp *teee*.

**Habits**: This attractive, active bird is found along wide rivers, mainly at montane elevations. In the Himalayas it occurs far above the timber line to 4,800 metres elevation. During winter it disperses widely and can be found at low elevations as well along rocky rivers and streams. Perches on the ground or on boulders or debris along the water, often cocking its tail.

**Distribution:** Oriental region into central Asia; partly migratory. An uncommon resident and winter visitor in northern parts of the mainland; vagrant in Hong Kong.

# CHESTNUT-BELLIED ROCK-THRUSH
## *Monticola rufiventris* 24 cm  F: Turdidae

**Description**: Male (photo) distinguished from following species by its chestnut chest and dark throat and mask; female brown with fine white scales on underparts.

**Voice**: A short, whistling song, *tii-teru;* also a chattering alarm call.

**Habits**: Mainly a montane resident, breeding in montane forest between 1,000 and 3,000 metres. During winter it disperses widely and turns up in the nearby lowlands. Breeds in closed forest, but often comes out to forest edges, to perch on a high exposed branch or a road-side wire, as this photo shows.

**Distribution:** Oriental region; partly migratory. An uncommon resident and winter visitor in northern parts of the mainland, including Hong Kong.

# BLUE ROCK-THRUSH
## *Monticola solitarius* 23 cm  F: Turdiae

**Description**: Photo shows male; some males have uniform dark blue plumage, with faint, pale scaling and black bill. Female is dark brown with fine buff scales.

**Voice**: A short, melodious song; also a soft, croaking call.

**Habits**: Breeds in rocky hills and in open forest with limestone outcrops, from the seacoast to low mountains at 1,800 metres. Outside breeding season, it disperses widely and can turn up in open country. It often settles on a prominent perch such as a rock, a rooftop or a pole, holding its body upright and bobbing down quickly. Flies out low to catch insects on the ground.

**Distribution:** Eurasia, Oriental region; migratory. A widespread resident and winter visitor recorded in all countries and territories; fairly common in northern parts; rarer further south.

# BLUE WHISTLING-THRUSH
## *Myiophoneus caeruleus* 32 cm  F: Turdidae

**Description:** Large thrush. Note faintly scaled blue plumage; some migrants have dark bill.

**Voice:** A rich, whistling song; also a harsh *scree*.

**Habits:** Found mainly in closed montane forest, from foothills to tree limit above 3,000 metres. During migration seen also in lowland rainforest and mangroves. Prefers dense, shady areas near rocky streams, where it perches low on a rock or fallen log. In spite of its size and beautiful plumage, this is a shy and elusive bird, not easy to view well.

**Distribution:** Oriental region, into central Asia; northern populations migrate south. A widespread resident and winter visitor on mainland, including Hong Kong; locally common in Thailand, but generally scarce.

# CHESTNUT-CAPPED THRUSH
## *Zoothera interpres* 17 cm  F: Turdidae

**Description:** Diagnostic combination of slaty-grey upperparts and tail with chestnut cap. Captive photo.

**Voice:** A melodious song that has been compared to the White-rumped Shama's, but pitched higher.

**Habits:** A lowland rainforest bird apparently restricted to primary forest in very low densities. There are few records of this species, but it has been seen by some observers on the trails of Malaysian national parks like Taman Negara and the Danum Valley (Sabah). Shy and retiring, it moves low, hopping on or near the ground. Feeds on fallen fruit.

**Distribution:** Southeast Asia. A rare resident in south Thailand, Malaysia and parts of the southeast Philippines; not recorded in Brunei.

## ORANGE-HEADED THRUSH
### *Zoothera citrina* 22 cm  F: Turdiae

**Distribution:** Oriental region; migratory, reaching Sumatra (Indonesia). An uncommon resident and passage migrant in the north, including Hong Kong; an uncommon winter visitor further south, including Singapore; a rare resident in montane Sabah (Borneo).

**Description:** Unmistakable; orange-rufous head and underparts diagnostic. Captive photo.

**Voice:** A clear and variable song with short repeated themes, also a low alarm call, *tjuck*.

**Habits:** Found in closed forest, from the lowlands to lower montane elevations; during migration also found in nearby scrub. A ground-dwelling bird, often seen hopping on the forest floor and sometimes on low branches. Sings from a higher perch. Feeds by turning fallen leaves to catch tiny invertebrate prey. Is generally shy and retiring and difficult to view well.

## SIBERIAN THRUSH
### *Zoothera sibirica* 24 cm  F: Turdidae

**Distribution:** Breeds in Northeast Asia; winters in Southeast Asia. An uncommon passage migrant in the north of the region, including Hong Kong; a locally fairly common winter visitor on the Malay Peninsula; rare in Singapore.

**Description:** Female (photo) distinguished with difficulty from other thrushes by head pattern and lack of white scales in rufous-brown upperparts. The male is unmistakable, with dark plumage and white supercilium ('eye-brow').

**Voice:** A quiet *chit* during migration.

**Habits:** An arboreal thrush found in closed forest, from the lowlands to the mountains, usually in small flocks. Feeds on the ground on insects, and high in fruiting trees. Quite shy; stays inside cover.

# COMMON BLACKBIRD
## *Turdus merula* 25 cm  F: Turdidae

**Description**: Photo shows male sunning, note yellow bill. Female a uniform dark brown, with pale throat.

**Voice**: A melodious song, also a harsh, rattling alarm call.

**Habits**: Found in open woodlands, scrub and cultivated areas in the lowlands as well as montane altitudes. An adaptable, locally tame species that comes into gardens. Seems to be expanding its range. Feeds on invertebrates on or near the ground; during winters also takes fruit.

**Distribution:** Eurasia; partly migratory. A fairly common resident in south China; a fairly common winter visitor in Hong Kong; an uncommon visitor in northern Indochina; rare in Thailand and Cambodia.

# ISLAND THRUSH (Mountain Blackbird)
## *Turdus poliocephalus* 22 cm  F: Turdidae

**Description**: Similar appearance to Black-breasted Thrush, *T. dissimilis,* of central Asia, but dark breast is paler. No overlap in ranges.

**Voice**: A clear, melodious song typical of the genus; also a rattling alarm call.

**Habits**: A strictly montane species within the region. On Pacific islands further east, also found in the lowlands. Found from 900 metres all the way to the limit of bushy vegetation above 3,500 metres. Moves low in the stunted montane forest, often dropping down to feed on the ground. Somewhat skulking habits, but sometimes sings from an open perch.

**Distribution:** Oriental region and Pacific islands. A locally common resident in high mountains in Sabah (Borneo), Taiwan and parts of the Philippines.

307

## EYE-BROWED THRUSH
### *Turdus obscurus* 23 cm  F: Turdidae

**Distribution:** Breeds in northern Siberia; winters in the Oriental region. A widespread but generally uncommon winter visitor in most of the region, including Hong Kong, Singapore and Brunei.

**Description:** Look for diagnostic white supersilium with orange-hued chest and flanks. Photo shows female; male has grey head and brighter flanks and chest.

**Voice:** During winter just a thin contact call, *tseep*.

**Habits:** Arboreal thrush found in a variety of wooded habitats from rainforest, mangroves and parks in the lowlands, to conifers at upper montane elevations. Although generally scarce, it can turn up locally in large numbers during peak migration in November-February, sometimes congregating in fruiting bushes and trees.

## FLYEATER (Golden-bellied Gerygone)
### *Gerygone sulphurea* 9 cm  F: Sylviidae

**Distribution:** Southeast Asia into Bali (Indonesia). A locally common resident in south Thailand, Malaysia, Singapore and most of the Philippines; not recorded in Brunei.

**Description:** Appearance plain, but is easy to recognise in the field, being very vocal. Taxonomic dispute over family: Lekagul & Round (1991) use the family Acanthizidae; Lim & Gardner (1997), the family Pardalotidae.

**Voice:** A slurred, wheezy song, usually a descending *zwee-zwee-zwee*.

**Habits:** Found mainly in mangroves in Thailand; in the rest of its range, found also in rainforest, coastal woodlands, and parks and gardens. Moves through the upper and middle storeys, gleaning invertebrates from the thin branches, with a quiet, constant call. The nest is a suspended pouch.

## CHESTNUT-CROWNED WARBLER
### *Seicercus castaniceps* 10 cm  F: Sylviidae

**Description**: Distinguished from the Mountain Tailorbird by its yellow wing stripe and white eyering.

**Voice**: A thin, whistling song of 3 to 6 notes.

**Habits**: This warbler is resident in montane forest from 1,200 to 2,400 metres. During winter in the north migrates to lower and warmer elevations. It moves low inside closed forest; sometimes also seen along forest edges. This individual is carrying food to the nest. Often part of montane bird waves, but being small and quick it can easily be overlooked when many birds move by at once.

**Distribution**: Oriental region; partly migratory. A locally fairly common resident in montane parts of the mainland; a rare winter visitor to Hong Kong.

## YELLOW-BREASTED WARBLER
### *Seicercus montis* 10 cm  F: Sylviidae

**Description**: A small bird; note lemon-yellow underparts, olive upperparts and rufous head.

**Voice**: A thin, high-pitched song, undulating up and down the scale.

**Habits**: A forest bird found in lower and upper montane rainforest between 900 and 2,200 metres. A restless feeder, constantly jumping through the thin branches of the middle and upper storeys, hunting for insects and larvae. Also participates in bird waves.

**Distribution**: Southeast Asia to Sumatra (Indonesia). A locally fairly common resident in montane parts of Malaysia and Palawan (Philippines).

# RADDE'S WARBLER
*Phylloscopus schwarzi* 14 cm  F: Sylviidae

**Description**: Distinguished with difficulty from the sympatric Dusky Warbler, *P. fuscatus* (12 cm), by its longer bill and legs, and tawny under tail coverts, showing well in this photograph.

**Voice**: A low *twit-twit* and a harsher *tschak-tschak*.

**Habits**: In winter quarters frequents a wide variety of wooded habitats except closed forest. Can be found in open deciduous forest, forest edges, scrub and grasslands with some cover. Often seen in foothills and at moderate elevations between sea level and 2,000 metres. Skulks low inside thickets like other members of this genus.

**Distribution**: Breeds in northern East Asia; winters in Southeast Asia. A locally fairly common winter visitor in parts of the mainland; rare in Hong Kong.

# INORNATE WARBLER
*Phylloscopus inornatus* 11 cm  F: Sylviidae

**Description**: Distinguished from other *Phylloscopus* warblers by a combination of prominent creamy supercilium (no additional crown-stripe) and double wing bar, showing well here.

**Voice**: A distinctive, ascending *wee-eest*.

**Habits**: During winter, from Sep–Apr, it settles in all wooded habitats from closed forest to open woodlands and parks and gardens. It can be found from coastal lowlands to upper montane elevations at 2,000 metres. An active bird, it feeds on insects, mainly in the tree tops, but can sometimes be seen fluttering through all levels of the forest.

**Distribution**: Breeds in temperate and subarctic Asia; winters in the Oriental region, reaching Sumatra. A widespread and generally common winter visitor throughout mainland, including Hong Kong; rare in Peninsular Malaysia and Singapore.

## ASHY-THROATED WARBLER
### *Phylloscopus maculipennis* 9 cm  F: Sylviidae

**Description:** Distinguished with difficulty from the White-tailed Leaf-warbler by its darker underparts with yellow wash on flanks and rump; also by its small black bill.

**Voice:** A high-pitched *zip* and a sweet *sweechoo*.

**Habits:** A strictly upper montane warbler breeding only between 2,100 and 3,050 metres. A so-called vertical migrant, northern populations move down to 800 metres during winter. In Thailand, only Doi Inthanon is high enough for this species where it is abundant near the summit. It occurs in closed forest, frequently seen low along forest edges, roads and trails.

**Distribution:** Oriental region; partly migratory. A locally common resident in upper montane parts of the mainland.

## ARCTIC WARBLER
### *Phylloscopus borealis* 12 cm  F: Sylviidae

**Description:** Distinguished with difficulty from other *Phylloscopus* warblers by its long, slender shape, greyish-olive plumage and one faint wing bar.

**Voice:** A hard *zheet*.

**Habits:** During migration, found mainly in the lowlands, in all kinds of woodlands, from primary rainforest to mangroves and even parks and gardens with large trees. Moves high in the thin branches, picking off tiny insects. Must be an abundant breeding bird in the Siberian land mass, judging from the large numbers that visit Southeast Asia during peak migration.

**Distribution:** Breeds in arctic and subarctic Eurasia; winters in the tropics. A widespread and common passage migrant and winter visitor in all countries and territories.

# EASTERN CROWNED WARBLER
## *Phylloscopus coronatus* 13 cm  F: Sylviidae

**Description**: Note diagnostic yellow vent contrasting with white belly; also look for dark crown-stripe; has thin yellow bar in wing.

**Voice**: A shrill *zweet*.

**Habits**: More arboreal than other migratory warblers. Is sometimes seen in parks and gardens, but is more likely to be found in closed forest, from mangroves and lowland forest into lower montane elevations reaching 1,800 metres. Flutters high through the trees hunting insects and grubs.

**Distribution**: Breeds in northern East Asia and winters in the Oriental region reaching Java (Indonesia). A widespread and locally common passage migrant and winter visitor in the region; uncommon in Hong Kong and Singapore.

# WHITE-TAILED LEAF-WARBLER
## *Phylloscopus davisoni* 11 cm  F: Sylviidae

**Description**: Note yellow wash in greyish supercilium and underparts; white in tail is difficult to see in the field.

**Voice**: A soft, metallic song.

**Habits**: Found in montane forest, upwards from 1,000 metres. Partly migratory, it moves to lower elevations during the cold season. Numerous in a suitable habitat and often seen in forest and forest edges, where it moves from the middle storey to just off the ground, feeding on small insects and grubs. Quite approachable; comes in close but quickly moves on, constantly flying from perch to perch.

**Distribution**: Oriental region; partly migratory. A widespread and locally common resident in montane parts of the mainland; not recorded in Cambodia; unconfirmed sightings in Hong Kong.

## MOUNTAIN LEAF-WARBLER (Island Leaf-warbler)
### *Phylloscopus trivigatus* 11 cm  F: Sylviidae

**Description**: Easily recognised by yellow underparts, black eye- and crown-stripes, and lack of wing bars.

**Voice**: A thin, high-pitched song; also a short, contact call: *twit*.

**Habits**: Occurs in montane rainforest between 800 and 3,000 metres, where it is often locally numerous and the only *Phylloscopus* warbler. Flies restlessly through the canopies and outer foliage of tall trees and low bushes in primary forest and forest edges. Constantly on the move, searching for insects and caterpillars, as this attractive photo from Fraser's Hill in Peninsular Malaysia shows.

**Distribution:** Sunda subregion into eastern Indonesia. A locally common resident in montane parts of Malaysia and the major Philippine islands.

## CLAMOROUS REED-WARBLER
### *Acrocephalus stentoreus* 18 cm  F: Sylviidae

**Description**: Distinguished from the following species with great difficulty by lack of streaks on breast.

**Voice**: A loud, warbling song and some harsher call notes; vocal.

**Habits**: Always found near water, usually lakes and marshlands with large reeds beds; also seen in scrub behind tidal mangroves. Solitary or in resident pairs; does not mix with other birds. Secretive and skulking; sometimes ventures out to sing from an open perch - often a reed stem - sitting in a characteristic, upright manner as seen in this photo.

**Distribution:** North Africa and east across the Oriental region into Australasia; mainly sedentary. An uncommon resident in Myanmar, southwest China and the Philippines; vagrant in Thailand and Vietnam.

# ORIENTAL REED-WARBLER
## *Acrocephalus orientalis* 18 cm  F: Sylviidae

**Description:** A large warbler. Distinguished from other *Acrocephalus* warblers in the region by its long bill, long wings and faint streaks on chest. Sometimes included under superspecies Great Reed-warbler, *A. arundinaceus*.

**Voice:** During migration, a penetrating alarm call: *chack*.

**Habits:** A marshland bird found around lowland swamps and flooded areas, and sometimes in scrub some distance from water. Seems to prefer marshes just behind the coast, where it can be abundant during peak migration, but it can turn up at any wetland site. Skulks among tall grasses; sometimes moves higher to feed on insects in bushes and small trees.

**Distribution:** Breeds in East Asia; winters in Southeast Asia. A widespread and common passage migrant and winter visitor throughout the region, including Hong Kong, Singapore and Brunei.

# COMMON TAILORBIRD
## *Orthotomus sutorius* 10 cm  F: Sylviidae

**Description:** Distinguished with difficulty from the following species by its grey-olive (less yellowish) upperparts, less rufous on crown and white underparts, including undertail coverts. Male (photo) has elongated tail.

**Voice:** A loud, repetitive *chee-rup, chee-rup*.

**Habits:** Frequents dry open woodlands, mangrove edges, gardens and parks; often seen in villages and towns up to lower montane elevations. A restless but friendly bird that hops low among scrub and ornamental plants catching insects. The tiny nest is built within one to three leaves 'tailored' together with spider webs and straw for shelter.

**Distribution:** Oriental region. A widespread and common resident on the mainland, including Hong Kong and Singapore.

## DARK-NECKED TAILORBIRD
*Orthotomus atrogularis* 11 cm  F: Sylviidae

**Description**: Female (photo) distinguished with difficulty from the Common Tailorbird by its more rufous crown and yellowish plumage, including undertail coverts. Male has prominent black patch on neck.

**Voice**: More high-pitched and trilling than Common Tailorbird's call: *trii-ip*.

**Habits**: Generally prefers more vegetated terrain than the Common Tailorbird; often seen in forest edges and clearings near dense secondary forest; seldom in gardens and never in open country. Otherwise, habits and behavior much like previous species.

**Distribution**: Oriental region. A widespread and common resident on the mainland, including Singapore; a locally fairly common resident of Borneo, including Brunei.

## ASHY TAILORBIRD
*Orthotomus ruficeps* 10 cm  F: Sylviidae

**Description**: Note ashy, grey body and red face. Male shown in photo; female has paler chest and white belly.

**Voice**: A penetrating trill: *treee-chip*.

**Habits**: Found mainly in tidal mangroves and sometimes in drier scrub just behind the coast; on Borneo moves into secondary lowland forest edges. An active and restless species seen hopping through the low mangrove bushes and trees, constantly chasing small insects and calling loudly. Nests inside a leaf, folded and sewn together, typical of its genus.

**Distribution**: Sunda sub-region. A fairly common resident in south Thailand, Myanmar, Malaysia, Singapore, Brunei and Sulu Island (Philippines).

## RUFOUS-TAILED TAILORBIRD
### *Orthotomus sericeus* 11 cm  F: Sylviidae

**Distribution:** Sunda sub-region. A widespread and locally fairly common resident in south Thailand, Myanmar, Malaysia, Singapore, Brunei and Palawan (Philippines).

**Description:** Note red crown, dark grey upperparts and white underparts; also look for rufous tail.

**Voice:** A powerful series of *tee-cher, tee-cher*.

**Habits:** Found in lowland forest edges and rural scrub. Often behind mangroves but not in flooded, tidal areas; occurs inland to 400 metres. Avoids closed forest. Often seen near villages, but not in open parks and gardens. Not as numerous as other tailorbirds. Skulks low inside dense scrub, but is very territorial and will respond strongly to a play-back of its call, coming forward to respond as this photo shows.

## MOUNTAIN TAILORBIRD
### *Orthotomus cuculatus* 12 cm  F: Sylviidae

**Distribution:** Oriental region. A locally fairly common resident in montane parts of the mainland; uncommon on the mountains of Borneo and the 3 largest Philippine islands.

**Description:** Distinguished from the Chestnut-crowned warbler by its slender build, lack of wing-bar and olive rump; otherwise unmistakable.

**Voice:** A high-pitched whistle of 4 to 6 thin notes, also a short trill.

**Habits:** A strictly montane species found only from 900 metres to upper montane elevations at 2,200 metres. It occurs in primary forest and forest edges, moving in the lower storey or slightly higher, often inside dense bamboos and creepers; not easy to observe. Always on the move; a familiar participant in montane bird waves.

## GREY-BREASTED PRINIA
*Prinia hodgsonii* 12 cm  F: Sylvidae

**Description**: Note the uniformly greyish head and breast contrasting with white throat.

**Voice**: A metallic song, vocal during the breeding season. A characteristic, high-pitched *hee-hee-hee*.

**Habits**: Found in dry forest edges, scrub and open grasslands, often in cultivated, rural areas near villages and roadsides. Occurs from the lowlands to 1,500 metres. Feeds on insects in grass and bushes and often visits flowering trees to feed on nectar as this photograph demonstrates.

**Distribution**: Oriental region. A widespread and common resident throughout most of the mainland.

## RUFESCENT PRINIA
*Prinia rufescens* 12 cm  F: Sylvidae

**Description**: Look for dark head contrasting with pale grey (not yellowish) underparts; also note relatively short tail.

**Voice**: A repeated *chiap-chiap;* also a buzzing call.

**Habits**: The most arboreal of the lowland prinias, found in wooded areas and along edges of closed forest; also seen in nearby plantations, but rarely in open country. Occurs mainly in the lowlands; recorded to 1,600 metres. It calls sitting low in the grass or in a bush and flies into cover with rapid wingbeats when disturbed.

**Distribution**: Oriental region. A widespread and fairly common resident throughout the mainland; no records from Singapore.

## PLAIN PRINIA (Tawny-flanked Prinia)
*Prinia inornata* 15 cm  F: Sylvidae

**Description:** Notice its pale grey face and underparts, and prominent whitish supercilium.

**Voice:** A buzzing *chee-cheerrr,* often from an exposed perch.

**Habits:** Prefers the wetter parts of open country. Found in tall grass near marshy areas, flooded fields, rivers or mangrove edges; occasionally also in drier areas to 800 metres. In Hong Kong, only really numerous around the Mai Po marshes. An active and vocal bird, it sits on tall grass stems singing and flies low to the next straw. Often a resident pair are seen together.

**Distribution:** Africa and the Oriental region. A widespread and common resident throughout most of the mainland, including Hong Kong.

## YELLOW-BELLIED PRINIA
*Prinia flaviventris* 13 cm  F: Sylvidae

**Description:** A slender and elegant warbler; note diagnostic bright yellow lower belly.

**Voice:** A short bubbling song, often from an exposed perch.

**Habits:** An open country species found in scrubland with long grass, often around marshy areas. A somewhat shy and skulking bird, it stays among the grasses where it builds its pouch-shaped nest near the ground. Sometimes comes out briefly to perch and sing in the open.

**Distribution:** Oriental region. A widespread and common resident in all countries and territories except the Philippines.

## HILL PRINIA
### *Prinia atrogularis* 18 cm  F: Sylviidae

**Description**: Distinguished from the similar Brown Prinia, *P. polychroa*, of the lowlands by its streaked breast and whitish supercilium; note very long tail.

**Voice**: A loud, repeated *cho-eep*.

**Habits**: This is a strictly montane species that takes over from the sympatric Brown Prinia at 900 metres and above, to the tree limit. In Peninsular Malaysia it occurs only at Gunung Tahan in Taman Negara (summit: 2,187m). Found along forest edges and in sub-alpine scrub and grassy areas. Often sings from an open perch or flies busily from perch to perch, its long tail dangling behind.

**Distribution**: Oriental region. A widespread and locally fairly common resident in montane parts of the mainland, excluding Hong Kong.

## ZITTING CISTICOLA
### *Cisticola juncidis* 11 cm  F: Sylviidae

**Description**: Distinguished from the following species by its plain head and white tip in tail.

**Voice**: A metallic *zitt-zitt*, sometimes uttered during display flights.

**Habits**: An open country species that has benefited from large-scale forest clearance in the region. One of the first birds to invade denuded areas and newly reclaimed land. Seems to prefer wet terrain; also seen near cultivated fields. Conspicuous and vocal during the breeding season, but otherwise usually seen fluttering low across the grassland before dropping back into cover.

**Distribution**: Africa, Eurasia into Australasia; northern populations migrate south. A common resident and winter visitor throughout the region except Borneo.

## BRIGHT-CAPPED CISTICOLA (Golden-headed Cisticola)
*Cisticola exilis* 11 cm  F: Sylviidae

**Description**: Breeding male (photo) unmistakable; non-breeding male distinguished with difficulty from previous species by the rufous wash on neck and flanks.

**Voice**: A buzzing hiss followed by a loud, bell-like note.

**Habits**: Habitat requirements are much like those of the previous species, but seems to prefer drier terrain and longer grass cover. Occurs from the lowlands locally into lower montane elevations. In non-breeding plumage it is very similar to the previous bird, and could have been overlooked in part of its range. This individual carries material to a pouch nest low in the grass.

**Distribution**: Oriental region, Australasia. A common resident in parts of the mainland, as well as Taiwan and the Philippines; recently confirmed in Hong Kong and Laos.

## SLATY-BELLIED TESIA
*Tesia olivea* 9 cm  F: Sylviidae

**Description**: Distinguished with difficulty from the sympatric but rarer Grey-bellied Tesia, *T. cyaniventer*, by its golden yellow (not olive-green) crown. The Chestnut-headed Tesia, *T. castaneocoronata*, has a chestnut head and yellow throat.

**Voice**: A loud and musical song.

**Habits**: One of 3 peculiar, short-tailed *Tesia* warblers found in northern parts of the region, inside dense primary forest above 900 metres. Moves low on or just off the ground, often in wet areas and gullies with dense bamboo and creepers. Good views of this babbler-like skulker are hard to come by.

**Distribution**: Oriental region. A scarce resident in north-western montane parts of the mainland.

## BORNEAN STUBTAIL
*Urosphena whiteheadi* 10 cm  F: Sylviidae

**Description**: Note small size and almost complete lack of tail; also look for buff supercilium and face.

**Voice**: A high-pitched *tzi-tzi-tzeee*.

**Habits**: A forest bird found in primary forest at Kinabalu, Gunung Mulu and other high Borneo mountains above 2,000 metres. Always moves just above the ground, skulking under cover of dense undergrowth; not really shy. Although this bird seems fairly numerous, its nest has never been found.

**Distribution**: Borneo endemic. A locally fairly common resident in mountains on Sabah and Sarawak.

## SUNDA BUSH-WARBLER (Mountain Bush-warbler *C. montanus*)
*Cettia vulcania* 13 cm  F: Sylviidae

**Description**: Note fairly long tail and cream throat and supercilium. Sometimes considered conspecific with Brownish-flanked Bush-warbler, *C. fortipes*, of South China and the Himalayas.

**Voice**: A weak, whistling song and a sharper alarm call *trr-trr*.

**Habits**: Strictly montane; found only in montane rainforest above 1,500 metres and upwards to the tree limit. Occurs on Mount Kinabalu and Gunung Mulu. Frequents primary forest with dense undergrowth of ferns and creepers, where it lives under cover; rarely seen flying. Feeds on tiny invertebrates. No nesting records.

**Distribution**: Southeast Asia from Borneo into eastern Indonesia. A generally uncommon resident on mountains in Sabah and Sarawak.

## BROWN-CHESTED FLYCATCHER
*Rhinomyias brunneata* 15 cm  F: Muscicapidae

**Description:** Distinguished with difficulty from other *Rhinomyias* flycatchers by its chunky build and diagnostic yellow lower mandible.

**Voice:** Usually silent during migration; harsh *churrs* reported.

**Habits:** Breeds in bamboo thickets and thick undergrowth in dense forest. During migration usually found in lowland rainforest, but can also turn up at lower montane elevations and in coastal scrub. An inconspicuous species, possibly overlooked during surveys. Perches low and has been observed to fly down to the forest floor, appearing somewhat like the babbler F: Timaliidae.

**Distribution:** Oriental region. Resident in South China, excluding Hong Kong; an uncommon winter visitor to Peninsular Malaysia and Singapore; rare in Thailand. Vulnerable to global extinction.

## GREY-CHESTED FLYCATCHER
*Rhinomyias umbratilis* 15 cm  F: Muscicapidae

**Description:** Bright white throat is diagnostic, contrasting sharply with brownish-grey band across chest.

**Voice:** A liquid song of 2 to 6 rising notes.

**Habits:** Found in lowland rainforest, in both primary and adjacent mature secondary forest. Also occurs in wet patches and peat swamp forest. Inconspicuous; perches low and is often stationary for long periods. Flies out occasionally to catch insects in the air or from thin branches in the undergrowth. Never lands on the ground.

**Distribution:** Sunda subregion. An uncommon resident in south Thailand, Malaysia and Brunei.

## DARK-SIDED FLYCATCHER
### *Muscicapa sibirica* 13 cm  F: Muscicapidae

**Description**: Distinguished with some difficulty from the following species by its small black (not yellowish) bill and streaks on flanks. The Grey-streaked Flycatcher, *M. griseisticta,* is larger (15 cm), more slender and has much more prominent streaking on underparts.

**Voice**: A clear *chi-up, chi-up.*

**Habits**: Breeds in upper montane forest, from 2,000 to 3,300 metres. Moves south during winter and settles in tropical lowlands. Seems to prefer somewhat more densely forested habitats than the following species and is less likely to turn up in open woodlands and gardens. Also seems to occur in smaller numbers.

**Distribution:** Breeds in northern East Asia and the Himalayas; winters in the Oriental region. A widespread but generally uncommon passage migrant and winter visitor throughout the region, including Hong Kong, Singapore, Brunei and Palawan (Philippines).

## ASIAN BROWN FLYCATCHER
### *Muscicapa dauurica* 12 cm (*M. latirostris*)  F: Muscicapidae

**Description**: Distinguished with difficulty from other *Muscicapa* flycatchers by its greyish plumage and lack of distinct streaks on underparts.

**Voice**: Sometimes a sibilant *tit-tit-tit;* usually quiet.

**Habits**: Frequents all types of wooded areas during migration, from montane forest edges to mangroves, deciduous woodlands, and parks and gardens. Usually seen singly, but during peak migration gathers in large numbers. An unobtrusive bird, it sits quietly at mid-storey level, occasionally flying out to catch tiny insects in the air, returning swiftly.

**Distribution:** Breeds in East Asia; winters in the Oriental region. A widespread and fairly common passage migrant and winter visitor throughout the region, including Hong Kong, Singapore and Brunei; rare in the Philippines; also resident in northwest Thailand.

## FERRUGINOUS FLYCATCHER
*Muscicapa ferruginea* 13 cm  F: Muscicapidae

**Description**: Note diagnostic reddish-brown wing coverts and flanks, contrasting with greyish head. Distinct eye-ring.

**Voice**: Usually quiet during migration.

**Habits**: Mainly montane; breeds at elevations between 600 and 3,000 metres. Disperses during migration, also into the lowlands. Occurs singly and in low densities. Found in closed forest, where it perches low, usually near a clearing or a small stream. Habitually uses the same perch making quick raids from there to catch minute insects in the air.

**Distribution**: Oriental region. Partly migratory; breeds in montane parts of south China and Taiwan. A widespread but scarce migrant throughout much of region, including Hong Kong and Singapore; vagrant in the Philippines.

## VERDITER FLYCATCHER
*Eumyias thalassina* 17 cm  F: Muscicapidae

**Description**: Distinguished from other blue flycatchers by its uniform greenish-blue plumage; note the black lores of this male contrast with its turquoise head; the faint pale scales on vent are obstructed here by a leaf.

**Voice**: A soft but penetrating warble.

**Habits**: Mainly resident in hilly terrain. In Thailand, occurs from the lowlands to upper montane elevations; in China between 1,200 and 3,000 metres. During the winter, December to February, northern populations will move to lower elevations. Tropical birds are sedentary. Easy to spot as it often perches high in the open near the forest edge, singing and flying out to catch insects in the air.

**Distribution**: Oriental region. A widespread and fairly common resident and winter visitor throughout the mainland, including Hong Kong; in Malaysia a mainly lower montane resident; uncommon in Brunei.

## INDIGO FLYCATCHER
*Eumyias indigo* 14 cm  F: Muscicapidae

**Description**: Distinguished with difficulty from other blue flycatchers by its comparatively small size, deep indigo blue plumage and characteristic black face with contrasting whitish forehead.

**Voice**: A ringing, squeaky call.

**Habits**: A strictly montane species found mainly between 1,500 and 3,000 metres, and occasionally down to 900 metres. Occurs at both Mount Kinabalu and Gunung Mulu. Seen inside primary forest and forest edges. Perches fairly low, from eye-level up into the middle storey. Catches flying insects from a perch among the trees. Not shy. Often moves with other birds in bird waves.

**Distribution**: Borneo, Sumatra and Java (Indonesia). A locally fairly common resident in montane parts of Sabah and Sarawak.

## YELLOW-RUMPED FLYCATCHER
*Ficedula zanthopygia* 13 cm  F: Muscicapidae

**Description**: Photo shows male; female is dull olive, but yellow rump shows clearly. Sometimes considered conspecific with the similar, but rarer, Narcissus Flycatcher, *F. narcissina*. Distinguished from that species by its white (not yellow) eyebrow.

**Voice**: A thin *pirip*.

**Habits**: Most of the population appear to winter in the tropics on the Malay Peninsula, and overfly the northern regions fairly quickly in fall and spring. Most common in September in Hong Kong. Settles in forest and along forest edges, from the lowlands to 800 metres. Also seen in coastal scrub and gardens, but can turn up almost anywhere during peak migration.

**Distribution**: Breeds in northern East Asia; winters in the Oriental region, reaching Sumatra. A locally and seasonally fairly common passage migrant and winter visitor in the region, including Hong Kong and Singapore.

## RUFOUS-GORGETTED FLYCATCHER
*Ficedula strophiata* 14 cm  F: Muscicapidae

**Description**: Note orange patch below throat. The breeding male of the more widespread Red-throated Flycatcher, *F. parva*, has full red throat and brownish grey (not blue) face, mantle and breast.

**Voice**: A harsh *trrt* and a metallic *pink*.

**Habits**: Resident in montane forest between 900 and 3,000 metres; outside of breeding season it disperses and moves to the lower montane zones. It prefers open sections of the forest and edges where it can hawk in the moss-covered vegetation, from a low perch as shown in this photograph.

**Distribution**: Oriental region, into central China. A locally fairly common resident and winter visitor in the north-western montane parts of the region.

## RUFOUS-BROWED FLYCATCHER
*Ficedula solitaris* 13 cm  F: Muscicapidae

**Description**: Note diagnostic white throat; from previous species also by smaller size, yellowish head and lack of mask.

**Voice**: A thin whistle of 3 descending notes.

**Habits**: Found in rainforest in the lower montane range, from 900 to 1,500 metres; in Thailand down to 400 metres. Prefers primary forest and is rarely seen at edges. Moves low inside the dark forest, perching on a stick just off the ground. Flies out quickly to hawk for minute insects. Generally unobtrusive and quiet. Sometimes sings with a faint voice.

**Distribution**: Southeast Asia into Sumatra (Indonesia). A generally scarce resident in montane parts of south Thailand, Myanmar and Peninsular Malaysia.

## SNOWY-BROWED FLYCATCHER
*Ficedula hyperythra* 11 cm  F: Muscicapidae

**Description**: Male (photo) has distinctive white eye-brow; female is uniformly dark brown.

**Voice**: A thin, high-pitched song of 3 to 4 notes, or a single *chee*.

**Habits**: Restricted to the insect-rich montane habitat, from 800 metres to the tree limit. Occurs above 1,200 metres in China. Found at Mount Kinabalu in Sabah upwards to 3,100 metres elevation. In Peninsular Malaysia, Fraser's Hill is too low for this bird, but it is locally common in the Cameron Highlands. Moves low, sometimes in the middle storey, but usually lower at eye-level. Also drops down to the ground like a small thrush, to pick up invertebrates. Easy to overlook, but friendly and confident.

**Distribution**: Oriental region. A widespread and locally fairly common resident in most upper montane parts of the region including the major Philippine islands; not recorded in Hong Kong.

## RUFOUS-CHESTED FLYCATCHER
*Ficedula dumetoria* 11 cm  F: Muscicapidae

**Description**: Immature (photo) similar to female, with faint streaks on breast. Note diagnostic contrast between rufous chest and white belly. Male similar to migratory Mugimaki Flycatcher, *F. mugimaki* (found higher in more open habitat), with black upperparts, and white supercilium and wing bar.

**Voice**: A faint high-pitched 3- to 4-note song.

**Habits**: Found in rainforest from the lowlands into lower montane elevations. Moves at eye-level or just off the ground and sometimes emerges near a trail. Is often associated with tiny forest streams and gullies with dense undergrowth. Shy and secretive, this bird quickly disappears into cover when spotted and good views are rare.

**Distribution**: Sunda subregion into eastern Indonesia. A locally scarce resident in south Thailand and Malaysia; rare in Brunei.

## LITTLE PIED FLYCATCHER
### *Ficedula westermanni* 11 cm  F: Muscicapidae

**Description**: Male (photo) is unmistakable, note especially prominent white supercilium. Female is a nondescript brown with paler underparts.

**Voice**: Quite vocal, with a thin *pi-pi-pi.*

**Habits**: A strictly montane species found in forest from 800 to 2,600 metres elevation, mainly in closed undisturbed forest, but also in forest edges and nearby gardens. Perches in the middle storey on an exposed stick, flying out to catch insects in the air.

**Distribution**: Oriental region. A widespread and common resident in most montane parts of the region including the larger Philippine islands.

## BLUE AND WHITE FLYCATCHER
### *Cyanoptila cyanomelana* 18 cm  F: Muscicapidae

**Description**: Photo shows captive male; female has blue replaced by brown. Distinguished from the similar resident White-tailed Flycatcher, *Cyornis concreta,* by sharp demarcation between dark blue/brown chest and white belly. Only member of its genus.

**Voice**: Usually silent during migration.

**Habits**: A forest bird that can be found in most wooded areas, from closed rainforest to open deciduous forest, as long as large trees are present. Mainly overflies the northern parts of region and settles in the wet tropical Sunda subregion for the winter, often inland at montane elevations up to 1,800 metres. Perches quite high in the upper storeys of large trees.

**Distribution**: Breeds in northern East Asia; winters in Oriental region, reaching Java (Indonesia). A widespread but uncommon passage migrant and winter visitor throughout the region; recorded in all countries and territories.

## LARGE NILTAVA
*Niltava grandis* 21 cm  F: Muscicapidae

**Description**: A large flycatcher. Male (photo) has dark blue underparts; also note paler crown and shoulder patch. Female is brown with distinct blue shoulder patch.

**Voice**: A clear whistle of 3 to 4 ascending notes.

**Habits**: A strictly montane bird found in rainforest and forest edges from 900 to 2,500 metres elevation. It sits lethargically in the middle storey, somewhat like a trogon, often calling softly. Usually seen in pairs. May occasionally fly out or drop to the forest floor to catch small invertebrate prey.

**Distribution**: Oriental region. A locally fairly common resident in montane parts of the mainland.

Morten Strange

## SMALL NILTAVA
*Niltava macgrigoriae* 14 cm  F: Muscicapidae

**Description**: Both sexes similar in plumage to previous species but easily recognized by much smaller size. Male (photo) has greyish (not all blue) belly.

**Voice**: A thin, high-pitched *twee-twee-ee-twee*.

**Habits**: Restricted to montane forest between 900 and 2,500 metres elevation. Generally moves lower inside denser vegetation, more skulking in habit than previous species. During the winter months sometimes shifts to lower elevations.

**Distribution**: Oriental region. A generally scarce resident in northwestern montane parts of the mainland.

B. Van Elegem

## PALE BLUE FLYCATCHER
*Cyornis unicolor* 18 cm  F: Muscicapidae

**Description**: Male (photo) distinguished with some difficulty from Verditer Flycatcher by its whitish (not all blue) underparts. Female is pale brown with greyish underparts.

**Voice**: A characteristic thrush-like descending song.

**Habits**: Occurs in closed forest, from the lowlands to 1,600 metres elevation, often in elevated foot hills, not below 200 metres in East Malaysia. A low density species, not really numerous anywhere. Habits and behavior are somewhat similar to Verditer Flycatcher.

**Distribution**: Oriental region. A widespread but generally scarce resident in northwestern parts of the mainland and Sunda subregion, excluding Singapore and Brunei.

## BORNEAN BLUE FLYCATCHER
*Cyornis superbus* 15 cm  F: Muscicapidae

**Description**: Male (photo) distinguished from the following species by its black mask. Female brown, with rufous rump and tail. Distinguished from Hill Blue Flycatcher *C. banyumas* of the Oriental region, including Borneo, by its supercilium and shining blue lower back.

**Voice**: No information.

**Habits**: Mainly a lower montane forest flycatcher found between 600 and 1,500 metres, but also found at lower elevations such as the Danum Valley where this rare photograph was taken. Turns up near rivers and forest streams, where it perches low inside dense forest, flying out to hawk for insects. Its nest has never been found.

**Distribution**: Borneo endemic. A scarce resident in Sabah and Sarawak; a single record from Brunei.

## MALAYSIAN BLUE FLYCATCHER
*Cyornis turcosa* 14 cm  F: Muscicapidae

**Description**: Male distinguished from other blue flycatchers within its range by its blue (not orange) throat. Female (photo) has white throat.

**Voice**: A thin, barely audible whistling song; also some harsher alarm notes *chrrrk*.

**Habits**: Rare in Peninsular Malaysia, but found with some luck in lowland rainforest in East Malaysia. Occurs in both primary forest and in mature secondary growth. Seems to prefer riverine habitats and is usually seen near a forested river or stream where it perches low on the edge of an overgrown clearing.

**Distribution**: Sunda subregion. In region, a scarce resident in Malaysia only. Near-threatened with global extinction.

## TICKELL'S BLUE FLYCATCHER
*Cyornis tickelliae* 15 cm  F: Muscicapidae

**Description**: Male (photo) similar to sympatric but montane Hill Blue Flycatcher *c.banyumas*, but rufous breast and white belly usually more of a contrast. Female has blue on upperparts replaced with grey.

**Voice**: A clear, whistling song of 5 to 7 notes; also a harsh alarm call *tac*.

**Habits**: Occurs in forest and along forest edges, from the lowlands into foothills at 600 metres elevation. Also recorded in nearby gardens. Prefers somewhat open areas around rivers and clearings, where it hawks for small flying insects from a low perch.

**Distribution**: Oriental region. A locally fairly common resident in Myanmar, Thailand, Indochina and Peninsular Malaysia.

# MANGROVE BLUE FLYCATCHER
*Cyornis rufigastra* 15 cm  F: Muscicapidae

**Distribution:** Southeast Asia into Sumatra (Indonesia). A locally fairly common resident in Malaysia and the Philippines; rare in Thailand, Singapore and Brunei.

**Description:** Female (photo) recognized by white patch around bill. Male lacks white lores and is distinguished (with difficulty) from other *Cyornis* flycatchers by its uniformly dark blue head.

**Voice:** A clear, melodious trill.

**Habits:** Strictly a mangrove bird on the Malay Peninsula and Borneo. Found in low tidal forest or nearby scrub in the Philippines. Also occurs in other forest and along forest edges. Inconspicuous but fairly tame. Perches low inside vegetation, flying out to catch tiny insects, often landing on the mud. Little studied although fairly numerous. Few nesting records.

# PYGMY BLUE FLYCATCHER
*Muscicapella hodgsoni* 10 cm  F: Muscicapidae

**Distribution:** Oriental region. An uncommon montane resident in Myanmar, west China and Malaysia; rare visitor to Thailand and Vietnam.

**Description:** Note tiny size and thin bill. Male (photo) has dark blue back and wings. Female has uniformly brown upperparts and pale rufous underparts.

**Voice:** A weak, high-pitched song.

**Habits:** A low density species found in montane forest above 800 metres. Northern birds seem to disperse somewhat to lower altitudes during winter. Easily overlooked due to small size and quiet habits. Can be spotted perching in the lower middle storey or just off the ground. Has a characteristic habit of restlessly flicking its tail upwards. Little studied. Few nesting records.

## GREY-HEADED FLYCATCHER
*Culicicapa ceylonensis* 12 cm   F: Muscicapidae

**Description**: Unmistakable. Note diagnostic yellow belly contrasting with grey head.

**Voice**: A fine, rising 3-note whistle; also a metallic rattle.

**Habits**: A restless and vocal bird that flutters about the middle storey catching flying insects. During the breeding season prefers closed submontane forest between 600 and 1,600 metres, and occasionally up to 2,200 metres. Also found in the lowlands in Peninsula Malaysia. Disperses widely, outside breeding period, into lowland forest, forest edges and mangroves. Often mixes with other insectivorous species in bird waves.

**Distribution**: Oriental region; partly migratory. A widespread and fairly common resident and winter visitor in much of the region, excluding Singapore; migrant only in Hong Kong; rare in Brunei.

## YELLOW-BELLIED FANTAIL
*Rhipidura hypoxantha* 13 cm   F: Rhipiduridae

**Description**: Unmistakable; only fantail with yellow. Note small size.

**Voice**: A thin, high-pitched whistle.

**Habits**: A montane forest bird, found in Thailand from 1,500 metres to the highest peaks; in China between 1,200 and 3,600 metres. Seems to prefer forest edges and narrow gaps in the forest near windfalls and trails where it can hawk for insects in the open space. Friendly and active. Perches in the middle storey or lower, often restlessly flicking and fanning its tail like other members of this family.

**Distribution**: Oriental region. A locally fairly common resident in northern montane parts of the mainland.

## WHITE-THROATED FANTAIL
### *Rhipidura albicollis* 19 cm  F: Rhipiduridae

**Description**: Distinguished from other fantails by black underparts contrasting with white throat.

**Voice**: A whistling, descending song; also a harsh *cheet*.

**Habits**: Strictly montane; occurs in forest between 900 and 2,600 metres; occasionally in the north down to 600 metres. A restless, vocal bird that flutters through the middle storey, never staying long in one spot. Often fans its tail. An inevitable member of montane bird waves.

**Distribution**: Oriental region. A common resident in most montane parts of the mainland and Borneo.

## PIED FANTAIL
### *Rhipidura javanica* 18 cm  F: Rhipiduridae

**Description**: Look for dark grey chest band.

**Voice**: A penetrating metallic squeak.

**Habits**: Mainly a mangrove bird, but throughout its range is also numerous in nearby secondary forest, coastal woodlands, scrub and even gardens. Usually associated with water. Jumps restlessly through the lower storey of vegetation, calling and fanning its tail. Makes short flights into the next cover. The nest is a tiny cup placed on a low branch.

**Distribution**: Southeast Asia into Bali (Indonesia). A common resident in the southern tropical parts of the region, including Singapore and Brunei.

# BLACK-NAPED MONARCH
## *Hypothymis azurea* 16 cm  F: Monarchidae

**Description**: Note bright blue upperparts and chest on male (photo); small black spot on top of head not visible here. Female has brown back, grey chest and lacks black spot on blue head.

**Voice**: A ringing *pwee-pwee-pwee*.

**Habits**: Frequents a variety of wooded habitats, from wet primary rainforest to deciduous forest and secondary growth, from the coast into lower montane elevations. Disperses widely outside breeding season, also into mangroves and disturbed areas. A restless and active bird that moves quickly from perch to perch in the lower to lower middle storey. Often participates in bird waves.

**Distribution**: Oriental region, partly migratory. A widespread resident and migrant in all countries and territories; locally fairly common, including Brunei; rare resident in Singapore; winter visitor only in Hong Kong.

# RUFOUS-WINGED FLYCATCHER (Rufous-winged Philentoma)
## *Philentoma pyrhopterum* 18 cm  F: Monarchidae

**Description**: Note diagnostic rufous wings and tail in female (photo). Male has pale blue head, chest and mantle.

**Voice**: A soft, 2-note whistle; also a harsher alarm call.

**Habits**: A lowland rainforest bird of primary forest and mature secondary forest, but not edges or clearings. Sits in the lower parts of the middle storey, flying out to catch insects in the air. A low density species, regularly seen but little studied. No nesting records.

**Distribution**: Sunda subregion. A local and generally scarce resident in south Thailand, Myanmar, Malaysia and Brunei; extinct in Singapore.

## ASIAN PARADISE-FLYCATCHER
*Terpsiphone paradisi* 22 cm + tail  F: Monarchidae

**Distribution**: Central and East Asia; Oriental region. Northern populations migrate south. A widespread and locally fairly common resident and migrant on the mainland and Borneo, including Brunei; migrant only in Hong Kong and Singapore.

**Description**: Distinguished from similar Japanese Paradise-flycatcher, *T. atrocaudata,* by bright rufous (not blackish rufous) wings and tail. Photo shows female. Male has elongated tail (20-25 cm); some males have white body and tail.

**Voice**: A whistling song; during migration a soft *theat.*

**Habits**: Found in all kinds of arboreal habitat, from primary lowland rainforest to deciduous woodlands at lower montane altitudes. During migration also seen in mangroves, forest edges and scrub. A successful species, found solitary or in pairs. During peak migration occurs locally, in relatively high densities for a forest bird. Perches in the middle storey and catches flying insects.

## BORNEAN WHISTLER
*Pachycephala hypoxantha* 16 cm  F: Pachycephalidae

**Distribution**: Borneo endemic. A locally fairly common mountain resident in Sabah and Sarawak.

**Description**: Unmistakable; note chunky build with olive upperparts and yellow underparts.

**Voice**: An intermittent, loud song.

**Habits**: A strictly montane forest bird found in rainforest from 900 to 2,600 metres, mainly closed undisturbed forest, but occasionally forest edges. Can be seen at Mt Kinabalu and Gunung Mulu. Perches in the middle storey, flying out to pick invertebrates from the foliage. Often seen mixing with other species in bird waves.

## MANGROVE WHISTLER
### *Pachycephala grisola* 17 cm  F: Pachycephalidae

**Description**: A nondescript, babbler-like whistler. Note pale grey underparts contrasting with rufous-brown wings and general lack of features.

**Voice**: A clear, long whistle *tu-tee-tee-tee-tew*.

**Habits**: Although associated with mangroves, this species shuns the tidal muddy areas of mangrove forests, preferring the adjacent coastal woodland habitat with casuarina trees, tall scrub and nearby cultivation. A solitary bird, it moves high in the small trees, flying babbler-style from perch to perch, often calling and catching insects and larvae along the way.

**Distribution**: Oriental region. Can be quite common locally, but generally scarce in southern coastal parts of the region, including Singapore, Brunei and Palawan (Philippines).

## ALPINE ACCENTOR
### *Prunella collaris* 17 cm  F: Pachycephalidae

**Description**: Note uniformly grey head and rufous flanks; western populations have white throat spotted with black.

**Voice**: A chipping, melodious song performed from the ground or in the air; also a trilling *chee-rip*.

**Habits**: One of 3 montane members of this family in the region, but the only one not associated with forest. A strictly alpine resident found between the treeline and the snowline. Usually seen above 3,400 metres; in winter down to 1,800 metres; in the Himalayas recorded to 6,400 metres. Perches on rocks and hops about on the ground feeding on seeds. Can be quite approachable.

**Distribution**: Eurasia. Found only in alpine regions of Myanmar, Yunnan (China) and Taiwan.

## WHITE WAGTAIL
*Motacilla alba* 19 cm  F: Motacillidae

**Description**: Plumage somewhat variable with sex, season and subspecies, but clear pied (not olive) shades always distinctive.

**Voice**: A frequent, shrill *tchizzik*.

**Habits**: Southeast Asia is the southern limit for this bird in Asia. While very numerous in the north, only a few travel south to the Malay Peninsula, Philippines and Borneo. This lively bird is found in open country, wagging its tail and making short low flights to catch insects and grubs.

**Distribution**: Breeds in temperate Eurasia; winters south. Resident in China and northern Vietnam; a common winter visitor elsewhere, including Hong Kong; rare in the tropics, including Singapore and Brunei.

## GREY WAGTAIL
*Motacilla cinerea* 19 cm  F: Motacillidae

**Description**: In winter plumage, distinguished from other wagtails by grey (not olive-brownish) mantle combined with white throat and pale yellow underparts.

**Voice**: A disyllabic *tzi-zick* on take-off.

**Habits**: Favours lower montane woodlands, preferably near a small shady stream. During migration can turn up at stagnant pools and larger rivers, from the lowlands to the mountains, but rarely on the coast. Mainly seen from September to April, but can be seen most months of the year. Moves along the water's edge, flicking its tail and picking up tiny invertebrates from the sand and gravel.

**Distribution**: Breeds in temperate Eurasia; winters in tropical regions of Africa, the Oriental region and Australasia. Migrant and winter visitor in all countries and territories; locally common.

## YELLOW WAGTAIL
*Motacilla flava* 18 cm  F: Motacillidae

**Description**: Distinguished from Grey Wagtail by colour of mantle and by dark rump and lack of wing band in flight. Distinguished from similar but rarer Citrine Wagtail, *M. citreola,* by no or very little yellow in face and on throat.

**Voice**: A loud *tswe-ep* in flight.

**Habits**: Locally abundant during peak migration, forming large flocks around coastal grasslands and dried up mudflats. Hundreds of individuals will converge at evening roosts. Can also be found inland in other short grass areas, usually near water. Seldom perches in trees; usually walks on the ground and flies off with an undulating flight pattern.

**Distribution**: Breeds in Eurasia and Alaska; winters in tropics from Africa and Oriental region into Australasia. A widespread and common passage migrant and winter visitor in all countries and territories.

## FOREST WAGTAIL
*Dendronanthus indicus* 18 cm  F: Motacillidae

**Description**: Distinguished fairly easily from other wagtails by prominent black-and-white pattern on wings and breast. Unique; the only member of its genus.

**Voice**: A soft *pink*.

**Habits**: Arboreal; during migration found in secondary forest, nearby tall scrub, cultivated areas and mangroves, usually near water. Mainly solitary. Usually seen along forest trails or near a clearing, but flies up into a tree when disturbed, swaying its body slowly from side to side in a peculiar fashion.

**Distribution**: Breeds in East Asia; winters in Oriental region. Mainly a locally fairly common passage migrant and winter visitor on the mainland, including Hong Kong and Singapore; rare in Sabah and south Philippines.

## OLIVE-BACKED PIPIT (Olive Tree-Pipit)
### *Anthus hodgsoni* 16 cm  F: Motacillidae

**Description:** Distinguished with difficulty from other pipits by streaked chest combined with faintly streaked olive-brownish back. Also note thin black crown stripe.

**Voice:** A hoarse *tseez* in flight.

**Habits:** An arboreal pipit found in open forest, secondary growth and plantations; also in meadows if trees are nearby. Mainly montane, occurs up to 3,600 metres during breeding season but in all elevations, also down to the coastal lowlands during migration. Feeds on the ground, but flies up into a tree to perch when flushed.

**Distribution:** Breeds in Himalayas and East Asia; winters in Oriental region. A fairly common winter visitor on the mainland, including Hong Kong; uncommon in parts of Philippines and Malaysia.

## RICHARD'S PIPIT
### *Anthus novaeseelandiae* 20 cm  F: Motacillidae

**Description:** Note diagnostic long legs and posture. Resident race considered by some a separate species, the Paddyfield Pipit, *A. rufulus*. Indistinguishable in field, apart from smaller size (16 cm).

**Voice:** A loud *chip* on take-off.

**Habits:** Strictly an open country bird, found in open fields and short grass areas, from coastal plains to lower montane elevations. Locally abundant during peak migration. Always feeds on the ground, sometimes flying up onto low perch. Nests in a small depression in the grass.

**Distribution:** East Asia, Oriental region, Australasia; northern populations migrate south. A widespread and common resident and migrant in all countries and territories.

## RED-THROATED PIPIT
### *Anthus cervinus* 17 cm  F: Motacillidae

**Description:** The male (photo) in breeding plumage shows reddish head and throat well. Immatures and females have less rufous colour on throat and are best recognized by black streaks on back and rump.

**Voice:** A thin but distinctive *sweeoo*.

**Habits:** During migration occurs in open country in the lowlands, often grasslands near the coast, especially in wet areas and cultivation. Feeds on the ground. From October to April it can be locally abundant, mainly in the northern parts where many winter.

**Distribution:** Breeds in subarctic Eurasia; migrates south reaching Africa and Borneo. A widespread and common passage migrant and winter visitor throughout the region, including Brunei and Hong Kong. Uncommon in Singapore and Malaysia; rare in the Philippines.

## ASHY WOOD-SWALLOW
### *Artamus fuscus* 18 cm  F: Artamidae

**Description:** No overlap in range with following species. Note grey (not white) underparts. Juvenile (right) mottled with brown.

**Voice:** A harsh *chreenk*.

**Habits:** An open country bird found in cleared areas, grassy fields and cultivation, mainly in the lowlands. Locally recorded to 1,800 metres. Perches high in the open. A social bird, always in small groups, chattering and making gliding, flapping flights for insects. Its broad, pointed wings give it a characteristic triangular shape in the air.

**Distribution:** Oriental region. A widespread, fairly common resident throughout the northern part of the mainland; not recorded in Hong Kong.

# WHITE-BREASTED WOOD-SWALLOW

*Artamus leucorhynchus* 18 cm  F: Artamidae

**Description**: Unmistakable. In flight its broad pointed wings and short tail give it a triangular shape.

**Voice**: Loud, harsh chatter.

**Habits**: Mainly a coastal species found in dry open woodlands, casuarinas, forest edges, coconut groves and other cultivated areas. Perches high in dead branches making flapping, gliding flights like a bee-eater catch insects. A very conspicuous and social bird, always in small vocal flocks, displaying and actively chasing crows and birds of prey.

**Distribution**: Southeast Asia into Australasia. A locally fairly common resident in Peninsular Malaysia (west coast), Borneo (including Brunei) and the Philippines.

# BROWN SHRIKE

*Lanius cristatus* 20 cm  F: Laniidae

**Description**: Distinguished from other shrikes by brown upperparts combined with pale rufous underparts. Note white supercilium separating black mask from grey (sometimes brown) crown.

**Voice**: A harsh *chak-chak-chak*.

**Habits**: An open country bird found around cleared land and cultivation; also in parks and gardens. Solitary, but during peak migration is locally abundant. In winter quarters, stakes out a territory and defends it against intruders. Perches low, dropping down into grass to catch small prey.

**Distribution**: Breeds in East Asia; winters in Oriental region, Australasia. A widespread and common passage migrant and winter visitor in all countries and territories.

## TIGER SHRIKE
*Lanius tigrinus* 19 cm  F: Laniidae

**Description**: In all plumages look for strong bill, fairly short tail and some black barring across back. Immature (photo) has white eye-ring. Breeding adult has black mask and grey crown.

**Voice**: A harsh chatter, often from inside cover.

**Habits**: More arboreal than other shrikes; found in lowland forest, secondary growth and dense coastal scrub. Usually perches low along forest edges. Generally inconspicuous; prefers to stay inside cover.

**Distribution**: Breeds in northern East Asia; winters in southeast Asia. Passage migrant and winter visitor in the region; fairly common in Thailand, Peninsular Malaysia and Singapore; otherwise scarce; vagrant in the Philippines.

## BURMESE SHRIKE
*Lanius collurioides* 20 cm  F: Laniidae

**Description**: Distinguished from other shrikes by combination of white underparts, brown mantle and black mask and forehead.

**Voice**: A staccato rattle.

**Habits**: Breeds in lower montane open woodlands between 900 and 1,800 metres. During winter disperses widely into deciduous forest edges and nearby scrub and cultivation. Perches low over grass and bushes, dropping down to catch small prey.

**Distribution**: Oriental region. Locally fairly common resident and winter visitor in parts of the mainland.

## LONG-TAILED SHRIKE
### *Lanius schach* 25 cm  F: Laniidae

**Distribution:** Oriental region, partly migratory. A common resident in most parts of the mainland, including Hong Kong, the Philippines and Singapore; vagrant in Sabah.

**Description:** Long, black tail diagnostic. Photo shows southern subspecies; northern races have black crown and brown mantle (not grey).

**Voice:** A low, squeaky song; also a harsh *keep*.

**Habits:** An open country species that seems to be expanding with the regional deforestation. Found in open fields and scrub, often near marshes. Quickly invades newly clear-felled or reclaimed areas. Perches low over long grass, suddenly pouncing on small prey below. Flies with undulating flight to next perch, long tail trailing behind.

## MOUNTAIN SHRIKE
### *Lanius validirostris* 22 cm  F: Laniidae

**Distribution:** Philippine endemic. A local and uncommon montane resident on the islands of Luzon, Mindoro and Mindanao.

**Description:** Distinguished from other shrikes by combination of all-grey cap, mantle and back, with warm rufous underparts.

**Voice:** Little information.

**Habits:** Occurs in forest edges and clearings in oak and pine forests; also in open secondary growth, scrub and along roadsides. World range is restricted to three Philippine islands, each with a different subspecies. These occur from 1,000 metres to the highest summits. Reported from Katanglad, Mindanao and Mt. Polis, Luzon, where it is surprisingly tame. Otherwise little studied.

## PHILIPPINE GLOSSY STARLING (Asian Glossy Starling)
*Aplonis panayensis* 20 cm  F: Sturnidae

**Description**: Unmistakable; within this region the only *Aplonis* starling. Note blackish-green sheen to plumage and red eye. Immature (left) heavily streaked.

**Voice**: A ringing whistle in flight and a metallic *ink* when perched.

**Habits**: An open country bird, well adapted to disturbed woodlands, towns, roadsides and gardens. Mainly arboreal; often feeds high in the trees but will land on the ground to take fallen fruit. Gregarious; always in flocks even during the breeding season when colonies form, nesting in cavities in buildings or trees.

**Distribution**: Oriental region. A common resident in parts of Myanmar, south Thailand, Malaysia, Singapore, Brunei and the Philippines.

## WHITE-SHOULDERED STARLING
*Sturnus sinensis* 20 cm  F: Sturnidae

**Description**: Combination of prominent white wing patch (broader in male, photo) and pale greyish-rufous plumage is diagnostic.

**Voice**: Harsh squeals.

**Habits**: Found in open country with some trees, cultivation, often near marshy areas. During migration also seen in coastal woodlands and mangroves. Nests mainly in crevices in buildings; sometimes in trees. Rarely comes to the ground. Outside breeding season moves about in small flocks. Not a high density species; seems to be declining in numbers.

**Distribution**: Oriental region, northeast India into Southeast Asia. Breeds in south China, including Hong Kong; winters in south. Generally scarce on the mainland, including Singapore; vagrant in Philippines; single record in Sabah (East Malaysia).

## PURPLE-BACKED STARLING (Daurian Starling)
*Sturnus sturninus* 19 cm  F: Sturnidae

**Description:** Distinguished from previous species by dark mantle and crown and narrow wing bar.

**Voice:** A quiet *neeah* in flight.

**Habits:** This species seems to overfly the subtropical region and settles in large numbers in the wet tropics from October to April, often in low-lying coastal areas. In winter quarters it is found in a wide variety of open wooded habitats, often in disturbed areas behind mangroves, cleared areas with some trees and cultivated areas; also in parks and gardens. Moves quickly in dense flocks, sometimes numbering hundreds, landing in fruiting trees, feeding in the high branches.

**Distribution:** Breeds in northern East Asia; winters in south reaching Sumatra. A common winter visitor to the Malay Peninsula, including Singapore; uncommon passage migrant further north, including Hong Kong.

## COMMON STARLING
*Sturnus vulgaris* 22 cm  F: Sturnidae

**Description:** Note diagnostic spotting in otherwise black plumage. Photo shows breeding plumage; non-breeding plumage is duller with more spots and dark bill.

**Voice:** A harsh *tje-er* during migration.

**Habits:** Occurs in open woodlands and cultivation. Locally abundant in towns and cities within its range. Notorious for having colonised the whole North American continent from a few birds released into Central Park in New York City. Today one of the most successful and numerous of all birds. In this region, however, only a few venture this far southeast.

**Distribution:** Breeds in temperate Eurasia; winters in south reaching the subtropics. Introduced in North America, New Zealand, and South Africa. A rare winter visitor in northern parts of mainland, including Hong Kong.

## ASIAN PIED STARLING
*Sturnus contra* 24 cm  F: Sturnidae

**Description**: Distinguished from following species by smaller size and black throat and cap contrasting with white cheeks.

**Voice**: A noisy rattle.

**Habits**: Occurs in open country, especially near low-lying marshy areas. Also found in plantations and open fields but not so common in towns. Perches in small trees and drops to the ground to feed on worms and larvae. Where numerous, it forms roosting flocks in the evening, typical behaviour for this family.

**Distribution**: Oriental region. A widespread and locally fairly common resident in parts of the mainland; introduced in Hong Kong.

## BLACK-COLLARED STARLING
*Sturnus nigricollis* 28 cm  F: Sturnidae

**Description**: Large size. Note diagnostic combination of white head and broad black collar.

**Voice**: A loud and squeaky song.

**Habits**: Found in all kinds of open country, from coastal villages to lower montane planes. Frequents scrub and cultivation, even seen in urban areas. This active and vocal starling has benefited from regional deforestation and seems to be expanding in numbers and range. The nest is a large, dense construction high in a tree.

**Distribution**: Oriental region. A widespread and common resident on much of the mainland, including Hong Kong; vagrant in Brunei.

## COMMON MYNA
*Acridotheres tristis* 25 cm  F: Sturnidae

**Description**: Unmistakable. Note chocolate body with black head and yellow facial skin.

**Voice**: A chattering and squeaky song.

**Habits**: An open country species largely associated with humans. Found in open woodlands, but mainly along roadsides, in cultivated areas and villages, where it can become very bold, even entering houses for food. Omnivorous and adaptable, the most numerous and successful bird in much of its range. Nests in crevices in buildings; roosts in large communal gatherings.

**Distribution**: Oriental region; introduced to New Zealand, Hawaii and South Africa. A widespread and common resident on much of the mainland, including Singapore; introduced in Hong Kong and Brunei.

## JUNGLE MYNA
*Acridotheres fuscus* 24 cm  F: Sturnidae

**Description**: Distinguished with some difficulty from following species by slaty grey (not black) plumage and short crest. The lower belly and vent, not visible from this angle, are pale grey.

**Voice**: Harsh chattering notes.

**Habits**: An open woodlands bird, slightly more arboreal than the next species; often seen in forest edges and clearings; also in the drier scrub behind tidal mangroves. Also occurs in rural cultivation and open fields where it can be observed following cattle and catching the insects they stir up.

**Distribution**: Oriental region. A widespread and fairly common resident in Myanmar and Peninsular Malaysia; uncommon in south Thailand only.

## WHITE-VENTED MYNA (Javan Myna)
*Acridotheres javanicus* 25 cm  F: Sturnidae

**Description**: Note black plumage with yellow bill, long crest and white vent. Patch in wing more visible in flight.

**Voice**: A variety of harsh chattering notes.

**Habits**: An open country species found in fields, villages and cities; also in open woodlands and forest edges, but never closed forest. Javan subspecies (with shorter crest) has established itself as by far the most numerous bird in Singapore, outnumbering the indigenous Common Myna and expanding north into Malaysia. Omnivorous; sometimes feeds on fruit high in the treetops and sometimes on ants in the grass below. Nests in cavities. Congregates in massive roosting flocks in the evening.

**Distribution**: Oriental region. A widespread and common resident in much of the Mainland; introduced in Singapore and southern Peninsular Malaysia.

## CRESTED MYNA
*Acridotheres cristatellus* 27 cm  F: Sturnidae

**Description**: Distinguished from previous species by larger size, ivory bill with rosy base and black vent.

**Voice**: A variety of loud calls. Caged birds can learn to 'talk'.

**Habits**: Found in all lowland habitats except closed forest. An adaptable species often seen in cultivated areas and near human habitation, where it sometimes nests inside crevices in buildings. Outside of the breeding season (which occurs April-July) it congregates in dense and noisy flocks each evening at roosting sites in large trees. During the day birds spread out to feed on the ground in open country or in fruiting trees.

**Distribution**: Oriental region. A common resident in north-eastern parts of the mainland, including Hong Kong; introduced in Penang (Malaysia), Manila (Philippines) and Singapore.

# GOLDEN-CRESTED MYNA
## *Ampeliceps coronatus* 22 cm   F: Sturnidae

**Distribution**: Oriental region. A scarce resident in Myanmar, Thailand, south China and Indochina; vagrant in northern Peninsular Malaysia.

**Description**: Distinguished from Hill Myna by smaller size and yellow crown. Photo shows captive male. Female has black throat and narrow yellow crown. The only member of its genus.

**Voice**: A whistle similar to the Hill Myna, but higher pitched.

**Habits**: Most starlings are open country birds, but this one and the Hill Myna live in closed forest. It can be found in lowland primary forest and forest edges, mainly in the lowlands into low hills. Recorded to 800 metres. Generally a low-density species, but in some locations it congregates in small flocks, settling in the top of fruiting trees. Seen often in Khao Yai National Park in Thailand.

# COLETO
## *Sarcops calvus* 30 cm   F: Sturnidae

**Distribution**: Philippine endemic. A locally fairly common resident on all major islands except Palawan.

**Description**: Unmistakable; the only member of its genus. Note bare pink skin around face. Underparts and wings black, mantel and back grey. Captive photo.

**Voice**: A metallic *kliing-kliing*; also mimics other birds.

**Habits**: An arboreal member of the starling family found in primary forest, nearby woodlands and cultivation. Often seen in large fruiting trees, together with pigeons and other frugivorous birds. The nest is built in a cavity in a tree or broken-off coconut trunk.

# HILL MYNA
## *Gracula religiosa* 30 cm  F: Sturnidae

**Description**: Large, powerful build. Distinguished from other black mynas by size, yellow wattles across neck, heavy flight silhouette and call. Forms its own genus with a Sri Lankan allospecies.

**Voice**: A penetrating whistle *ti-ongg;* also chatters softly and mimics.

**Habits**: An arboreal member of the starling family found in closed primary forest and forest edges; also in coastal coconut groves, often on offshore islands. Perches high, often on the top of a dead branch near the forest's edge, calling loudly. Always seen in pairs, sometimes a group. The nest is built in an abandoned woodpecker's hole or other tree cavity.

**Distribution**: Oriental region. A locally fairly common resident in much of the region, including Brunei and Palawan (Philippines); uncommon in Singapore.

# BROWN-THROATED SUNBIRD (Plain-throated Sunbird)
## *Anthreptes malacensis* 14 cm  F: Nectariniidae

**Description**: Male (top) has brown throat and metallic blue shoulder patch. Female (bottom) recognised with difficulty by strong bill and uniform olive-yellowish plumage.

**Voice**: A loud monotonous *chiff-chaff.*

**Habits**: Prefers rural cultivation, coconut groves, mature gardens and secondary growth. Found often near the coast and on offshore islands, never in closed forest. Feeds on nectar and tiny insects late in the morning, flying from flower to flower. The nest is a pouch with a side entrance, suspended low in a tree.

**Distribution**: Southeast Asia into eastern Indonesia. A widespread and common resident in southern parts of the mainland (including Singapore) and Borneo (including Brunei); fairly common in the Philippines.

## RED-THROATED SUNBIRD
*Anthreptes rhodolaema* 13 cm  F: Nectariniidae

**Description:** Much like Brown-throated Sunbird, but note reddish throat (male). Side view shows dull maroon wing patch (less metallic purple).

**Voice:** Typical sunbird-like chirps.

**Habits:** Restricted to closed lowland rainforest, both primary and nearby mature secondary growth. Often seen in Taman Negara, but otherwise rarely recorded. Moves in the middle and lower storey in a restless search for flowers and tiny fruits.

**Distribution:** Sunda subregion. A rare resident in south Thailand, Myanmar and Brunei; local and scarce in Malaysia; extinct in Singapore.

## RUBY-CHEEKED SUNBIRD
*Anthreptes singalensis* 11 cm  F: Nectariniidae

**Description:** Note rufous throat of female (photo). Male has metallic green cap, mantle and wing coverts.

**Voice:** A high-pitched *wee-eest*.

**Habits:** An adaptable species found in many forested habitats, from closed primary rainforest of the Sunda subregion to deciduous woodlands further north. Also found in secondary growth, mangroves, and cultivation near forest, but rarely seen in gardens. Feeds in trees or bushes with flowers or tiny fruits. Quickly shifts around the tree, often a few in the company of other sunbirds, white-eyes or bulbuls.

**Distribution:** Oriental region. A widespread and fairly common resident throughout most of the mainland and Borneo, including Brunei.

## PURPLE-THROATED SUNBIRD
*Nectarinia sperata* 10 cm  F: Nectariniidae

**Description**: Tiny size; the smallest of the sunbirds. Blackish upperparts contrasting with green cap and maroon belly are diagnostic (male, left). Female (right) a uniform dark olive.

**Voice**: A high-pitched series of chirps and whistles.

**Habits**: Found in wooded areas, from secondary rainforest and forest edges to plantations and mature gardens. This restless bird flutters about quickly in the canopies of small trees, where it feeds on flowers, tiny fruits and insects.

**Distribution:** Oriental region. A generally uncommon resident in parts of the mainland, including Peninsular Malaysia and Singapore. Fairly common locally in the Philippines and Borneo, including Brunei.

## COPPER-THROATED SUNBIRD
*Nectarinia calcostetha* 14 cm  F: Nectariniidae

**Description**: Fairly large, slender build. Male (photo) appears uniformly dark, but purple breast and belly and green cap shine in good light. Female has diagnostic greyish head and underparts; upperparts dark olive.

**Voice**: A characteristic long trill; also a rapid twitter.

**Habits**: A coastal specialist found exclusively in tidal mangrove forests and in casuarinas and coconut groves just behind the sea. A very local species that is sometimes quite numerous in the ideal habitat. A conspicuous, vocal and active bird. Visits flowering trees and bushes; often seen flying quickly from tree to tree in a frantic search for food.

**Distribution:** Southeast Asia to Java (Indonesia). A generally uncommon resident in southern parts of the mainland (including Singapore), on Borneo (including Brunei), and on Palawan (Philippines).

## OLIVE-BACKED SUNBIRD
### *Nectarinia jugularis* 11 cm  F: Nectariniidae

**Description:** Small size and long thin bill. Note the diagnostic blue throat and breast of male (left), missing in female (right).

**Voice:** High-pitched chirps and chatters *cheep, cheep, wheet*.

**Habits:** Found in all types of open woodlands and disturbed habitats from the coast to lower montane elevations. The most successful member of its family in the region. Numerous in parks and gardens, often visiting ornamental flowers and even potted plants on urban balconies. Flutters about, low in trees and bushes, tame and easy to observe, therefore well known. Sometimes mistaken for a hummingbird (a family not represented in Asia).

**Distribution:** Oriental region and east into northern Australia. A widespread and common resident throughout the region; vagrant in Hong Kong.

## PURPLE SUNBIRD
### *Nectarinia asiatica* 11 cm  F: Nectariniidae

**Description:** Female (photo) distinguished with difficulty from other sunbirds by greyish (not yellow or olive) belly; male is dark purple with black wings.

**Voice:** A loud *chweet*.

**Habits:** Found in deciduous woodlands, cultivation, scrub and gardens but avoids closed rainforest. Usually seen solitary or a resident pair together. Visits flowering bushes and low trees feeding on nectar, small insects and spiders. Flutters about quickly and with great agility while calling frequently.

**Distribution:** Oriental region. A widespread and fairly common resident in Myanmar, Thailand, south China and Indochina.

## APO SUNBIRD
### *Aethopyga boltoni* 10 cm  F: Nectariniidae

**Description**: Overlaps in range and altitude with another more numerous endemic, the Grey-hooded Sunbird, *A. primigenius,* but documentation and descriptions are incomplete.

**Voice**: A repeated rising and falling series of short notes.

**Habits**: A strictly montane forest bird found at elevations above 1,500 metres. Moves in the upper storey of primary and mature secondary forest. It is regularly spotted at Mt Apo National Park and at Mt Katanglad, where basic eco-tourism facilities are available.

**Distribution:** Philippine endemic. A scarce resident in montane parts of the island of Mindanao. Near-threatened with global extinction.

## LOVELY SUNBIRD
### *Aethopyga shelleyi* 9 cm  F: Nectariniidae

**Description**: Male (photo) is unmistakable. Female has olive upperparts with greyish yellow underparts and yellow rump.

**Voice**: A melodious whistle and repeated *tweet-tweet*.

**Habits**: Found in forest, along forest edges and in nearby cultivation. Occurs mainly in the lowlands; also recorded at montane elevations below 2,000 metres. Found in all major lowland nature reserves. Behaviour and nesting habits much like other members of this family and genus.

**Distribution:** Philippine endemic. A widespread and fairly common resident on most major islands.

## GOULD'S SUNBIRD
### *Aethopyga gouldiae* 11 cm  F: Nectariniidae

**Distribution:** Oriental region into central China. A locally fairly common resident in montane parts of Myanmar, southwest China, Laos and Vietnam; a winter visitor only in Thailand; vagrant in Hong Kong.

**Description:** Male (photo) distinguished from following species by full red breast and mantle. Female has distinct yellow rump.

**Voice:** A high-pitched *chit*.

**Habits:** Strictly montane in breeding season, usually found above 1,200 metres; in the Himalayas as high as 4,200 metres. Feeds on flowers in the stunted montane trees and rhododendrons. Also visits gardens near forest to feed on ornamental flowers as shown in photo. During the winter months it disperses widely and has been recorded down to 400 metres.

## GREEN-TAILED SUNBIRD
### *Aethopyga nipalensis* 11 cm  F: Nectariniidae

**Distribution:** Oriental region. A locally common resident in upper montane parts of Myanmar, Thailand, Yunnan (China), Laos and Vietnam.

**Description:** Distinguished from following species by yellow (not grey) underparts. Photo shows subspecies endemic to Doi Inthanon (Thailand); note scarlet band across bright yellow lower breast. Other populations are duller, without red on breast.

**Voice:** A high-pitched, thin *psss-t*.

**Habits:** A strictly upper montane forest bird found in closed forest, along edges and in nearby gardens, from 1,800 to 3,300 metres. Moves quickly from the highest treetops to the lowest bushes in a frantic search for nectar and small insects. Several are often seen together, keeping in contact with constant thin whistles, has no fear of humans.

# FORK-TAILED SUNBIRD
## *Aethopyga christinae* 10 cm   F: Nectariniidae

**Description**: Male (photo) has peculiar elongated tail showing well in photo. Throat and upper breast are dark maroon. Female is olive with yellowish underparts and grey crown.

**Voice**: A high-pitched trill and various twitters; also a loud and frequent contact call *chiff-chiff* while feeding.

**Habits**: Found in open woodlands, cultivation and gardens. Numerous locally within its small range in ideal habitat. Feeds restlessly on flowers. The nest is a woven pouch suspended from a branch in a tree.

**Distribution**: Mainland Southeast Asia only. A locally common resident in Vietnam and southeast China, including Hong Kong.

# BLACK-THROATED SUNBIRD
## *Aethopyga saturata* 11 cm   F: Nectariniidae

**Description**: Note the black head with blue cap, maroon mantle and elongated tail of male (top). Female (bottom) is drab olive.

**Voice**: A sharp, chirping call when feeding and flying.

**Habits**: A forest bird found mainly in lower montane closed forest, from 600 to 1,800 metres, and occasionally down to 300 metres. Feeds on flowers and small insects at all levels, often high in the canopy but also down to eye-level near the edges. Readily ventures into nearby gardens and camps where it visits ornamental flowers and bushes. Quick and restless, but tame and easy to observe.

**Distribution**: Oriental region. A locally fairly common resident in elevated areas of the mainland.

# CRIMSON SUNBIRD
*Aethopyga siparaja* 11 cm  F: Nectariniidae

**Description:** Male (top) distinguished from Scarlet Sunbird by bluish black (not red) tail. Female (bottom) has reddish tinge on throat.

**Voice:** A high-pitched chirp *chit-chit-chew*.

**Habits:** Frequents forest edges and secondary growth; also found in nearby cultivation. Visits flowers at canopy level in the forest or low ornamental plants, often seen in mature gardens and orchid nurseries. Like most sunbirds it is sedentary to one area, visiting the same flowers late every morning.

**Distribution:** Oriental region. A widespread and locally fairly common resident in much of the region, including Singapore, Brunei and parts of the Philippines.

# SCARLET SUNBIRD (Temminck's Sunbird)
*Aethopyga temminckii* 11 cm  F: Nectariniidae

**Description:** Male (photo) distinguished from Crimson Sunbird by red (not black) tail. Female drab olive with reddish tinge to tail. The Javan subspecies, *A. mystacalis,* considered by some to be full species, with this name.

**Voice:** A high-pitched *cheet-cheet*.

**Habits:** Found in rainforest and forest edges. Occurs mainly in the lowlands on the Malay Peninsula; on Borneo primarily between 600 and 2,000 metres. Lives almost exclusively on nectar extracted from small flowers in the upper or middle storeys of the forest. Rarely seen in cultivated areas.

**Distribution:** Sunda subregion. An uncommon resident in Malaysia; in East Malaysia, resident mainly at lower montane elevations; rare in south Thailand.

## LITTLE SPIDERHUNTER
*Arachnothera longirostra* 16 cm  F: Nectariniidae

**Description**: Distinguished from the Thick-billed Spiderhunter, *A. crassirostris*, by thin bill, and by pale throat and bright yellow underparts contrasting with dark olive upperparts.

**Voice**: A penetrating *chiit* in flight.

**Habits**: An adaptable and successful forest bird found in primary forest, secondary growth and nearby cultivation. A secretive and skulking bird, not easy to observe; most often seen moving quickly through the dense undergrowth, calling loudly. Feeds on nectar and small invertebrates, regularly visiting flowering bushes and scrub, especially wild banana flowers.

**Distribution**: Oriental region. A locally fairly common resident in much of the region, including Brunei, Singapore and parts of the Philippines.

## LONG-BILLED SPIDERHUNTER
*Arachnothera robusta* 22 cm  F: Nectariniidae

**Description**: Note massive bill and faint streaking on breast.

**Voice**: A loud *chit-chit*.

**Habits**: Found in primary rainforest and forest edges, mainly in the lowlands and lower hills, occasionally as high as 1,200 metres. Moves at canopy level feeding on nectar, spiders and insects. Although a low-density species, it is noisy, conspicuous and can quite easily be seen at certain sites, such as the Taman Negara HQ (Malaysia) where it visits ornamental trees. This and the next 3 photographs were taken there.

**Distribution**: Sunda subregion. An uncommon resident in Malaysia and Brunei; rare in the extreme south of Thailand.

# SPECTACLED SPIDERHUNTER
*Arachnothera flavigaster* 22 cm  F: Nectariniidae

**Description:** Yellow eye-ring is diagnostic; also note shorter and stronger bill.

**Voice:** A loud *chi-chip*.

**Habits:** Found in lowland rainforest, from sea level to 600 metres; on Borneo recorded to 1,600 metres. Often ventures out of the forest to feed in cultivated areas such as banana and coconut groves near rural villages. Conspicuous and quarrelsome it chases other nectar-feeders away from its favourite patch. The nest is a small pouch of spider webs fixed under a large leaf or two smaller leaves sewn together; typical of the genus.

**Distribution:** Sunda subregion. A generally scarce resident in south Thailand and Malaysia; rare in Brunei; extinct in Singapore.

# YELLOW-EARED SPIDERHUNTER
*Arachnothera chrysogenys* 18 cm  F: Nectariniidae

**Description:** Note conspicuous yellow patch below eye. Also distinguished from previous species by smaller size and paler underparts.

**Voice:** A penetrating squeaky *chick*.

**Habits:** Fairly adaptable. Found both in primary rainforest and in nearby disturbed forest and cultivation. Often seen flying high between canopies, calling loudly. Sometimes flies down briefly to the lower storeys near the forest edge to feed on nectar, spiders and small seeds.

**Distribution:** Sunda subregion. A locally fairly common resident in south Thailand, Myanmar and Malaysia; rare in Brunei and Singapore.

## GREY-BREASTED SPIDERHUNTER
*Arachnothera affinis* 18 cm  F: Nectariniidae

**Description**: Distinguished from other lowland spiderhunters by dark greyish-olive plumage and faint streaks on breast.

**Voice**: A variety of high-pitched chatters.

**Habits**: Found in primary rainforest, mature secondary growth and along forest edges from the lowlands to lower montane elevations. A restless bird, it moves through the middle and upper storeys of the forest, and occasionally lower down. Shifts quickly from tree to tree, searching for small insects and nectar.

**Distribution:** Sunda subregion. A locally fairly common resident in south Thailand, Myanmar, Malaysia and Brunei; extinct in Singapore.

## STREAKED SPIDERHUNTER
*Arachnothera magna* 19 cm  F: Nectariniidae

**Description**: Distinguished from other spiderhunters by large chunky build and bold black streaks in plumage.

**Voice**: A loud chatter.

**Habits**: Mainly montane, usually found inside primary montane forest. Occurs between 900 and 2,000 metres in northern parts of range, but sometimes lower. Also seen in nearby disturbed areas such as roadsides and gardens, feeding on cultivated flowers. Locally numerous; a heavy and noisy bird that is easy to spot and often quite tame.

**Distribution:** Oriental region. A common resident in montane parts of the mainland.

## SCARLET-BREASTED FLOWERPECKER
*Prionochilus thoracicus* 10 cm  F: Dicaeidae

**Description**: Male (photo) distinguished from other flowerpeckers by black head and red patch on black breast. Female lacks black patterns but has reddish tinge on breast.

**Voice**: Metallic clicks typical of the family.

**Habits**: A lowland rainforest bird found in primary as well as mature secondary forest. Usually moves high in the middle or upper storeys, feeding on flowers and small fruit and insects; seldom seen at eye-level. Little studied, although colourful and conspicuous. Few nesting records; often missed during surveys.

**Distribution**: Sunda sub-region. A generally scarce resident in south Thailand, Malaysia and Brunei.

## YELLOW-BREASTED FLOWERPECKER
*Prionochilus maculatus* 10 cm  F: Dicaeidae

**Description**: Note diagnostic dark streaks on yellow breast and small orange crown; sexes similar.

**Voice**: Metallic clicks and a softer *tsweet-tsweet*.

**Habits**: Found in primary and secondary rainforest and nearby scrub, from the lowlands into lower montane elevations. Visits flowering and fruiting trees and bushes from the canopies down to eye-level; often seen feeding with other flowerpeckers on Mistletoe plants and Rhododendrons along the trails.

**Distribution**: Sunda sub-region. A fairly common resident in south Thailand, Myanmar, Malaysia and Brunei; extinct in Singapore.

## CRIMSON-BREASTED FLOWERPECKER
*Prionochilus percussus* 10 cm  F: Dicaeidae

**Description**: Look for diagnostic red patch on breast of male (photo). The similar Yellow-rumped Flowerpecker, *P. xanthopygius,* endemic to Borneo, has smaller patch and yellow rump. Female is olive green with yellow stripe down belly.

**Voice**: Like that of other flowerpeckers.

**Habits**: Found in lowland rainforest and forest edges, often near other flowerpecker species. Moves quickly through the middle storey, sometimes moving lower near clearings to feed on flowering or fruiting trees and bushes. Little studied; no nesting records.

**Distribution**: Sunda subregion. A locally fairly common resident in Peninsular Malaysia, but generally scarce; uncommon in south Thailand; occurs in Myanmar; vagrant in Borneo, including Brunei.

## THICK-BILLED FLOWERPECKER
*Dicaeum agile* 10 cm  F: Dicaeidae

**Description**: Note diagnostic broad streaks on underparts; sexes similar.

**Voice**: A thin *pseeow*.

**Habits**: Found in rainforest and deciduous forest from lowlands into lower montane elevations, mainly in tall primary forest. Stays at upper storey and canopy level and is difficult to observe. More sluggish than other flowerpeckers. Has a peculiar habit of twisting its tail slowly from side to side.

**Distribution**: Oriental region. A locally common resident in Thailand, but generally scarce; rare in Peninsular Malaysia; vagrant in Singapore.

## YELLOW-VENTED FLOWERPECKER
*Dicaeum chrysorrheum* 10 cm  F: Dicaeidae

**Description**: Prominent thin streaks on pale underparts and yellow rump are diagnostic; sexes similar.

**Voice**: A short, harsh *sweest;* seems less vocal than other flowerpeckers.

**Habits**: Found in wooded areas, often secondary forest and edges near primary growth; seldom seen inside closed forest. An active feeder, it visits fruiting and flowering trees and bushes, usually at canopy level, but sometimes lower.

**Distribution**: Oriental region. A widespread and locally fairly common resident throughout much of the mainland; rare in Singapore; uncommon in Brunei and East Malaysia.

## ORANGE-BELLIED FLOWERPECKER
*Dicaeum trigonostigma* 9 cm  F: Dicaeidae

**Description**: Male (top) unmistakable; note bright orange underparts and bluish head and wings. Female (bottom) is plain olive with yellow tinge around tail.

**Voice**: A frequent metallic *chick*.

**Habits**: Found in dense wooded areas, often near lowland primary rainforest. Usually seen along disturbed edges and roadsides, in secondary growth and nearby cultivation. Moves in a jerky flight on tiny whirling wings across the whole strata of the forest, from the highest canopies, to bushes just off the ground. Active, tame and delightful to observe.

**Distribution**: Oriental region. A locally common resident in Myanmar, south Thailand, Malaysia, Singapore, Brunei and the Philippines.

## SCARLET-BACKED FLOWERPECKER
*Dicaeum cruentatum* 9 cm  F: Dicaeidae

**Description**: Male (photo) distinguished from other flowerpeckers by red crown and back. Female is dull brown with red vent only.

**Voice**: A frequent metallic *tick*, often in flight.

**Habits**: An adaptable and successful member of this family, found in all kinds of wooded habitat except closed forest. Seen in gardens, urban parks and open country with scattered trees. Flies restlessly from one treetop to the next, often detected only by its clicking call. The nest is a small woven pouch with a side entrance suspended from a branch high inside a tree, typical of the family.

**Distribution:** Oriental region. A widespread and common resident in most of the region, including Hong Kong, Singapore and Brunei.

## BLACK-SIDED FLOWERPECKER
*Dicaeum monticolum* 8 cm  F: Dicaeidae

**Description**: Male (photo) unmistakable within range. Female is dull grey. Possibly conspicific with following species, however this listing follows both Smythies (1981) and MacKinnon & Phillipps (1993).

**Voice**: A sharp metallic *tick*.

**Habits**: Occurs in most elevated parts of Sabah and Sarawak, from 300 to 2,100 metres. Can be found in both Mulu National Park (Sarawak) and on Mt. Kinabalu (Sabah) where this photograph was taken. Occurs in forest and along forest edges. Like other members of this family it often feeds high in the trees on fruits of parasitic mistletoe plants and flowers. Also catches small insects on its hectic rounds.

**Distribution:** Borneo endemic. A fairly common resident in montane parts of Sabah and Sarawak.

## BUFF-BELLIED FLOWERPECKER (Fire-breasted Flowerpecker)
*Dicaeum ignipectus* 9 cm  F: Dicaeidae

**Description**: Note yellowish buff underparts contrasting with grey head of female (photo). Male has diagnostic glossy dark green upperparts; some subspecies have a red patch on buff underparts.

**Voice**: Like other flowerpeckers.

**Habits**: Strictly montane and given the right habitat and elevation the most numerous flowerpecker. Resident between 900 and 2,200 metres; in China occurring up to 3,950 metres. Somewhat nomadic in northern parts of range, moving lower during winter. Found in forest and along forest edges, feeding on flowers and small fruit.

**Distribution**: Oriental region. A locally fairly common resident in montane parts of the mainland; uncommon in Philippine mountains; mainly a winter visitor to Hong Kong.

## ORIENTAL WHITE-EYE
*Zosterops palpebrosus* 11 cm  F: Zosteropidae

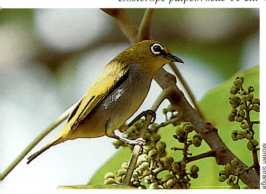

**Description**: Distinguished with difficulty from other white-eyes by brighter upperparts and dark, almost black lores.

**Voice**: A frequent, high-pitched chatter.

**Habits**: Found in secondary growth, open woodlands, mangroves and cultivation; in the north also in closed forest up to 1,800 metres; in the Sunda subregion only along the coast. Here the inland forest habitat is taken up by the very similar Everett's White-eye *Z. everetti*. Always seen in flocks, moving restlessly through the trees, feeding on flowers, insects and small fruits.

**Distribution**: Oriental region. A widespread and common resident throughout the mainland; Singapore population considered escapees; rare in coastal Sarawak (East Malaysia); vagrant in Brunei.

## BLACK-CAPPED WHITE-EYE
*Zosterops atricapilla* 11 cm  F: Zosteropidae

**Description**: Unmistakable. Note grey underparts and black forehead.

**Voice**: Soft chatter like other white-eyes.

**Habits**: A montane rainforest bird occurring from 900 to 3,000 metres. Can be seen well at Mt. Kinabalu (Sabah) and Mulu (Sarawak). An active bird constantly on the move through the canopies and the middle storey of the forest in small flocks, chattering and searching for minute food items.

**Distribution:** Borneo and Sumatra. A locally fairly common resident in the mountains of Sabah and Sarawak.

## MOUNTAIN WHITE-EYE
*Zosterops montanus* 12 cm  F: Zosteropidae

**Description**: Note characteristic sharp contrast between yellow throat and upper breast; white belly is seen well from this angle.

**Voice**: High-pitched chatter.

**Habits**: Restricted to montane elevations above 1,000 metres. Mt. Apo and Mt. Katanglad (Mindanao) and Mt. Polis (Luzon) are all good locations for this species. Feeds actively in forest and along forest edges, from treetop to ground level. Often moves in small flocks and with other birds, taking mainly small fruits and berries as this photo illustrates.

**Distribution:** The Philippines and Indonesia. A locally common resident in the mountains of the major Philippine islands.

## MOUNTAIN BLACK-EYE (Blackeye)
*Chlorocharis emiliae* 14 cm  F: Zosteropidae

**Description:** Unmistakable; fairly large; only white-eye with black eye ring.

**Voice:** A melodious thrush-like song, also a twittering contact call.

**Habits:** An upper montane specialist locally abundant, especially on Mt. Kinabalu, from 2,800 to 3,600 metres at the tree line. On other mountains it has been recorded down to 1,200 metres. Hops through the stunted montane trees, somewhat like a Common Iora. Feeds mainly on insects which it pecks from the foliage; also takes some small fruits.

**Distribution:** Borneo endemic. A locally common resident in the mountains of Sabah and Sarawak.

## EURASIAN TREE-SPARROW
*Passer montanus* 15 cm  F: Passeridae

**Description:** Distinguished from other sparrows by brown cap and streaked back.

**Voice:** A thin, monotonous *chip-chip*.

**Habits:** One of very few birds to be exclusively associated with humans; does not occur in any truly wild habitats. Abundant in towns, villages and rural as well as urban developments, where it feeds on grain and food scraps on the ground. During the breeding season it also takes many insects. Nests in cavities in buildings or in trees. Always seen in pairs or a small group and can become totally tame.

**Distribution:** Eurasia; introduced in other regions, e.g. Australia and USA. A widespread and common resident in all countries and territories; has most recently expanded to the Philippines and Borneo, including Brunei.

## PLAIN-BACKED SPARROW
*Passer flaveolus* 15 cm  F: Passeridae

**Description**: Male (photo) distinguished from the previous species by smooth chestnut mantle and pale forehead. Female is a plain pale brown.

**Voice**: A monotonous *chip*, more resonant than the Tree Sparrow's.

**Habits**: Another member of this family that is widespread in the region, but not nearly as successful as the previous species. Occurs in disturbed habitats, clearings, rural roadsides and cultivation, but shuns houses and buildings. Seen perching low in bushes and trees, often in resident pairs, the male chipping away as shown in the photo.

**Distribution**: Mainland Southeast Asia only. A widespread but generally scarce resident in Myanmar, Thailand and Indochina; also found in Peninsular Malaysia, except in the extreme south.

Morten Strange

## BAYA WEAVER
*Ploceus philippinus* 15 cm  F: Ploceidae

**Description**: Photos shows female at nest. Breeding male has blackish face and golden cap.

**Voice**: A sparrow-like *chip* near nest; also a harsh, chattering song with a mixed variety of whistling and wheezy notes.

**Habits**: Found in open woodlands, usually near brackish or freshwater wetlands with long grass. The carefully woven nest with its long entrance tube is built in colonies suspended high in trees near water. In spite of what the Latin name seems to indicate, this species is absent from the Philippines. In fact the family is not represented there nor on Borneo.

**Distribution**: Oriental region. A widespread and locally fairly common resident in large areas of the mainland, including Singapore.

Morten Strange

## STREAKED WEAVER
*Ploceus manyar* 14 cm  F: Ploceidae

**Description**: Photo shows male. Distinguished from other weavers in all plumages by dark streaks on chest.

**Voice**: Like the Baya Weaver.

**Habits**: Frequents open country, grassy marshes and paddy fields. Moves through the terrain in large flocks, feeding among tall grasses. Nests in dense colonies quite different from Baya Weaver: the nest is a rounded (not elongated) ball with a short entrance, placed low among grasses and bushes. An active weaver colony is a delightful spectacle of birds flying to and from the site building, calling and displaying.

**Distribution**: Oriental region. A local and generally uncommon resident in parts of the mainland; recently recorded breeding in Singapore.

## ASIAN GOLDEN WEAVER
*Ploceus hypoxanthus* 15 cm  F: Ploceidae

**Description**: The beautiful golden plumage of the male (photo) is unmistakable. Female distinguished with difficulty from the two previous species by massive bill, very thick at base.

**Voice**: Like previous species.

**Habits**: Found in lowland freshwater marshes, rivers and lakes with tall grasses and nearby wet paddy fields. Behaviour and nesting habits much like the Streaked Weaver. A low-density species which does not occur in any great numbers within its small range. Seems to be declining in numbers and is now regarded as near-threatened with global extinction.

**Distribution**: Southeast Asia into Sumatra and Java. A local and uncommon resident in southern parts of Myanmar, Thailand, Cambodia and Vietnam.

## RED AVADAVAT
*Amandava amandava* 10 cm  F: Estrildidae

**Description**: Male (photo) has reddish head and underparts with fine white spots. Female is duller but with bright red rump.

**Voice**: A shrill *speep,* often uttered in flight.

**Habits**: Found in open country with long grass cover, often near wet areas, cultivation and rural gardens. Mainly occurs in the lowlands and low hills, recorded to 1,500 metres. Often seen near other munias, feeding on seeds among tall grasses; during breeding season also takes insects as food for young. A popular cagebird. Although quite tame, good views are not easy. Usually seen flying by, fast and low.

**Distribution:** Oriental region into eastern Indonesia. A widespread but uncommon resident in parts of the mainland; introduced in Hong Kong and Manila (Philippines) and Kota Kinabalu (Sabah).

## WHITE-RUMPED MUNIA (White-backed Munia)
*Lonchura striata* 11 cm  F: Estrildidae

**Description**: Distinguished from White-bellied Munia, *L. leucogastra,* by a white lower back that flashes on take-off.

**Voice**: A trilled *prrit.*

**Habits**: Found in wooded terrain and overgrown open country, cultivation and gardens. A forest edge bird of the Sunda subregion and the Philippines. This successful species seems to have benefited from forest clearance and increased in numbers. Feeds on seeds low in the grass, but flies up into trees to roost. Builds a large, ball-shaped nest within dense foliage.

**Distribution:** Oriental region. A widespread and common resident all through the mainland, including Hong Kong; rare in Singapore.

## SCALY-BREASTED MUNIA (Spotted Munia)
*Lonchura punctulata* 11 cm  F: Estrildidae

**Description**: Unmistakable. Note diagnostic scaly underparts.

**Voice**: A faint *kee-dee*.

**Habits**: An open country bird, it frequents grassy fields, open woodlands, cultivation and gardens. Moves about in small flocks, often feeding among roadside grasses or picking up seeds from lawns and field edges. Quite tame. Flies short distances, calling softly; congregates in larger flocks at evening roosts in taller trees. The nest is a messy ball of vegetation in a bush.

**Distribution**: Oriental region; introduced elsewhere. A widespread and common resident on the mainland, including Hong Kong and Singapore, and in parts of the Philippines.

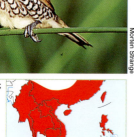

## CHESTNUT MUNIA (Black-headed Munia)
*Lonchura malacca* 11 cm  F: Estrildidae

**Description**: Unmistakable. Note diagnostic black head missing in juveniles.

**Voice**: A shrill *preeep*.

**Habits**: An open country species found in small flocks in fields, long grass areas and cultivation. Forms dense flocks in prime habitat, but often just small groups, sometimes in the company of other munias. Flies low, with an undulating flight pattern, in packed groups. Feeds low in the grass or on the ground, mainly on seeds.

**Distribution**: Oriental region; somewhat nomadic outside breeding season. A locally common resident in Malaysia, Singapore, Brunei and the Philippines; less common in northern part of its range, including Hong Kong.

## WHITE-HEADED MUNIA
*Lonchura maja* 11 cm  F: Estrildidae

**Description:** Its white head contrasting with chestnut body is diagnostic.

**Voice:** A thin *peep*.

**Habits:** An open country bird often associated with coastal marshes; also found in dry fields, rural cultivation and low scrub. Outside breeding season forms dense flocks roaming across flat grasslands, often with other munia species. Pecks seeds from low straws or from the ground along grassy edges.

**Distribution:** Sunda subregion to Bali (Indonesia). A locally fairly common resident in Peninsular Malaysia and Singapore; uncommon in south Thailand.

## BLACK-HEADED GREENFINCH
*Carduelis ambigua* 14 cm  F: Fringillidae

**Description:** Male (photo) unmistakable. Female has grey (not black) head and lacks streaks on breast. Photo shows south Vietnam subspecies treated by Vo Quy & Nguyen Cu (1995) as endemic species Vietnamese Greenfinch, *C. spinoides*.

**Voice:** A twittering *treee,* and a thin, metallic *tit-tit*.

**Habits:** Found in open woodlands at montane elevations above 1,200 metres, often in conifers and also in nearby cultivation and gardens. Somewhat nomadic during winter; generally moves to lower elevations. Can be seen in small flocks, chattering softly while feeding on seeds low in trees and bushes.

**Distribution:** Oriental region; mainly sedentary. A locally fairly common resident in northwestern montane parts of region; a rare winter visitor to Thailand.

## VINACEOUS ROSEFINCH
### *Carpodacus vinaceus* 15 cm  F: Fringillidae

**Description:** Distinguished from other rosefinches (*Carpodacus spp*) by dark crimson (not pink) plumage.

**Voice:** A hard *pwit* or *sieh* and a simple song lasting about two seconds.

**Habits:** One of 17 species of rosefinch in China, but the only one found on the island of Taiwan, where it occurs at upper montane elevations between 2,300 and 2,900 meters. Found in the Himalayas to 3,400 meters but moves down to 1,200 meters in winter. Occurs in mixed montane forest with conifers and deciduous trees, often at the edge of woodlands where it comes down low to feed on seeds as shown in this photo.

**Distribution:** Oriental region into central China. A locally fairly common resident in montane parts of Myanmar, southwest China and Taiwan.

## BROWN BULLFINCH
### *Pyrrhula nipalensis* 17 cm  F: Fringillidae

**Description:** Unmistakable. Note brown cap, small thick bill and white rump; bright white vent sometimes shows well.

**Voice:** A thin, piping call.

**Habits:** A montane member of the northern-based family of finches, otherwise poorly represented in the tropics. Occurs in mixed forest on the mountains, often in open woodlands with pines, from 1,300 metres upwards; in China occurs to 3,600 metres and moves lower in winter. The High Pines area at Fraser's Hill in Malaysia, where this photograph was taken, is a favourite spot to watch for this special species. Nesting activity has been reported.

**Distribution:** Oriental region. An uncommon upper montane resident in the extreme north of Vietnam, Peninsular Malaysia, Myanmar, South China and Taiwan, excluding Hong Kong.

## WHITE-CHEEKED BULLFINCH (Philippine Bullfinch)
*Pyrrhula leucogenis* 16 cm  F: Fringillidae

**Description:** Unmistakable within range, the only *Pyrrhula* in the Philippines.

**Voice:** A fluty whistle of 2 to 3 notes.

**Habits:** Found in montane forest and forest edges above 1,200 metres, often in resident pairs. Regularly observed in small numbers at both Mt. Apo and Mt. Katanglad on Mindanao. Also ventures into nearby cultivated areas. Feeds on small berries in fruiting trees, sometimes in the company of Mountain White-eyes.

Pete Morris

**Distribution:** Philippine endemic. A scarce resident in montane parts of Luzon and Mindanao.

## YELLOW-BREASTED BUNTING
*Emberiza aureola* 15 cm  F: Emberizidae

**Description:** Distinguished from other buntings in all plumages by yellow underparts, mainly streaked on flanks, and characteristic head pattern.

**Voice:** A short *tzip* and a trilled *trseet*.

**Habits:** The only member of this large mainly temperate and subarctic family to penetrate the tropics. During winter, from October to April, it settles in open country with some trees, often in marshy areas. During peak migration, flocks numbering hundreds have been observed roosting in reed beds. More often seen flying overhead in small groups calling softly. Feeds on the ground, often in paddy fields and other cultivated areas.

Tim Loseby

**Distribution:** Breeds in northern Eurasia; winters in the south. A common passage migrant and winter visitor throughout most of the mainland, including Hong Kong; rare in Peninsular Malaysia and Singapore; a single record in Sarawak.

# GLOSSARY

**Adult**: mature plumage bird.

**Allospecies**: two closely related species replacing each other geographically.

**Aquatic**: growing or living in water.

**Arboreal**: living in trees.

**Australasia**: a faunal region that includes Eastern Indonesia, New Guinea, Australia, New Zealand and the southwest Pacific.

**Birdwave**: a mixed species flock, feeding on invertebrates, while moving through the forest.

**Casque**: an enlargement on the upper part of the bill of hornbills.

**Conspecific**: of the same species.

**Coronal**: along edge of crown.

**Crepuscular**: active in the weak light at dusk and dawn.

**Deciduous**: leafless for part of the year, in the cold or the dry season.

**Diagnostic**: a feature that establishes identification of a species.

**Dimorphic**: having two distinctive plumage types.

**Dipterocarp**: a hardwood tree of the Dipterocarpaceae family.

**Diurnal**: active by day.

**Doi**: Thai for mountain.

**Echolocate**: to navigate in total darkness by sound.

**Extinct**: no longer present in area concerned.

**Feral**: escaped and living wild.

**Frugivorous**: feeding on fruit.

**Genera**: the plural of genus.

**Genus**: divisions into which a bird family is divided.

**Gregarious**: congregating in social flocks.

**Gunung**: Malay for mountain.

**Immature**: used here to refer to any plumage stage older than juvenile and younger than adult.

**Insectivorous**: feeding on insects.

**Juvenile**: bird that has just fledged from the nest.

**Kelong**: offshore fishing platform.

**Khao**: Thai for hill.

**Local**: unevenly distributed.

**Migrant**: a species that has moved temporarily away from its breeding area, usually to a warmer climate.

**Monotypic**: the sole representative of its species, genus or family.

**Montane**: pertaining to mountains; used here to refer to areas above 900 metres elevation.

**Nocturnal**: active by night.

**Nomadic**: moving outside resident range when not breeding.

**Non-breeding visitor**: can be found at any time during the year, but no evidence of breeding.

**Ocellus**: an eye-like spot in the plumage; the plural is ocelli.

**Oriental**: a faunal region including south and southeast Asia.

**Paddy**: wet rice field.

**Palearctic**: a faunal region encompassing Europe, north Africa and northern Asia, south to the Yangtze River; here used synonymously with Eurasia.

**Passerine**: a perching bird of the order Passeriformes; includes all families from Broadbills to end of sequence.

**Pelagic**: relating to the seas or oceans, often living far from land.

**Pied**: patterned in black and white.

**Plume**: an elongated display feather.

**Primary forest**: original, virgin forest.

**Race**: synonymous with subspecies.

**Raptor**: the popular term for a bird of prey, from the order Falconiformes, for example the Accipitridae or Falconidae family.

**Resident**: a species breeding or believed to be breeding in that area.

**Secondary forest**: logged or otherwise disturbed forest.

**Sedentary**: present in its breeding area all year; antonym of migratory.

**Shorebird**: a long-legged water bird of the suborder Charadii, primarily the Charadriidae or Scolopacidae family.

**Stenotopic**: confined to one type of habitat

**Storey**: a level in the forest.

**Straggler**: a bird found outside its usual geographical range.

**Streamer**: a greatly elongated tail feather.

**Subspecies**: a population visibly distinguishable from other populations of same species (sometimes only in the hand).

**Sunda**: a faunal subregion covering the Malay Peninsula, Borneo, Sumatra, Java and Bali.

**Supercilium**: eye-stripe.

**Sympatric**: same distribution.

**Terrestrial**: living on the ground.

**Vagrant**: very rare, irregular and accidental in occurrence.

**Wader**: popular term for shorebird.

**Wattle**: a patch of coloured skin hanging from head or neck.

# Selected bibliography

The following works were consulted in the preparation of this book. Additional information was extracted and compiled from articles which appeared in the Oriental Bird Club publications *OBC Bulletin* and *The Forktail*.

Attenborough, D. (1998), *The Life of Birds*, BBC Books, London.

Coates, B.J., Bishop, K.D. and Gardner, D. (1997), *A Guide to the Birds of Wallacea*, Dove Publications, Queensland.

Collar, N.J., Crosby, M.J. and Stattersfield, A.J. (1994), *Birds to Watch 2; The World List of Threatened Birds*, BirdLife International, Cambridge.

De Schauensee, R.M. (1984), *The Birds of China*, Smithsonian Institution Press, Washington, D.C.

del Hoyo, J., Elliott, A. and Sargatal, J. (eds.) (1992-97), *Handbook of the Birds of the World*, vol. 1–4, Lynx Editions, Barcelona.

Diamond, A.W. and Lovejoy, T.E. (1985), *Conservation of Tropical Forest Birds*, ICBP, Cambridge.

Dickinson, E.C., Kennedy, R.S. and Parkes, K.C. (1991), *The Birds of the Philippines*; British Ornithologists' Union Checklist No 12.

Dymond, N. (1995), *Some Prime Birding Sites in Vietnam*, N. Dymond, Shetland.

Flegg, J. and Madge, S. (1995), *Photographic Field Guide—Birds of Australia*, New Holland, London.

Gee, B. (1997), 'The Philippines Winter 1996/1997', B. Gee, London.

Gonzales P.C. and Rees, C.P. (1988), *Birds of the Philippines*, Haribon Foundation, Manila.

Gosler, C. (1991), *The Photographic Guide to Birds of the World*, Reed International Books Limited, London.

Grewal, B. (1993), *Birds of India—A Photographic Guide*, Guidebook Company Limited, Hong Kong.

Grewal, B. (1995), *A Photographic Guide to Birds of India and Nepal*, New Holland, London.

Gro-Nielsen, L. (1997), *A Survey of the Avifauna in Primary Forest Compared with the Avifauna in Different Types of Secondary Forest*, University of Århus, Denmark.

Hails, C.J. and Jarvis, F. (1987), *Birds of Singapore*, Times Editions, Singapore.

Howard, R. and Moore, A. (1991), *A Complete Checklist of Birds of the World*, Academic Press Limited, England.

Inskipp, T., Lindsey, N. and Duckworth W. (1996), *An Annotated Checklist of the Birds of the Oriental Region*, Oriental Bird Club, England.

Jepson, P. and Ounsted R. (eds.) (1997), *Birding Indonesia*, Periplus Editions (HK) Ltd, Singapore.

Jyarajasingam, J. and Pearson, A. (1999), *A Field Guide to the Birds of West Malaysia and Singapore*, Oxford University Press, London.

King, B., Woodcock, M.W. and Dickinson, E.C. (1975), *A Field Guide to the Birds of South-East Asia*, Collins, London.

Lekagul, B. and Round, P.D. (1991), *A Guide to the Birds of Thailand*, Saha Kharn Bhaet Co., Bangkok.

Lewis, A., Morris, P. and Higgins, N. (1989), Thailand and Malaysia Dec 1988 - Aug 1989, Higgins, Lewis and Morris, England.

Lim, K. S. and Gardner, D. (1997), *Birds: An Illustrated Field Guide to the Birds of Singapore*, Sun Tree Publishing, Singapore.

MacKinnon, J. and Hicks, N. (1996), *A Photographic Guide to Birds of China*, New Holland, London.

MacKinnon, J. and Phillipps, K. (1993), *A Field Guide to the Birds of Borneo, Sumatra, Java and Bali*, Oxford University Press, London.

Medway, Lord and Wells, D. R. (1976), *The Birds of the Malay Peninsula*, vol. 5, Penerbit University Malaya, Kuala Lumpur.

Poonswad, P. and Kemp, A. C. (eds.) (1993), *Manual to the Conservation of Asian Hornbills*, Hornbill Project, Thailand.

Quy, V. and Cu, N. (1995), *Checklist of the Birds of Vietnam*, Vietnam National University, Hanoi.

Rabor, D.S. (1977), *Philippine Birds and Mammals*, University of the Philippines Science Education Center, Quezon City.

Robson, C. (2000), *A Field Guide to the Birds of South-East Asia*, New Holland, London.

Sargeant, D. (1992), *A Birders Guide to the Philippines*, D. E.Sargeant, England.

Smythies, B.E. (1981), *The Birds of Borneo*, The Malayan Nature Society, Kuala Lumpur.

Sonobe, K. and Usui, S. (Eds.) (1993), *A Field Guide to the Waterbirds of Asia*, Wild Bird Society of Japan, Tokyo.

Strange, M. (1998), *Birds of South-east Asia*, New Holland, London.

Strange, M. (1998), *Tropical Birds of Southeast Asia*, Periplus Editions (HK) Ltd, Singapore.

Strange, M. and Jeyarajasingam, A. (1993), *Birds: A Photographic Guide to the Birds of Peninsular Malaysia and Singapore*, Sun Tree Publishing, Singapore.

Sun, H., Seng, K.H., Omaliss, K., Heng, N. and Poole, C. (1998), *The Birds of Cambodia*, the Royal Government of Cambodia, Phnom Penh.

Van Marle, J.G. and Voous, K.H. (1988), *The Birds of Sumatra*, British Ornithologists' Union Checklist No. 10.

Viney, C., Phillipps, K. and Lam, C. Y. (1994), *Birds of Hong Kong*, Government Publications Centre, Hong Kong.

Vowles, G.A. and Vowles, R.S. (1997), *An Annotated Checklist of the Birds of Brunei*, Centro de Estudos Ornitologicos no Algarve.

Wheatley, N. (1996), *Where to Watch Birds in Asia*, Christopher Helm, London.

Most of these publications include more extensive lists of relevant books and papers. Unpublished trip reports produced by travelling birdwatchers are often another valuable source of current and first-hand information. Four such reports covering some of the less-visited sites are listed here, and more are available from the Oriental Bird Club. See website for useful internet links.

The following two societies continuously publish news on Southeast Asian birds, and provide specialised information:

Oriental Bird Club
The Lodge
Sandy
Bedfordshire SG19 2DL
U.K
Website: http://www.orientalbirdclub.org/

BirdLife International
Wellbrook Court
Girton Road
Cambridge CB3 ONA
U.K.
Tel: 44-1223 277318
Fax: 44-1223 277200
E-mail: birdlife@birdlife.org.uk

Since new titles on Asian birdlife appear every year, check with Nature's Niche for the latest publications.

Nature's Niche Pte Ltd
Botanic Garden Shop
1 Cluny Road
Singapore 259569
Tel: 65-475 2319
Fax: 65-475 1597
E-mail: nniche@singnet.com.sg

# INDEX OF COMMON NAMES

Accentor, Alpine 337
Adjutant, Greater 59
Adjutant, Lesser 60
Argus, Great 92
Avadavat, Red 371
Avocet, Pied 124
Babbler, Abbott's 267
Babbler, Black-capped 265
Babbler, Buff-breasted 265
Babbler, Chestnut-rumped 274
Babbler, Chestnut-winged 274
Babbler, Golden 272
Babbler, Grey-headed 273
Babbler, Grey-throated 273
Babbler, Horsfield's 267
Babbler, Mountain 268
Babbler, Rufous-crowned 269
Babbler, Scaly-crowned 269
Babbler, Short-tailed 266
Babbler, Sooty-capped 268
Babbler, White-chested 266
Babbler, White-hooded 286
Barbet, Black-browed 199
Barbet, Blue-eared 202
Barbet, Blue-throated 200
Barbet, Brown 203
Barbet, Coppersmith 202
Barbet, Fire-tufted 196
Barbet, Golden-naped 201
Barbet, Golden-throated 199
Barbet, Gold-whiskered 197
Barbet, Green-eared 197
Barbet, Lineated 196
Barbet, Moustached 200
Barbet, Red-crowned 198
Barbet, Red-throated 198
Barbet, Yellow-crowned 201
Barwing, Formosan 287
Barwing, Spectacled 287
Baza, Black 71
Baza, Jerdon's 70
Bee-eater, Blue-bearded 187
Bee-eater, Blue-tailed 185

Bee-eater, Blue-throated 186
Bee-eater, Chestnut-headed 184
Bee-eater, Green 185
Bee-eater, Red-bearded 186
Besra 78
Bittern, Black 55
Bittern, Cinnamon 55
Bittern, Great 56
Bittern, Schrenck's 54
Bittern, Yellow 54
Blackbird, Common 307
Black-eye, Mountain (Blackeye) 368
Bleeding-heart, Luzon 144
Bleeding-heart, Mindoro 144
Bluebird, Asian Fairy 255
Booby, Brown 44
Booby, Masked 43
Booby, Red-footed 43
Broadbill, Banded 216
Broadbill, Black-and-red 215
Broadbill, Black-and-yellow 216
Broadbill, Dusky 215
Broadbill, Green 218
Broadbill, Long-tailed 217
Broadbill, Silver-breasted 217
Brown-dove, White-eared 137
Bulbul, Ashy 248
Bulbul, Black 249
Bulbul, Black-and-white 235
Bulbul, Black-crested 236
Bulbul, Black-headed 235
Bulbul, Buff-vented 246
Bulbul, Chestnut 248
Bulbul, Cream-vented 242
Bulbul, Finsch's 243
Bulbul, Flavescent 240
Bulbul, Grey-bellied 237
Bulbul, Grey-eyed 246
Bulbul, Hairy-backed 245
Bulbul, Light-vented (Chinese Bulbul) 238
Bulbul, Mountain 247

Bulbul, Ochraceous 244
Bulbul, Olive-winged 241
Bulbul, Puff-backed 239
Bulbul, Puff-throated 244
Bulbul, Red-eyed 242
Bulbul, Red-whiskered 237
Bulbul, Scaly-breasted 236
Bulbul, Sooty-headed 238
Bulbul, Spectacled 243
Bulbul, Straw-headed 234
Bulbul, Streak-eared 241
Bulbul, Streaked 247
Bulbul, Stripe-throated 239
Bulbul, Yellow-bellied 245
Bulbul, Yellow-vented 240
Bullfinch, Brown 374
Bullfinch, White-cheeked (Philippine Bullfinch) 375
Bunting, Yellow-breasted 375
Bushchat, Grey 303
Bushchat, Pied 302
Bush-lark, Singing (Australasian Bushlark) 223
Bush-warbler, Sunda (Mountain Bush-warbler C. montanus) 321
Buttonquail, Barred 93
Buzzard, Common 79
Chat, River 303
Cisticola, Bright-capped (Golden-headed Cisticola) 320
Cisticola, Zitting 319
Cochoa, Green 301
Coleto 350
Coot, Common 99
Cormorant, Great (Cormorant) 44
Cormorant, Little 45
Coucal, Greater 158
Coucal, Lesser 159
Crake, Baillon's 95
Crake, Red-legged 95
Crake, Ruddy-breasted (Ruddy Crake) 96
Crake, White-browed 96
Crane, Common 93
Crane, Sarus 94

Crow, House 259
Crow, Large-billed 260
Cuckoo, Asian Emerald 153
Cuckoo, Brush 152
Cuckoo, Drongo 154
Cuckoo, Indian 151
Cuckoo, Little Bronze (Malayan Bronze Cuckoo) 154
Cuckoo, Oriental 151
Cuckoo, Plaintive 152
Cuckoo, Violet 153
Cuckoo-dove, Little 140
Cuckoo-shrike, Large (Black-faced Cuckoo-shrike) 228
Curlew, Eastern 109
Curlew, Eurasian 108
Curlew, Little 109
Cutia 284
Darter (Oriental Darter) 45
Dollarbird 188
Dove, Collared 141
Dove, Emerald (Green-winged Pigeon) 143
Dove, Peaceful (Zebra Dove) 143
Dove, Spotted 142
Dowitcher, Asian 116
Drongo, Ashy 250
Drongo, Black 249
Drongo, Bronzed 251
Drongo, Crow-billed 250
Drongo, Greater Racket-tailed 252
Drongo, Lesser Racket-tailed 251
Drongo, Spangled (Hair-crested Drongo) 252
Duck, Mandarin 68
Duck, Philippine (Philippine Mallard) 65
Duck, Spot-billed 64
Duck, Tufted 68
Duck, White-winged 69
Dunlin 121
Eagle, Black 80
Eagle, Greater Spotted 80
Eagle, Philippine 81
Eagle, Rufous-bellied 82

Eagle, Steppe 81
Eagle-owl, Barred 161
Egret, Cattle 50
Egret, Chinese 51
Egret, Great 51
Egret, Little 52
Egret, Plumed (Intermediate Egret) 52
Falconet, Black-thighed 84
Falconet, Collared 84
Fantail, Pied 334
Fantail, White-throated 334
Fantail, Yellow-bellied 333
Finchbill, Collared 234
Finfoot, Masked 99
Fireback, Crested 89
Fireback, Crestless 89
Fireback, Siamese 90
Fish-eagle, Grey-headed 74
Fish-owl, Brown 162
Fish-owl, Buffy 162
Flowerpecker, Black-sided 365
Flowerpecker, Buff-bellied (Fire-breasted Flowerpecker) 366
Flowerpecker, Crimson-breasted 363
Flowerpecker, Orange-bellied 364
Flowerpecker, Scarlet-backed 365
Flowerpecker, Scarlet-breasted 362
Flowerpecker, Thick-billed 363
Flowerpecker, Yellow-breasted 362
Flowerpecker, Yellow-vented 364
Flycatcher, Asian Brown 323
Flycatcher, Blue and White 328
Flycatcher, Bornean Blue 330
Flycatcher, Brown-chested 322
Flycatcher, Dark-sided 323
Flycatcher, Ferruginous 324
Flycatcher, Grey-chested 322
Flycatcher, Grey-headed 333
Flycatcher, Indigo 325
Flycatcher, Little Pied 328
Flycatcher, Malaysian Blue 331
Flycatcher, Mangrove Blue 332
Flycatcher, Pale Blue 330

Flycatcher, Pygmy Blue 332
Flycatcher, Rufous-browed 326
Flycatcher, Rufous-chested 327
Flycatcher, Rufous-gorgetted 326
Flycatcher, Rufous-winged (Rufous-winged Philentoma) 335
Flycatcher, Snowy-browed 327
Flycatcher, Tickell's Blue 331
Flycatcher, Verditer 324
Flycatcher, Yellow-rumped 325
Flycatcher-shrike, Bar-winged 226
Flycatcher-shrike, Black-winged 227
Flyeater (Golden-bellied Gerygone) 308
Forktail, Slaty-backed 300
Forktail, White-crowned 300
Forktail. Chestnut-naped 299
Frigatebird, Great 46
Frigatebird, Lesser 46
Frogmouth, Gould's 166
Frogmouth, Javan 167
Frogmouth, Large 165
Frogmouth, Palawan 167
Frogmouth, Philippine 166
Fruit-dove, Black-naped 138
Fruit-dove, Jambu 138
Fruit-dove, Yellow-breasted 137
Fruit-hunter, Black-breasted (Black-breasted Triller/Jeffery) 301
Fulvetta, Brown 290
Fulvetta, Grey-cheeked 291
Fulvetta, Mountain 290
Fulvetta, Rufous-winged 289
Fulvetta, Streak-throated 289
Gadwall 66
Garganey 66
Godwit, Bar-tailed 110
Godwit, Black-tailed 110
Goldenback, Common (Common Flameback) 209
Goldenback, Greater 214
Goose, Cotton Pygmy 69
Goose, Grey-lag 61
Goshawk, Crested 78

Grebe, Little (Red-throated Little Grebe) 42
Greenfinch, Black-headed 373
Greenshank, Common 112
Greenshank, Nordmann's (Spotted Greenshank) 113
Griffon, Himalayan 74
Ground-cuckoo, Coral-billed 158
Gull, Brown-headed 127
Gull, Common Black-headed 127
Gull, Herring 128
Hanging-parrot, Blue-crowned 150
Hanging-parrot, Vernal 149
Hawk-cuckoo, Hodgson's 150
Hawk-eagle, Blyth's 83
Hawk-eagle, Changeable 82
Hawk-eagle, Mountain 83
Hawk-owl, Brown 163
Heron, Great-billed 47
Heron, Grey 47
Heron, Little (Striated Heron) 48
Heron, Purple 48
Honey-buzzard, Oriental (Crested Honey-buzzard) 71
Honeyguide, Malaysian 203
Hoopoe 188
Hornbill, Black 193
Hornbill, Brown 189
Hornbill, Bushy-crested 190
Hornbill, Great 194
Hornbill, Helmeted 195
Hornbill, Oriental Pied (Asian Pied Hornbill) 193
Hornbill, Plain-pouched 192
Hornbill, Rhinoceros 194
Hornbill, Rufous 195
Hornbill, Rufous-necked 190
Hornbill, White-crowned 189
Hornbill, Wreathed 192
Hornbill, Wrinkled 191
Hornbill, Writhed 191
Hwamei 280
Ibis, Black-headed 60
Ibis, Glossy 61
Iora, Common 231
Iora, Green 230
Jacana, Bronze-winged 100
Jacana, Pheasant-tailed 100
Jay, Crested 255
Jay, Eurasian 256
Junglefowl, Red 90
Kestrel, Eurasian 85
Kingfisher, Banded 181
Kingfisher, Black-backed (Oriental Dwarf Kingfisher) 179
Kingfisher, Black-capped 182
Kingfisher, Blue-eared 179
Kingfisher, Brown-winged 180
Kingfisher, Collared 183
Kingfisher, Common 178
Kingfisher, Crested 177
Kingfisher, Pied 178
Kingfisher, Rufous-backed 180
Kingfisher, Stork-billed 181
Kingfisher, White-throated 182
Kite, Black 72
Kite, Black-shouldered (Black-winged Kite) 72
Kite, Brahminy 73
Knot, Great 118
Knot, Red 118
Koel, Common Asian 155
Lapwing, Grey-headed 102
Lapwing, Northern 102
Lapwing, Red-wattled 103
Lapwing, River 103
Laughingthrush, Black 278
Laughingthrush, Black-throated 279
Laughingthrush, Chestnut-capped 280
Laughingthrush, Chestnut-crowned 282
Laughingthrush, Greater Necklaced 278
Laughingthrush, Grey-sided 279
Laughingthrush, Masked (Black-faced Laughingthrush) 276
Laughingthrush, Mountain Morrison 281
Laughingthrush, Red-tailed 282

Laughingthrush, Sunda  276
Laughingthrush, White-browed  281
Laughingthrush, White-crested  277
Laughingthrush, White-throated  277
Leafbird, Blue-winged  233
Leafbird, Golden-fronted  232
Leafbird, Greater Green  232
Leafbird, Lesser Green  231
Leafbird, Orange-bellied  233
Leaf-warbler, Mountain (Island Leaf-warbler)  313
Leaf-warbler, White-tailed  312
Leiothrix, Red-billed (Peking Robin)  284
Liocichla, Red-faced  283
Magpie, Black-billed  257
Magpie, Green (Common Green Magpie)  257
Magpie, Short-tailed (Indo-Chinese Green Magpie)  256
Malkoha, Chestnut-bellied  155
Malkoha, Chestnut-breasted  157
Malkoha, Green-billed  156
Malkoha, Raffles's  156
Malkoha, Red-billed  157
Mallard  65
Marsh-harrier, Eastern  77
Martin, Plain  224
Mesia, Silver-eared  283
Minivet, Grey-chinned  229
Minivet, Scarlet  230
Minivet, Small  229
Minla, Blue-winged  288
Minla, Chestnut-tailed  288
Monarch, Black-naped  335
Moorhen, Common  98
Munia, Chestnut (Black-headed Munia)  372
Munia, Scaly-breasted (Spotted Munia)  372
Munia, White-headed  373
Munia, White-rumped (White-backed Munia)  371
Myna, Common  348
Myna, Crested  349
Myna, Golden-crested  350
Myna, Hill  351
Myna, Jungle  348
Myna, White-vented (Javan Myna)  349
Needletail, Brown (Brown-backed Needletail)  171
Night-heron, Black-crowned  53
Night-heron, Malayan  53
Nightjar, Grey  168
Nightjar, Indian  169
Nightjar, Large-tailed  168
Nightjar, Savanna  169
Niltava, Large  329
Niltava, Small  329
Noddy, Brown  133
Nuthatch, Blue  263
Nuthatch, Velvet-fronted  263
Oriole, Black-and-crimson  254
Oriole, Black-hooded  254
Oriole, Black-naped  253
Oriole, Dark-throated  253
Osprey  70
Owl, Barn  159
Owl, Short-eared  165
Owlet, Collared  163
Owlet, Spotted  164
Oystercatcher, Common  101
Paintedsnipe, Greater (Greater Painted Snipe)  101
Palm-swift, Asian  173
Paradise-flycatcher, Asian  336
Parakeet, Alexandrine  146
Parakeet, Blossom-headed  148
Parakeet, Long-tailed  148
Parakeet, Red-breasted  147
Parakeet, Rose-ringed  147
Parrot, Blue-naped  146
Parrot, Blue-rumped  149
Partridge, Bar-backed  86
Partridge, Scaly-breasted (Chestnut-breasted/Chestnut-necklaced)  87
Peacock-pheasant, Malaysian  91
Peacock-pheasant, Palawan  91

Peafowl, Green 92
Pelican, Spot-billed 42
Phalarope, Red-necked 125
Pheasant, Kalij 88
Piculet, Rufous 204
Piculet, Speckled 204
Pigeon, Green Imperial 139
Pigeon, Little Green 136
Pigeon, Mountain Imperial 140
Pigeon, Nicobar 145
Pigeon, Pied Imperial 139
Pigeon, Pink-necked (Pink-necked Green Pigeon) 136
Pigeon, Pompadour 135
Pigeon, Thick-billed (Thick-billed Green Pigeon) 135
Pigeon, Wedge-tailed 134
Pigeon, Yellow-vented 134
Pintail, Common (Northern Pintail) 63
Pipit, Olive-backed (Olive Tree-Pipit) 340
Pipit, Red-throated 341
Pipit, Richard's 340
Pitta, Azure-breasted (Steere's Pitta) 221
Pitta, Bar-bellied 222
Pitta, Blue-headed 218
Pitta, Blue-winged 220
Pitta, Eared 223
Pitta, Garnet 220
Pitta, Gurney's 222
Pitta, Hooded 221
Pitta, Mangrove 219
Pitta, Whiskered (Koch's Pitta) 219
Plover, Common Ringed 105
Plover, Grey 104
Plover, Kentish 106
Plover, Little Ringed 105
Plover, Malaysian 106
Plover, Mongolian (Lesser Sand-plover) 107
Plover, Pacific Golden (Lesser Golden Plover) 104
Pochard, Common 67

Pond-heron, Chinese 49
Pond-heron, Javan 49
Pratincole, Oriental 126
Pratincole, Small 126
Prinia, Grey-breasted 317
Prinia, Hill 319
Prinia, Plain (Tawny-flanked Prinia) 318
Prinia, Rufescent 317
Prinia, Yellow-bellied 318
Quail, Blue-breasted 86
Racquet-tail, Blue-crowned 145
Rail, Slaty-breasted 94
Redshank, Common 111
Redshank, Spotted 111
Redstart, Plumbeous 298
Reed-warbler, Clamorous 313
Reed-warbler, Oriental 314
Reef-egret, Pacific (Reef Egret) 50
Rhabdornis, Stripe-headed (Stripe-headed Creeper) 264
Robin, Magpie (Oriental Magpie Robin) 296
Robin, Siberian Blue 295
Robin, White-tailed 299
Rock-thrush, Blue 304
Rock-thrush, Chestnut-bellied 304
Roller, Indian 187
Rosefinch, Vinaceous 374
Rubythroat, Siberian 295
Ruff 123
Sanderling 122
Sandpiper, Broad-billed 123
Sandpiper, Common 115
Sandpiper, Curlew 122
Sandpiper, Green 113
Sandpiper, Marsh 112
Sandpiper, Sharp-tailed 121
Sandpiper, Terek 114
Sandpiper, Wood 114
Sand-plover, Greater 107
Scimitar-babbler, Chestnut-backed 270
Scops-owl, Collared 160
Scops-owl, Oriental 160

Scops-owl, Philippine 161
Sea-eagle, White-bellied (White-bellied Fish-Eagle) 73
Serpent-eagle, Crested 76
Serpent-eagle, Philippine 76
Shama, Black 297
Shama, White-rumped 296
Shama, White-vented (Palawan Shama) 297
Shelduck, Ruddy 63
Shikra 79
Shortwing, White-browed 294
Shoveler, Northern 67
Shrike, Brown 342
Shrike, Burmese 343
Shrike, Long-tailed 344
Shrike, Mountain 344
Shrike, Tiger 343
Shrike-babbler, Black-eared 285
Shrike-babbler, Chestnut-fronted 286
Shrike-babbler, White-browed 285
Sibia, Black-headed 292
Sibia, Long-tailed 292
Sibia, Rufous-backed 291
Snipe, Common 117
Snipe, Swinhoe's 117
Sparrow, Plain-backed 369
Sparrowhawk, Japanese 77
Spiderhunter, Grey-breasted 361
Spiderhunter, Little 359
Spiderhunter, Long-billed 359
Spiderhunter, Spectacled 360
Spiderhunter, Streaked 361
Spiderhunter, Yellow-eared 360
Spoonbill, Asian 57
Starling, Asian Pied 347
Starling, Black-collared 347
Starling, Common 346
Starling, Philippine Glossy (Asian Glossy Starling) 345
Starling, Purple-backed (Daurian Starling) 346
Starling, White-shouldered 345
Stilt, Black-winged 124

Stint, Little 119
Stint, Long-toed 120
Stint, Rufous-necked 119
Stint, Temminck's 120
Stonechat 302
Stork, Black 58
Stork, Black-necked 59
Stork, Milky 56
Stork, Painted 57
Stork, Woolly-necked 58
Stubtail, Bornean 321
Sunbird, Apo 355
Sunbird, Black-throated 357
Sunbird, Brown-throated (Plain-throated Sunbird) 351
Sunbird, Copper-throated 353
Sunbird, Crimson 358
Sunbird, Fork-tailed 357
Sunbird, Gould's 356
Sunbird, Green-tailed 356
Sunbird, Lovely 355
Sunbird, Olive-backed 354
Sunbird, Purple 354
Sunbird, Purple-throated 353
Sunbird, Red-throated 352
Sunbird, Ruby-cheeked 352
Sunbird, Scarlet (Temminck's Sunbird) 358
Swallow, Barn 224
Swallow, Pacific 225
Swallow, Red-rumped 226
Swallow, Wire-tailed 225
Swamphen, Purple 98
Swift, House (Little Swift) 172
Swift, Silver-rumped 172
Swiftlet, Black-nest 170
Swiftlet, Edible-nest 170
Swiftlet, White-bellied (Glossy Swiftlet) 171
Tailorbird, Ashy 315
Tailorbird, Common 314
Tailorbird, Dark-necked 315
Tailorbird, Mountain 316
Tailorbird, Rufous-tailed 316
Tattler, Grey-tailed 115

Teal, Common 64
Tern, Black-naped 131
Tern, Bridled 131
Tern, Caspian 130
Tern, Common 130
Tern, Great crested 132
Tern, Gull-billed 129
Tern, Lesser Crested 133
Tern, Little 132
Tern, Whiskered 128
Tern, White-winged 129
Tesia, Slaty-bellied 320
Thick-knee, Beach 125
Thrush, Chestnut-capped 305
Thrush, Eye-browed 308
Thrush, Island (Mountain Blackbird) 307
Thrush, Orange-headed 306
Thrush, Siberian 306
Tit, Great 260
Tit, Sultan 262
Tit, White-fronted 261
Tit, Yellow-browed 262
Tit, Yellow-cheeked 261
Tit-babbler, Fluffy-backed 275
Tit-babbler, Striped 275
Treecreeper, Brown-throated 264
Treeduck, Lesser (Lesser Whistling-duck) 62
Treeduck, Wandering (Wandering Whistling-duck) 62
Treepie, Racket-tailed 259
Treepie, Rufous 258
Treepie, Sunda 258
Tree-sparrow, Eurasian 368
Treeswift, Grey-rumped 173
Treeswift, Whiskered 174
Triller, Pied 228
Trogon, Diard's 175
Trogon, Philippine 175
Trogon, Red-headed 177
Trogon, Red-naped 174
Trogon, Scarlet-rumped 176
Trogon, Whitehead's 176
Turnstone, Ruddy 116

Turtle-dove, Oriental 141
Turtle-dove, Red (Red Collared-dove) 142
Vulture, Red-headed 75
Vulture, White-rumped (White-backed Vulture) 75
Wagtail, Forest 339
Wagtail, Grey 338
Wagtail, White 338
Wagtail, Yellow 339
Warbler, Arctic 311
Warbler, Ashy-throated 311
Warbler, Chestnut-crowned 309
Warbler, Eastern Crowned 312
Warbler, Inornate 310
Warbler, Radde's 310
Warbler, Yellow-breasted 309
Watercock 97
Waterhen, White-breasted 97
Water-redstart, Luzon 298
Weaver, Asian Golden 370
Weaver, Baya 369
Weaver, Streaked 370
Whimbrel 108
Whistler, Bornean 336
Whistler, Mangrove 337
Whistling-thrush, Blue 305
White-eye, Black-capped 367
White-eye, Mountain 367
White-eye, Oriental 366
Wood-kingfisher, Blue-capped 184
Wood-kingfisher, Spotted 183
Wood-owl, Spotted 164
Wood-partridge, Black (Black Partridge) 85
Wood-partridge, Crested (Crested Partridge) 88
Wood-partridge, Ferruginous (Ferruginous Partridge) 87
Woodpecker, Banded 208
Woodpecker, Black-and-buff 210
Woodpecker, Black-headed 206
Woodpecker, Brown-capped (Sunda Woodpecker) 213
Woodpecker, Buff-rumped 210

Woodpecker, Checker-throated 208
Woodpecker, Crimson-winged 207
Woodpecker, Fulvous-breasted 212
Woodpecker, Great Slaty 211
Woodpecker, Heart-spotted 213
Woodpecker, Laced 205
Woodpecker, Olive-backed 209
Woodpecker, Orange-backed 214
Woodpecker, Rufous 205
Woodpecker, Rufous-bellied 212
Woodpecker, White-bellied 211
Wood-shrike, Large 227
Wood-swallow, Ashy 341
Wood-swallow, White-breasted 342
Wren-babbler, Eye-browed 271
Wren-babbler, Mountain 271
Wren-babbler, Pygmy 272
Wren-babbler, Striped 270
Yellownape, Greater 206
Yellownape, Lesser 207
Yuhina, Chestnut-crested 293
Yuhina, Stripe-throated 293
Yuhina, White-bellied 294

# INDEX OF SCIENTIFIC NAMES

*Accipiter badius* 79
*Accipiter gularis* 77
*Accipiter trivirgatus* 78
*Accipiter virgatus* 78
*Aceros leucocephalus* 191
*Aceros nipalensis* 190
*Acridotheres cristatellus* 349
*Acridotheres fuscus* 348
*Acridotheres javanicus* 349
*Acridotheres tristis* 348
*Acrocephalus orientalis* 314
*Acrocephalus stentoreus* 313
*Actenoides bombroni* 184
*Actenoides lindsayi* 183
*Actinodura morrisoniana* 287
*Actinodura ramsayi* 287
*Aegithina tiphia* 231
*Aegithina viridissima* 230
*Aerodramus fuciphagus* 170
*Aerodramus maximus* 170
*Aethopyga boltoni* 355
*Aethopyga christinae* 357
*Aethopyga gouldiae* 356
*Aethopyga nipalensis* 356
*Aethopyga saturata* 357
*Aethopyga shelleyi* 355
*Aethopyga siparaja* 358
*Aethopyga temminckii* 358
*Aix galericulata* 68
*Alcedo atthis* 178
*Alcedo meninting* 179
*Alcippe brunneicauda* 290
*Alcippe castaneceps* 289
*Alcippe cinereiceps* 289
*Alcippe morrisonia* 291
*Alcippe peracensis* 290
*Amandava amandava* 371
*Amaurornis phoenicurus* 97
*Ampeliceps coronatus* 350
*Anas acuta* 63
*Anas clypeata* 67
*Anas crecca* 64
*Anas luzonica* 65
*Anas platyrhynchos* 65
*Anas poecilorhyncha* 64
*Anas querquedula* 66
*Anas strepera* 66
*Anastomus oscitans* 57
*Anhinga melanogaster* 45
*Anorrhinus galeritus* 190
*Anous stolidus* 133
*Anser anser* 61
*Anthracoceros albirostris* 193
*Anthracoceros malayanus* 193
*Anthreptes malacensis* 351
*Anthreptes rhodolaema* 352
*Anthreptes singalensis* 352
*Anthus cervinus* 341
*Anthus hodgsoni* 340
*Anthus novaeseelandiae* 340
*Aplonis panayensis* 345
*Apus affinis* 172

*Aquila clanga* 80
*Aquila nipalensis* 81
*Arachnothera affinis* 361
*Arachnothera chrysogenys* 360
*Arachnothera flavigaster* 360
*Arachnothera longirostra* 359
*Arachnothera magna* 361
*Arachnothera robusta* 359
*Arborophila brunneopectus* 86
*Arborophila charltonii* 87
*Ardea cinerea* 47
*Ardea purpurea* 48
*Ardea sumatrana* 47
*Ardeola bacchus* 49
*Ardeola speciosa* 49
*Arenaria interpres* 116
*Argusianus argus* 92
*Artamus fuscus* 341
*Artamus leucorhynchus* 342
*Asio flammeus* 165
*Athene brama* 164
*Aviceda jerdoni* 70
*Aviceda leuphotes* 71
*Aythya ferina* 67
*Aythya fuligula* 68
*Batrachostomus auritus* 165
*Batrachostomus chaseni* 167
*Batrachostomus javensis* 167
*Batrachostomus septimus* 166
*Batrachostomus stellatus* 166
*Berenicornis comatus* 189
*Botaurus stellaris* 56
*Brachypteryx montana* 294
*Bubo sumatranus* 161
*Bubulcus ibis* 50
*Buceros bicornis* 194
*Buceros hydrocorax* 195
*Buceros rhinoceros* 194
*Buteo buteo* 79
*Butorides striatus* 48
*Cacomantis merulinus* 152
*Cacomantis variolosus* 152
*Cairina scutulata* 69
*Calidris acuminata* 121
*Calidris alba* 122

*Calidris alpina* 121
*Calidris canutus* 118
*Calidris ferruginea* 122
*Calidris minuta* 119
*Calidris ruficollis* 119
*Calidris subminuta* 120
*Calidris temminckii* 120
*Calidris tenuirostris* 118
*Caloenas nicobarica* 145
*Caloperdix oculea* 87
*Calorhamphus fuliginosus* 203
*Calyptomena viridis* 218
*Caprimulgus affinis* 169
*Caprimulgus asiaticus* 169
*Caprimulgus indicus* 168
*Caprimulgus macrurus* 168
*Carduelis ambigua* 373
*Carpococcyx renauldi* 158
*Carpodacus vinaceus* 374
*Celeus brachyurus* 205
*Centropus bengalensis* 159
*Centropus sinensis* 158
*Certhia discolor* 264
*Ceryle lugubris* 177
*Ceryle rudis* 178
*Cettia vulcania* 321
*Ceyx erithacus* 179
*Ceyx rufidorsa* 180
*Chalcophaps indica* 143
*Charadrius alexandrinus* 106
*Charadrius dubius* 105
*Charadrius hiaticula* 105
*Charadrius leschenaultii* 107
*Charadrius mongolus* 107
*Charadrius peronii* 106
*Chlamydochaera jefferyi* 301
*Chlidonias hybridus* 128
*Chlidonias leucopterus* 129
*Chlorocharis emiliae* 368
*Chloropsis aurifrons* 232
*Chloropsis cochinchinensis* 233
*Chloropsis cyanopogon* 231
*Chloropsis hardwickii* 233
*Chloropsis sonnerati* 232
*Chrysococcyx maculatus* 153

*Chrysococcyx minutillus* 154
*Chrysococcyx xanthorhynchus* 153
*Chrysocolaptes lucidus* 214
*Ciconia episcopus* 58
*Ciconia nigra* 58
*Cinclidium leucurum* 299
*Circus spilonotus* 77
*Cissa chinensis* 257
*Cissa thalassina* 256
*Cisticola exilis* 320
*Cisticola juncidis* 319
*Cochoa viridis* 301
*Collocalia esculenta* 171
*Copsychus cebuensis* 297
*Copsychus malabaricus* 296
*Copsychus niger* 297
*Copsychus saularis* 296
*Coracias benghalensis* 187
*Coracina novaehollandiae* 228
*Corvus macrorhynchos* 260
*Corvus splendens* 259
*Corydon sumatranus* 215
*Coturnix chinensis* 86
*Criniger finschii* 243
*Criniger ochraceus* 244
*Criniger pallidus* 244
*Crypsirina temia* 259
*Cuculus fugax* 150
*Cuculus micropterus* 151
*Cuculus saturatus* 151
*Culicicapa ceylonensis* 333
*Cutia nipalensis* 284
*Cyanoptila cyanomelana* 328
*Cymbirhynchus macrorhynchos* 215
*Cyornis rufigastra* 332
*Cyornis superbus* 330
*Cyornis tickelliae* 331
*Cyornis turcosa* 331
*Cyornis unicolor* 330
*Cypsiurus balasiensis* 173
*Dendrocitta occipitalis* 258
*Dendrocitta vagabunda* 258
*Dendrocygna arcuata* 62
*Dendrocygna javanica* 62
*Dendronanthus indicus* 339

*Dicaeum agile* 363
*Dicaeum chrysorrheum* 364
*Dicaeum cruentatum* 365
*Dicaeum ignipectus* 366
*Dicaeum monticolum* 365
*Dicaeum trigonostigma* 364
*Dicrurus aeneus* 251
*Dicrurus annectans* 250
*Dicrurus hottentottus* 252
*Dicrurus leucophaeus* 250
*Dicrurus macrocercus* 249
*Dicrurus paradiseus* 252
*Dicrurus remifer* 251
*Dinopium javanense* 209
*Dinopium rafflesii* 209
*Dryocopus javensis* 211
*Ducula aenea* 139
*Ducula badia* 140
*Ducula bicolor* 139
*Dupetor flavicollis* 55
*Egretta alba*
(*Casmerodius albus*) 51
*Egretta eulophotes* 51
*Egretta garzetta* 52
*Egretta intermedia*
(*Mesophoyz intermedia*) 52
*Egretta sacra* 50
*Elanus caeruleus* 72
*Emberiza aureola* 375
*Enicurus leschenaulti* 300
*Enicurus ruficapillus* 299
*Enicurus schistaceus* 300
*Ephippiorhynchus asiaticus* 59
*Esacus magnirostris* 125
*Eudynamys scolopacea* 155
*Eumyias indigo* 325
*Eumyias thalassina* 324
*Eurylaimus javanicus* 216
*Eurylaimus ochromalus* 216
*Eurystomus orientalis* 188
*Falco tinnunculus* 85
*Ficedula dumetoria* 327
*Ficedula hyperythra* 327
*Ficedula solitaris* 326
*Ficedula strophiata* 326

*Ficedula westermanni* 328
*Ficedula zanthopygia* 325
*Fregata ariel* 46
*Fregata minor* 46
*Fulica atra* 99
*Gallicolumba luzonica* 144
*Gallicolumba platenae* 144
*Gallicrex cinerea* 97
*Gallinago gallinago* 117
*Gallinago megala* 117
*Gallinula chloropus* 98
*Gallirallus striatus* 94
*Gallulax caerulatus* 279
*Gallus gallus* 90
*Gampsorhynchus rufulus* 286
*Garrulax albogularis* 277
*Garrulax canorus* 280
*Garrulax chinensis* 279
*Garrulax erythrocephalus* 282
*Garrulax leucolophus* 277
*Garrulax lugubris* 278
*Garrulax milnei* 282
*Garrulax mitratus* 280
*Garrulax morrisonianus* 281
*Garrulax palliatus* 276
*Garrulax pectoralis* 278
*Garrulax perspicillatus* 276
*Garrulax sannio* 281
*Garrulus glandarius* 256
*Gelochelidon nilotica* 129
*Geopelia striata* 143
*Gerygone sulphurea* 308
*Glareola lactea* 126
*Glareola maldivarum* 126
*Glaucidium brodiei* 163
*Gorsachius melanolophus* 53
*Gracula religiosa* 351
*Griniger phaeocephalus* 245
*Grus antigone* 94
*Grus grus* 93
*Gyps bengalensis* 75
*Gyps himalayensis* 74
*Haematopus ostralegus* 101
*Halcyon chloris* 183
*Halcyon pileata* 182

*Halcyon smyrnensis* 182
*Haliaeetus leucogaster* 73
*Haliastur indus* 73
*Harpactes ardens* 175
*Harpactes diardii* 175
*Harpactes duvaucelii* 176
*Harpactes erythrocephalus* 177
*Harpactes kasumba* 174
*Harpactes whiteheadi* 176
*Heliopais personata* 99
*Hemicircus canente* 213
*Hemiprocne comata* 174
*Hemiprocne longipennis* 173
*Hemipus hirundinaceus* 227
*Hemipus picatus* 226
*Heterophasia annectens* 291
*Heterophasia melanoleuca* 292
*Heterophasia picaoides* 292
*Hieraaetus kienerii* 82
*Himantopus himantopus* 124
*Hirundapus giganteus* 171
*Hirundo daurica* 226
*Hirundo rustica* 224
*Hirundo smithii* 225
*Hirundo tahitica* 225
*Hydrophasianus chirurgus* 100
*Hypothymis azurea* 335
*Hypsipetes castanotus* 248
*Hypsipetes charlottae* 246
*Hypsipetes criniger* 245
*Hypsipetes flavala* 248
*Hypsipetes madagascariensis* 249
*Hypsipetes malaccensis* 247
*Hypsipetes mcclellandii* 247
*Hypsipetes propinquus* 246
*Ichthyophaga ichthyaetus* 74
*Ictinaetus malayensis* 80
*Indicator archipelagicus* 203
*Irena puella* 255
*Ixobrychus cinnamomeus* 55
*Ixobrychus eurhythmus* 54
*Ixobrychus sinensis* 54
*Kenopia striata* 270
*Ketupa ketupu* 162
*Ketupa zeylonensis* 162

*Lacedo pulchella* 181
*Lalage nigra* 228
*Lanius colluriodes* 343
*Lanius cristatus* 342
*Lanius schach* 344
*Lanius tigrinus* 343
*Lanius validirostris* 344
*Larus argentatus* 128
*Larus brunnicephalus* 127
*Larus ridibundus* 127
*Leiothrix argentauris* 283
*Leiothrix lutea* 284
*Leptoptilos dubius* 59
*Leptoptilos javanicus* 60
*Limicola falcinellus* 123
*Limnodromus semipalmatus* 116
*Limosa lapponica* 110
*Limosa limosa* 110
*Liocichla phoenicea* 283
*Lonchura maja* 373
*Lonchura malacca* 372
*Lonchura punctulata* 372
*Lonchura striata* 371
*Lophura diardi* 90
*Lophura erythropthalma* 89
*Lophura ignita* 89
*Lophura leucomelana* 88
*Loriculus galgulus* 150
*Loriculus vernalis* 149
*Luscinia calliope* 295
*Luscinia cyane* 295
*Macronous gularis* 275
*Macronous ptilosus* 275
*Macropygia ruficeps* 140
*Malacopteron affine* 268
*Malacopteron cinereum* 269
*Malacopteron magnirostre* 268
*Malacopteron magnum* 269
*Megalaima asiatica* 200
*Megalaima australis* 200
*Megalaima australis* 202
*Megalaima chrysopogon* 197
*Megalaima faiostricta* 197
*Megalaima franklinii* 199
*Megalaima haemacephala* 202

*Megalaima henricii* 201
*Megalaima lineata* 196
*Megalaima mystacophanos* 198
*Megalaima oorti* 199
*Megalaima pulcherrima* 201
*Megalaima rafflesii* 198
*Meiglyptes tristis* 210
*Meiglyptes tukki* 210
*Melanochlora sultanea* 262
*Melanoperdix nigra* 85
*Merops leschenaulti* 184
*Merops orientalis* 185
*Merops philippinus* 185
*Merops viridis* 186
*Metopidius indicus* 100
*Microhierax caerulescens* 84
*Microhierax fringillarius* 84
*Milvus migrans* 72
*Minla cyanouroptera* 288
*Minla strigula* 288
*Mirafra javanica* 223
*Monticola rufiventris* 304
*Monticola solitarius* 304
*Motacilla alba* 338
*Motacilla cinerea* 338
*Motacilla flava* 339
*Mulleripicus pulverulentus* 211
*Muscicapa dauurica* 323
*Muscicapa ferruginea* 324
*Muscicapa sibirica* 323
*Muscicapella hodgsoni* 332
*Mycteria cinerea* 56
*Mycteria leucocephala* 57
*Myiophoneus caeruleus* 305
*Napothera crassa* 271
*Napothera epilepidota* 271
*Nectarinia asiatica* 354
*Nectarinia calcostetha* 353
*Nectarinia jugularis* 354
*Nectarinia sperata* 353
*Nettapus coromandelianus* 69
*Niltava grandis* 329
*Niltava macgrigoriae* 329
*Ninox scutulata* 163
*Numenius arquata* 108

*Numenius madagascariensis* 109
*Numenius minutus* 109
*Numenius phaeopus* 108
*Nycticorax nycticorax* 53
*Nyctyornis amictus* 186
*Nyctyornis athertoni* 187
*Oriolus chinensis* 253
*Oriolus cruentus* 254
*Oriolus xanthonotus* 253
*Oriolus xanthornus* 254
*Orthotomus atrogularis* 315
*Orthotomus cuculatus* 316
*Orthotomus ruficeps* 315
*Orthotomus sericeus* 316
*Orthotomus sutorius* 314
*Otus lempiji* 160
*Otus megalotis* 161
*Otus sunia* 160
*Pachycephala grisola* 337
*Pachycephala hypoxantha* 336
*Pandion haliaetus* 70
*Parus major* 260
*Parus semilarvatus* 261
*Parus spilonotus* 261
*Passer flaveolus* 369
*Passer montanus* 368
*Pavo muticus* 92
*Pelargopsis amauroptera* 180
*Pelargopsis capensis* 181
*Pelecanus philippensis* 42
*Pellorneum capistratum* 265
*Pericrocotus cinnamomeus* 229
*Pericrocotus flammeus* 230
*Pericrocotus solaris* 229
*Pernis ptilorhynchus* 71
*Phaenicophaeus chlorophaeus* 156
*Phaenicophaeus curvirostris* 157
*Phaenicophaeus javanicus* 157
*Phaenicophaeus sumatranus* 155
*Phaenicophaeus tristis* 156
*Phalacrocorax carbo* 44
*Phalacrocorax niger* 45
*Phalaropus lobatus* 125
*Phapitreron leucotis* 137
*Philentoma pyrhopterum* 335

*Philomachus pugnax* 123
*Phylloscopus borealis* 311
*Phylloscopus coronatus* 312
*Phylloscopus davisoni* 312
*Phylloscopus inornatus* 310
*Phylloscopus maculipennis* 311
*Phylloscopus schwarzi* 310
*Phylloscopus trivigatus* 313
*Pica pica* 257
*Picoides hyperythrus* 212
*Picoides macei* 212
*Picoides moluccensis* 213
*Picumnus innominatus* 204
*Picus chlorolophus* 207
*Picus erythropygius* 206
*Picus flavinucha* 206
*Picus mentalis* 208
*Picus miniaceus* 208
*Picus puniceus* 207
*Picus vittatus* 205
*Pithecophaga jefferyi* 81
*Pitta baudii* 218
*Pitta ellioti* 222
*Pitta granatina* 220
*Pitta gurneyi* 222
*Pitta kochi* 219
*Pitta megarhyncha* 219
*Pitta moluccensis* 220
*Pitta phayrei* 223
*Pitta sordida* 221
*Pitta steerii* 221
*Platylophus galericulatus* 255
*Plegadis falcinellus* 61
*Ploceus hypoxanthus* 370
*Ploceus manyar* 370
*Ploceus philippinus* 369
*Pluvialis fulva* 104
*Pluvialis squatarola* 104
*Pnoepyga pusilla* 272
*Polyplectron emphanum* 91
*Polyplectron malacense* 91
*Pomatorhinus montanus* 270
*Porphyrio porphyrio* 98
*Porzana cinerea* 96
*Porzana fusca* 96

*Porzana pusilla* 95
*Prinia atrogularis* 319
*Prinia flaviventris* 318
*Prinia hodgsonii* 317
*Prinia inornata* 318
*Prinia rufescens* 317
*Prioniturus discurus* 145
*Prionochilus maculatus* 362
*Prionochilus percussus* 363
*Prionochilus thoracicus* 362
*Prunella collaris* 337
*Psarisomus dalhousiae* 217
*Psilopogon pyrolophus* 196
*Psittacula alexandri* 147
*Psittacula eupatria* 146
*Psittacula krameri* 147
*Psittacula longicauda* 148
*Psittacula roseata* 148
*Psittinus cyanurus* 149
*Pteruthius aenobarbus* 286
*Pteruthius flaviscapis* 285
*Pteruthius melanotis* 285
*Ptilinopus jambu* 138
*Ptilinopus melanospila* 138
*Ptilinopus occipitalis* 137
*Ptilolaemus tickelli* 189
*Pycnonotus atriceps* 235
*Pycnonotus aurigaster* 238
*Pycnonotus blanfordi* 241
*Pycnonotus brunneus* 242
*Pycnonotus cyaniventris* 237
*Pycnonotus erythropthalmos* 243
*Pycnonotus eutilotus* 239
*Pycnonotus finlaysoni* 239
*Pycnonotus flavescens* 240
*Pycnonotus goiavier* 240
*Pycnonotus jocosus* 237
*Pycnonotus melanicterus* 236
*Pycnonotus melanoleucos* 235
*Pycnonotus plumosus* 241
*Pycnonotus simplex* 242
*Pycnonotus sinensis* 238
*Pycnonotus squamatus* 236
*Pycnonotus zeylanicus* 234
*Pyrrhula leucogenis* 375

*Pyrrhula nipalensis* 374
*Rallina fasciata* 95
*Recurvirostra avosetta* 124
*Reinwardtipicus validus* 214
*Rhabdornis mystacalis* 264
*Rhaphidura leucopygialis* 172
*Rhinomyias brunneata* 322
*Rhinomyias umbratilis* 322
*Rhinoplax vigil* 195
*Rhipidura albicollis* 334
*Rhipidura hypoxantha* 333
*Rhipidura javanica* 334
*Rhyacornis bicolor* 298
*Rhyacornis fuliginosus* 298
*Rhyticeros corrugatus* 191
*Rhyticeros subruficollis* 192
*Rhyticeros undulatus* 192
*Riparia paludicola* 224
*Rollulus rouloul* 88
*Rostratula benghalensis* 101
*Sarcogyps calvus* 75
*Sarcops calvus* 350
*Sasia abnormis* 204
*Saxicola caprata* 302
*Saxicola torquata* 302
*Saxicola ferrea* 303
*Seicercus castaniceps* 309
*Seicercus montis* 309
*Serilophus lunatus* 217
*Sitta azurea* 263
*Sitta frontalis* 263
*Spilornis cheela* 76
*Spilornis holospilus* 76
*Spizaetus alboniger* 83
*Spizaetus cirrhatus* 82
*Spizaetus nipalensis* 83
*Spizixos semitorques* 234
*Stachyris chrysaea* 272
*Stachyris erythroptera* 274
*Stachyris maculata* 274
*Stachyris nigriceps* 273
*Stachyris poliocephala* 273
*Sterna albifrons* 132
*Sterna anaethetus* 131
*Sterna bengalensis* 133

*Sterna bergii* 132
*Sterna caspia* 130
*Sterna hirundo* 130
*Sterna sumatrana* 131
*Streptopelia chinensis* 142
*Streptopelia decaocto* 141
*Streptopelia orientalis* 141
*Streptopelia tranquebarica* 142
*Strix seloputo* 164
*Sturnus contra* 347
*Sturnus nigricollis* 347
*Sturnus sinensis* 345
*Sturnus sturninus* 346
*Sturnus vulgaris* 346
*Sula dactylatra* 43
*Sula leucogaster* 44
*Sula sula* 43
*Surniculus lugubris* 154
*Sylviparus modestus* 262
*Tachybaptus ruficollis* 42
*Tadorna ferruginea* 63
*Tanygnathus lucionensis* 146
*Tephrodornis virgatus* 227
*Terpsiphone paradisi* 336
*Tesia olivea* 320
*Thamnolaea leucocephala* 303
*Threskiornis melanocephalus* 60
*Treron curvirostra* 135
*Treron olax* 136
*Treron pompadora* 135
*Treron seimundi* 134
*Treron sphenura* 134
*Treron vernans* 136
*Trichastoma abbotti* 267
*Trichastoma malaccense* 266
*Trichastoma rostratum* 266
*Trichastoma sepiarium* 267
*Trichastoma tickelli* 265
*Tringa brevipes* 115
*Tringa cinereus* 114
*Tringa erythropus* 111
*Tringa glareola* 114
*Tringa guttifer* 113
*Tringa hypoleucos* 115
*Tringa nebularia* 112

*Tringa ochropus* 113
*Tringa stagnatilis* 112
*Tringa totanus* 111
*Turdus merula* 307
*Turdus obscurus* 308
*Turdus poliocephalus* 307
*Turnix suscitator* 93
*Tyto alba* 159
*Upupa epops* 188
*Urosphena whiteheadi* 321
*Vanellus cinereus* 102
*Vanellus duvaucelii* 103
*Vanellus indicus* 103
*Vanellus vanellus* 102
*Yuhina everetti* 293
*Yuhina gularis* 293
*Yuhina zantholeuca* 294
*Zoothera citrina* 306
*Zoothera interpres* 305
*Zoothera sibirica* 306
*Zosterops atricapilla* 367
*Zosterops montanus* 367
*Zosterops palpebrosus* 366